Fusion reflects the way instructors want to teach the integrated developmental reading and writing course. We *know* because *we* asked.

Fusion: Integrated Reading and Writing, Book 1, is the first text in a one-of-a-kind series that connects the reading and writing processes in every chapter. The authors use parallel strategies to teach students how to analyze readings and generate writing. Throughout, grammar instruction is integrated with writing instruction using high-interest readings.

How research drove this text's development
We wanted to find out *how* instructors expect to teach the combined course, and what they need in order to teach it more effectively. **Fusion** is the direct result of extensive research conducted across the country, which indicated that a textbook addressing instructors' needs would:

- Provide instructor support, with particular attention paid to teaching reading
- Cover two levels of writing (paragraph and essay development)
- Present lessons following a pattern of reading, writing, analyzing, and grammar
- Provide support for those teaching in a learning community
- Integrate a variety of interesting readings
- Incorporate online technology (**Aplia™**) to promote skill development and allow for tracking of learning outcomes
- Promote persistence and retention by giving students a chance to move through the developmental sequence more quickly

The *Fusion: Integrated Reading and Writing* series includes **Book 1** for courses at the paragraph level and **Book 2** for courses at the essay level.

"I can't wait to teach from this book. You have done an excellent job of building the reading skills and showing how the reading directly correlates to the writing."
— Claudia Swicegood, Rowan-Cabarrus Community College

Preview

Integrated reading and writing guidance in every chapter

Fusion's integrated approach is reciprocal and reinforcing. For each rhetorical mode, students are taught specific reading strategies as well as writing strategies presented as modes of thought. The authors also employ parallel strategies that incorporate timelines, graphic organizers, and outlining for teaching reading and writing. For instance, students are prompted to fill in a chart with sights, sounds, and tastes that they identify in a description. Later, they use the chart to list sensory details they plan to include in a writing assignment.

Parallel reading and writing strategies are introduced in Chapter 1, "The Reading-Writing Connection." Students learn about the STRAP strategy (subject, type, role, audience, purpose) for analyzing reading and writing assignments.

The STRAP Strategy

You can use the STRAP strategy to analyze your writing and reading assignments. The strategy consists of answering questions about these five features: *subject, type, role, audience,* and *purpose.* Once you answer the questions, you'll be ready to get to work. This chart shows how the strategy works:

For Reading Assignments		For Writing Assignments
What specific topic does the reading address?	**Subject**	What specific topic should I write about?
What form (*essay, text chapter, article*) does the reading take?	**Type**	What form of writing (*essay, article*) will I use?
What position (*student, responder, concerned individual*) does the writer assume?	**Role**	What position (*student, citizen, employee*) should I assume?

Next, they learn about the traits, which are used as a pedagogical tool throughout the text to keep students focused on the reading-writing connection.

LO2 Using the Traits for Reading and Writing

You can use the traits of writing to help you gain a full understanding of reading assignments and develop your own paragraphs and essays. The traits identify the fundamental or basic elements in written language, including ideas, organization, voice, word choice, sentence fluency, and conventions. Pages 00-00 discuss in detail how to use the traits when reading, and pages 00-00 discuss in detail how to use the when writing.

INSIGHT
Using the traits answers these two questions: "What elements should I look for in each of my reading assignments?" and "What elements should I consider when developing my writing assignments?"

The Traits in Action

This chart shows the connection between using the traits for reading and writing assignments.

Read to identify . . .	The Traits	Write to shape . . .
▪ the topic. ▪ the thesis (main point). ▪ the key supporting details. ▪ the quality of the beginning, middle, and ending parts.	**Ideas**	▪ a thesis or focus. ▪ your thoughts on the topic. ▪ effective supporting details. ▪ an effective beginning, middle, and ending.

Instruction on concepts and skills— in this case, the traits—is followed by brief exercises that immediately reinforce how the topic applies to both reading and writing.

Respond for Reading To get a feel for using the traits, answer the questions below for "Cross-Cultural Miscues" on page 282.

NOTE: The questions on this page cover the first three traits.

Questions to Answer for Reading

Ideas:	What is the topic of this paragraph or essay? *A comparison of American English and British English*
	What specific details stand out? Name two.
Organization:	How does the paragraph start? *With a topic sentence that states the main idea*
	What is included in the middle part? *Details showing the differences between American and British English*
	How does it end? *With a final thought about the main idea*
Voice:	Does the writer seem interested in and knowledgeable about the topic? Why or why not?

Extra Practice: Answer the questions above for "A View from Mount Ritter" on pages 00-00.

Respond for Writing To get a feel for using the traits for writing, answer the questions below for this assignment:

▪ Write a process paragraph explaining how to use a social networking site such as Facebook. Your writing is intended for older adults who have little experience with the Internet.

Questions to Answer for Writing

Ideas:	What topic will you write about?
	What main point about the topic could you focus on? (*Is your topic easy to do, does it have a special feature or part, etc.?*)
	What types of details could you include (*explanations, examples, descriptions, personal thoughts,* etc.)? Name two.
Organization:	How could you begin your writing?
	How will you organize your details (*by time order, by order of importance, by logic*)?

"This book does a nice job integrating reading and writing strategies. At the same time, it is accessible, engaging, and interesting."

—Katherine McEwen,
Cape Fear Community College

Visual presentation of concepts

A CLOSER LOOK at Considering the Evidence and Purpose

As you saw on page 259, cause-effect relationships are not always as simple as they might at first seem. It is important when reading to recognize the link between cause and effect and to make sure it is a reasonable one.

Identify Which of the following cause-effect patterns comes closest to the organization of the paragraph on the previous page? balanced

1. Cause-Focused	2. Effect-Focused	3. Balanced
Topic Sentence	Topic Sentence	Topic Sentence
Causes	Causes	Causes
Effects	Effects	Effects
Closing Sentence	Closing Sentence	Closing Sentence

Consider How does the topic sentence help you learn from this paragraph?

_____

_____

What purpose might the writer have had for explaining this cause-effect relationship?

_____

_____

What other reasons could there be for change
unit?

_____

_____

What else would you like to know about the su

_____

_____

Students benefit from—and often prefer—visual reinforcement. ***Fusion*** incorporates process charts, graphic organizers, checklists, photographs, and illustrations throughout the text to give students the visual cues that engage them and help them understand the material.

Reading

Reading narratives can be an extremely enjoyable experience. After all, who doesn't enjoy a good story? You can also learn a lot about life from narratives.

LO2 Learning About Reading Strategies

These two strategies—following the key actions and answering the 5 W's and H—will help you read narrative texts.

Strategy 1:
Following the Key Actions

When reading a narrative, it's important that you follow the key actions in the order they occur. A graphic organizer called a time line works well for this purpose. On it, you can identify the main actions of a story chronologically, or by time.

Time Line

1.	(Key actions in order)
2.	
3.	
4.	
5.	

Strategy 2:
Answering the 5 W's and H

In one way, you can simply enjoy a narrative that holds your interest from beginning to end as a good story. But to truly understand a narrative, you need to identify the key actions. To do this, you can answer the 5 W's and H about the story. (This is a strategy used by reporters when they gather details for a news story.)

5W's and H

Who was involved in the experience?

What happened?

When did it happen?

Where did it happen?

Why did it happen?

How did it happened?

Tip
Sometimes you will not find answers to all of these questions, but stories usually reveal most of the 5 W's and H details.

"The graphic organizers will help students think about the text they read as well as prepare them for writing."
—Gina Henderson, Tallahassee Community College

Brief, approachable learning units . . .

Every chapter has several assignments, each typically designed on one or two pages with a clear learning objective and a clear stopping point. This purposeful design allows students to approach each assignment as a single manageable task, addressing a challenge faced by many developmental students—the ability to stay focused.

Reviewers praised this section on Learning Reading Strategies in Chapter 11, "Classification," which introduces a strategy, illustrates it, presents a visual strategy for diagramming ideas, and ends with a brief practice exercise.

A few pages later, students learn how to write a classification paragraph, beginning with planning, as shown here, then moving to other brief units that discuss writing, revising, editing, and correcting (incorporating the chapter's grammar instruction on using transitions and subject-verb agreement).

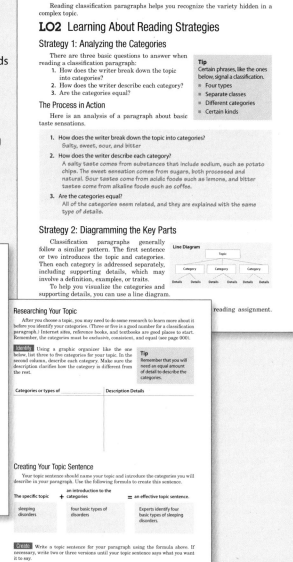

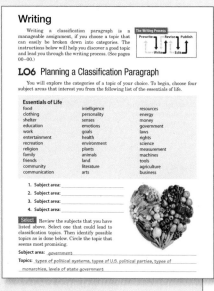

"The greatest strength is its consistency in format and use of visuals. I think it does a great job of making the text appealing to a college audience."
—Ray Orkwis, Northern Virginia Community College

. . . with a cohesive blend of explanation and graphics

Here in Chapter 17, "Sentence Basics," all instruction on the use of prepositional phrases appears on a cohesive two-page spread. Note the use of graphical organizers and the integration of vocabulary at the bottom of the page on the right.

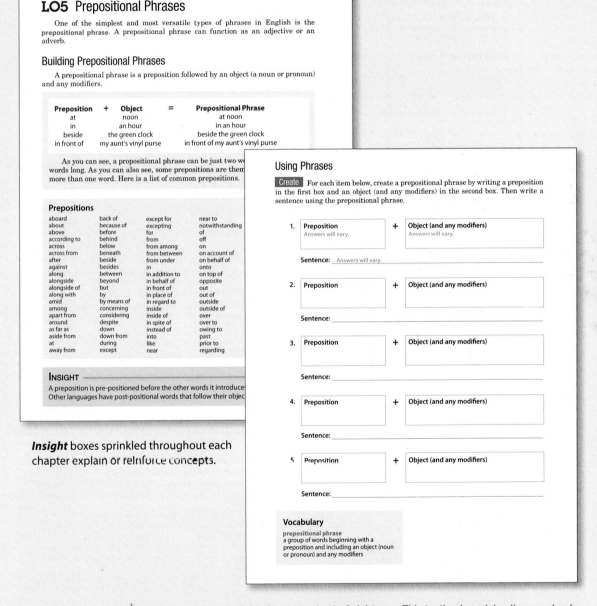

Insight boxes sprinkled throughout each chapter explain or reinforce concepts.

Grammar instruction in every modes chapter

Fusion integrates relevant grammar coverage in the context of students' reading and writing assignments. Additional practice and instruction appears in the book's Workshop section, which includes in-depth discussions on working with words, sentences, and mechanics.

LO8 Editing the Writing

Pronouns and their antecedents, the words that are replaced by the pronouns, must agree in three ways: in number, in person, and in gender. This page covers basic pronoun antecedent agreement

Basic Pronoun-Antecedent Agreement

Number

Somebody needs to bring his or her laptop to the meeting.

(The singular pronouns *his* or *her* agree with the singular antecedent *somebody*.)

Person

If students want to do better research, they should talk to a librarian.

(The third-person pronoun *they* agrees with the antecedent *students*.)

Gender

Chris picked up his lawn mower from his parents' garage.

(The masculine pronoun *his* agrees with the antecedent *Chris*.)

Practice Read the sentences below. Correct the pronouns so that they agree with their antecedents in number, person, and gender.

1. The musicians strummed his guitars.   *their*
2. After Shauna finished washing the dishes, it sparkled.   *they*
3. If the waitress wants a better tip, he should be more poli   *she*
4. As the basketball players walked onto the court, he wave   *they*
5. Mrs. Jackson started their car.   *her*
6. Everyone can attend the extra study session if they need   *he or she needs*
7. Eric poured root beer in their favorite mug.   *his*

Additional Practice: For additional practice, see pages 00–00.

Apply Read your cause-effect paragraph, watching for agreeme pronouns and their antecedents. Correct any pronoun-antecedent that you find.

In Chapter 12, "Cause and Effect," students learn about pronoun-antecedent agreement.

In Chapter 13, "Comparison," students receive instruction on the use of commas.

"I was very impressed with the guidance provided in each chapter on drafting paragraphs, revising, and editing. Although grammar cannot be taught effectively as a stand-alone topic, I also felt the grammar mini-lessons given during the editing process would be useful to students. Surely, something will stick!"
—Jon Bell, Pima College

LO9 Editing the Writing

Commas tell the reader when to pause, making the writing easy to follow.

Commas After Introductory Words

Many sentences naturally start with the subject. Some sentences, however, start with an introductory phrase or clause. A comma is used to separate a long introductory word group from the rest of the sentence. When you read sentences like these out loud, you will naturally pause after the introductory words. That tells you that a comma is needed to separate these words from the rest of the sentence. See the examples that follow.

Introductory Word Groups:

After my third birthday, my brother was born. (prepositional phrase)

When he arrived on the scene, life changed for me. (dependent clause)

Punctuation Practice Read the sentences below, out loud. Listen for the natural pause after an introductory phrase or clause. Place a comma to set off the introductory words.

1. When my younger brother was born, I was jealous.
2. Before he showed up, I had Mom all to myself.
3. At the beginning of our relationship, we didn't get along very well.
4. As the years passed, my brother stopped being a pest and became a friend.
5. As a matter of fact, we both came to love basketball.
6. Without my younger brother, I wouldn't have anyone to push my basketball skills.
7. Taking that into account, our long rivalry has helped us both.
8. Since our teenage years, we've become best friends.
9. Although we still tease each other, we're not being vicious.
10. When we bump fists, I sometimes remember when we bumped heads.

Apply Read your comparison-contrast paragraph and look for sentences that begin with introductory phrases or clauses. If you do not find any, add an introductory phrase or clause to a few sentences to vary their beginnings. Does this help your writing read more smoothly? Remember to use a comma to separate a long introductory word group from the rest of the sentence. (For more information, see page 000.)

Pedagogy that emphasizes critical thinking and vocabulary

Purposeful use of learning aids throughout the text reinforces key concepts, promotes skill development, and encourages students to think analytically.

Consider the Traits boxes remind students of the traits used for reading and writing. They appear in Review and Enrichment sections at the end of each forms chapter, providing additional professional writing samples to read and react to, along with ideas for additional student writing assignments.

Thought-provoking quotes, followed by a **What do you think?** question, engage students in critical thinking about a chapter-related topic. In the narration chapter, students reflect on lessons learned through life experience.

Review and Enrichment

On the next seven pages you will find a multi-paragraph personal narrative to read and respond to followed by a number of narrative writing ideas to choose from. Completing these activities will help you form a better understanding of narration.

> "Experience is a hard teacher because she gives you the test first, the lesson afterwards."
> —Vernon Saunders Law

Prereading

Many of your most memorable experiences involve family members. You may have become reacquainted with a brother or a sister. You may have had to deal with the passing of a beloved family member, or you may find yourself in conflict with someone in your immediate or extended family.

Identify Think of two family members (immediate or extended) who have influenced you in a significant way. Then list one or two experiences with that person that stand out in your mind. Share your thoughts with your classmates.

Person: _____

Experiences: _____

Person: _____

Experiences: _____

CONSIDER THE TRAITS

As you read the narrative that follows, focus first on the **ideas**—the main point and supporting details in the story. Then consider the **organization**—the way the opening, the middle, and closing parts are constructed. Also think about the author's **voice**—the overall tone of the writing. And finally, ask yourself if these traits combine to produce an effective reading experience.

What do you think?

Explain what you think Vernon Saunders Law means in the quotation at the top of the page? Also explain how the quotation relates to personal narratives. Share your thoughts with your classmates.

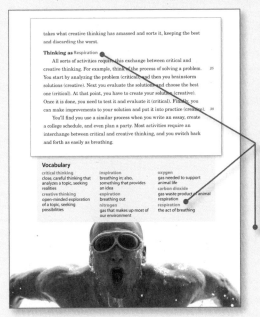

takes what creative thinking has amassed and sorts it, keeping the best and discarding the worst.

Thinking as Respiration

All sorts of activities require this exchange between critical and creative thinking. For example, think of the process of solving a problem. You start by analyzing the problem (critical), and then you brainstorm solutions (creative). Next you evaluate the solutions and choose the best one (critical). At that point, you have to create your solution (creative). Once it is done, you need to test it and evaluate it (critical). Finally, you can make improvements to your solution and put it into practice (creative).

You'll find you use a similar process when you write an essay, create a college schedule, and even plan a party. Most activities require an interchange between critical and creative thinking, and you switch back and forth as easily as breathing.

Vocabulary

critical thinking close, careful thinking that analyzes a topic, seeking realities	**inspiration** breathing in; also, something that provides an idea	**oxygen** gas needed to support animal life
creative thinking open-minded exploration of a topic, seeking possibilities	**expiration** breathing out	**carbon dioxide** gas waste product of animal respiration
	nitrogen gas that makes up most of our environment	**respiration** the act of breathing

Important or challenging words are defined on the page on which they are introduced. In addition, integrated vocabulary exercises provide students practice in figuring out the meaning of unfamiliar words using context clues.

Vocabulary Practice

Explain or define the following words in the essay by using context clues and your understanding of word parts. (See pages 24–25.) Also list the clues or word parts that help you define the terms.
- expansive (line 10)
- discerning (line 13)
- extracting (line 19)
- amassed (line 21)

Integrated inference activities give students opportunities to think critically about the reading selections.

Drawing Inferences

An *inference* is a logical conclusion that you draw from evidence in the text. To practice drawing inferences, answer the following questions about the essay you just read. Afterward, share your responses with your classmates.

1. What inferences can you draw from the line "Not surprisingly, many Romantic poets enjoyed their melancholy" (lines 38–39)?
2. Read the following statement: "Consider, too, that though people were fond of stabbing each other, they were forbidden to take a look inside the dead man afterward—a hobby that da Vinci later popularized." Judging from this statement, infer the author's opinion about violence against living people and dissection of dead people.

> "The vocabulary boxes with the readings are helpful."
> —Kathy Tyndall, Wake Technical Community College

Aplia™ for *Fusion, Book 1*

Active learning motivates students to read, practice, and apply the material.

Through diagnostic tests, succinct instruction, and engaging assignments, **Aplia™** for *Fusion: Integrated Reading and Writing* reinforces key concepts and provides students with the practice they need to build fundamental reading, writing, and grammar skills. More than 1,000,000 students at over 1,300 institutions have used the program to learn course material across the disciplines.

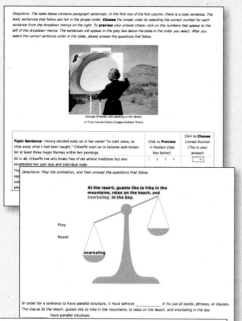

- Diagnostic tests provide an overall picture of a class' performance, allowing instructors to instantly see where students are succeeding and where they need additional help.

- Diagnostic reports allow the instructor to view class progress on a student-by-student and topic-by-topic basis.

- Assignments include immediate and constructive feed-back, reinforcing key concepts and motivating students to improve their reading and writing skills.

- Question structure reinforces the reading and writing strategies covered in the book, and many assignments incorporate a visual component to illustrate key concepts.

- Grades are automatically recorded in the **Aplia** grade-book, keeping students accountable while minimizing time spent grading.

Contact your Cengage Learning representative for assistance with packaging access to **Aplia** with each new student text. For more information and a demonstration, go to **www.aplia.com/developmentalenglish.**

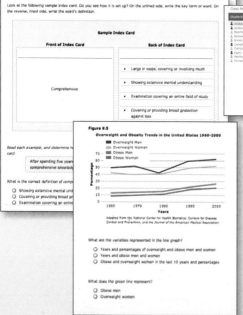

Aplia for *Fusion* is available in two versions—one to accompany ***Fusion, Book 1,*** and the other to accompany ***Fusion, Book 2.***

Fusion

Integrated Reading and Writing **Book 1**

KEMPER / MEYER / VAN RYS / SEBRANEK

Dave Kemper

Verne Meyer
Dordt College

John Van Rys
Redeemer University College

Pat Sebranek

WADSWORTH
CENGAGE Learning™

Australia • Brazil • Japan • Korea • Mexico • Singapore • Spain • United Kingdom • United States

WADSWORTH
CENGAGE Learning™

Fusion: Integrating Reading and Writing, Book 1

Dave Kemper, Verne Meyer, John Van Rys, and Pat Sebranek

Senior Publisher: Lyn Uhl

Director of Developmental Studies: Annie Todd

Senior Development Editor: Leslie Taggart

Development Editor: Margaret Manos

Assistant Editor: Beth Rice

Editorial Assistant: Matthew Conte

Media Editor: Amy Gibbons, Christian Biagetti

Marketing Manager: Sophie Teague

Marketing Coordinator: Brittany Blais

Marketing Communications Manager: Linda Yip

Content Project Manager: Rosemary Winfield

Art Director: Cate Barr

Manufacturing Planner: Betsy Donaghey

Rights Acquisition Specialist: Timothy Sisler

Production Service: Sebranek, Inc.

Text Designer: Sebranek, Inc.

Cover Designer: Sebranek, Inc.

Cover Image: Sebranek, Inc.

Compositor: Sebranek, Inc.

Sebranek, Inc.: Steve J. Augustyn, Colleen Belmont, Chris Erickson, Mariellen Hanrahan, Dave Kemper, Tim Kemper, Rob King, Chris Krenzke, Lois Krenzke, Mark Lalumondier, April Lindau, Janae Sebranek, Lester Smith, Jean Varley

For product information and technology assistance, contact us at **Cengage Learning Customer & Sales Support, 1-800-354-9706.**

For permission to use material from this text or product, submit all requests online at **cengage.com/permissions.** Further permissions questions can be emailed to **permissionrequest@cengage.com.**

Library of Congress Control Number: 2011942007

ISBN-13: 978-1-133-31215-4

ISBN-10: 1-133-31215-2

Annotated Instructor's Edition:
ISBN-13: 978-1-133-31216-1
ISBN-10: 1-133-31216-0

Wadsworth
20 Channel Center Street
Boston, MA 02210
USA

Cengage Learning is a leading provider of customized learning solutions with office locations around the globe, including Singapore, the United Kingdom, Australia, Mexico, Brazil and Japan. Locate your local office at **international.cengage.com/region**

Cengage Learning products are represented in Canada by Nelson Education, Ltd.

For your course and learning solutions, visit **www.cengage.com.**

Purchase any of our products at your local college store or at our preferred online store **www.cengagebrain.com.**
Instructors: Please visit **login.cengage.com** and log in to access instructor-specific resources.

Credits begin on page 564, which constitutes an extension of this copyright page.

Printed in the U.S.A.
1 2 3 4 5 6 7 15 14 13 12 11

Fusion 1 Brief Contents

To the Student

Our mission with **Fusion: Integrated Reading and Writing, Book 1 and Book 2,** is to help you function, and even flourish, as a college reader and writer. *Book 1* focuses on sentences and paragraphs, and *Book 2* focuses on essays. As you work through the chapters in each book, you will learn skills that take the mystery out of understanding reading assignments and developing effective writing assignments. And by providing just the right amount of practice and enrichment, we make sure that you can remember and apply these skills in all your classes.

It's important for you to understand the special connection between reading and writing. Both help you learn and improve your communication skills. Reading gives you ideas for writing, and writing helps you understand your reading more fully. The connections go on and on. Studying reading and writing together, or in an integrated way, makes perfect sense. For the first time, you may truly connect to the written language—and do so much more quickly and effectively than if you had to take separate reading and writing courses. What is more exciting is this: Your work in this book will give you the confidence and motivation to learn in any setting.

Logical Organization

Fusion introduces you to key concepts in a logical and meaningful way. Part 1 introduces you to the fundamentals of academic reading and writing. Part 2 addresses the important forms of reading and writing that you will do in your college classes. Part 3 introduces you to the basics of research, including summarizing and report writing. And parts 4–6 cover the conventions or rules for using the language correctly and provide plenty of practice activities.

- Part I: Reading and Writing for Success
- Part II: Reading and Writing Essays
- Part III: Research
- Part IV: Sentence Workshops
- Part V: Word Workshops
- Part VI: Punctuation and Mechanics Workshops
- Appendix/Glossary

SPECIAL NOTE Helpful "See" references in parts 2 and 3 connect you to the other parts during your reading and writing. This truly makes *Fusion* an integrated text.

Research-Based Approach

Fusion reflects the best research on reading, writing, and learning, so you can be confident that if you follow the explanations and guidelines in each chapter, you will succeed. Here are the key features in the text:

- **Manageable assignments:** The work in each chapter is broken down into manageable exercises that will help you stay on task and do your best work.

- **Easy-to-follow format:** Each chapter opens with important background information, continues with helpful instruction and practice, and concludes with a review or a reflection activity to help you think about what you have learned.

- **Integrated skills work:** In *Fusion*, you will learn how to approach reading and writing as processes. But you will also practice important skills and strategies within each process. Learning these skills in context helps you better understand and apply them.

- **Interesting models:** Each chapter in parts 2 and 3 provides interesting professional and student models for you to read and react to. Many of the professional models come from academic texts so you can experience the types of reading you will be assigned in your classes.

- **Reading-writing connection:** The key traits of the written language are integrated throughout each chapter to help you understand the special connection between reading and writing.

- **Visual format:** *Fusion* is visually appealing and clear, designed to prepare you for college-level reading and writing.

- **Collaborative learning:** You will be encouraged to work together on many of the reading and writing activities to enrich your learning experience.

Andresr, 2011 / Used under license from Shutterstock.com

The Reading-Writing Connection

These pages from Chapter 7—Narration—show, in part, how reading and writing are covered in *Fusion*.

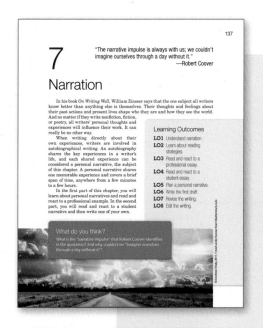

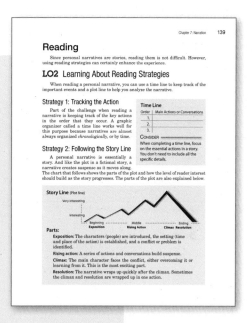

Writing

In this part of the chapter, you will write a narrative about a memorable experience from your past. Be sure to use the writing process to help you do your best work. (See pages 70–75.)

The Writing Process
Prewrite · Revise · Publish
Write · Edit

LO5 Prewriting: Planning a Narrative

These two pages will help you gather and focus your thoughts for writing.

Selecting a Topic

Select List four experiences from your own life to consider for a personal narrative. Identify important experiences that covered a brief span of time, from a few minutes to a few hours. Then choose one of the experiences to write about.

1. _____
2. _____
3. _____
4. _____

Identifying the Key Actions

Think carefully about the actions and conversations related to your experience.

Identify Use a time line to list the main actions in chronological order.

Time Line
1.
2.
3.

CONSIDER THE PAST
If you have trouble recalling details about the experience, complete one of these activities.

- Talk about the experience with a classmate or with someone else associated with it.
- Review any photographs or videos of the experience.
- Write nonstop about the experience for 5-7 minutes to see what actions and

LO6 Writing the First Draft

In a first draft, you follow your plan and organize your details to create a narrative. The sample narrative below is about a memorable moment in the writer's life.

Read Read the narrative, noting how the writer created effective opening and closing parts. Also note how he developed his ideas in the middle part. Are all of the details arranged chronologically? Does the writer include any personal thoughts and feelings about the experience?

Remembering Gramps

Opening paragraph
It was sometime after eight o'clock on a Saturday morning when I received the call about my grandfather's death. I was already awake, cracking eggs into a skillet, when my cell phone buzzed on the countertop. A little early for a phone call, I thought. It was my mom. "Are you awake?" she asked, her voice cracking. Sensing her distress, I asked, "What's wrong?" She told me my grandfather had suffered a stroke during the night and didn't make it.

Middle paragraph 1
After talking through the funeral plans, I wobbled over to my cushy, leather couch and stared blankly at the circulating blades on the ceiling fan. Memories of my grandfather spun around in my head, like the time he taught me how to throw a curveball, and the fishing trip we took together on the Gulf Coast, and the day he poured me a Coke, but instead mistakenly handed me his glass of bourbon and ice.

Middle paragraph 2
Of course, those were old memories. By the time I reached college, Grandpa wasn't as active anymore. Tired and overworked from his years of hard labor at the steel yard, his back eventually gave out and his joints swelled up with arthritis. He lived alone in the modest two-bedroom home he built for my grandmother after they married. But even after she was gone, he never lost the sparkle in his brown eyes. Nor did he lose his sense of humor, punctuated by a deep baritone laugh.

Closing paragraph
And so I sat there, staring at the ceiling and reminiscing about Grandpa. Sure, I had a lump in my throat, and tears filled my eyes; but I felt thankful for the times we had together and hopeful that one day I could be as good a grandfather as he had been to me. I owed him that much—and so much more.

LO7 Revising the Writing

Revising your first draft involves adding, deleting, rearranging, and reworking parts of your writing. Revision often begins with a peer review.

Peer Review

Sharing your writing is especially important when you are reviewing and revising a first draft. The feedback will help you change and improve your essay.

Peer Review Sheet

Narrative title: Remembering Gramps

Writer: Colin Lindau

Reviewer: Colleen Belmont

1. Which part of the narrative seems to work best—opening, middle, or closing? Why?
   Opening, because it makes you want to read the rest and find out what is going to happen.

2. Which part of the narrative needs work—opening, middle, or closing? Why?
   Middle, because you want more details about the relationship between the writer and the grandfather.

3. Which details in the story caught your attention? Name three.
   a. buzzing phone
   b. cracking voice
   c. modest two-bedroom home

4. Does the wri... Yes, a short... attention.

5. Identify a ph... Lines 9 and...

Respond Comp... draft of a classma... comments helpful...

Adding Specific Verbs and Modifiers

You can strengthen your narrative by adding specific verbs and modifiers. Such improvements energize your writing.

Verbs		Modifiers	
General	Specific	General	Specific
grew	swelled	baseball (hat)	flat-billed New York Yankees (hat)
came	advanced	curly (hair)	wavy auburn (hair)
run	sprint	sweet (sauce)	tangy barbeque (sauce)
lives	roams		
wear	don		

Revising in Action

Read aloud the first draft and then the revised version of the following excerpt. Using specific verbs and adjectives adds life to the writing.

wobbled   cushy, leather   circulating   ceiling
I walked over to my couch and stared blankly at the blades on the fan.

Revise Improve your writing, using the following checklist and a classmate's comments on the response sheet. Continue working until you can check off each item in the list.

Revising Checklist

Ideas
☐ 1. Do I focus on one specific experience or memory?
☐ 2. Do I include sensory details and dialogue?
☐ 3. Do I use specific verbs and modifiers?

Organization
☐ 4. Does the narrative have an opening, a middle, and a closing?
☐ 5. Is the story organized chronologically?
☐ 6. Have I used transitions to connect my sentences?

Voice
☐ 7. Is my interest in the story obvious to the reader?
☐ 8. Does my writing voice sound natural?

LO8 Editing the Writing

The main work of editing is correcting your revised first draft.

Quotation Marks and Dialogue

Dialogue enlivens a story and reveals the personalities of its characters. When you write conversations between people, using their exact words, place quotation marks before and after the **direct quotation.** However, when you write *about* what someone has said, not using the speaker's exact words, omit the quotation marks before and after the **indirect quotation.** See the examples that follow.

Direct Quotation
Before we left class, Mr. Lopez said, "Next week's final will be comprehensive."

Indirect Quotation
Mr. Lopez told the class that the final will be comprehensive.

Note: The word *that* often indicates dialogue that is being reported rather than quoted.

Punctuation Practice Read the sentences below. Indicate where quotation marks ("") should be placed before and after the speaker's exact words in direct quotations. If the sentence contains no direct quotations, write "C" for correct on the blank following the sentence. The first example has been done for you.

1. On my way out today, Jessie said, I forgot my cell phone. _____
2. Who is your favorite actress, asked Veronica. _____
3. The salesperson suggested that I should take the truck for a test-drive. _____
4. Frank said that if we want to make it in time, we should leave by noon. __C__
5. Pull over to the side of the road, said the police officer. _____
6. After glancing at her test score, Jillian said, Spring break can't come soon enough. _____
7. And with this new cell phone model, said the salesperson, you can play music, get driving directions, and check your e-mail. _____
8. Jana said that she is in love with her new summer dress. _____

Apply Read your narrative. If you included any dialogue (with direct quotations), make sure that it is properly marked with quotation marks. If you did not include any dialogue, consider adding some.

Part I:

Reading and Writing for Success

Part I: Reading and Writing for Success

1

The Reading-Writing Connection

Reading and writing are really two sides of the same coin, meaning they are "different but closely related." You read to learn, and you write to learn. You use reading to help you with your writing. You use writing to help you understand your reading. Reading is thinking; writing is thinking. The connections go on and on.

This chapter introduces the reading-writing connection and offers three strategies that will help you with your college-level reading and writing assignments: (1) using questions to identify the key parts of assignments, (2) using the traits of writing to help you analyze your reading and develop your writing, and (3) using graphic organizers to arrange ideas in your reading and writing.

The next four chapters in this section take a closer look at academic reading and writing.

Learning Outcomes

LO1 Understand reading and writing assignments.

LO2 Use the traits for reading and writing.

LO3 Use graphic organizers for reading and writing.

LO4 Review the reading-writing connection.

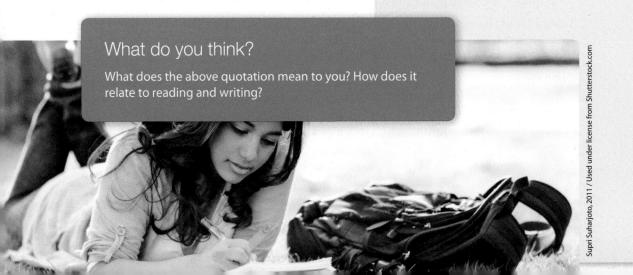

What do you think?

What does the above quotation mean to you? How does it relate to reading and writing?

LO1 Understanding Reading and Writing Assignments

At the start of a reading or writing assignment, you should identify exactly what is expected of you. The main features of an assignment are similar to the key features in a recipe. If you forget any one of them, the final product will suffer.

The STRAP Strategy

You can use the STRAP strategy to analyze your writing and reading assignments. The strategy consists of answering questions about these five features: *subject, type, role, audience,* and *purpose*. Once you answer the questions, you'll be ready to get to work. This chart shows how the strategy works:

For Reading Assignments		For Writing Assignments
What specific topic does the reading address?	**Subject**	What specific topic should I write about?
What form (*essay, text chapter, article*) does the reading take?	**Type**	What form of writing (*essay, article*) will I use?
What position (*student, responder, concerned individual*) does the writer assume?	**Role**	What position (*student, citizen, employee*) should I assume?
Who is the intended reader?	**Audience**	Who is the intended reader?
What is the goal of the material?	**Purpose**	What is the goal (*to inform, to persuade*) of the writing?

The STRAP Strategy in Action

Suppose you were given the following reading assignment.

Assignment: Read the paragraph on page 138. Then identify the 5 W's (*who? what? when? where?* and *why?*) of the experience that the writer shares. Below are the answers to the STRAP questions for this assignment.

Subject:	Working for a lady on evenings and Saturdays
Type:	Narrative paragraph
Role:	Adult looking back at school years
Audience:	Readers in general
Purpose:	To share a personal experience

Respond for Reading   Analyze the following reading assignment by answering the STRAP questions that follow it.

Assignment: Read "Crime-Scene Investigation of Blood" on page 210. Then list the steps in involved in the process.

Subject: What specific topic does the reading address?
steps for processing a bloodstain

Type: What form (*paragraph, article, textbook chapter*) does the reading take?
textbook chapter

Role: What position (*observer, participant, expert, student*) does the writer assume?
expert

Audience: Who is the intended audience (*students, general readers, experts*)?
students

Purpose: What is the goal of the text (*to inform, to persuade, to entertain, to describe*)?
to inform

Additional Practice: Use the questions above to analyze this assignment:

- Read the descriptive essay on page 129. Then identify the specific topic of the description and at least five or six sensory details that stand out to you.

Respond for Writing   Analyze the following writing assignment by answering the STRAP questions that follow it.

Assignment: Write a paragraph explaining how to use a social networking Web site such as Facebook. Your writing is intended for older adults who have little experience with social media.

Subject: What specific topic does the writing assignment address?

Type: What form (*paragraph, essay, blog posting*) should my writing take?

Role: What position (*teacher, student, observer, participant*) should I assume?

Audience: Who is the intended audience (*classmates, older adults, general audience*)?

Purpose: What is the goal of my writing (*to persuade, to explain, to classify*)?

Additional Practice: Use the STRAP questions above to analyze this assignment.

- Think of one of your favorite interests (working out, fashion, cars, reality television, and so on). Then write an essay classifying different categories or types for a specific topic related to this interest. For example, if you enjoy working out, perhaps you could classify different types of leg exercises.

LO2 Using the Traits for Reading and Writing

You can use the traits of writing to help you gain a full understanding of reading assignments and develop your own paragraphs and essays. The traits identify the key elements of written language, including ideas, organization, voice, word choice, sentence fluency, and conventions. Pages 29-64 discuss how to use the traits when reading, and pages 87-108 discuss how to use them when writing.

INSIGHT

Using the traits answers these two questions: "What elements should I look for in each of my reading assignments?" and "What elements should I consider when developing my writing assignments?"

The Traits in Action

This chart shows the connection between using the traits for reading and writing assignments.

Read to identify . . .	The Traits	Write to shape . . .
■ the topic. ■ the thesis (main point). ■ the key supporting details.	**Ideas**	■ a thesis or focus. ■ your thoughts on the topic. ■ effective supporting details.
■ the quality of the beginning, middle, and ending parts. ■ the organization of the supporting details.	**Organization**	■ an effective beginning, middle, and ending. ■ a logical, clear presentation of your supporting details.
■ the level of the writer's interest in and knowledge about the topic.	**Voice**	■ a voice that sounds interesting, honest, and knowledgeable.
■ the quality of the words. (Are they interesting and clear?)	**Word Choice**	■ words that are specific, clear, and fitting for the assignment.
■ the effectiveness of the sentences. (Do they flow smoothly, and are they clear?)	**Sentence Fluency**	■ smooth-reading, clear, and accurate sentences.
■ to what degree the writing follows conventions (and why or why not).	**Conventions**	■ paragraphs or essays that follow the conventions or rules.

Note Design, or the appearance of a text, is sometimes included in a list of the traits. The key consideration of design is readability: Does the design add to or take away from the reading of a text?

Respond for Reading To get a feel for using the traits, answer the questions below for the paragraph "Cross-Cultural Miscues" on page 282.

> NOTE: The questions on this page cover the first three traits of effective reading and writing.

Questions to Answer for Reading

Ideas: What is the topic of this paragraph or essay? A comparison of American English and British English

What specific details stand out? Name two.

Organization: How does it start? With a topic sentence that states the main idea

What is included in the middle part? Details showing the differences between American and British English

How does it end? With a final thought about the main idea

Voice: Does the writer seem interested in and knowledgeable about the topic? Why or why not?

Extra Practice: Answer the questions above for "A View from Mount Ritter" on pages 129-130.

Respond for Writing To get a feel for using the traits for writing, answer the questions below for this assignment:

■ Write a paragraph explaining how to use a social networking Web site such as Facebook. Your writing is intended for older adults who have little experience with the Internet.

Questions to Answer for Writing

Ideas: What topic will you write about?

What main point about the topic could you focus on?

What types of details could you include (*explanations, examples, descriptions, personal thoughts,* etc.)? Name two.

Organization: How could you begin your writing?

How will you organize your details (*by time order, by order of importance, by logic*)?

Voice: How will you sound in your writing (*formal and factual, informal and friendly, or somewhere in between*)? Explain.

Extra Practice: Answer the questions above for this writing assignment:

■ Think of one of your favorite interests (*working out, fashion, cars, reality television, and so on*). Then write a paragraph classifying different categories or types for a specific topic related to this interest. For example, if you enjoy working out, perhaps you could classify different types of leg exercises.

LO3 Using Graphic Organizers for Reading and Writing

Graphic organizers help you map out ideas or concepts and are commonly used to organize the ideas that you collect for writing assignments. You can use the same organizers to "chart" the key information in reading assignments.

Charting a Reading Assignment

Provided below is a line diagram that charts the key points in the classification paragraph "Effective Discipline" on page 234.

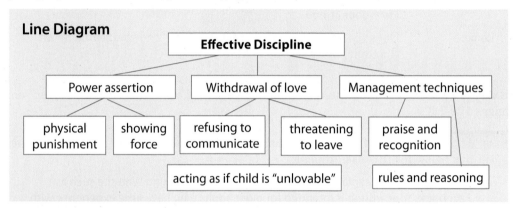

Respond for Reading   Use a line diagram to chart the key points in the classification paragraph "My Condiments to the Chef" on page 241.

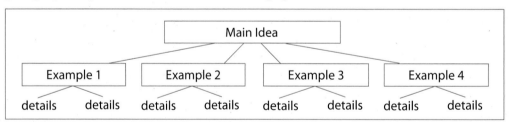

Respond for Writing   Use a line diagram to chart the main categories or examples for a specific topic related to one of your favorite interests. (You've already done some planning for this assignment on the previous page.)

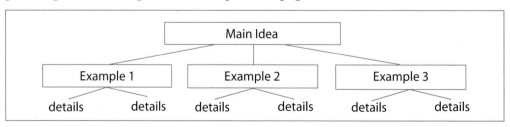

Sample Graphic Organizers

Time Line Use for personal narratives to list actions or events in the order they occurred.

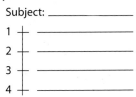

Process Diagram Use to collect details for science-related writing, such as the steps in a process.

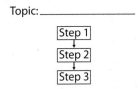

Line Diagram Use to collect and organize details for informational essays.

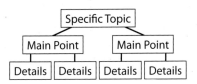

Venn Diagram Use to collect details to compare and contrast two topics.

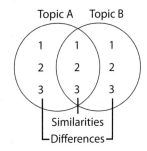

Cause-Effect Organizer Use to collect and organize details for cause-effect essays.

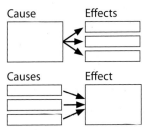

Problem-Solution Web Use to map out problem-solution essays.

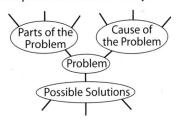

Evaluation Chart Use to collect supporting details for essays of evaluation.

Subject: _____

Points to Evaluate	Supporting Details
1	
2	
3	
4	

Cluster Use to collect details for informational essays.

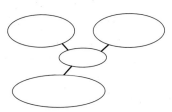

LO4 Reviewing the Reading-Writing Connection

Compete these activities as needed to help you better understand the reading-writing connection.

Understand the Assignment Answer these questions about the STRAP strategy. (See pages 4–5.)

- What is the STRAP strategy? A learning strategy for analyzing reading and writing assignments
- What does each letter in STRAP stand for? subject, type, role, audience, and purpose

Assignment: Use the STRAP strategy to analyze "Text Messaging and Driving Don't Mix." (page 308.)

Subject: text messaging while driving

Type: paragraph

Role: concerned individual, student

Audience: general audience

Purpose: to persuade

Use the Traits Answers these questions about the traits of writing. (See pages 6–7.)

- Which is the first and most important trait?

  ideas

- Which traits deals with the arrangement of details in writing?

  organization

- Which trait deals with the rules for using the language correctly?

  conventions

Assignment: Write a paragraph in which you describe a favorite place. Be sure to include specific details arranged so they are easy to follow.

Ideas: _____

_____

Organization: _____

_____

Voice: _____

_____

2

> "To read without reflecting is like eating without digesting."
> —Edmund Burke

Academic Reading and Learning

We all do it sometimes. We listen without really hearing, letting someone's words breeze past us like mere puffs of air. Honest listening means paying attention, hearing what is being said, considering it, and providing some sort of response.

The same is true with reading. It isn't enough to just let our eyes roam casually across the page and forget the words there as quickly as we read them. Instead, we must actively engage the text, paying attention, considering what it means. Active reading means thinking about the words as we read them, connecting them to what we have read before, predicting what the text will say next, and evaluating the ideas as they present themselves.

In this chapter, you will learn strategies for learning the most from your academic reading.

Learning Outcomes

LO1 Read to learn.
LO2 Understand the reading process.
LO3 Use basic reading strategies.
LO4 Read critically.
LO5 Improve vocabulary.
LO6 Read graphics.
LO7 Review reading and learning.

What do you think?

How is the Burke quotation above related to the introductory paragraphs of this chapter?

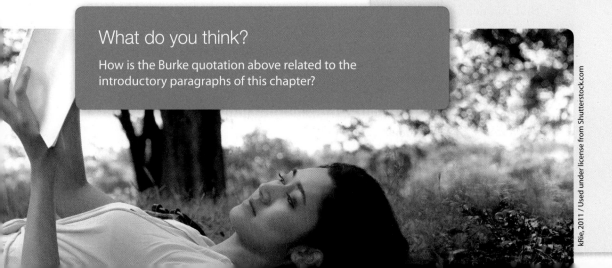

kRie, 2011 / Used under license from Shutterstock.com

> "Today a reader, tomorrow a leader."
> —Margaret Fuller

LO1 Reading to Learn

To be the best musicians, or athletes, or public speakers, people study the techniques of that skill and put those techniques into practice. You'll find that academic reading has its own techniques that can help you best understand and remember what you read.

Traits

In effective text, the reader will find strong ideas, logical organization, a clear voice, precise words, and smooth sentences. These traits are the working parts of a text.

Effective Academic Reading

Follow the guidelines listed below for all of your reading assignments.

1. **Divide the assignment into doable parts.** Don't try to read long texts all at once. Instead, try to read for 15–30 minutes at a time.

2. **Find a quiet place.** You'll need space to read and write without distractions. (Quiet background music is okay, if it helps you stay on task.)

3. **Gather your materials.** Have on hand a notebook, related handouts, Web access, and so on.

4. **Approach your reading as a process.** Academic reading requires that you do a number of things, usually in a certain order. (See pages 13–16.)

5. **Use proven reading strategies.** For example, taking notes and annotating a text gets you actively involved in your reading. (See pages 17–20.)

6. **Know what to look for when you read.** There are key ideas or elements that you need to identify in order to understand a text. (See pages 22–23.)

7. **Summarize what you have learned.** Also note any concepts or explanations that you don't understand. (See page 21.)

8. **Review your reading from time to time.** Doing this will help you internalize the information so you can apply it in your writing and class work.

Practice Choose the star below that best describes your academic-reading skills. Then, in a brief paragraph, explain your choice. In your paragraph, consider which of the guidelines above you do or do not follow.

Weak ★ ★ ★ ★ ★ Strong

LO2 Understanding the Reading Process

If you cook, you know how important it is to follow the steps in a recipe. The more difficult the recipe, the more important it is to follow the steps. Otherwise you risk leaving out an essential ingredient.

You can apply a step-by-step process to your academic reading, as well. Following the steps will help you learn the most from your reading.

> **Think about it.**
> Reading allows you to discover what other people are thinking about important subjects.

The Steps in the Process

The process described below helps you pace yourself and read thoughtfully. See pages 14–15 for a closer look.

Process	Activities
Prereading	First become familiar with the text and establish a starting point for reading.
Reading	Read the assignment once to get a basic understanding of the text. Use reading strategies such as the ones on pages 17–20.
Rereading	Complete additional readings and analysis as needed, until you have a clear understanding of the text's key elements or traits.
Reflecting	Evaluate your reading experience: *What have you learned? What questions do you have about the material? How has this reading changed or expanded what you know about the topic?*

The Process in Action

This graphic shows the reading process in action. The arrows show how you may move back and forth between the steps. For example, after beginning your reading, you may refer back to something in your prereading.

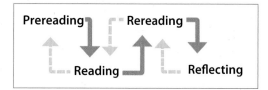

Practice What observations can you make about the reading process after reviewing the information above? One observation is provided below; list three or four more on your own paper.

Academic reading can't be done quickly.

A CLOSER LOOK at the Process

Each step in the reading process requires a special type of thinking and planning. Following these steps will help you become a more confident reader and learner.

Prereading addresses what you should do *before* your actual reading. A coach reviews scouting reports in order to prepare for an opponent; prereading helps you to prepare for a reading assignment. Here are the basic prereading tasks.

- **Review the title.** Many readers give the title very little thought. Bad move. The title often identifies the topic of the reading and helps you understand the author's attitude or feeling about it.

- **Learn about the author.** Read the brief biography that may be provided with the text. Or check online for information about the writer. This information may help you appreciate the author's approach or point of view taken in the text.

- **Preview the text.**
  - Read the first paragraph or two to get a general idea about the topic, the level of language used, the writer's tone, and so on.
  - Next, skim the text for headings, bold words, and graphics.
  - Then read the final paragraph or two to see how the text ends.
  - Finally, consider the author's purpose and audience.

- **Establish a starting point for reading.** Once you have done all of these things, write down your first thoughts about the text. Consider what you already know about the topic, what questions you have, and what you expect to learn.

Consider

Prereading is more important when you are assigned to read essays, articles, and other longer texts, and less important when you are assigned to read an individual paragraph.

Reading a text requires your undivided attention. These are your goals during the first reading.

- **Confirm the author's purpose and audience.** Is the material intended to explain, describe, or persuade? And does it address general readers, college students, professionals, or so on?
- **Identify the focus or main idea** of the text. (See page 32.)
- **Locate the evidence**—the facts and details that support the main idea. (See page 92.)
- **Consider the conclusion**—the closing thoughts of the writer.

Rereading a text helps you to better understand its main points. These are your goals during your rereading.

- **Confirm your basic understanding of the text.** Are you still sure about the main idea and support? If not, adjust your thinking.
- **Analyze the development of the ideas.** Is the topic timely or important? Does the main idea seem reasonable? What types of support are provided—facts, statistics, or examples? Does the conclusion seem logical?
- **Consider the organization of the material.** How does the writer organize his or her support? (See page 49.)
- **Check the voice and style of the writing.** Does the writer seem knowledgeable about the topic and interested in it? Are the ideas easy to follow?

Reflecting helps you fine-tune your thinking about the material. Writing about your reading is the best way to reflect on it. These are your goals during this step.

- **Explain what you have learned.** What new information have you gained? How will you use it? Does this new information change your thinking?
- **Explore your feelings about the reading.** Did the reading surprise you? Did it disappoint you? Did it answer your questions?
- **Identify what questions you still have.** Then try to answer them.

CONSIDER ▬▬▬▬▬▬▬▬▬▬▬▬▬▬▬▬▬▬▬▬▬▬▬▬▬▬▬▬▬▬▬▬▬▬

Try summarizing the text. Doing so will help you determine how well you understand it. (See page 21.)

Apply Use this process for your next reading assignment. Afterward discuss the experience with your classmates.

Other Reading Processes

Two other reading processes—KWL and SQ3R—are variations on the reading process described on the previous pages.

KWL

KWL stands for what I *know*, what I *want* to know, and what I *learned*. Identifying what you know (K) and want to know (W) occurs during prereading. Identifying what you learned (L) occurs after your reading, rereading, and reflecting.

Using a KWL Chart

1. Write the topic of your reading at the top of your paper. Then divide the paper into three columns labeled **K, W, and L**.
2. In the **K** column, identify what you already know.
3. In the **W** column, identify the questions you want answered.
4. In the **L** column, note what you have learned.

Topic:		
K	W	L
Identify what you **KNOW**.	Identify what you **WANT** to know.	List what you **LEARNED**.

SQ3R

SQ3R is a thorough reading process, very similar to prereading, reading, rereading, and reflecting. The letters SQ3R stand for *survey, question, read, recite,* and *review*.

Using SQ3R

Survey: When you survey, skim the title, headings, graphics, and first and last paragraphs to get a general idea about the text.

Question: During this step, ask questions about the topic that you hope the text will answer.

Read: While you do the reading, take careful notes, reread challenging parts, look up unfamiliar words, and so on.

Recite: At the end of each page, section, or chapter, state out loud what you have learned. (This could involve answering the 5 W's and H—*who? what? when? where? why?* and *how?*) Reread as necessary.

Review: After reading, you study your notes, answer questions about the reading, summarize the text, and so on.

LO3 Using Basic Reading Strategies

To make sure that you gain the most from each reading assignment, carry out the reading strategies on the next few pages.

Forming Personal Responses

To thoughtfully interact with a text, you need to write about it. Reserve part of your class notebook for these personal responses. Personal responses to a text help you think about it—to agree with it, to question it, to make connections with it. The following guidelines will help you do this:

INSIGHT

If you are a visual person, you may understand a text best by clustering or mapping its important points. (See page 89 for a sample cluster.)

- **Write several times,** perhaps once before you read, two or three times during the reading, and one time afterward.

- **Write freely and honestly** to make genuine connections with the text.

- **Respond to points of view** that you like or agree with, information that confuses you, connections that you can make with other material, and ideas that seem significant.

- **Label and date your responses.** You can use these entries to prepare for exams or complete other assignments.

- **Share your discoveries.** Your entries can provide conversation starters in discussions with classmates.

Types of Personal Responses

Here are some specific ways to respond to a text:

Discuss	Carry on a conversation with the author or a character to get to know her or him and yourself a little better.
Illustrate	Create graphics or draw pictures to help you figure out parts of the text.
Imitate	Continue the article or story line, trying to write like the author.
Express	Share your feelings about the text, perhaps in a poem.

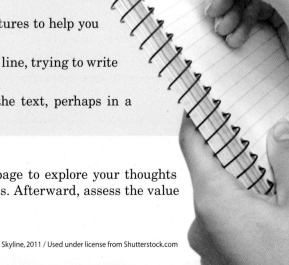

Practice   Follow the guidelines on this page to explore your thoughts about one of your next reading assignments. Afterward, assess the value of forming personal responses to a text.

Annotating a Text

To annotate means "to add comments or make notes in a text." Annotating a text allows you to interact with the ideas in a reading selection. Here are some suggestions:

- Write questions in the margins.
- Underline or highlight important points.
- Summarize key passages.
- Define new terms.
- Make connections to other parts.

> NOTE:
>
> Annotate reading material only if you own the text or if you are reading a photocopy.

Annotating in Action

Here is an example of one student's annotations of a paragraph from *Psychology: A Journey,* a college-level psychology textbook by Dennis Coon and John O. Mitterer.

Good question. I'd think so.

A century ago!

I don't think I could do that for science.

This seems to prove their theory.

A bad pun. But I wonder how the conclusion was wrong.

Don't feelings of hunger originate in the stomach? To find out, Walter Cannon and A.L. Washburn (1912) decided to see if stomach contractions cause hunger. In an early study, Washburn trained himself to swallow a balloon, which could be inflated through an attached tube. (You, too, will do anything for science, right?) This allowed Cannon to record the movements of Washburn's stomach. When Washburn's stomach contracted, he reported that he felt "hunger pangs." In view of this, the two scientists concluded that hunger is nothing more than the contractions of an empty stomach. (This, however, proved to be an inflated conclusion.)

From COON/MITTERER. *Psychology: A Journey,* 4E. © 2001 Wadsworth, part of Cengage Learning, Inc.

INSIGHT

Highlighting or underlining alone are not good ways to annotate, because you may forget later why you marked that text. It is important to also write notes in the margin as reminders of what you were thinking while reading.

Annotate   Carefully read the paragraph below. Then, if you own this book, annotate the text according to the following directions:

- Circle the main point of the paragraph.
- Underline or highlight two ideas that you either agree with, question, or are confused by. Then make a comment about each idea in the margin.
- Circle one or two words that you are unsure of. Research those words, and then define or explain them.

The Reading Process

Prereading — Rereading

Reading — Reflecting

With knowledge obtained from the Greeks, the Romans realized that *1*
some diseases were connected to filth, contaminated water, and poor *2*
sanitation. They began the development of sanitary systems by building *3*
sewers to carry away waste and aqueducts (waterways) to deliver clean *4*
water. They drained swamps and marshes to reduce the incidence *5*
of malaria. They created laws to keep streets clean and eliminate *6*
garbage. The first hospitals were also established in ancient Rome when *7*
physicians began caring for injured soldiers or ill people in their homes. *8*

From SIMMERS. *Diversified Health Occupations*, 7E. © 2009 Delman Learning, a part of Cengage Learning, Inc.

Taking Effective Notes

Taking notes helps you to focus on reading material and understand it more fully. Notes change information you have read about to information that you are working with. Of course, taking effective notes makes studying for an exam much easier.

Note-Taking Tips

- Use your own words as much as possible.
- Record only key points and details rather than complicated sentences.
- Consider **boldfaced** or *italicized* words, graphics, and captions as well as the main text.
- Employ abbreviations and symbols to save time (vs., #, &, etc.).
- Decide on a system to organize or arrange your notes so they are easy to follow.

An Active Note-Taking System

To make your note taking more active, use a two-column system. One column (two-thirds of the page) is for your main notes, and the other column (one-third of the page) is for comments, reactions, and questions.

INSIGHT

Note taking should be more than writing down what you read. It should also be connecting with and questioning new information.

Two-Column Notes

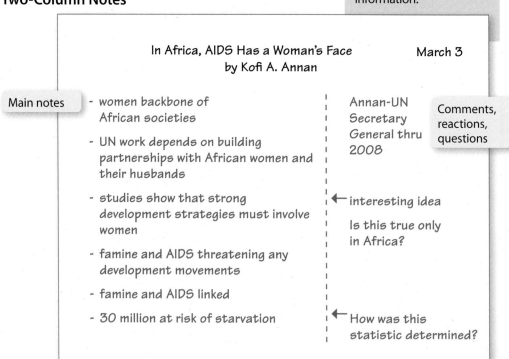

In Africa, AIDS Has a Woman's Face   March 3
by Kofi A. Annan

Main notes

- women backbone of African societies

- UN work depends on building partnerships with African women and their husbands

- studies show that strong development strategies must involve women

- famine and AIDS threatening any development movements

- famine and AIDS linked

- 30 million at risk of starvation

Annan-UN Secretary General thru 2008

Comments, reactions, questions

← interesting idea

Is this true only in Africa?

← How was this statistic determined?

Summarizing a Text

Summarizing a reading assignment will tell you how well you understand the information. Summarizing means "to present the main points in a clear, concise form using your own words." Generally speaking, a summary should be about one-third as long as the original.

Summarizing Tips

- Start by clearly stating the main point of the text.
- Share only the essential supporting facts and details (names, dates, times, and places) in the next sentences.
- Present your ideas in a logical order.
- Tie all of your points together in a closing sentence.

Example Summary

The example below summarizes a two-page essay by Kofi A. Annan concerning the suffering caused by AIDS and famine in southern Africa.

Main points (underlined)

Essential supporting facts

Closing sentence (underlined)

The Face of AIDS

Famine and AIDS are threatening the agricultural   1
societies in southern Africa. Tragically, women, the
main unifying force in African societies, make up 59% of
individuals worldwide infected by the HIV virus. With so
many women suffering from AIDS, the family structure   5
and the agricultural infrastructure are suffering severely.
These conditions have significantly contributed to the famine
conditions and resulting starvation. Any traditional survival
techniques used by African women in the past won't work for
these twin disasters. International relief is needed, and it   10
must provide immediate food and health aid. A key focus of
health aid must be the treatment of women infected with HIV
and preventative education to stop the spread of the disease.
The future of southern Africa depends on the health and
leadership of its women.   15

Practice On your own paper, summarize one of the paragraphs on pages 109–361 or a paragraph provided by your instructor. Use the tips above as a guide.

LO4 Reading Critically

Critical reading involves a lot of analyzing and evaluating. Analyzing refers to, among other things, classifying and comparing ideas as well as looking for cause-effect relationships. Evaluating refers to weighing the value of a text and considering its strengths and weaknesses.

INSIGHT

When you analyze or evaluate a text, you are involved in higher-level thinking. At the same time, other types of thinking like remembering and understanding also come into play.

Bloom's New Taxonomy

Whenever you are asked to . . .	Be prepared to . . .
Remember	collect basic information, identify key terms, and remember main points.
Understand	explain what you have learned, give examples, and restate information.
Apply	identify crucial details, organize key points, and model or show understanding.
Analyze	carefully examine the topic, classify the main points, show cause-effect relationships, and make comparisons.
Evaluate	judge the value of information, identify strengths and weaknesses, and argue for or against the ideas.
Create	develop something new from what you have learned.

Practice Study the chart above. Then explain in a brief paragraph how many of these thinking skills you apply to your own academic reading.

A CLOSER LOOK at Critical Reading

When reading critically, you are, in effect, asking and answering thoughtful questions about a text. Here are some thoughtful questions that a critical reader may ask about a nonfiction text:

Asking Critical Questions

- What is the purpose of the reading (to inform, to entertain, to persuade)?
- Who is the intended audience (general readers, students, professionals)?
- What parts does the text include (title, headings, graphics, introduction, and so on)?
- What logical pattern of reasoning does it follow? (See below.)
- What is the focus or main idea in the reading? (See pages 30–31.)
- How is the focus supported or developed (facts, examples, definitions, and so on)?
- What parts of the text seem especially important and why?
- What questions do you still have about the topic?
- How will you use this information?

Logical Patterns of Reasoning

Almost all texts that you read will follow either deductive or inductive patterns of reasoning. **Deductive thinking** moves from a general focus (topic sentence) to specific supporting details. Most texts follow this form of thinking. **Inductive thinking** moves from specific facts and details to a general conclusion.

Use these questions to check for deductive thinking.

- Does the text start with a thesis (main point or major premise)?
- Do the details logically support or follow from the focus?
- Does the conclusion logically follow the ideas that come before it?

Use these questions to check for inductive thinking.

- Does the text start with a series of facts, examples, and explanations?
- Do they logically lead up to the general conclusion?
- Does the general conclusion make sense in terms of the preceding evidence (facts, examples, and so on)?

Apply Use the "critical questions" on this page as a general guide for your next information reading assignment. Afterward, share your reading experience with your classmates.

LO5 Improving Vocabulary

To understand and benefit from your academic reading, you need to understand the words used in each text.

Keeping a Vocabulary Notebook

Proactive means "acting in advance" or "acting before." Keeping a vocabulary notebook is proactive because you are taking control of your vocabulary building. The note card to the right shows the kinds of information to include for words you list in your notebook.

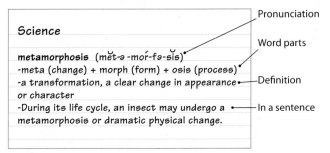

Pronunciation

Word parts

Science

metamorphosis (mĕt-ə-mor-fə-sĭs)
-meta (change) + morph (form) + osis (process)
-a transformation, a clear change in appearance —Definition
or character
-During its life cycle, an insect may undergo a ——In a sentence
metamorphosis or dramatic physical change.

Create In your vocabulary notebook, list two or three challenging words from one of your next reading assignments. For each word, include the types of information shown above. Continue adding new words from your reading selections.

Using Context

Avoid the temptation to skip new words in your reading. Instead, try to figure out what the new words mean in *context*—looking for clues in the other words and ideas around them. Use these examples of context clues as a guide:

- **Cause-effect relationships:** Suggesting the use of seat belts didn't work, so the state officials made seat-belt use *mandatory.*
- **Definitions built into the text:** Dr. Williams is an *anthropologist,* a person who scientifically studies the physical, social, and cultural development of humans.
- **Comparisons and contrasts:** Lynn Dery lives in New York, so she is used to a fast-paced life; Mandy Williams lives in the country, so she is used to a more *serene* lifestyle.
- **Words in a series:** Spaghetti, lasagna, and *ziti* all have their own special shape.
- **Synonyms (words with the same meaning):** Hector's essay contains too many *banal,* overused phrases.
- **Antonyms (words with the opposite meaning):** Mrs. Wolfe still seemed strong and energetic after the storm, but Mr. Wolfe looked *haggard.*
- **The tone of the text:** The street was filled with *bellicose* protesters who pushed and shoved their way through the crowd. The scene was no longer peaceful and calm, as the marchers promised it would be.

Define Define each italicized word above using the clues in the sentences. Afterward, check your definitions in a dictionary.

Understanding Word Parts

You may have heard of the following terms: *roots* (base words), *prefixes*, and *suffixes*. Many words in our language are made up of combinations of these word parts. (See pages 549–557 for a listing of common word parts.)

- **Roots** like *liber* (as in liberate) or *scope* (as in telescope) are the starting points for most words.
- **Prefixes** like *anti* (as in antibiotic) or *un* (as in unreal) are word parts that come before roots to form new words.
- **Suffixes** like *dom* (as in boredom) or *ly* (as in hourly) are word parts that come after roots to form new words.

Sample Words

The following examples show how multiple word parts can be combined to form words.

Transportation **combines . . .**
- the prefix *trans* meaning "across" or "beyond,"
- the root *port* meaning "carry,"
- and the suffix *tion* meaning "act of."

So, *transportation* **means "the act of carrying across or beyond."**

Biographic **combines . . .**
- the root *bio* meaning "life,"
- the root *graph* meaning "write,"
- and the suffix *ic* meaning "nature of" or "relating to."

So, *biographic* **means "relating to writing about real life."**

Micrometer **combines . . .**
- the root *micro* meaning "small"
- and the root *meter* meaning "measure."

So, a *micrometer* **is "a device for measuring small distances."**

Identify   Using the examples above as a guide, analyze and define these words.
- nominate (nomin + ate)
- hemisphere (hemi + sphere)
- senile (sen + ile)
- translucent (trans + luc + ent)

LO6 Reading Graphics

In many of your college texts, a significant portion of the information will be given in charts, graphs, diagrams, and drawings. Knowing how to read these types of graphics, then, is important to your success as a college student. Follow these reading guidelines.

- **Scan the graphic.** Consider it as a whole to get an overall idea about its message. Note its type (bar graph, pie graph, diagram, table, and so forth), its topic, its level of complexity, and so on.
- **Study the specific parts.** Start with the main heading or title. Next, note any additional labels or guides (such as the horizontal and vertical guides on a bar graph). Then focus on the actual information displayed in the graphic.
- **Question the graphic.** Does it address an important topic? What is its purpose (to make a comparison, to show a change, and so on)? What is the source of the information? Is the graphic out of date or biased in any way?
- **Reflect on its effectiveness.** Explain in your own words the main message of the graphic. Then consider its effectiveness, how it relates to the surrounding text, and how it matches up to your previous knowledge of the topic.

Analysis of a Graphic

Review the bar graph below. Then read the discussion to learn how all of the parts work together.

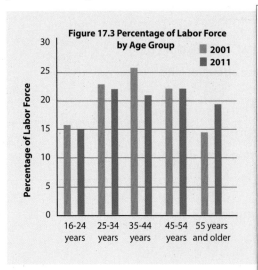

Discussion: This bar graph compares the labor force in 2001 to the labor force in 2011 for five specific age groups. The heading identifies the subject or topic of the graphic. The horizontal line identifies the different age groups, and the vertical line identifies the percentage of the labor force for each group. The key in the upper right-hand corner of the graphic explains the color-coded bars. With all of that information, the graphic reads quite clearly—and many interesting comparisons can be made.

React   Read and analyze the following graphics, answering the questions about each one on your own paper. Use the information on the previous page as a guide.

Graphic 1

1. This graphic is called a pictograph rather than a bar graph. What makes it a "pictograph"?

   The use of pictures in place of bars
   _____

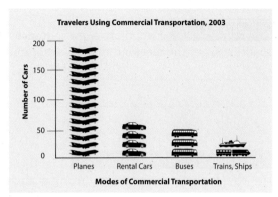

2. What is the topic of this graphic?

   Travelers Using Commercial Transportation in 2003
   _____

3. What information is provided on the horizontal line? On the vertical line?

   Horizontal: Modes of Transportation; Vertical: Number of Cars
   _____

4. What comparisons can a reader make from this graphic?

   _____

Graphic 2

1. This graphic is called a line diagram, and it maps a structure. What structure does this diagram map?

   The structure of the U.S. Federal
   _____

   Government
   _____

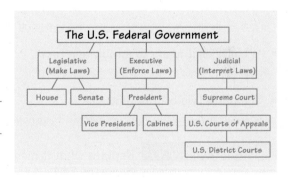

2. From the following items, choose the two working parts in this diagram: *words, lines, symbols.*

   words, lines
   _____

3. What are the three main branches in this graphic?

   Legislative, Executive, and Judicial
   _____

LO7 Reviewing Reading and Learning

On your own paper, respond to each set of directions to review the concepts covered in this chapter.

Reading to Learn Explain in a few sentences how you should approach your academic reading to get the most out of each assignment. (See page 12.)

_____

_____

_____

Understanding the Reading Process List the four steps in the reading process. Identify two things that you should do during each step. (See pages 13–15.)

1. _Prereading_____

2. _Reading_____

3. _Rereading_____

4. _Reflecting_____

Using Reading Strategies Answer the following questions about reading strategies. (See pages 17–21.)

■ What does it mean to respond personally to a text?

To make personal observations about a text in writing or note taking

■ What does it mean to annotate a text?

To add comments or make notes in the actual text

■ What are two-column notes?

A note-taking system that reserves space for main notes and personal observations

Improving Vocabulary Explain what it means to use context clues to figure out the meaning of new words. (See page 24.)

To look for clues near a difficult word to discover its meaning in the context of a reading

_____

Reading Graphics Explain why it is important to know how to read graphics. (See pages 26–27.)

Much of the information in college texts is presented graphically

_____

3

The Traits of Academic Reading

"Reading is a basic tool of the living of a good life."
—Joseph Addison

Here's one thing you know for sure: As a college student, you will do a lot of reading. Because reading is so important, you need to know the best way to understand and learn from each assignment. The last chapter, "Academic Reading and Learning," provided a starting point by discussing important skills such as note taking and vocabulary building. This chapter takes a closer look at reading.

You will learn about the traits or building blocks of a reading assignment. The basic traits include ideas, organization, voice, word choice, and sentences. Knowing how to identify and analyze these traits will make you a better reader. And becoming a better reader will help you succeed in all of your classes.

Remember: Reading may be your most important learning tool in college, so you need to know how to learn from your reading assignment.

Learning Outcomes

LO1 Ideas
LO2 Organization
LO3 Voice
LO4 Word choice and sentences
LO5 Review

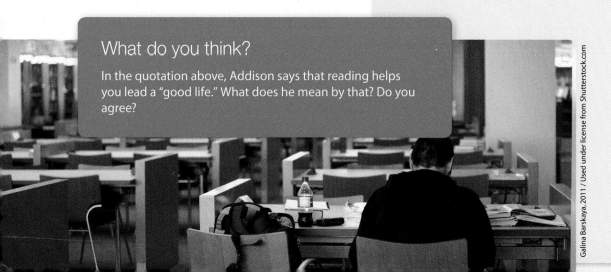

What do you think?

In the quotation above, Addison says that reading helps you lead a "good life." What does he mean by that? Do you agree?

Galina Barskaya, 2011 / Used under license from Shutterstock.com

LO1 Ideas

Ideas are the key trait in everything that you read. Every other trait—organization, voice, word choice—depends on the ideas. In this section you will learn about identifying the main idea and supporting details in a text.

Identifying the Main Idea

Almost every thing that you read—be it an essay, an article, or a textbook chapter—develops a main idea. This idea is usually stated in the topic sentence in paragraphs and in the thesis statement in essays or other longer texts.

There are times, however, when the main idea comes later in the text, perhaps as a concluding or closing statement. You may also read some essays or articles where the main idea is only **implied**, rather than stated directly. You may even read some longer texts that have more than one main idea or a main idea and one or two **secondary** ideas.

INSIGHT

Every piece of writing needs a spark to ignite or start a piece of writing. A main idea serves this purpose.

What the Main Idea Tells You

In a *narrative* text, the main idea will tell you what experience the writer is going to share:

- "My final moments on stage during the musical *Grease* are ones I'll never forget."

In an *informational* text, the main idea will tell you what the author is going to explain or discuss:

- "One word in medical reports strikers fear into people everywhere, and that word is pandemic."

In a *persuasive* text, the main idea will tell you what claim or opinion the writer is going to argue for:

- "Text messaging should be banned in all states because it is making U.S. roads dangerous."

SPECIAL NOTE: The way that a sentence is worded might tell you that it states the main idea: "It has been more than two years since my telephone rang with the news . . . ," "There are several steps . . . ," or "All the flavors a person can taste are made up of . . . ."

Vocabulary

implied
suggested rather than stated directly

secondary
lesser, not primary

Steps to Identifying the Main Idea

Follow the steps below to help you identify the main idea in a text. In paragraphs, you usually need to look no further than the first sentence—the topic sentence. In an essay, you usually will find the main idea stated in the thesis in one of the opening paragraphs. These steps will help you identify the main idea.

Steps to Follow

1. Study the title, and the first and last sentences of paragraphs. For essays, study the title and first and last paragraphs.

2. Then read the paragraph from start to finish. For an essay read the opening few paragraphs to gain a general understanding of the topic.

3. Next, in a paragraph, look for a sentence (usually the first one) that directs the writing. In an essay, look for this sentence at the end of one of the opening paragraphs.

4. Write this statement down, or underline it if you own the text or are reading a copy. (If you can't find such a statement, try to state it in your own words.)

5. Read the paragraph again (or the essay completely) to make sure that this statement makes sense as the main idea. In a paragraph, each new sentence should support or develop this idea. In an essay, each new paragraph should support or develop it.

6. If your thinking changes, identify or write down what you now believe to be the main idea.

INSIGHT

A paragraph is really an essay in miniature. That is, it should contain the same traits or working parts. Essays, of course, provide more information because the support comes in the form of paragraphs rather than sentences. (See the graphic on page 54 to see how the two forms compare.)

The Structure of a Topic Sentence or Thesis Statement

A topic sentence or thesis statement usually consists of two parts: (1) a specific topic plus (2) a particular feeling or idea about it. Here are three examples:

- "The United States must invest in wind power *(topic)* to resist our dependence on fossil fuel *(feeling/opinion).*"
- "Captain Chesley 'Sully' Sullenberger *(topic)* performed an emergency landing in the Hudson River *(idea).*"
- "The Don Quixote statuette my dad gave me *(topic)* isn't worth much to other people *(feeling).*"

In Context

Example 1

Study the following paragraph in which the writer explains Braille.

Communicating by Braille

Braille is a system of communication used by the blind. It was   1
developed by Louis Braille, a blind French student, in 1824. The code
consists of an alphabet using combinations of small raised dots. The
dots are imprinted on paper and can be felt, and thus read, by running
the fingers across the page. The basic unit of the code is called a "cell,"   5
which is two dots wide and three dots high. Each letter is formed by
different combinations of these dots. Numbers, punctuation marks, and
even a system for writing music are also expressed by using different
arrangements. These small dots, which may seem insignificant to the
sighted, have opened up the entire world of books and reading for the   10
blind.

Discussion: A paragraph, by definition, is a group of sentences sharing ideas about a main point, which is usually stated in the topic sentence. The topic sentence in the above paragraph is underlined. It identifies the topic *(Braille)* and an important idea about it *(is a system of communication used by the blind).* The sentences in the body of the paragraph give facts about the topic.

Example 2

Read the following paragraph, in which the writer recalls a memorable gym teacher.

Duck-Walking

Mr. Brown, my middle school gym teacher, did not allow any fooling around in his classes. Unfortunately, two of my friends learned this the hard way. At the end of the first day of flag football, Mr. Brown blew his whistle. Most of us knew enough to stop and fall in line. He had made it very clear on the first day of class that when he blew his whistle, we had to stop our activity. Immediately. Kerry Schmidt and Jesse Johnson ignored the whistle and continued throwing a football. With fire in his eyes, Mr. Brown quickly sent the rest of us in. We all watched from the locker room doorway while Mr. Brown made Kerry and Jesse duck-walk on the football field. By the time they went 20 yards, they were really struggling. He sent them in after another 10 yards when their duck-walk had turned into more of a crawl. We couldn't help giving a few duck calls when they limped into the locker room, but we didn't quack too loudly because we didn't want Mr. Brown to make us walk like a duck or another other type of animal.

1

5

10

Discussion: The topic sentence, which is underlined above, identifies the topic (*Mr. Brown*) and a feeling about him (*did not allow any fooling around in his classes*). The sentences in the body describe one experience that supports the topic sentence.

Example 3

Read the title, opening paragraph, and numbered main points in an essay from a book entitled *Focus on College and Career Success.*

Be Advised! Advising Mistakes Students Make

One of the most important relationships you'll have as a college   *1*
student is the one you build with your academic advisor. In your college
this person may be an advisor, a counselor, or a faculty member who can
steer you toward courses you can handle and instructors you can learn
best from. An advisor can keep you from taking classes that bog you down   *5*
academically or unnecessary ones that take you extra time to earn your
degree. <u>Here's a list of advising mistakes students make from real advisors
who work with college students every day</u>.

    1. Not using the campus advising office or your faculty advisor. . . .   *10*

    2. Not planning ahead. . . .

    3. **Procrastinating**. . . .

    4. Skipping **prerequisites**. . . .

"Be Advised! Advising Mistakes Students Make," from STALEY/STALEY. *FOCUS on College and Career Success,* 1E. © 2012 Wadsworth, a part of Cengage Learning, Inc.

Discussion: The title and general comments in the opening paragraph about the topic lead up to the thesis statement (underlined). Each of the numbered points that follow identifies an advising mistake. So clearly, the underlined statement is the thesis of the essay.

Vocabulary

procrastinating
putting off doing
something

prerequisites
courses that are
needed

Example 4

Read the title and opening part of a section from *Sociology: Your Compass for a New World* in which the authors discuss clothing as a symbol of status.

Status and Style

Often rich people engage in **conspicuous** displays of **consumption**,   *1*
waste and leisure not because they are necessary, useful, or pleasurable
but simply to impress their peers and inferiors (Veblen, 1899). This is
evident if we consider how clothing acts as a sort of language that signals
one's status to others (Lurie, 1981).   *5*

For thousands of years, certain clothing styles have indicated rank. In
ancient Egypt, only people in high positions were allowed to wear sandals.
The ancient Greeks . . .

European laws governing the dress styles of different groups fell into
disuse after about 1700. That is because a new method of control emerged   *10*
as Europe became wealthier. . .

Today we have different ways of using clothes to signal status.
Designer labels loudly proclaim the dollar value of garments. . . .

"Status and Style" from BRYM/LIE. *Sociology: Your Compass for a New World, 2E.* © 2006
Thompson, a part of Cengage Learning, Inc.

Discussion: The underlined statement in the opening paragraph essentially restates the claim made in the title—which suggests that it is the main point or thesis of the text. The start of the next three paragraphs show that the underlined idea will be explored in the main part of the text.

Vocabulary

conspicuous consumption
wasteful spending to show off

Practice   Identify the topic sentence in the two paragraphs that follow. For the essay on page 38, identify the thesis statement. Then explain each of your choices (how the statement relates to the other sentences in the text).

Tip

Use the guidelines on page 32 to help you find the topic sentence or thesis statement for each sample text.

Practice 1

Defying Gravity

Unlike race cars or trains, roller coasters do not rely on powerful engines for speed. Instead, roller coasters let gravity do much of the work. (Gravity is the force that constantly pulls objects of mass toward the ground.) When a roller-coaster track slopes down, the passenger cars accelerate forward because gravity pulls the front car downward. When the track tilts up, the cars decelerate because gravity pulls the back car downward. But gravity is not the only factor in maintaining speed. Another factor is momentum. On most roller coasters, the first drop is the tallest and steepest. Coasters are designed this way to create enough momentum to carry the forward through the rest of the track. Momentum is especially needed to make it up hills and through loops, as gravity pulls the cars in the opposite direction. This tug-of-war between gravity and momentum makes for exciting rides.

1

5

10

Topic sentence: Unlike race cars or trains, roller coasters do not rely on powerful engines for speed.

_____

Explain your choice: _____

_____

_____

_____

Practice 2

The Value of Serving

Community service requirements give students life-changing   *1*
experiences not available in the classroom. First, they learn the
importance of basic job skills such as being on time, teamwork, and
completing tasks. Volunteer Anna Hernandez said, "I had to be at the
senior center right at 3:00 p.m. when the board games started. The   *5*
residents expected me to be there." Community service work also helps
students appreciate the problems and challenges facing Burlington. Scott
Thompson, part of a clean-up crew, never realized how thoughtless people
can be until he started cleaning up after them. As he stated, "Some people
really trash the parks." Most importantly, students learn about giving   *10*
back. For many students, community service is the first time they have
helped people in the community. According to Ms. Sandra Williams, the
community service advisor, "Working in the community shows students
that a lot of people need help." Critics feel that this requirement seems
almost like a punishment. However, participants quickly discover the   *15*
value of their efforts. Essentially, community service gives students a taste
of real life at just the right time.

Topic sentence: Community service requirements give students life-changing experiences

 not available in the classroom.

_____

Explain your choice: _____

_____

_____

_____

Practice 3

Dietary Diversity

Whatever your cultural heritage, you have probably sampled Chinese, Mexican, Indian, Italian, and Japanese foods. If you belong to any of these ethnic groups, you may eat these **cuisines** regularly. Each type of ethnic cooking has its own nutritional benefits and potential drawbacks.

Mediterranean Diet Several years ago **epidemiologists** noticed something unexpected in the residents of regions along the Mediterranean Sea: a lower incidence of deaths from heart disease. . . .

Ethnic Cuisines The cuisine served in Mexico features rice, corn, and beans, which are low in fat and high in nutrition. However, the dishes Americans think of as Mexican are far less healthful. . . .

African American cuisine traces some of its roots to food preferences from west Africa (for example, peanuts, okra, and black-eyed peas). . . .

The mainland Chinese diet, which is plant-based, high in carbohydrates, and low in fats and animal protein, is considered one of the most healthful in the world. . . .

Many Indian dishes highlight healthful ingredients such as vegetables and legumes (beans and peas). However, many also use ghee (a form of butter) or coconut oil; both are rich in saturated fats. . . .

1

5

10

15

"Dietary Diversity" from HALES. *An Invitation to Health,* 7E. © 2012 Brooks/Cole, a part of Cengage Learning, Inc.

Thesis statement: Each type of ethnic cooking has its own nutritional benefits and potential drawbacks.

_____

Explain your choice: _____

_____

_____

_____

Vocabulary

cuisines
manners or styles of preparing food

epidemiologists
medical professionals who study the causes and control of diseases

Recognizing and Analyzing Supporting Details

The main idea serves as the starting point for writing. The supporting details explain or develop this idea. To gain a complete understanding of a reading assignment, you must be able to identify and understand the supporting information.

Recognizing the Types of Support

The next two pages demonstrate different types of supporting details that you will find in informational texts. The examples come from an article about the Crazy Horse Memorial in South Dakota.

> "The great gift we can bestow in others is a good example."
> —Thomas Morrell

■ **Facts and statistics** give specific details about a main point or topic.

The head of Crazy Horse will be 87 feet high, which is 20 feet higher than any of the heads of the presidents at Mount Rushmore.

■ **Explanations** move the discussion along.

There is no verifiable photograph of Crazy Horse. What will be captured in the carving is the spirit of this man.

■ **Examples** show or demonstrate something.

Crazy Horse was that last leader to surrender to the U.S. military, and he did so because the people who followed him were suffering so much. *(This example shows that Crazy Horse tried to stay true to the Lakota ways of life as long as he could.)*

■ **Descriptions** or observations show how something or someone appears.

Crazy Horse will be seen leaning over his horse's head, pointing his left hand toward his sacred lands.

- **Reasons** answer the question "Why?" about something.

  > Crazy Horse is being memorialized because he was known as a courageous fighter, a humble man, a giver and provider, and someone true to the Lakota way of life.

- **Quotations** share the specific thoughts of people knowledgeable about the main point.

  > "The development of this memorial is not without controversy. For example, descendants of Crazy Horse feel that the family wasn't properly consulted at the outset of the project," stated local historian Marcie Smith.

- **Reflections** offer the writer's personal thoughts and feelings.

  > Because of Crazy Horse's private nature, one can only assume that he would have had little interest in such a memorial.

- **Analysis** shows the writer's critical thinking about the topic.

  > The memorial seems like a good idea, a way to honor a great man. Unfortunately, it is also a reminder of the difficult history of Native Americans.

Additional Support

Listed below are other types of support that you may find in your reading assignments.

- **Analogies** often compare something unfamiliar with something familiar.
- **Definitions** explain complex terms.
- **Experiences** share events in the writer's life, sometimes in the form of flashbacks.
- **Anecdotes** provide a slice of life (a brief story) to illustrate something.
- **References** to experts or studies add authority to an essay.

INSIGHT

A text may contain any combination of supporting details, and in any number. Knowing this will help you follow its development.

Supporting Details in Context

Here is a paragraph from a student essay in which the writer identifies an unusual plant, the banyan tree. The writer uses *facts, explanations,* and *examples* in his explanation.

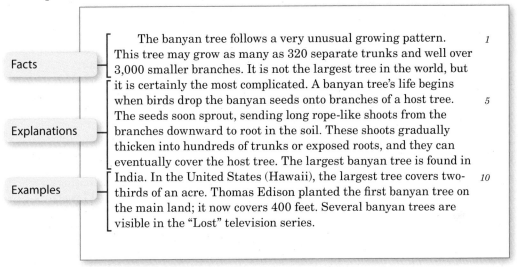

Facts

Explanations

Examples

> The banyan tree follows a very unusual growing pattern. *1*
> This tree may grow as many as 320 separate trunks and well over
> 3,000 smaller branches. It is not the largest tree in the world, but
> it is certainly the most complicated. A banyan tree's life begins
> when birds drop the banyan seeds onto branches of a host tree. *5*
> The seeds soon sprout, sending long rope-like shoots from the
> branches downward to root in the soil. These shoots gradually
> thicken into hundreds of trunks or exposed roots, and they can
> eventually cover the host tree. The largest banyan tree is found in
> India. In the United States (Hawaii), the largest tree covers two- *10*
> thirds of an acre. Thomas Edison planted the first banyan tree on
> the main land; it now covers 400 feet. Several banyan trees are
> visible in the "Lost" television series.

Here is another paragraph from a textbook, *Sociology: Your Compass for a New World*. The writer discusses religious sects using *explanations, examples,* and *analysis*.

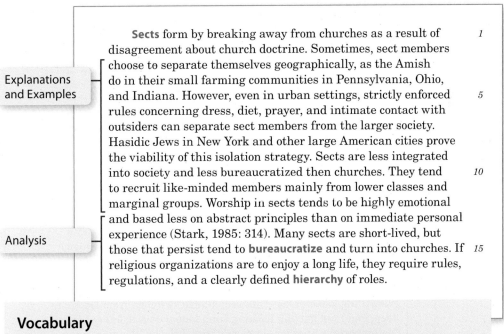

Explanations and Examples

Analysis

> **Sects** form by breaking away from churches as a result of *1*
> disagreement about church doctrine. Sometimes, sect members
> choose to separate themselves geographically, as the Amish
> do in their small farming communities in Pennsylvania, Ohio,
> and Indiana. However, even in urban settings, strictly enforced *5*
> rules concerning dress, diet, prayer, and intimate contact with
> outsiders can separate sect members from the larger society.
> Hasidic Jews in New York and other large American cities prove
> the viability of this isolation strategy. Sects are less integrated
> into society and less bureaucratized then churches. They tend *10*
> to recruit like-minded members mainly from lower classes and
> marginal groups. Worship in sects tends to be highly emotional
> and based less on abstract principles than on immediate personal
> experience (Stark, 1985: 314). Many sects are short-lived, but
> those that persist tend to **bureaucratize** and turn into churches. If *15*
> religious organizations are to enjoy a long life, they require rules,
> regulations, and a clearly defined **hierarchy** of roles.

Vocabulary

sects	**bureaucratize**	**hierarchy**
groups forming distinct units within larger groups	to make into a group of governing officials	a group of people with authority

Lastly, here is a personal essay in which student writer Eric Dawson explains his fascination with car racing. He uses *reflections, explanations, descriptions,* and *analysis* to share his story.

The Thrill of Victory

My fascination started the first time I saw my dad race. That was back in 1982. Ever since then, racing has been my main interest. I will never forget the afternoon when my dad told me I could drive, and that he would build a race car for me. That was probably the most exciting day of my life. That was the day my dad passed down the legacy of racing to me.

Reflections

You wouldn't believe the feeling that I had the first day I hit the track with my brand-new Buick stock car. I was a 13-year-old kid with absolutely no driving experience, being strapped into a 400-horsepower stock car. It was a very scary but exciting experience. All it took was one afternoon at the track, and I was hooked. I became the youngest driver ever to race at the Lake Geneva Raceway.

Explanation and Description

I guess you could say that my first year racing was a big learning experience. Driving race cars was not as easy as it appeared. I finished 18th overall out of 70 cars. It was a rough year. Because of my age and inexperience, many people had little or no faith in me, and I was sponsorless all season. Racing is a very expensive sport. Without some type of sponsorship or financial backing, it is almost impossible to maintain a race team. After that year, my future looked grim. I had no money and no sponsorship offers, but I did have some respectable finishes.

I managed to get enough funds together to build a new and more competitive car for the following season. The racing year started off great. I pulled off two second-place finishes in the first two races. Then disaster struck. I was leading the final race of the night, when my brand-new Monte Carlo hit an oil slick and slid headfirst into the wall, at just over 100 miles per hour. My car was destroyed. I was sent to the hospital with a broken wrist and a separated shoulder. I thought my racing career was over. I had spent every nickel I had on this car, and I was still sponsorless.

Analysis

Just when I thought I was through with racing, a miracle happened. When I returned from the hospital, there were two men waiting to speak to me. The men were from B. F. Goodrich. They not only wanted to sponsor me, but also wanted to give me a new race car. My future did a 180-degree turnaround.

This year will be my third year with B. F. Goodrich, and everything looks great. This year I have switched from Dodge to Jeep, and I am getting backing from Mopar Performance. Jeep Motorsports is another of my sponsors. It looks like all my hard work and dedication is starting to pay off.

1

5

10

15

20

25

30

35

40

Practice Identify the type of support used in the underlined information. Use pages 39–40 as a guide. (The first one is done for you.)

1. <u>By the 1800s, there were believed to be between 3,000 and 5,000 wolves living in the state</u>. (Wydeven). Around the same time, many European settlers arrived in the area.

   fact/statistic

2. When I was in first grade, our circus field trip was one huge disappointment. <u>First of all, I couldn't see much of anything because we were sitting in one of the last rows.</u> I could barely make out tiny figures scurrying around the three rings.

   reason, example, or explanation

3. Rent control is a main factor in determining the number of homeless a city will have. <u>For example, the number of homeless in Santa Monica, California, is so great that the city has been called "The Homeless Capital of the West Coast."</u>

   example

4. The emotional outburst known as road rage is a factor in as many as two-thirds of nonfatal accidents. . . . <u>Psychologist Arnold Nerenberg of Whittier, California, a specialist in motorway mayhem, estimates 1.78 billion episodes of road rage occur each year.</u> . . . (Adapted from *An Invitation to Health*, p422.)

   reference

5. <u>Webster's defines "eclectic" (i-klek'-tik) as selecting elements from different sources or systems.</u> Eclectic suggests variety. But what a great way to say variety. Variety sounds so plain, so Brand X. But eclectic is rich with imagination.

   definition

6. <u>My grandmother's rose garden was a symphony of color, and she was the conductor.</u> Shears in hand, she would step confidently toward the rose trellis and spread her hands. With a quick downbeat, her sheers sliced through the sharp thorns.

   analogy

Practice Here is part of an essay by Lois Krenske in which she discusses an unusual happening in nature, whale **strandings**. Try to identify different types of support used in each paragraph. Work on this activity with one or more of your classmates if your instructor allows it.

Suicide by Strandings

Mass whale suicides, or "strandings," as they are called, occur with disturbing consistency. Many men have tried to understand these bizarre suicides. Even Aristotle, the ancient Greek philosopher, considered them. Although he decided the suicides may indeed happen "without any apparent reason," modern biologists are not so easily convinced.   *1*

5

explanations; examples; quotations

One researcher has pointed out that the whales are descended from land-dwelling animals. He decided the whales may simply be "remembering" their ancient roots and beach themselves to go home. This habit, however, would have put the whales close to extinction years ago. The idea had to be dismissed.   *10*

references; reasons; explanations

A newer theory suggests that the whales blindly follow the earth's magnetic forces. The whales travel wherever these forces lead, almost as if they were following a road map. Unfortunately, the magnetic flow will sometimes **intersect** the shore and guide the whales along a collision course with the beach.   *15*

reasons; explanations

Biologists realize, of course, that none of these findings are complete explanations. They feel that the strandings must have a number of causes. To make this point, they compare beached whales to crashed planes. One theory will never explain them all.

reflections; analysis

Vocabulary

strandings
occurrences of swimming onto a beach

intersect
cut across, form a cross

Analyzing the Support

Identifying the different details in a reading assignment is the first step. You should also decide how effective they are. Reading without analyzing the details is like attempting to play soccer without defining the boundaries of the field: One of the key elements is missing.

A Guide to Careful Analysis

Use the following questions as a guide when you analyze the support in a paragraph or an essay that you read. Your answers will help you better understand the text and judge its value.

Questions to Ask

1. What supporting evidence seems especially strong? Why?

   _____

2. Does this information seem reliable and well researched? Explain.

   _____

3. What evidence, if any, does not seem that effective? Explain?

   _____

4. How would you rate the overall quality of the supporting information and why?

   Weak ★ ★ ★ ★ ★ Strong

   _____

5. What have you learned from this text?

   _____

6. What questions do you still have about it?

   _____

INSIGHT

Answering questions like these helps you connect with your reading assignment and remember the key points in it.

> "The book to read is not the one which thinks for you, but the one which makes you think."
> —Harper Lee

Analysis in Action

Here is a paragraph that shares a story about coming to America. The topic sentence is underlined. The supporting information includes explanations and descriptions. The analysis follows the paragraph.

I saw the pain in Frances Opeka's eyes when she talked about fleeing Yugoslavia when the Russian and communist troops were moving in. Sometime, in May of 1945, at 4:00 a.m., my grandfather's brother knocked on the window of Frances' home and said, "If you're coming with us, we're leaving in a half an hour." So my grandma, who was seven months pregnant, and my great-aunt (Frances) woke up my grandma's three children and left. They didn't have time to say good-bye to their parents, relatives, or friends. They just left. Their first stop was a camp in Austria and then they went to Italy where they lived for five difficult years in a refugee camp. Living conditions were primitive, to say the least. At times, they slept on the cold ground or if they were lucky, they slept on a thin covering of hay. At night, France would often go without her coat because she wanted to cover her pregnant sister to keep her warm. For food, they usually received bread and soup. They would cup their hands around the bread so they would not lose even a crumb. To get a potato was a treat. Germs and colds spread easily in the camp, so they all went through their sick times. My great-uncle Greg had the measles and being so young, he thought he was going to die. My grandma and great-aunt had high fevers multiple times. Well, my grandmother had her child, my mother, and her family was the first one that was allowed to come to America.

Sample Analysis

Main point as stated in the topic sentence (underlined): Fleeing her homeland was a painful experience for the writer's great-aunt.

1. What supporting information is especially strong? Why?

   The information held my interest because it showed what the family had to do to remain free. One detail that stands out is this one: The family left early in the morning without saying goodbye to anyone. Also, not wasting even a crumb of bread showed how hungry they were.

2. Does this information seem reliable and well-researched?

   This information comes from one of the refugees, so it should
   be reliable. But Frances Opeka is recalling something that
   happened a long time ago, so some of the details might be
   fuzzy. The experience of people fleeing communist rule could be
   checked on the Internet to learn more about this time.

3. What evidence, if any, does not seem that effective? Why?

   For the most part, the story seems realistic and believable.
   There were no really questionable ideas shared. Anyway, why
   would anyone try to make this up?

4. How would you rate the overall quality of the supporting
   information and why?

   Weak ★ ★ ★ (★) ★ Strong

   The supporting information got my attention because the story
   is so dramatic. But at times, more details would have made it
   better. For example, how did the family actually get to Austria
   and Italy?

5. What have you learned from this text?

   The end of World War II did not bring an end to the suffering of
   people in Europe. For this family, the suffering continued for at
   least five more years.

6. What questions do you still have about it?

   Two questions were identified in question 4. Also, I would like to
   know how many people attempted to flee Yugoslavia, and how
   many actually succeeded.

Practice Analyze the following paragraph. To get started, carefully read the paragraph; then underline the topic sentence and consider the different types of support that it includes. Next, answer the analysis questions that follow the paragraph.

Drug Deal

I was an eyewitness to a drug deal, and the smoothness and quickness   *1*
of the transaction will be in my mind forever. I was busy at work when
I happened to observe the deal. My work place, a restaurant, opens onto
an alley. About 25 feet from the rear of the restaurant is a dumpster. I
was taking a break and glanced out the back door. I saw a well-dressed   *5*
man come from the left and a raggedy-looking man come from the right.
They both met by the dumpster in clear view of me. The both looked
around, watching for anyone who might be in the alley. Then they quickly
exchanged packages and checked what they received. The slick man
flipped through the roll of bills he received and nodded. The raggedy   *10*
man checked his package and gave a quick nod. Both men slipped their
packages in their pockets and after a few quick glances, each went the way
he had come. The whole incident took about 45 seconds.

Analysis

1. What main point is stated in the topic sentence or thesis statement?
   Witnessing a drug deal made a major impact on the writer.

2. What supporting evidence seems especially strong? Why?

3. Does this information seem reliable and well-researched? Explain.

4. What evidence, if any, does not seem that effective? Why?

5. How would you rate the overall quality of the supporting information and why?
   Weak ★ ★ ★ ★ ★ Strong

6. What have you learned from this text? What questions do you have about it?

Special Challenge Analyze the essay on page 42 by answering the questions above about it.

LO2 Organization

When you read, remember that the ideas and organization work together to create meaning. Unless the ideas are organized, it would be almost impossible to follow them.

Common Patterns of Organization

Factual texts may follow one of these basic patterns. Knowing how these patterns work will help you follow the ideas in a text.

- **Chronological** – Paragraphs that recall experiences or explain how something works or how to do something usually follow chronological or time order.

- **Spatial** –Paragraphs that describe something or someone are often organized spatially or by location, working from top to bottom, right to left, and so on.

- **Logical** –Paragraphs that simply present supporting ideas in a sensible or reasonable order are organized logically.

- **Cause-effect** – Paragraphs that explain the relationship between causes and effects usually explore the causes first, then the effects.

- **Comparison-contrast** – Paragraphs that compare show the similarities and differences between two ideas. Comparative essays may discuss one subject first, then the next subject; they may discuss all of the similarities between the two and then their differences; or they make a point-by-point comparison.

- **Problem-solution** – Paragraphs that explore a particular problem often begin with a summary of the problem, follow with possible solutions, and then focus on the best solution.

- **Order of importance (argumentative)** – Paragraphs that support a claim or an opinion may be organized from the most important argument to the least important or the other way around. Objections to the claim or arguments often come first or last.

INSIGHT

While a text usually follows one main pattern, other patterns may be used in a few specific parts.

The Patterns in Action

Each paragraph that follows shows how a writer uses a common pattern of organization to arrange his or her ideas.

Chronological Order

This paragraph narrates an interesting historical story about growing up in the American frontier. (The words and phrases in italics show that time order is used.)

Francis Anne Slocum

Francis Anne Slocum was born in Rhode Island in March of 1773. The *1* next year her family moved to Pennsylvania. There, *until she was five,* she lived a happy childhood. But *on November 2, 1778,* Delaware Indians raided her home during the absence of the father. No one was hurt, but Francis was taken from the family and lost for 57 years. Then *in January of 1835,* a fur *5* trader named Colonel Ewing stopped at the house of a widow of the Chief of the Miami Indians. Colonel Ewing became interested in the mistress of the house because her features and coloring seemed different to him. Ewing *later* learned she was born of white parents and that her father's name was Slocum. He announced this discovery in a Lancaster, Pennsylvania, newspaper. *10* *Eventually*, one of Francis's brothers read the article and was *soon* reunited with his long-lost sister.

Comparison-Contrast

This paragraph compares and contrasts two main types of lightbulbs by first identifying their similarities and then discussing their differences.

See the Light

To select a lightbulb, you need to understand the differences between the *1* traditional incandescent bulb and the new compact fluorescent ones. Both bulbs are similar in that they come in many shapes, sizes, and brightnesses. But they are different in many important ways. For example, the new compacts have some limitations in their usability. Because of their odd shape, *5* they may not fit in the bulb sockets on some lamps. Compacts also may not work well in very cold temperatures , and they can't be used with a dimmer switch. On the other hand, compact bulbs are four times more efficient than incandescent ones. A 15-watt compact bulb produces as many lumens of light as a 60-watt incandescent bulb. Cost is another factor to consider. A compact *10* may cost about $15.00 while an incandescent can be purchased for a dollar. However, the compact burns less electricity and lasts seven to ten times longer. So in the long run, it should be less expensive. This information may help you decide what bulbs to choose in your own room or apartment.

Cause-Effect

This paragraph identifies the causes and effects of job opportunities in journalism. (The words in italics identify the cause-effect order used.)

Wanted: Newspaper Jobs

Students interested in journalism may want to consider other professions.   1
The *cause* is simple: Fewer and fewer people are buying newspapers. Many individuals, especially young people, are getting their news on the Internet. Fewer buyers of newspapers and magazines mean less income from sales. Fewer readers also mean fewer ad dollars, which is a major source of revenue.   5
As a result, newspapers are going out of business or cutting back and magazines are folding. This situation has forced publishers to re-form their companies. Newspapers are now offering electronic alternatives to their print products, but readers get this news for free or pay a small fee that in no way offsets the huge losses the companies are facing. The *effect* of this situation   10
on journalists is predictable: There are not enough jobs for experienced journalists, let alone college graduates. However, not all is lost. The Internet may offer exciting new career choices in the Information Age, especially for people who understand and appreciate the power of electronic communications.

Problem-Solution

This problem-solution paragraph discusses a serious issue in older urban dwellings, lead poisoning. (The words in italics show the pattern of organization used.)

Dangers of Lead Poisoning

Young children unprotected from almost any amount of lead may   1
suffer serious health problems. Lead poisoning can lead to everything from headaches to periods of confusion to learning problems. Inner-city dwellings built before 1960 may contain lead-based paints, the major source of the *problem*. If the lead paint is peeling, very young children will eat the paint   5
chips. Even the dust from this paint can be harmful. Unfortunately, once someone suffers from lead poisoning, there are no complete cures. The best *solutions* for families are **preventative**, such as daily house cleaning and regularly washing of hands. Long-term solutions include painting over the old lead paint, but without sanding beforehand. The Mayo Clinic Web site on lead   10
poisoning reminds renters that they have rights protecting their health and safety. Landlords are required by law to find and address sources of lead.

Vocabulary

preventative
a remedy that prevents something

Practice   Label the main pattern of organization used in the following paragraphs. Use pages 49–51 as a guide for your work.

Those Were the Days

1. The old man grumbled a bit as he wiped his eyes with the back of his gnarled hand. From his perch above the crowd, he watched the proceeding. He then glanced at his wife standing a short distance away. She, too, was old, but he still saw her as a much younger woman. His thoughts went back. He recalled the black and white dishes on which she had so proudly served him home-cooked meals. The chairs, the tables, the curtains, things that had made their home—all raced before his eyes. Then the auctioneer's voice brought his thoughts back to the present. He shifted in the seat of his old John Deere tractor. It was now being auctioned off and would soon be plowing someone else's field. Then the other machinery was to be sold, piece by piece. Within the next hour or so, the things he had worked for all his life would be gone. A half century of thoughts and feelings went with everything on display.

Pattern of organization:

chronological

Religion and School

2. Americans have the right to practice the religion of their choice, but practicing religion in public schools touches on sensitive ground. Religion in public schools goes against the Constitution of the United States. Most specifically and importantly, the First Amendment clearly states its desire to leave religion out of public schooling. The establishment clause in this amendment says there can be no official religion. The free-exercise clause states how one people can practice whatever religion they choose. If religious education were **mandated** in public schools, both of these rights would be violated. In addition, the Fourteenth Amendment contains an equal protection clause that makes clear the separation of church and state. The Supreme Court has also voiced its opinion that having religion affiliated with public schooling is unconstitutional. So it is clear that the writers of the Constitution wanted to keep religion separate from public institutions such as the education system.

Pattern of organization:

order of importance

TV and Your Health

3. Regardless of where they live, Americans spend most of their leisure time watching television: on average, more than 30 hours a week. Yet the more time spent in front of the TV, the greater the risk of obesity and related chronic diseases. Compared with other **sedentary** activities, such as reading, writing, or driving, watching TV lowers **metabolic** rate, so people burn fewer calories. Every hour spent watching television may increase your risk of dying prematurely from any cause by 11 percent, from **cardiorespiratory** disease by 18 percent, and from cancer by 9 percent, according to recent research. Compared with those who watched less than two hours per day, individuals who watched more than four hours had an 80 percent greater risk of premature death from heart-related causes.

"TV and Your Health" from HALES. *An Invitation to Health,* 7E. © 2012 Brooks/Cole, a part of Cengage Learning, Inc.

Pattern of organization:

cause-effect

About Race

4. Race is often the first thing people think of when they hear the word diversity. But some experts say race is a relatively modern idea. Centuries ago people tended to classify other people by status, religion, or language, for example, not by race. Actually, most of us are a blend of **enthnicities**, and how we perceive ourselves may be different from the way others see us. People may assume that a Pacific Islander with light-brown skin, dark hair, and dark eyes, for example, is Hispanic. And a classmate you may assume is White may think of himself as black. Or consider this: If you have a Chinese mother and a White father, you may not know which "race box" to check on standard forms. Should you choose Mom or Dad? Biologists tell us that there's more variation within a race than there is between races. Race isn't biological, they say, but *racism* is real.

"About Race" from STALEY/STALEY. *FOCUS on College and Career Success,* 1E. © 2012 Wadsworth, a part of Cengage Learning, Inc.

Pattern of organization:

logical

Vocabulary

mandated
required or commanded by

sedentary
requiring much sitting

metabolic
dealing with the chemical processes occurring within an organism to sustain life

cardiorespiratory
of or relating to the heart and the respiratory system

enthnicities
ethnic character and background

Another Approach to Organization

The patterns of organization refer to the main part of a text, in which the supporting evidence is presented. There are, of course, beginning and ending parts to a text as well. When analyzing a text, keep this three-part structure in mind.

Three-Part Structure

Paragraph Structure

Topic Sentence
- Names the topic and focus

Body Sentences
- Provide supporting sentences
- Follow a pattern of organization

Closing Sentence
- Wraps up the paragraph

Essay Structure

Beginning Part
- Introduces the topic
- Provides background information
- Identifies the main point or thesis

Middle Part
- Supports or develops the main point
- Follows one or more patterns of organization

Ending Part
- Summarizes the key ideas
- Restates the thesis
- Provides final thoughts or analysis

Considering the Three Main Parts

Use these questions as a guide when considering the beginning, middle, and ending parts in a paragraph or an essay. Your answers will contribute to your overall understanding of the text.

Questions to Ask

1. What type of information is given in the topic sentence or opening paragraph (in an essay)? Consider naming the topic, giving background information, starting the main point.

   _____

2. What types of supporting details are included?

   _____

3. How are the details in the main part organized?

   _____

4. What type of information is given in the closing sentence or ending part—summary of key ideas, restatement of the main point, final thoughts, and so on.

   _____

5. Does the organization make the text easy or hard to follow? Explain.

   _____

Practice   Answer the above questions for each of these paragraphs. (Work on this activity with a classmate if your instructor allows it.)

- "Drug Deal" (page 48)

   _____

   _____

- "See the Light" (page 50)

   _____

   _____

LO3 Voice

Another main trait of a text is voice—the special way in which the writer speaks to the reader. It may help to think of voice as the personality in a piece of writing. Most informational texts will speak to you in one of three ways:

- **Academic voice:** Writers of professional materials use a serious academic voice.
- **Personal voice:** Writers of essays, articles, and blog postings often use a casual personal voice.
- **Satiric voice:** Occasionally, writers sometimes use a satiric voice when they want to criticize or make fun of someone or something.

> "Voice is the aspect of writing closest to the writer."
> —Dan Kirby

A Basic Guide to Voice

Academic Voice

An academic voice is used in most textbooks, professional journals, and in thoughtful, serious research. An academic uses **formal English** and sounds serious and objective (sticking to the facts). The following informational text uses an academic voice.

> According to the Sierra Club, pollutants from farm run-off are steadily seeping into streams, lakes, reservoirs, and wells. Because much of the drinking water comes from these sources, warnings are posted in a number of U.S. and Canadian communities, and many more postings might be needed in the future (Sierra Club, 2005). As the Sierra Club argues, the pollution and related warnings are serious, and failure to heed them could be deadly. . . .

1

5

SPECIAL NOTE: Serious texts may contain brief personal introductions or brief passages containing the writer's personal thoughts and feelings and still be academic in voice.

formal English
a serious, straightforward style used in most academic writing including textbooks; characterized by objectivity (sticking to the facts)

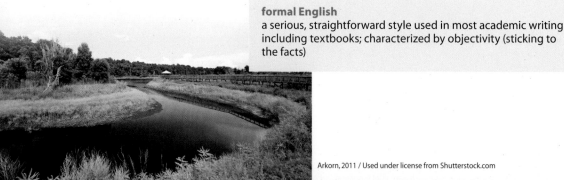

Arkorn, 2011 / Used under license from Shutterstock.com

Personal Voice

A personal voice used in personal essays, articles in popular magazines, and personal blog postings uses **informal English** and sounds somewhat relaxed and subjective (including the writer's personal thoughts and feelings). The following description uses a personal voice.

One Capewell photograph is proudly displayed in our house. It' a black-and-white photograph of two people neatly attired in their best military uniforms, and it was taken during World War II in a small studio in Leicester, England. . . . What makes this photograph so special to our family is the occasion that prompted it. It's my great-grandparents' wedding picture. They were both on leave to get married. Their honeymoon had to wait until after the war. This photograph is one of the few keepsakes that we have left from their military experience and wedding day, and we take very special care of it.

1

5

Satiric Voice

A satiric voice is used in essays and commentaries in which the writer speaks humorously or **sarcastically** about someone or something. A satire may be objective or subjective. The following passage from a personal blog posting uses a satiric voice. (King Arne refers to Arne Duncan, the Department of Education Secretary.)

All Hail to the King

King Arne made a visit to Milwaukee, and at one point during his visit, he toured a downtown public high school. A photograph in the newspaper shows the king marching down a hall with his attendants following close behind.

The king was impatient with his subjects here because in his estimation, they weren't making enough school improvements. And of course, when the king speaks, everyone listens because the king controls the coffers (stimulus money). He has $10 billion to invest in education, and this is only part of the money for education that he controls. (Talk about a power high).

1

5

informal English
a relaxed style used in most personal essays; characterized by subjectivity (the writer's personal thoughts and feelings)

satiric
the use of humor, fake praise, or sarcasm to make fun of someone or something

sarcastically
the act of making critical comments

Practice Carefully read the following passages. Then identify the voice used in each one—academic, personal, or satiric.

1. I recently sat in on a meeting that made my eyes droop and my toes curl. The purpose of the meeting was clear, but it dragged on and on without anything getting accomplished. And here's why: One person wouldn't stop talking. . . .

   Voice: satiric or personal

   _____

2. Several factors contributed to the tragedy in Walkerton, Ontario, including human error. First, according to *The Edmonton Journal,* a flaw in the water treatment system allowed water to enter Walkerton's well (Blackwell, 2001). Even after the manure washed in Walkerton's well, the chlorine should have killed the bacteria. . . .

   Voice: academic

   _____

3. Then there comes an odor in the cafeteria. No more than an odor. It is a heavy choking presence that overpowers the senses and settles on the skin leaving a thin greasy film. The food line lurches forward once more and doomed students mover closer to their noon meal. . . .

   Voice: academic

   _____

4. On a cold August morning, the stars blanketed the night sky over the outskirts of Quito, Ecuador. I stood on the street corner, shaking underneath my wool sweater, waiting for a guide to show me around this massive market. . . .

   Voice: personal

   _____

5. The major danger associated with texting is the distraction it causes to the driver. When a driver's eyes are concentrating on a phone instead of the road, he or she is more likely to get in an accident. Some critics say teenage drivers are the problem, but 20 percent of adults in a recent AAA study admitted regularly texting while driving. . . .

   Voice: academic

   _____

LO4 Word Choice and Sentences

Two other important traits are word choice and sentences.

Word Choice

Word choice is closely connected to voice, in that the words used help create the writer's voice. For example, textbook writers will naturally use many specific words associated with the topic. These content-specific words help create the academic voice in the text. Personal essayists, on the other hand, usually rely on more familiar words, which helps create a more personal or conversational voice.

Academic passage with content-specific words (underlined)

Wind farms are a clean energy source. Unlike power plants, which   *1*
emit dangerous pollutants, wind farms release no pollution into the air,
meaning less smog, less acid rain, and fewer greenhouse emissions. The
American Wind Energy Association reports that running a single wind
turbine has the potential to displace 2,000 tons of carbon dioxide, or the   *5*
equivalent of one square mile of forest trees.

Passage from a personal essay with mostly familiar words:

There was this old guy I used to know. His name was Jimmy, but I   *1*
called him "Admiral" because he had been in some war. He was about five
feet tall and smelled of cigar smoke mixed with coffee and other scents I
didn't recognize. He had smoke-stained teeth that were crooked. His white
hair always looked like it needed to be washed, and he wore the same   *5*
wrinkled clothes. But he had beautiful blue eyes, the deepest blue I've ever
seen.

Practice   Team up with a classmate to find one passage (two or three sentences) in a paragraph in this book that uses many content-specific words. Write the passage down and underline these words. Then write down a passage from a paragraph that seems more personal and uses very familiar terms. Be prepared to discuss your findings.

Sentences

Sentences come in all shapes and sizes. Some of them are very brief and direct. Others flow along very smoothly like a lazy country stream. Then, of course, there are sentences that are very complex that require multiple readings to understand.

Academic Sentences

The sentences in most textbooks are often long and complex, sometimes containing many ideas. These sentences suggest that the writer has been very careful her or his thinking. This makes sense because textbooks must share information thoroughly and accurately. Here are some longer sentences from academic texts. In each one, the core sentence is underlined. Notice all of the additional information added to each one.

Public housing was built in Chicago because of the Great Migration, the name given to the movement of African Americans from the South to the North.

Over time, the first musical instruments, which were stone and clay sound-producing objects, evolved into wind instruments including flutes and windpipes.

While North American wealth grew out of the Industrial Revolution, today's capitalism is a system largely based on consumerism—an attitude that values the purchase of goods in the belief that it is necessary.

In the past couple of decades, the status of the stewardess (i.e., the position of the stewardess in relation to others) has changed. In the era of shoe searches, deep discount no-frill service, and packaged peanut snacks, little of the glamour remains.

Sentences in Personal Essays

The sentences in personal essays are usually simpler than the ones that you will find in academic texts. As such, they are easier to follow and move along rather quickly. As a general rule, you will find more variety in the sentence length and structure. Notice how easy it is to read the following passages from personal essays.

The burnt smell of oil was the first thing I would notice in my grandfather's garage. On the right wall, he had pictures of the Smith Family. Some days, I would study all of the smiling faces on the pictures.

I had locked myself in the walk-in freezer. I knew I would get out. Someone *had* to open the door. But when? All around me, I saw frozen shrimp, crab legs, and lobsters. I couldn't even eat any of it.

My Indian culture is important to me, but that doesn't mean that I don't value my independence. During this semester, I have had a chance to think about my life. And I realize that I am an Indian and an American.

Have questions about your love life? Wonder what fashions to wear this fall? Want to know about the latest in hip food? Trendy magazines geared for young women address "deep" issues like these. Am I the only female that is both embarrassed and offended by these magazines?

Practice   Carefully read the following sets of sentences. Then identify each set as either academic or personal in structure. (Word choice, of course, plays a role in the level of difficulty or complexity in these sentences.)

1. The fourth type of Latin American music known as urban popular music combines a dynamic sound with calls for social change that appeals to many young listeners.

   Sentence style: academic

2. It's laundry night for me, and the Laundromat is buzzing, thumping, whirring. All the seats by the window are taken, as usual. The vending machines are doing overtime. A very pregnant young woman is folding clothes. Her toddler son is trying to climb into a dryer.

   Sentence style: personal

3. Waking up is hard. I'd rather dream I've won the tournament than get up and face the scale. But I'm hopeful. I've been strict and focused, in the gym and at the table. This tournament is the toughest one for the year, by far.

   Sentence style: personal

4. The Dutch fear of Islamic extremism has also increased, brought on in part by international attacks such as September 11 (2001) and later attacks in Madrid and London. This fear was further intensified when two well-know Dutch politicians were assassinated.

   Sentence style: academic

5. Sethe lives in house number 124, a house generally believed to be haunted and "full of baby venom" (Morrison 3). The child's ghost living in the house throws things around, shakes the floor, and stomps up the stairs.

   Sentence style: academic

Special Challenge   Find two sentences in the models in *Fusion 1* that are clearly academic because of their length and complexity. Then find two sentences that are personal in structure. Share your work with your classmates.

LO5 Reviewing the Traits of Reading

Respond to each set of directions to review the concepts covered in this chapter.

Ideas   Answer the following questions about the ideas in writing. (Pages 30–48.)

1. What is the first step to follow to find the main idea in a paragraph? The last step?

   Study the title, and the first and last sentences; Reread the paragraph and review the main idea

2. What is the name of the sentence that contains the main idea in a paragraph?

   topic sentence

3. What two parts does this sentence usually contain?

   (1) a specific topic plus (2) a particular feeling or idea about it

4. What is the purpose of supporting details in a paragraph?

   To support the main idea

5. What are four types of supporting details?

6. What type of support includes the writer's personal thoughts and feelings?

   reflections

Organization   Explain the following patterns of organization. (See pages 49–55.)

Chronological   When details are organized according to the time in which they occurred

Spatial   When details are organized according to their location

Comparison-contrast   When details are organized in a manner that shows the similarities and

differences between two ideas

Order of importance   When details are organized from the most important to the least important

or the other way around

Organization Explain the three-part structure in a paragraph.

Paragraphs have three distinct parts—a topic sentence, body sentences, and a closing sentence.

Create a graphic that will help you remember these three parts.

Voice Answer the following questions about voice. (see pages 56–58.)

1. What is voice in writing?

   The writer's unique way of speaking to the reader

2. What is meant by academic voice? (Find an example in one model.)

   A formal style that sounds serious and objective

3. What is meant by a personal voice? (Find an example in one model.)

   An informal style that sounds somewhat relaxed and subjective

4. What is meant by a satiric voice?

   A humorous or sarcastic style that may be objective or subjective

Word Choice and Sentences Answer the following questions about word choice and sentences. (See pages 59–62.)

1. What are the main features of academic word choice and sentences?

2. What are the main features of personal word choice and sentences?

4

"The pen is the tongue of the mind."
—Miguel de Cervantes

Academic Writing and Learning

You may not consider yourself a writer, but chances are you write more than you realize. Think about how many text messages, social media posts, or e-mails you have responded to in the last week alone. All of these examples involve using written words to communicate. Indeed, writing is an essential communication tool, especially with today's technology at your fingertips.

For a lot of you, this social aspect of writing comes naturally, while writing in the classroom is more difficult. Do not feel alone. Academic writing challenges even the most experienced writers. This chapter will outline guidelines and strategies to help make the demands of academic writing more manageable. Along the way, you will learn that writing is more than a way to share ideas—it is also a tool for *learning* new ideas.

Learning Outcomes

LO1 Write to learn.
LO2 Write to share.
LO3 Understand the writing process.
LO4 Use writing strategies.
LO5 Think critically and logically.
LO6 Review academic writing and learning.

What do you think?

In the quotation above, Miguel de Cervantes refers to a pen as "the tongue of the mind." What do you think he means by that? How does it relate to writing?

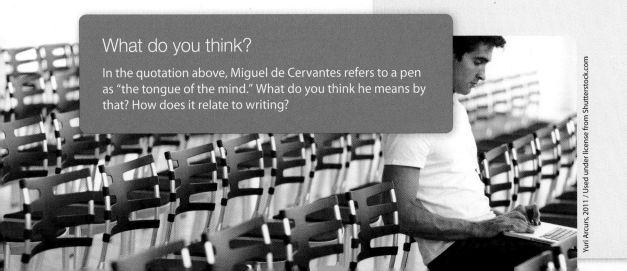

> "Don't think and then write it down. Think on paper."
> —Harry Kemelman

LO1 Writing to Learn

When athletes and other entertainers perform at exceedingly high levels, you often hear them talk about entering "The Zone," a special place where the mind slows down and achieving something extraordinary feels ordinary.

Experienced writers will tell you that writing allows you to enter a similar state of mind. The act of filling up a page triggers their thinking and leads to meaningful learning. The key is to rid your mind of distractions and let your thoughts flow onto the paper.

Changing Your Attitude

If you think of writing in just one way—as an assignment to be completed—you will never discover its true value. Writing works best when you think of it as a learning tool. A series of questions, a list, or a quick note can be a meaningful form of writing if it helps you think and understand. If you make writing an important part of your learning routine, you'll change your attitude about writing (for the better), and you'll become a better thinker and learner.

Keeping a Class Notebook

Keeping a class notebook or journal is essential if you are going to make writing an important part of your learning routine. Certainly, you can take notes in this notebook, but it is also helpful to reflect on what is going on in the class. These writing activities will help you think about your course work.

- Write freely about anything from class discussions to challenging assignments.
- Explore new ideas and concepts.
- Argue for and against any points of view that came up in class.
- Question what you are learning.
- Record your thoughts and feelings about an extended project.
- Evaluate your progress in the class.

Reflect Write freely for 5 to 10 minutes about your writing experiences. Consider how you feel about writing, your strengths and weaknesses as a writer, if you have ever used writing to learn, and so on. Then share your thoughts with your classmates.

LO2 Writing to Share Learning

The second important function of writing is to *share* what you have learned. When you write to learn, you write to gather your thoughts and make conclusions about subjects. But when you write to share, you present what you have learned to an audience, including your instructors and classmates. Writing to share involves making your writing clear, complete, and ready to be read by others.

A Learning Connection

As this graphic shows, improved thinking is the link between the two functions of writing. Writing to learn involves exploring and forming your thoughts, and writing to share learning involves clarifying and fine-tuning those thoughts.

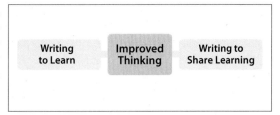

INSIGHT

Following the steps in the writing process is the best way to develop writing to share. This process helps you pace yourself so you don't try to do everything all at once. (See pages 68–73.)

The Range of Writing

The forms of writing to share cover a lot of territory, as you can see in the chart to the right. As a college student, your writing will likely cover the entire spectrum, with a focus on the more formal forms, such as essays and reports.

React Answer these questions about the chart: What forms of writing do you most often engage in? How does your writing approach change at different points along the spectrum?

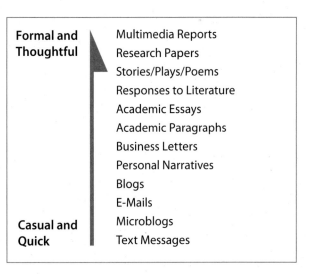

Formal and Thoughtful

Multimedia Reports
Research Papers
Stories/Plays/Poems
Responses to Literature
Academic Essays
Academic Paragraphs
Business Letters
Personal Narratives
Blogs
E-Mails
Microblogs
Text Messages

Casual and Quick

LO3 Understanding the Writing Process

Attempting to start and finish a writing project all at once can cause you undue stress. A writing project is much more manageable when you approach it as a process. This section will introduce you to the steps in the writing process.

The Steps in the Process

You cannot change a flat tire with one simple action. It takes a number of steps to get the job done right. The same goes for writing. If you expect to complete a paper in one general attempt, you (and your instructor) will be disappointed in the results. On the other hand, if you follow the writing process, you'll complete the job in the right way—one step at a time.

Process	Activities
Prewriting	Start the process by (1) selecting a topic to write about, (2) collecting details about it, and (3) finding a focus to direct your writing.
Writing	Then write your first draft, using your prewriting plan as a general guide. Writing a first draft allows you to connect your thoughts about a topic.
Revising	Carefully review your first draft and have a classmate read it as well. Change any parts that need to be clearer, and add missing information.
Editing	Edit your revised writing by checking for style, grammar, punctuation, and spelling errors.
Publishing	During the final step, prepare your writing to share with your instructor, your peers, or another audience.

Reasons to Write

Always use the writing process when you are writing to share learning and when you are writing certain personal forms. You don't need to use it when you are simply writing to learn.

Reason	Forms	Purpose
Writing to share learning	Informational paragraphs, summaries	To show your understanding of subjects you are studying
Personal writing	Personal paragraphs, blog postings, short stories, plays	To share your personal thoughts, feelings, and creativity with others

Reflect   Explain how the writing process explained above compares with your own way of completing assignments. Consider what you normally do first, second, third, and so on.

"If you start in the right place and follow all the
steps, you will get to the right end."
—Elizabeth Moon

The Process in Action

As the chart to the right indicates, there can be forward and backward movement between the steps in the writing process. For example, after writing a first draft, you may decide to collect more details about your topic, which is actually a prewriting activity.

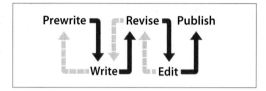

Points to Remember

When using the writing process, you need to understand the following points.

1. All the steps require some type of writing. Prewriting (planning), revising, and editing are as much writing activities as composing the first draft is.

2. It is unlikely that the process will work the same for any two writing assignments. For one assignment, you may struggle with gathering details. For another, you may have trouble starting the first draft.

3. No two writers develop their writing in the same way. Some writers need to talk about their writing early on, while others would rather keep their ideas to themselves. Some writers need to step away from their writing. Other writers can't stop until they produce a first draft. Your own writing personality will develop as you gain more writing experience.

4. All the information about the writing process won't make you a better writer unless you make a sincere effort to use it. You wouldn't expect to play the piano just by reading about it—you must follow the instructions and practice. The same holds true for writing.

INSIGHT

When you respond to a writing prompt on a test, use an abbreviated form of the writing process. Spend a few minutes gathering and organizing your ideas; then write your response. Afterward, read what you have produced and quickly revise and edit it.

Create   Make a chart that shows your own process—the one you described on page 68. Share your chart with your classmates.

A CLOSER LOOK at the Process

Each step in the writing process requires a special type of thinking. Following these steps will help you become a more confident writer and learner.

Prewriting is the first step in the writing process. In many ways, it is the most important step because it involves all of the decisions and planning that come before writing a first draft. If you plan well, you will be well prepared to work through the rest of the process. These are the basic prewriting tasks.

- **Identify a meaningful writing idea.** Choose a topic that meets the requirements of the assignment and that truly interests you. Begin your topic search by writing freely about the assignment or by simply listing your ideas.

- **Collect plenty of details.** Explore your own thoughts and feelings about the topic. Then gather additional information, either through firsthand experience (observations, interviews, and so on) or by reading about the topic in books, magazines, and on the Internet.

- **Establish a focus.** Just as a skilled photographer focuses or centers the subject before taking a photograph, you must identify a special part or feeling about the topic before writing your first draft. This focus, or emphasis, is usually expressed in a topic sentence. (See pages 32–38.)

- **Choose a pattern of arrangement.** Once you have established a focus, decide what details to include in your writing and how to organize them. You can arrange your details chronologically (by time), logically, by order of importance, and so on. (See pages 49–51.)

- **Organize your information.** With a pattern of arrangement in mind, you can organize your details in one of three basic ways:
  - Make a quick list of main points and support.
  - Create an outline—a more formal arrangement of main points and subpoints.
  - Fill in a graphic organizer—arranging main points and details in a chart or diagram. (See page 9.)

Supri Suharjoto, 2011 /
Used under license from Shutterstock.com

Drafting is the next step in the writing process. You have one important task during this step—to connect your thoughts and ideas about your topic. Just put these thoughts on paper so you have something to work with. They do not have to be perfectly worded. Here is a basic guide to drafting.

- **Strike while you're hot.** Write your first draft while your planning is still fresh in your mind.

- **Refer to your prewriting.** Use all of your planning and organizing as a basic writing guide. But also be open to new ideas as they come to mind.

- **Write as much as you can.** Keep writing until you get all of your ideas on paper, or until you come to a natural stopping point. Concentrate on forming your ideas rather than on making everything correct.

- **Form a meaningful whole.** A meaningful whole for a paragraph means a topic sentence, body sentences, and a closing sentence.

- **Pay special attention to each part.** All three parts—the opening, the middle, and the closing—play important roles in your writing. Give each part special attention. (See pages 74–79.)

Opening Sentence
The opening gets the reader's interest and states your thesis.

- **Look back to move forward.** Stop and reread what you have written to help you add new ideas.

- **Write naturally and honestly.** "Talk" to your readers, as if a group of classmates were gathered around you.

Middle
The middle supports your thesis.

- **Remember, it's a draft.** A first draft is your first look at a developing writing idea. You will have plenty of opportunities to improve upon it later in the process.

Closing
The closing offers important final thoughts about the topic.

A CLOSER LOOK at the Process (continued)

Revising is the third step in the process. During this step, you shape and improve the ideas in your first draft. Here is a basic guide to revising.

- **Step away from your draft.** Your time away will help you see your first draft more clearly, and with a fresh outlook.

- **Revisit your purpose.** Are you writing to explain, to persuade, to describe, or to share?

- **Read your draft many times.** Read it silently and out loud to get an overall impression of your work.

- **Have peers read it.** Their comments and questions will help you decide what changes to make.

- **Check your overall focus.** Decide if your focus still works and if you have provided enough support for it.

- **Review each part.** Be sure that the opening sets the proper tone for your writing, the middle part supports your focus, and the closing provides worthy final thoughts about the topic.

- **Know your basic moves.** There are four basic ways to make changes— adding, cutting, rewriting, or reordering information. Each change or improvement that you make will bring you closer to a strong finished paper.

Add information to . . .
- make a main point more convincing.
- complete an explanation.
- improve the flow of your writing.

Rewrite information if it . . .
- seems confusing or unclear.
- appears too complicated.
- lacks the proper voice.

Cut information if it . . .
- doesn't support the thesis.
- seems repetitious.

Reorder information if it . . .
- seems out of order.
- would make more sense in another spot.

- **Plan a revising strategy.** Decide what you need to do first, second, and third, and then make the necessary changes.

Editing is the fourth step, when you check your revised writing for style and correctness. Editing becomes important *after* you have revised the content of your writing. Here is a basic guide to editing.

- **Start with clean copy.** Do your editing on a clean copy of your revised writing; otherwise, things get too confusing.
- **Check first for style.** Make sure that you have used the best words, such as specific nouns and verbs and smooth-reading sentences.
- **Then check for correctness.** Start by checking your spelling, then move on to end punctuation, and so on.
- **For spelling, read from the last word to the first.** This strategy will force you to look at each word. (A spell checker will not catch every error.)
- **Circle punctuation.** This strategy will force you to look at each mark.
- **Refer to an editing checklist.** You'll find an example on page 127. Also refer to pages 363–539 for sentence, grammar, punctuation, and mechanics rules.
- **Use editing symbols.** These symbols provide an efficient way to mark errors.

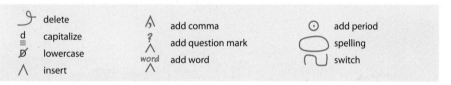

- **Get help.** Ask a trusted classmate to check for errors as well. You are too close to your writing to notice everything.

Publishing is the final step in the writing process. During this step, you prepare your writing before submitting or sharing it.

- **Prepare a final copy.** Incorporate all of your editing changes.
- **Follow design requirements.** Format your final copy according to the requirements established by your instructor.
- **Proofread the text.** Check your writing one last time for errors.

LO4 Using Writing Strategies

The writing strategies and instruction on the next 10 pages will help you write strong paragraphs.

Creating an Effective Topic Sentence

The topic sentence is the most important sentence in a paragraph, because it introduces the topic and establishes a focus for the rest of the writing. In most cases, the topic sentence is also the first sentence of the paragraph. Use this formula to create effective topic sentences for your paragraphs.

A specific topic		a specific feeling, feature, or part		An effective topic sentence
arrival of Hernán Cortéz in Mexico	**+**	marked the beginning of the end for the Aztec empire	**=**	The arrival of Hernán Cortéz in Mexico marked the beginning of the end of the Aztec empire.

Patryk Kosmider, 2011 / Used under license from Shutterstock.com

INSIGHT

A topic sentence is sometimes called a controlling sentence, because it establishes boundaries for your writing and helps you decide what information to include about your topic. A paragraph without a topic sentence lacks direction and can steer readers off course.

Analyzing the Topic Sentence

Analyze   Carefully read the following paragraph, paying special attention to how the topic sentence controls the direction of the paragraph. Then answer the questions below.

There are three main types of solar eclipses, each of which occurs   *1*
when the moon passes between the sun and the earth. The first type is
called a total solar eclipse. During a total solar eclipse, the moon blocks
out the entire central portion of the sun, resulting in the sky darkening as
if it were night. The second type is called a partial solar eclipse. With this   *5*
type, only part of the sun's surface is blocked out, and the sky may dim
slightly. Finally, an annular solar eclipse occurs when the sun and moon
are exactly in line, but the moon appears smaller than the sun. As a result,
the sun looks as if it has a bright ring around a dark center. Despite their
differences, all three types of solar eclipses do share one thing in common: *10*
They are rare to see, since the moon only passes between the sun and
earth twice a year on average.

1. What specific topic is introduced in the topic sentence?

   solar eclipses

2. What special part or feature about the topic is stated in the topic sentence?

   three main types of solar eclipses

3. How does the topic sentence control the direction of the other details in this paragraph?
   It establishes a direction for the rest of the paragraph by limiting the topic to the
   three types of solar eclipses.

4. How would you rate this topic sentence and why?

   Weak ★ ★ ★ ★ ★ Strong

Developing the Middle Part

In the middle paragraphs, you develop all of the main points that support your topic statement. Use your planning (quick list, outline, graphic organizer) as a general guide when you develop this part of a paragraph. Here are a few tips for getting started.

- **Keep your topic sentence in mind as you write.** All of your details should support or explain this statement.
- **Use plenty of details** to fully explain your ideas.
- **Use your own words,** except on those few occasions when you employ a quotation to add authority to your writing.
- **Be open to new ideas that occur to you,** especially if they will improve your paragraph.
- **Try any of the basic writing moves** that are appropriate to your topic.

Basic Writing Moves

The paragraphs in the middle part of a paragraph should, among other things, *explain, describe, define, classify,* and so on. What follows is a list and definitions of these basic writing moves.

Narrating	sharing an experience or a story
Describing	telling how someone or something appears, acts, or operates
Explaining	providing important facts, details, and examples
Illustrating	providing examples to support a main point
Analyzing	carefully examining a subject or breaking it down
Comparing	showing how two subjects are similar and different
Defining	identifying or clarifying the meaning of a term
Reflecting	connecting with or wondering about
Evaluating	rating the value of something
Arguing	using logic and evidence to prove something is true
Classifying	breaking down a subject into categories, or types

Special Challenge   Read two different paragraphs in this book. On your own paper, list the different moves that the writer uses in the middle sentences of the paragraph. For example, the writer may *explain* in one or more sentences, *reflect* in another, and so on.

Analyzing the Middle Sentences

Analyze   Carefully read the following paragraph, paying special attention to the middle sentences. Then answer the questions below.

There are three main types of solar eclipses, each of which occurs   *1*
when the moon passes between the sun and the earth. The first type is
called a total solar eclipse. During a total solar eclipse, the moon blocks
out the entire central portion of the sun, resulting in the sky darkening as
if it were night. The second type is called a partial solar eclipse. With this   *5*
type, only part of the sun's surface is blocked out, and the sky may dim
slightly. Finally, an annular solar eclipse occurs when the sun and moon
are exactly in line, but the moon appears smaller than the sun. As a result,
the sun looks as if it has a bright ring around a dark center. Despite their
differences, all three types of solar eclipses do share one thing in common: *10*
They are rare to see, since the moon only passes between the sun and
earth twice a year on average.

1. How do the middle sentences relate to the topic sentence?

   They expand on the focus of the topic sentence—the three main types of solar eclipses.

2. Do the middle sentences do enough to support the topic sentence? Explain.

   _____

3. What basic writing move (or moves) does the writer use in this paragraph? (See previous page.)

   analyzing and classifying_____

4. How would you rate the middle sentences and why?

   Weak ★ ★ ★ ★ ★ Strong

   _____

Writing a Strong Closing

While the opening part of your writing offers important *first* impressions, the closing part offers important *final* impressions. More specifically, the closing helps the reader better understand and appreciate the importance of your topic sentence.

The Basic Parts

Consider the strategies below when writing your closing. Note that it may take more than one sentence to appropriately close a paragraph.

- Remind the reader of the focus of the topic sentence.

  > Exploring the basics of sleeplessness makes it clear why we have sleep disorder clinics: There are a lot of people who aren't getting a good night's sleep.

- Summarize the main point.

  > As you can see, sometimes young adults seem to be everywhere and nowhere at the same time.

- Reflect on the explanation or argument you've presented in the middle part.

  > Let's make all of our roads a safer place; the time has come to make text messaging while driving illegal in every state.

- Offer a final thought to keep the reader thinking about the topic.

  > With all the senses to appeal to, chefs can make every dish a unique work of art.

INSIGHT

You may need to write two or three versions of your closing before it says exactly what you want it to say.

Example Closing Sentence

Analyze   Carefully read the same paragraph, paying special attention to the closing sentence. Then answer the questions below.

> There are three main types of solar eclipses, each of which occurs *1*
> when the moon passes between the sun and the earth. The first type is
> called a total solar eclipse. During a total solar eclipse, the moon blocks
> out the entire central portion of the sun, resulting in the sky darkening as
> if it were night. The second type is called a partial solar eclipse. With this *5*
> type, only part of the sun's surface is blocked out, and the sky may dim
> slightly. Finally, an annular solar eclipse occurs when the sun and moon
> are exactly in line, but the moon appears smaller than the sun. As a result,
> the sun looks as if it has a bright ring around a dark center. Despite their
> differences, all three types of solar eclipses do share one thing in common: *10*
> They are rare to see, since the moon only passes between the sun and
> earth twice a year on average.

1. In what way does the closing sentence remind the reader of the topic sentence?

   It restates the ideas discussed in the topic sentence.

   _____

2. What basic closing strategy (or strategies) does the writer use in this paragraph? (See the previous page.)

   It reminds the reader of the focus of the topic sentence.

   _____

3. How would you rate the end of this paragraph and why?

   Weak ★ ★ ★ ★ ★ Strong

   _____

   _____

Understanding Strong Writing

The traits (ideas, organization, voice, and so on) are the key ingredients in writing. Each one contributes to a successful essay or report. (See pages 89–108.)

The traits-based checklist below serves as a guide to strong writing. Your writing will be clear and effective when it can "pass" each point. This checklist is especially helpful during revising, when you are deciding how to improve your writing.

> "The first draft is the down draft—you just get it down. The second draft is the up draft—you fix it up."
> —Anne Lamont

INSIGHT

Word choice and sentence fluency are not as important early on in the revising process, when you are focused on content. But they do become important later on, during editing.

A Guide to Strong Writing

Ideas

☐ 1. Does an interesting and relevant topic serve as a starting point for the writing?

☐ 2. Is the writing focused, addressing a specific feeling about or a specific part of the topic? (Check the topic sentence.)

☐ 3. Are there enough specific ideas, details, and examples to support the thesis?

☐ 4. Overall, is the writing engaging and informative?

Organization

☐ 5. Does the writing form a meaningful whole—with opening, middle, and closing parts?

☐ 6. Does the writing follow a logical pattern of organization?

☐ 7. Do transitions connect ideas and help the writing flow?

Voice

☐ 8. Does the writer sound informed about and interested in the topic?

☐ 9. Does the writer sound sincere and genuine?

Word Choice

☐ 10. Does the word choice clearly fit the purpose and the audience?

☐ 11. Does the writing include specific nouns and verbs?

Sentence Fluency

☐ 12. Are the sentences clear, and do they flow smoothly?

☐ 13. Are the sentences varied in their beginnings and length?

React Carefully read the following paragraph. Then answer the questions below.

Cutting Down the Atmosphere

Trees make up an essential part of the earth's ecosystem, but rapid *1*
deforestation is having harmful effects on the planet. Deforestation refers
to the clearance of forests through logging and burning. The main cause
of deforestation is the use of trees for lumber and fuel. Forests are also
cut down to make room for farming. But while deforestation can provide *5*
a short-term boost to struggling economies, it is also causing harm to
the environment. Adverse effects of deforestation include erosion of soil,
disruption of the water cycle, loss of biodiversity, and flooding and drought.
The most harmful effect, though, may be on the climate. Deforestation
leads to a greater accumulation of carbon dioxide in the atmosphere, which *10*
in turn may warm the planet. Those who practice deforestation must
determine if the economic benefits outweigh the negative impact on the
earth.

Ideas

☐ **1.** Is the topic relevant and interesting?

☐ **2.** Is the topic sentence clear?

☐ **3.** Does the paragraph contain a variety of specific details?

Organization

☐ **4.** Does the topic sentence include the key elements of an effective opening?

☐ **5.** Do the middle sentences follow a logical pattern of organization?

Voice

☐ **6.** Does the writer sound informed and interested in the topic?

☐ **7.** Does the writer sound sincere and honest?

Using Standard English

Standard English (SE) is English that is considered appropriate for school, business, and government. You have been learning SE throughout your years in school. The chart that follows shows the basic differences between non-Standard English (NS) and SE.

Differences in . . .	NS	SE
1. Expressing plurals after numbers	10 mile	10 miles
2. Expressing habitual action	He always be early.	He always is early.
3. Expressing ownership	My friend car . . .	My friend's car . . .
4. Expressing the third-person singular verb	The customer ask . . .	The customer asks . . .
5. Expressing negatives	She doesn't never . . .	She doesn't ever . . .
6. Using reflexive pronouns	He sees hisself . . .	He sees himself . . .
7. Using demonstrative adjectives	Them reports are . . .	Those reports are . . .
8. Using forms of *do*	He done it.	He did it.
9. Avoiding double subjects	My manager he . . .	My manager . . .
10. Using *a* or *an*	I need new laptop. She had angry caller.	I need a new laptop. She had an angry caller.
11. Using the past tense of verbs	Carl finish his . . .	Carl finished his . . .
12. Using *isn't* or *aren't* versus *ain't*	The company ain't . . .	The company isn't . . .

"Standard English is not a language—
but a variety of English among many."
—Peter Trudgill

Read   Carefully read the following narrative paragraph. As you will see, it contains underlined examples of non-standard variations of American English (NS).

> Riding up the mountain trail, my thighs ached and my lungs *1*
> burned, but I couldn't be happier. Fifty feet in front of me pedaled my
> brother, Keith, fresh off his tour with the Marines. This mountain biking
> adventure was his idea. The green, forest-lined trail be bumpy, with sharp
> turns and steep descents. It ain't for beginners. At one point we hit patch *5*
> of fog and I lost sight of Keith. It felt as if we were riding through clouds.
> Keith couldn't even see hisself. The ghostly air be damp and smelled like
> rain. I slowed down and called for my brother. "Are you still up there?"
> "Would I be anywhere else?" he yelled back. When the fog disappeared,
> we stopped for a breather on a ridge that overlooked a vast valley. A *10*
> sea of pointy evergreens stretched for miles, ending near the peak of a
> distant mountain. While I snack on my peanut butter granola bar, Keith
> he glanced over at me. "This is fun, isn't it?" he commented. "It's good
> having you back, man," I responded. With that we hopped on our bikes and
> continued our adventure. *15*

Discuss   In small groups or as a class, identify the number that describes each underlined NS form, using the chart on page 82 as a guide. Then explain how to express each one using Standard English (SE).

LO5 Thinking Critically and Logically

Critical thinking is careful, logical thinking—the kind of thinking that you should use for your academic writing. Here are some questions that will help you to think critically and logically about your writing projects.

Asking Critical Questions

- What is the purpose of my writing (to inform, to entertain, to persuade)?
- Who is my intended audience (general readers, my instructor, my peers)?
- Can my topic be separated into parts? If so, what are they?
- How well do I know my topic?
- What will the reader gain from reading about this topic?
- What logical pattern of thinking should I follow? (See below.)
- What will be the focus, or topic sentence, of my paragraph? (See pages 74–75.)
- How will I support my topic sentence?

Logical Patterns of Thinking

Most of your academic writing will follow either a deductive or an inductive pattern of thinking. **Deductive thinking** moves from a general focus to specific supporting details. This is the most common pattern of thinking that you will use. **Inductive thinking** moves from specific facts and details to a general conclusion.

Use these questions to check for deductive thinking.

- Do I include a topic and a focus in my topic sentence?
- Do the details logically support or follow from my topic sentence?
- Does the conclusion logically follow the ideas that come before it?

Use these questions to check for inductive thinking.

- Do I start with a series of facts, examples, and explanations?
- Do the details logically lead up to a general conclusion?
- Is the general conclusion reasonable?

Apply For your next writing assignment, use the questions on this page as a general guide to critical and logical thinking.

A CLOSER LOOK at Logic

Logic is the science of reasonable and accurate thinking. Your writing will be logical if it contains relevant and provable evidence.

Reliable and Logical Evidence

Observation: I happily waited in line with scores of others at the Columbia Public Market.

Quotation: Christie George of Willis Bakery said, "Our booth has generated goodwill for our business."

Statistic: The number of markets in the United States increased by 18.3 percent from 2004 to 2006.

Explanation: According to the United States Department of Agriculture . . .

Faulty Logic

Exaggerating the Facts: Eating fast food causes obesity, even if you eat it once or twice a month.

Distracting the Reader: Processed food is not only bad for your health, but it looks gross and the wrappers add to the problem of littering.

Offering Extremes: If you don't start buying locally grown food, all farmers will lose their jobs.

Telling Only Part of the Truth: Eating fresh, locally grown food is the only way to eat healthy.

Appealing to a Popular Position: You should eat locally grown food because a lot of celebrities are saying it's a good idea.

Practice Write two or three of your own examples of faulty logic (without naming the type). Then exchange your work with a partner and discuss each other's examples.

_____

_____

LO6 Reviewing Academic Writing and Learning

Writing to Learn Answer the following questions about writing to learn. (See page 66.)

1. How is writing to learn different from traditional writing assignments?

   Writing to learn means uses writing to learn new information, rather than to simply complete an assignment.

2. What are some ways you can write to learn using a class notebook? Name two.

Understanding the Writing Process Answer the following questions about the writing process. (See pages 68–73.)

1. What are the steps in the writing process?

   Prewriting, writing, revising, editing, publishing

2. Explain the forward and backward movement of this process?

   A writer may move back and forth between the steps in the process.

3. Which step deals with planning to write? With improving the first draft?

   Prewriting; revising

Using Writing Strategies Answer the following questions about the writing strategies and instruction covered in this chapter. (See pages 74–83.)

1. What are the three main parts of an academic paragraph?

   A topic sentence, body sentences, and a closing sentence

2. What is Standard English?

   English that is considered appropriate for school, business, and government.

3. How can the guide to strong writing help you?

   Your writing is clear and effective when it "passes" each point in the checklist.

Thinking Critically and Logically Answer the following questions about critical and logical thinking. (See pages 84–85.)

1. What is critical thinking?

   Careful, logical thinking that is recommended for academic writing

2. What is meant by faulty logic? Give one example.

   Illogical or exaggerated evidence

5

The Traits of Academic Writing

"Good writing is also about making good choices when it comes to picking the tools you plan to work with."
—Stephen King

Writing is basically forming your thoughts on paper. Since you have plenty of thoughts and feelings, shouldn't writing then be an easy and natural thing to do? After all, how difficult can it be to record what you are thinking? Well, as you know, it can actually be quite a challenge. The problem that you and many others may face is understanding how to form your thoughts on paper.

In chapter 4, you learned that writing is a process. (See pages 68–73.) This process gives you a step-by-step structure that will help you develop your thoughts on paper. This chapter introduces you to the traits or working parts of academic writing. The traits include ideas, organization, voice, word choice, sentences, and conventions.

Together, the writing process and the traits of writing will help you develop your best thoughts on paper.

Learning Outcomes

LO1 Ideas
LO2 Focus
LO3 Organization
LO4 Voice
LO5 Word choice and sentences
LO6 Conventions
LO7 Review

What do you think?

In the quotation above, what "tools" do you think King is referring to? Are any tools identified in the introduction to this chapter? Explain.

LO1 Ideas

Ideas are the first and most important trait to consider when you are writing. Without ideas you have nothing to work with. Just as a cook needs ingredients to make something, a writer needs ideas to develop a piece of writing. When choosing ideas, you need to consider a topic first, then details to support it.

> "As soon as you connect with your true subject, you will write."
> —Joyce Carol Oates

Selecting a Topic

Always try to select a topic that attracts you; otherwise, you will have a hard time working with it through the steps in the writing process. Granted, your choices may be limited for many of your writing assignments. Even so, do your best to select a topic that truly has some meaning to you.

Limiting Your Choices

In most cases, a writing assignment will identify a general subject area, and your first job is to find a specific writing idea related to this subject. This graphic shows how the selecting process should work from the general subject area to a specific topic.

Assignment: Write a paragraph explaining a stress-related condition.

INSIGHT ————

A topic for a research report must be broad enough to offer plenty of information. For a more limited assignment (a one- or two-page essay), the topic should be more specific.

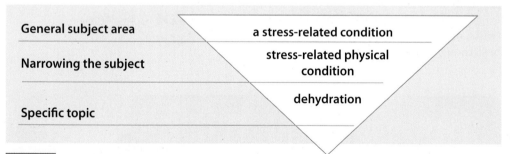

General subject area	a stress-related condition
Narrowing the subject	stress-related physical condition
Specific topic	dehydration

Select Identify a specific topic for the following assignment.

Assignment: Write a paragraph explaining an important environmental problem.

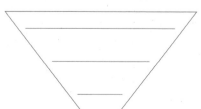

1. General subject area
2. Narrow this subject
3. Specific topic

Selecting Strategies

Always review your class notes, textbook, and Web sites for possible topics. You may also want to try one of the selecting strategies that follow.

- **Clustering** Begin a cluster (or web) with a nucleus word or phrase related to the assignment. (The general subject area or narrowed subject would work.) Circle it and then cluster related words around it. As you continue, you will identify possible writing ideas.

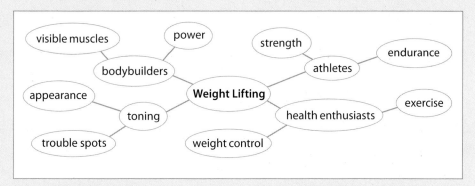

- **Listing** Freely list ideas as you think about your writing assignment. Keep going as long as you can. Then review your list for possible topics.
- **Developing a Dialogue** Write nonstop for 5–10 minutes about your assignment to discover possible topics. Begin by writing down a particular thought about the assignment.

Practice Use one of the strategies explained above to identify possible topics related to one of the following general subject areas:

exercise   popular music   careers   freedom/rights   technology

Gathering Details

To write about a topic, you need plenty of supporting details. Some of these details may come from your own thoughts about the topic. Other details will come from reading and learning about the topic.

Identifying What You Already Know

To learn what you already know about a topic, try one of these strategies.

- **Clustering** Create a cluster with your topic as the nucleus word. (see page 89.)
- **Listing** List your thoughts and ideas about your topic as well as questions that come to mind. Keep your list going as long as you can.
- **Freewriting** Write nonstop for 5-8 minutes to see what ideas you can discover about your topic. Go where your thoughts take you, one after another.
- **Discussing** Create a dialogue (written conversation) about your topic. In this dialogue, talk about your topic. Keep the dialogue going as long as you can. Here's one way to get started:

  (Your name): Luis, do you know anything about (your topic)?

  Luis: I know a little bit. How about you?

Collect   Use one of the strategies above to gather your thoughts about a topic you identified on the last page. (Select an activity different from the one you used on page 89.)

_____

_____

_____

_____

CONSIDER THE TRAITS

Remember that at this stage, the most important trait is ideas. Gather them, discover them, hunt them down. More is better.

> "Knowledge is of two kinds. We know subjects ourselves, or we know where we can find information about it."
> —Samuel Johnson

Learning More About a Topic

Your own thoughts will not be enough for many writing assignments. You will need to collect addition information through research. You can read about a topic or learn about it some other way. You can also try one of these strategies.

Answering Key Questions Create a list of questions about the topic that you would like to answer during your research. Let's say that you are writing about an event. You could list questions based on the 5 W's and H to answer.

- **When** did the event take place?

  _____

- **What** exactly happened?

  _____

- **Who** was involved?

  _____

- **Why** did it occur?

  _____

- **Where** did it take place?

  _____

- **How** did everything go? (Were there any problems?)

  _____

Analyzing You can explore your topic from different angles by answering these questions.

- What parts does my topic have? *(Break it down.)*

  _____

- What do I see, hear, or feel when I think about my topic? *(Describe it.)*

  _____

- What is it similar to and different from? *(Compare it.)*

  _____

- What value does it have? *(Evaluate it.)*

  _____

- How useful is it? *(Apply it.)*

  _____

Collect Use either of the above strategies to discover more about the topic you worked with on the last page. (Answer at least three of the questions after doing some quick research.)

  _____

  _____

Understanding Supporting Details

When you collect information, you need to know that there are different types of details that you can use in your writing. These details will help you explain or support your topic.

Types of Details

The following list identifies the common types of details.

- **Facts and statistics** give specific information that can be checked.

  Peregrine falcons have the same mate for life and produce three or four eggs each season.

- **Examples** demonstrate or show something.

  Main point: Americans responded in many ways during the latest oil crisis.

  Example: Many homeowners in the Northeast voluntarily turned down their home thermostats.

- **Definitions** explain new terms.

  A pandemic is an "infectious disease covering a wide geographic area and affecting a large part of the population."

- **Quotations** provide the thoughts of people knowledgeable about the topic.

  Chris Woolston of the Consumer Health Interactive says, " Fatty, unbalanced, and oversized. That, in a nutshell, is the American diet."

- **Reasons** answer the question "Why?" about an idea.

  Huck and Jim both escaped from civilization. They were both fleeing from an unbearable situation.

Identify List two or three different types of details that you could use to support the topic you have been working with in this chapter.

_____

_____

_____

Levels of Details

List two or three different types of details that you could use to support the topic you have been working with in this chapter.

- **Level 1:** A **controlling sentence** names a topic (usually a topic sentence) or makes a main point.
- **Level 2:** A **clarifying sentence** explains a level 1 sentence.
- **Level 3:** A **completing sentence** adds details to complete the point.

Details in Action

In the passage that follows, the level 1 sentence (a topic sentence) is supported by two level 2 sentences. Each level 2 sentence is supported by two level 3 sentences.

> **(Level 1)** Cartoons helped to shape the way I think. **(Level 2)** Most   1
> of them taught me never to take life too seriously. **(Level 3)** Many of the
> characters made their way through life with smirks on their faces. **(Level
> 3)** And all but a few of them seized the day, living for the moment. **(Level
> 2)** In an offhanded way, cartoons also provided me with a guide on how   5
> to act. **(Level 3)** Good versus evil was usually clearly defined. **(Level 3)**
> Other cartoons stressed the importance of loyalty.

Identify Identify After reading the following passage, label its levels of detail. Work on this activity with a partner if your instructor allows it.

> (Level 1   ) Jim Thorpe was one of the star athletes   1
> representing the United States in the 1912 Summer Olympics in Sweden.
> (Level 2   ) Thorpe, a Native American, was an extremely versatile
> athlete, but he was especially skilled in track and field. (Level 3   )
> He won a gold medal in the pentathlon, a track-and-field event of five   5
> parts. (Level 3   ) He also won a gold medal in the decathlon, a ten-
> part track-and-field event.

Special Challenge Write a brief paragraph describing a favorite television show. Label your sentences with a 1, 2, or 3, depending on the level of detail they include. (Your paragraph may or may not have level 3 details.)

LO2 Focus or Thesis

Focus is not one of the basic traits of writing, but it is included here because it helps you plan how to use the ideas that you collect.

Choosing a Focus

A focus is a particular feeling or part of the topic that you want to emphasize.

Let's say you are writing about the food in your school's union. More specifically, you want to complain about the huge amount of food that goes to waste. Your feelings about the waste could serve as the focus for your writing.

Topic: food in your school union

Focus: amount of food that is wasted

Your writing will be hard to follow if it lacks focus. So it's important to identify a clear and reasonable focus. To try to describe everything about the food in the union would be unreasonable, because there would be too much to say.

Evaluating a Focus

Your writing will hard to follow if it lacks focus. As a result, it's important to identify a clear and reasonable focus. To try to describe every activity related to an annual community event would be too general; whereas, focusing on one or two unique activities would seem reasonable.

Review Rate the effectiveness of each focus below by circling the appropriate star. Consider whether the focus is clear, reasonable, and worth developing. Explain each of your choices.

1. **Topic:** sports drinks **Focus:** the best choice during long workouts
   weak ★ ★ ★ ★ ★ strong _____

   _____

2. **Topic:** society's view of beauty **Focus:** seems good
   weak ★ ★ ★ ★ ★ strong _____

   _____

3. **Topic:** cultural comparisons between Korea and the United States **Focus:** contrasting views on cleanliness
   weak ★ ★ ★ ★ ★ strong _____

   _____

Forming a Topic Sentence

State your focus in a **topic sentence** for a paragraph and in a **thesis statement** in an essay. The following formula can be used to write a topic sentence or thesis statement. The following example is for an informational paragraph.

A specific topic		A particular feeling, feature, or part		An effective topic sentence or thesis statement
arrival of Hernán Cortés in Mexico	**+**	marked the beginning of the end of the Aztec empire	**=**	The arrival of Hernán Cortés in Mexico marked the beginning of the end of the Aztec empire.

Create   Identify a focus and then write a topic sentence or thesis statement for each of the following assignments. The first one is done for you.

1. **Writing assignment:** Paragraph describing a specific style of clothing

   Specific topic: Zoot suit

   Focus: _Popular during the swing era_

   Topic sentence: _The zoot suit (specific topic) became a popular fashion symbol in the swing era (a particular feature)._

2. **Writing assignment:** Paragraph explaining how to do something

   Specific topic: Using chopsticks

   Focus: _____

   Topic sentence: _____

   _____

3. **Writing assignment:** Paragraph analyzing a popular type of cooking

   Specific topic: Cajun cooking

   Focus: _____

   Thesis statement: _____

   _____

4. **Writing assignment:** Paragraph exploring technology and education

   Specific topic: Electronic textbooks

   Focus: _____

   Thesis statement: _____

   _____

Vocabulary

topic sentence
the controlling idea in paragraph

thesis statement
the controlling idea in an essay

LO3 Organization

You should next think about the pattern of organization that you plan to use to develop your topic sentence (or thesis statement). Here's one way to do this:

1. **Study your topic sentence or thesis.** It will usually indicate how to organize your details. Consider the following topic sentence

   > Eating locally grown produce will improve the local economy.

   This topic sentence suggests arranging the information by order of importance (see below) because the writer is trying to prove a point.

2. **Then review the details you have gathered.** Decide which details support your topic sentence; also decide on the best pattern of organization to arrange them. For the example topic sentence, the writer would arrange his or her details (reasons) from most important to least important or the other way around.

Patterns of Organization

Listed below are some of the common patterns that you will use in your writing.

- Use **chronological order** (time) when you are sharing a personal experience, telling how something happened, or explaining how to do something.
- Use **spatial order** (location) for descriptions, arranging information from left to right, from top to bottom, from the edge to the center, and so on.
- Use **order of importance** when you are taking a stand or arguing for or against something. Arrange your reasons either from most important to least important or the other way around.
- Use **logical order** if you want to follow your topic sentence or thesis statement with supporting details (reasons, examples, and so on) that naturally and logically follow one another.
- Use **compare-contrast organization** when you want to show how one topic is different from and similar to another one.

CONSIDER THE TRAITS

Think about your purpose as you choose a pattern of organization. Often, your working thesis statement will suggest how you should organize details.

Choose Study each of the following topic sentences and thesis statements. Then choose the best method of organization to develop it. The first one is done for you. (Work on this activity with a classmate if your instructor allows it.)

1. **Topic sentence:** The bottom of the hill in my childhood neighborhood offered everything young boys wanted.

   Appropriate method of organization: _spatial order_

   Explain: _The topic sentence suggests that the writer will describe the area_

   at the bottom of the hill, so using spatial order seems appropriate.

   _____

2. **Topic sentence:** In most cases, people involved in recreational fishing should use barbless hooks.

   Appropriate method of organization: _order of importance_

   Explain: _The topic sentence suggests that the writer will argue in favor of barbless hooks._

   The supporting details should follow order of importance.

   _____

3. **Topic sentence:** To become an effective leader, a person must develop three main traits.

   Appropriate method of organization: _logical order_

   Explain: _The topic sentence suggests that the writer will describe the three traits of_

   becoming an effective leader, so logical organization seems appropriate.

   _____

4. **Thesis statement:** Meeting my grandmother for the first time rates as one of my most important personal encounters.

   Appropriate method of organization: _chronological order_

   Explain: _The topic sentence suggests that the writer will share an experience, so_

   chronological order seems appropriate.

   _____

5. **Thesis statement:** (Choose one that you wrote on page 95.)

   Appropriate method of organization: _____

   Explain: _____

   _____

   _____

Arranging Your Details

Here are three basic strategies for arranging the supporting details after selecting a pattern of organization.

- **Make a quick list** of main points.
- **Create an outline**—an organized arrangement of main points and subpoints.
- **Fill in a graphic organizer,** arranging main points and details in a chart or diagram. (See pages 8–9.)

Using a Quick List

A quick list works well when you are writing a short piece or when your planning time is limited. Here is a quick list for a descriptive paragraph about zoot suits. (The list organizes details in spatial order, from top to bottom.)

Sample Quick List

Topic sentence: The zoot suit became a popular fashion symbol in the swing era.
- begins with a stylish wide-brimmed hat turned down
- follows with an oversized, tapered long jacket
- under jacket, a dress shirt with a tie
- pleated pants taper to narrow bottoms
- ends with two-tone, thin-soled shoes

Create   Write a topic sentence and a quick list for a narrative paragraph about a funny, scary, or otherwise significant personal experience. Include four to six details in your list, organized chronologically.

Topic sentence:

_____

_____

Quick list:

_____

_____

_____

_____

Using an Outline

An outline shows how ideas fit together for your writing. Topic and sentence outlines follow specific guidelines: If you have a "I," you must at least have a "II." If you have an "A," you must at least have a "B," and so on. You can also change or simplify an outline to meet your needs. Outlines are often used to arrange the ideas in essays and other longer pieces of writing.

Simplified Outline

Here is the first part of a simplified outline that includes main points stated in complete sentences and supporting details stated as phrases.

> **Thesis statement:** Humpback whales are by far the most playful and amazing whale species.
>
> 1. Most observers note that humpbacks appear to enjoy attention.
>   - lift bodies almost completely out of water (breaching)
>   - slap huge flippers against the water
>   - thrust their flukes (tail portion) straight out of water
>
> 2. Humpback whales "sing" better than other whales.
>   - song lasts up to 30 minutes
>   - head pointed toward ocean floor when singing
>   - seem to engage in group singing

Develop Create a simplified outline for an essay about becoming a leader. A thesis statement and three main points are provided. Put the main points in the most logical order, and make up two or three details to support each one. (Work on this activity with a classmate if your instructor allows it.)

Thesis statement: To become an effective leader, a person must develop three main traits.

Main points: Leaders must earn the respect of others. Leaders must display good work habits. Leaders must be confident..

1. _____
   - _____
   - _____
   - _____

2. _____
   - _____
   - _____
   - _____

LO4 Voice

Voice is the personality in writing—how the writer speaks to the reader. Your college instructors will expect you to use an academic voice for most of your writing. In some cases, however, you will be able to use a more personal voice.

- **Academic voice:** An academic voice sounds serious, and it is the one that you should use for informational essays and reports. This passage is written using an academic voice.

> Wisconsin farmers and hunters have serious concerns about the large number of wolves in the state. While wolves are extremely shy and don't pose a threat to humans, they do threaten livestock. With wolf populations on the rise since the mid-1990s, wolf attacks on livestock have been increasing.

INSIGHT

Generally speaking, an academic voice speaks in the third person *(he, she, it, they, and so on)*. It follows the rules for Standard English (see page 82), it is objective (meaning that it sticks to the facts), and it chooses words that sound more formal *(he would* rather than *he'd)*.

- **Personal voice:** A personal voice sounds more relaxed and conversational. It is generally used for narratives and personal essays. This passage is written using a personal voice.

> I was generally a brave little kid, but there were two things that scared me: storms and spiders. The storms that scared me were the ones when tornado warnings were issued and everybody would have to go in the basement. I'd always go to the bathroom, partly because of my nervous reaction, and partly because I thought it was the safest place.

INSIGHT

A personal voice speaks in the first-person *(I, my, we,* etc.). It generally follows the rules for Standard English, it is subjective (meaning it includes personal thoughts and feelings), and it is more relaxed with word choice *(they're* instead of *they are)*.

Create   Write two or three sentences about school or a job that sound academic. Then rewrite these sentences to make them sound more personal. Afterward, share your writing with your classmates.

_____

_____

_____

Working with Voice

Your individual writing voice, or special way of saying things, will develop through practice and experience. In other words, you won't write with "voice" just by learning about it. You must work on it. Here are a few things that you can do.

- **Practice writing.** Write nonstop for at least 10 minutes a day. Write about anything and everything. This practice will help you feel more comfortable with writing, which will help you write with more voice.

- **Become a regular reader.** Read newspapers, magazines, blogs, books. As you read, you will learn about different ways of expressing yourself.

- **Watch for good models.** If you really like the sound of something you read, try to write a brief passage like it.

- **Know your topics.** If you know a lot about a topic, it's easier to sound interested and knowledgeable.

- **Know your purpose and assignment.** For informational paragraphs and essays, you will need to sound more formal and academic. For narratives and personal essays, you should sound more conversational and personal.

- **Be honest.** And keep things simple. This may be easier said than done. As editor Patricia T. O'Conner says, "Simplicity takes practice."

Practice   Write nonstop for 5 to 10 minutes (time yourself) about any topic or topics, but be sure not to stop. (If you draw a blank, write "I'm stuck" until some new ideas come to mind.) Afterward, count the number of words you have written. Continue this practice daily or every other day and the number of words that you can write will increase dramatically. In the process, your individual writing voice will begin to develop.

LO5 Word Choice and Sentences

The words and sentences that you use carry the meaning in your writing. So it is important that they are clear, interesting, and honest. Also be sure that they fit the type of writing that you are doing. As you learned on the last two pages, the language you use for an informational paragraph will be different from the language you use in a narrative recalling a personal experience.

Using the Best Words

Generally speaking, specific words (*LeBron soars*) are better to use than general ones (*the basketball player jumps*). And fresh words (a *drop-dead* beauty) are usually better to use than overused ones (a *real* beauty).

Specific Nouns and Verbs

It's especially important to use specific nouns and verbs because they carry the most meaning in your sentences. The charts below show different examples of general versus specific nouns and verbs.

General nouns:	personal computer	adventure	performer
Specific nouns:	iMac	bungee jumping	Jennifer Lopez

General verbs:	laugh	run	look	build
Specific verbs:	giggle	sprint	inspect	erect

Study List examples of specific nouns and verbs that come to mind when you inspect the photograph to the right. Afterward, compare lists with your classmates.

Samot, 2011 / Used under license from Shutterstock.com

Specific Nouns	Specific Verbs

What to Watch For with Words

If the words you use help to create clear and interesting paragraphs, essays, and reports, then you have probably used the right ones. The following information discusses word-related issues to consider:

Watch for . . .

- **Vague adjectives** (modifiers of nouns) such as *neat, big, pretty, small, cute, fun, bad, nice, good, great,* and *funny.* Use more specific adjectives instead.

  > **Vague adjective:** Josie makes a good pizza crust.
  >
  > **Specific adjective:** Josie makes a thin and crisp pizza crust.

- **Too many adjectives in general.** Being "adjective happy" detracts from rather than adds to writing.

  > **Too many adjectives:** Part-time help can complete high-profile, high-impact workplace tasks without adding full-time employees.
  >
  > **Fewer adjectives:** Part-time help can complete important tasks without adding full-time employees. (simpler and clearer)

- **Too many "be" verbs** (*is, are, was, were, and so on*). Instead, use specific action verbs.

  > **"Be" verb:** Laura is a powerful diver.
  >
  > **Specific action verb:** Laura dives powerfully.

- **The same word used over and over.** Such repetition calls undo attention to the word.

  > **Overuse of a word:** I noticed a woman dressed in a crisp, navy blue suit. The woman appeared to be in charge. I soon realized that the woman was the owner.
  >
  > **Variety added:** I noticed a woman dressed in a crisp, navy blue suit who appeared to be in charge. I soon realized that she was the owner.

- **Words used incorrectly.** Words such as *their, they're,* and *there* and *it* and *it's* are commonly misused.

  > Most engineers get their (not they're or there) training on the job.
  >
  > Jogging has its (not it's) most impact if it's (not its) done regularly.

Create Write your own example for at least three of the problems discussed above. For each one, provide a new sentence with improved word choice. Afterward, share your work with your classmates.

Writing Clear Sentences

To write strong, clear sentences, you must first understand the basics. By definition, a simple sentence expresses a complete thought and contains a subject and a verb. But not all sentences are "simple." There are compound sentences, complex sentences, as well as other types.

The most common sentence errors include fragments *(incomplete sentences),* comma splices *(two sentences connected only with a comma),* and run-on sentences *(two sentences joined without punctuation).* The examples that follow show what is and what isn't a sentence. (See pages 409–427 for more explanations and practice activities.)

A Basic Guide to Sentences

Correct sentences

Simple sentence:	Jackson chews his fingernails. *(one complete idea)*
Compound sentence:	Max watches the presentation, but his mind is really somewhere else. *(two complete ideas)*
Complex sentence:	Sonja takes quick notes, while Connie sketches tiny flowers. *(one main idea and one subordinate or lesser idea)*

Sentence errors

Fragment:	Popcorn all over the floor. *(no verb)*
	Popcorn *spilled* over the floor. *(verb added)*
Fragment:	Couldn't help laughing. *(no subject)*
	We couldn't help laughing. *(subject added)*
Comma Splice:	Josie and I ordered coffee, we decided to split a cookie. *(missing a connecting word or end punctuation)*
	Josie and I ordered coffee, *and* we decided to split a cookie. *(connecting word added)*
Run-on:	Taking my dog for a walk frustrates me he has to sniff every tree and shrub in front of him. *(no punctuation)*
	Taking my dog for a walk frustrates me. He has to sniff every tree and shrub in front of him. *(punctuation added)*

Develop Write for 5 minutes about your favorite late night snack (or snacks). Then use the information above to check your sentences for correctness. Ask a classmate to check them as well. Correct any sentence errors that you find.

Checking Your Sentences for Style

There are other issues to consider when it comes to writing effective sentences. The information that follows identifies four of them.

Watch for . . .

- **Short, choppy sentences.** Too many short sentences in a row will sound choppy. To correct this problem, combine some of the ideas.

   > **Choppy sentences:** A Harley roared past us. The cycle was jet black. It stopped in front of a food stand. The food stand sells fresh fish tacos.
   >
   > **Combined sentences:** A jet-black Harley roared past us and stopped in front of a food stand that sells fresh fish tacos.

- **Sentences with the same beginning.** (This problem often creates choppy sentences.) To correct this problem, vary some of your sentence beginnings and lengths.

   > **Sentences with no variety:** Keeping a daily planner is important. It keeps track of your schedule. It lists your assignments. It helps you plan your time during the day.
   >
   > **Varied sentences:** Keeping a daily planner is important. In addition to keeping track of your schedule, it lists your assignments and helps you plan your time.

- **Sentences with passive verbs.** With a passive verb, the subject is acted on rather than doing the action. (See pages 462–463 for more information and activities.) To fix this problem, change the passive verbs into active ones.

   > **Passive verb:** The 16-ounce porterhouse steak was *attacked* by the Chihuahua.
   >
   > **Active verb:** The Chihuahua *attacked* the 16-ounce porterhouse steak.

Check   Use the following strategy to evaluate the sentences that you used in the activity on page 104.

1. List the opening words in your sentences. Decide if some sentence beginnings need to be varied.

   _____

2. List the number of words in each sentence. Decide if some sentence lengths need to be varied.

   _____

3. List the main verbs used. Decide if you need to replace any overused "be" verbs (*is, are, was, were*) with action verbs.

   _____

LO6 Conventions

The conventions are the rules for grammar, usage, and mechanics that you need to follow in your writing. But be sure to focus on the correctness of your writing at the best time, when you have completed the revising of your writing. Once all of your ideas are in place, then checking for the conventions becomes important.

Getting Started

If you're working on a computer, do your correcting on a printout of your work. Then enter the changes on the computer. Be sure to save the edited printout so you have a record of the changes you've made.

If you're working with pen and paper, do your editing on a neat copy of your revised writing. Then make a new copy of your writing and save the edited copy. Once you develop a final copy, be sure to proofread it for correctness before you submit it.

Strategies for Editing

When checking for errors, examine your writing word for word and sentence by sentence. The following strategies will help you edit thoroughly and effectively.

- Work with a clean copy of your writing, one that includes your revising changes.
- Check one element at a time—spelling, punctuation, and so on.
- For spelling, start at the bottom of the page to force yourself to look at each word. (Remember that your spell-checker will not catch all errors.)
- For punctuation, circle all the marks to force yourself to look at each one.
- Read your work aloud at least once, noting any errors as you go along.
- Refer to a list of common errors.
- Have an editing guide (see pages 362–539 in this text) and a dictionary handy.
- Ask a trusted classmate to check your work as well.

Preview When you have questions about punctuation, grammar, or any other convention, turn to pages 362–539. This part of the book is divided into three major workshops. Answer the following questions about this section.

1. What are the names of the three workshops in this section?

2. How will these workshops prove helpful when you are editing your writing?

3. Which one or two of these workshops will you probably turn to more than the others? Why?

Using Editing Strategies

You can use editing symbols to mark errors in your writing. Listed below are some of the most common symbols.

C chicago	Capitalize a letter.	first my ∧ speech	Insert here.
Ḟall	Make lowercase.	∧ ∧ ∧	Insert a comma, a colon, or a semicolon.
Mr Ford	Insert (add) a period.	∨ ∨ ∨	Insert an apostrophe or quotation marks.
Sp. or (recieve)	Correct spelling.	? ! ∧ ∧	Insert a question mark or an exclamation point.
Mr. Lott he	Delete (take out) or replace.	(possible worst)	Switch words or letters.

Edit   Use the editing symbols above to mark the errors in the following piece and show how they should be corrected.

When we lived on Maple street, we had a neighbor who seemed to   1
have two personalities his name was Mr. Bunde. I worked for him one
Summer while I was in grade school, cutting his lawn and doing other yard
work. After a few months of working for him I'd had more than enough. In
general, he was a nice enough guy and he likes to joke around some of the   5
                                        liked
time. Unfortunately, it was hard to tell if he was really kidding or if his
mood was suddenly changing. When he was in one of his moods I couldn't
do anything rite. Sometimes he would complain about other neighbors and
     right   knew
he would expect me to agree with him, even though he new they were my
friends. I not only have to concentrate on my work but I also had to be on   10
            had
my guard, trying to predict Mr. Bunde's mood. Why did I have to work for
him ?

LO7 Reviewing the Traits of Writing

Respond to each set of directions to review the concepts in this chapter.

Ideas Answer the following questions about this section. (See pages 88–93.)

- What does it mean to narrow a subject?

  To move from a general subject area into a specific subject area

- What are four different types of supporting details?

  facts and statistics, examples, definitions, quotations, reflections

Identifying a Focus Explain the importance of a topic sentence in a paragraph. (See pages 94–95.)

The topic sentence introduces the subject and includes a particular feeling or idea

about it, which establishes boundaries for the remainder of the paragraph.

Organization List the first four patterns listed in this section. Explain each one. (See pages 96–99.)

1. _____

2. _____

3. _____

4. _____

Voice Explain the following two types of writing voices. (See pages 100–101.)

- Academic Voice: Preferable for most forms of academic writing; follows the rules of

  Standard English; reflects knowledge about the subject

- Personal Voice: Used for sharing personal thoughts and stories; less formal than

  academic voice; conversational in tone

Word Choice and Sentences Answer the following questions about this section. (See pages 102–105.)

- Why is it important to use specific nouns and verbs? Specific nouns and

  verbs carry the most meaning in writing.

- Why should you vary some of your sentence beginnings and lengths? _____

  Sentence variety helps sentences flow from one to the next.

Conventions Explain when in the writing process you should check for conventions and why the "timing" is important. (See pages 106–107.)

Checking conventions should be the last step in the writing process. If you check them earlier in the

process, you may not give enough attention to the other steps.

Part II:

Reading and Writing Paragraphs

Part II: Reading and Writing Paragraphs

6

> "As we read we discover the importance of physical details. . . ."
> —John Gardner

Description

Have you ever thought about what makes dogs and cats different? It's more than just size: Some cats are very large, and some dogs are quite tiny. Both are mammals. Both are pets. Both have four legs and a tail. Both are primarily carnivorous. Unlike dogs, however, cats possess retractable claws, and they purr. Dogs have shoulder blades, which cats do not, and, or course, dogs bark.

Details help us to tell the two creatures apart. The more descriptive details that are presented, the more we learn about the subjects, and the more confidently we can talk about them.

In this chapter, you will read and react to professional and student descriptive paragraphs. Then you will write a descriptive paragraph of your own. In the process, you should come to value the importance of descriptive details in all forms of communication.

Learning Outcomes

LO1 Understand description.

LO2 Learn about reading strategies.

LO3 Read and react to a professional paragraph.

LO4 Read and react to a student paragraph.

LO5 Practice reading skills.

LO6 Plan a description paragraph.

LO7 Write the first draft.

LO8 Revise the writing.

LO9 Edit the writing.

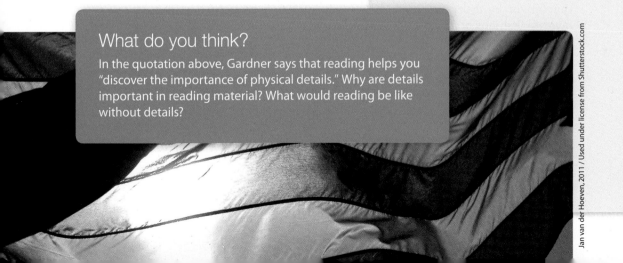

What do you think?

In the quotation above, Gardner says that reading helps you "discover the importance of physical details." Why are details important in reading material? What would reading be like without details?

LO1 Understanding Description

In the film *Enter the Dragon,* Bruce Lee describes thinking as a finger pointing at the moon. "Don't concentrate on the finger," he says, "or you will miss all that heavenly glory." Notice how Lee's description uses a few well-chosen details—the finger, the moon, the heavenly glory—to convey its message.

Descriptive writing relies upon these sorts of details. The purpose of such writing is not merely to list, however. Instead, it is to choose the best details and present them in the best manner to describe the subject. Descriptive writing helps readers to feel they have experienced the subject for themselves.

> "A good description is a magician that can turn an ear into an eye"
> —Unknown

Many Purposes

For this reason, other types of writing often include some description. A narrative (story) may describe a scene and a character. An explanation may use description in its examples. Process writing may describe each step. Classifications and comparisons may use description to make their subjects easier to understand.

Description in Academic Texts

Your reading assignments in academic texts will seldom be pure descriptions. But even within a typical explanation or analysis, there's a good chance some description will occur. For example, in an analysis of the traditional family, a sociologist might provide a description of a day in the life of the family members. In an explanation of gender differences, a health expert might provide a detailed description of each gender.

INSIGHT

Descriptions don't have to include every detail. Rather, authors usually choose the key details to picture the subject they are writing about.

Practice Think of a favorite magazine or Web site. Then name two or three topics that might be described in it. For example, *People Magazine* might describe the favorite fashions of an up-and-coming actress.

_____

_____

_____

Reading

Reading descriptions can be entertaining and enlightening. They can create powerful images in your head and help you visualize topics.

LO2 Learning About Reading Strategies

To best understand descriptive writing, pay attention to the details included and the order they are presented.

Strategy 1: Identifying Details

Descriptive texts typically include sensory details—the sights, sounds, smells, tastes, and textures of a subject. Use a chart like the one below to note the sensory details in the descriptive texts you read. You can also use this chart to gather sensory details for your own descriptive writing.

Sensory Chart

Sights	Sounds	Smells	Tastes	Textures

Strategy 2: Considering Organization

The order in which details are revealed also plays an important role in the effectiveness of descriptive writing. Common descriptive organizations include the following.

> **INSIGHT**
>
> Not every description will appeal to every sense. A description of a meal might focus on tastes, smells, sights, and textures, but not at all on sound.

- **Spatial Organization:** Details are arranged by location—top to bottom, right to left, foreground to background, or so on. Settings are often described this way.
- **Chronological Organization:** Details are presented according to the passage of time. Events are typically described this way.
- **Logical Order:** The details simply follow one another predictably or naturally. Academic texts often use this order to explain or define.

LO3 Reading and Reacting to a Professional Paragraph

Read In this description paragraph, the author describes a statue he has rescued. Use the reading process to get the most from the paragraph, along with the reading strategies on the last page. (See pages 14–15.)

NOTE: Don Quixote (Kē-hō'-tē) is the hero of a Spanish novel by the same name. He is an impractical knight "battling" life's injustice, but failing miserably.

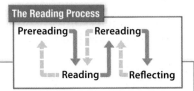

The Reading Process

Prereading → Reading → Rereading → Reflecting

A Battered Statue

The Don Quixote statuette my dad gave me isn't worth much. It is a *1* statue of a gaunt old man in battered armor sitting astride a swayback horse. The helmet on Quixote's head is dented, its visor bent above bushy eyebrows, squinting eyes, a wide wedge of a nose, and an unruly mustache and beard. His breastplate and shield are so worn that whatever emblems *5* they once held have been lost. The statue looks like roughcast pewter, but when I accidentally knocked it over, it smashed on the floor, revealing itself to be painted plaster. I scooped up the jaggy chunks and did my best to stick them back together. Now a few seams of seeping glue and off-color paint crisscross the figure, and electrician's tape clings to the bent lance. *10* Despite these flaws, despite dust and cobwebs, Quixote still manages to stare out with a look of hope. The statuette wasn't worth much when Dad gave it to me, and it's worth even less now. But somehow, after all this time and all this glue and tape, the statue means even more to me.

React Answer the following questions. Then discuss your responses with your classmates.

1. What is the main idea of this paragraph?

   The Quixote statue isn't worth much, but it means a lot to the writer.

2. What are two or three sensory details that you especially like?

   _____

3. Does the paragraph follow one pattern of organization? Explain. (See page 113.)

   spatial organization

4. How would you rate this paragraph?

   Weak ★ ★ ★ ★ ★ Strong

   _____

A CLOSER LOOK   at Description

As noted in the chapter introduction, most descriptive writing tries to do more than merely describe. Descriptive writing often communicates an attitude or a feeling.

Identifying Tone

To recognize an author's tone or attitude in descriptive writing, it may help to make a chart like the one below. List descriptive words in the first column and your thoughts about their effect in the second. (An example is included.)

Word	Effect
battered	Adds to a sense of worthlessness or uselessness

Identify Use a chart like the one above to analyze the tone of the description paragraph on page 114. List at least three or four descriptive words.

Understanding Mood

Mood is the feeling generated in the reader. A writer's tone can help to create a particular mood. In "A Battered Statue," for example, the author uses words with a tone of wear and defeat. And the paragraph moves from a description of Quixote as a character, to the broken plaster of the statuette, to the rebuilding of it.

One way to understand the mood of a descriptive piece is to freewrite about to see how it makes you feel.

Freewrite Write nonstop for about 5 minutes about the paragraph you have just read. Consider how the statue is described and how the details make you feel about it. This writing will help you identify the mood of the piece.

_____

_____

_____

LO4 Reading and Reacting to a Student Paragraph

Read   Read the following description paragraph about a dog. Remember to use the steps in the reading process to help you gain a full understanding of the text. (See pages 14–15.)

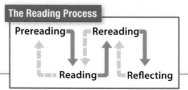

The Reading Process

Prereading   Rereading

Reading   Reflecting

A Small Package

    My family recently gave me a Chihuahua from a rescue shelter. He's a   *1*
cute little guy, just over six pounds, with short white fur, big brown spots
on both sides of his body. In contrast to most Chihuahuas whose ears stand
straight up, my dog has floppy ears. He's considered an "apple-headed,
deer-faced" Chihuahua, which means his forehead is domed instead of flat,   *5*
and his muzzle is long instead of short. Like most Chihuahuas, he barks
(okay, yaps) a lot whenever someone comes to the door, or when a neighbor
gets near the yard, or even when a family member enters or leaves the
room. Chihuahuas are noisy, mainly because they're nervous. Imagine
being only ankle high to the people you live with. You'd bark too! Similarly,   *10*
Chihuahuas are smart and easily trained. They love to do tricks for their
masters. I've taught my little guy more than twenty tricks, including
"Come" and "Hush." Those last two are helpful for keeping peace when
someone comes to the door.

React   Answer the following questions about the paragraph. Then discuss your answers with your classmates.

1. What is the main idea of this paragraph?

   The writer describes his Chihuahua.
   _____

2. What are two or three sensory details that you especially like?

   _____

   _____

3. What is the most important thing that you learned in this paragraph?

   _____

   _____

4. How would you rate this paragraph and why?

   Weak ★ ★ ★ ★ ★ Strong

   _____

A CLOSER LOOK at the Content

The content is the information covered in a paragraph or an essay. Studying the content is how you learn from reading material.

Analyzing the Details

Now that you have read two descriptive paragraphs, it is helpful to see how many different types of sensory details are used in each one. Such an analysis will show you how effectively each description captures the topic and if any important senses have not been covered.

Create Complete a sensory chart for each descriptive paragraph that you have just read. Then decide if the important senses have all been covered. Afterward, compare your findings with those of your classmates.

A Battered Statue

Sights	Sounds	Smells	Tastes	Textures

A Small Package

Sights	Sounds	Smells	Tastes	Textures

Personal Reflections

Both of the descriptive paragraphs describe topics that belong to the writers. As such, they are written from a personal point of view. When writers have a personal attachment to a topic, they will often include their personal reflections (thoughts and feelings) about it. These reflections add another level of meaning to the paragraphs.

Identify Write down at least one personal reflection from each of the paragraphs. Consider what each of these ideas has to say about the writer and his relationship to the topic.

"A Battered Statue"

_____

_____

"A Small Package"

_____

_____

LO5 Practicing Reading Skills

Reading is a great way to build your vocabulary and practice important thinking skills. The activities below will help you work on both.

Vocabulary: Using Context

Page 24 explains one strategy—using context clues—that will help you understand new words in your reading. Context clues are clues provided by the words and ideas around unfamiliar words.

Using Context: In the first paragraph (page 114), the word *gaunt* is used (line 2). The other descriptive words in the sentence help you understand what *gaunt* might mean.

"It is a statue of a *gaunt* old man in battered armor sitting astride a swayback horse." (Descriptive words like *old, battered,* and *swayback* suggest that *gaunt* means something like tired or thin.)

Identify Use context clues to explain or define the italicized words from the paragraph on page 114.

1. The helmet on Quixote's head is dented, its visor bent above bushy eyebrows, squinting eyes, a wide wedge of a nose, and an *unruly* mustache and beard.

    Context clues (words or ideas that help explain *unruly*): _____

    Meaning: _____

2. The statue looks like roughcast *pewter,* but when I accidentally knocked it over, it smashed on the floor, revealing itself to be painted plaster.

    Context clues (words or ideas that help explain *pewter*): _____

    Meaning: _____

Reading Critically: Noting Signal Words

Writers use signal words or transitions to direct the reader. They tell the reader to keep going, stop and take note, or turn here. For example, when writers want to show how things compare, they may use signal words such as *similarly, just as,* and *like most*. And when writers want to show how things are different, they may use signal words such as *in contrast, on the other hand, yet,* and *even though*.

Identify Carefully reread the paragraph on page 116. Then answer the following questions.

What, if any, signal words or transitions in this paragraph identify comparisons? What words identify contrasts?

Signal words that compare: *looks like,* Signal words that contrast: *but somehow*

Writing

It is time now to begin planning and writing your own description paragraph about a person, place, or thing that is important to you. Remember to use the writing process to help you do your best work.

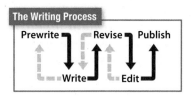

LO6 Planning a Description Paragraph

According to one old tale, a boy was asked to bring a wizard something no one had ever seen before. The boy brought an egg. When the chick inside hatched out, the wizard was the first to see it.

The point is that your descriptive paragraph doesn't have to be about something unusual. What makes a description effective instead is how you see the topic and present it to your readers.

Selecting a Topic

To select a topic, you can start by listing items in the general categories of person, place, or thing. Then jot down one or more specific examples of each. Circle the one you would like to write about. See one student's example below.

Select List two or three possible topics for each of the categories below. A sample topic for each category is provided. Circle the one you would like to describe.

Person	Place	Thing
Teachers	Shops	Pets
Ms. Rucki	Starbucks	parakeet
Neighbors	Apple Store	Cars
Mr. Vogt	Restaurants	my first one
Wilson Kendall	Staniford's Pizza	Clothes
Celebrities	Parks	leather jacket
Matt Damon	North Beecham	
Others	Hoversten State Park	

List Create your own chart of people, places, and things. Circle the item you feel most excited about as the topic for your description paragraph.

Gathering Details

Sensory details help readers to "picture" your subject in their own minds. In the example below, a student used a sensory chart to list details about her first car. Part of her sensory chart is shown below. Notice the tone of her words.

Sensory Details

Sights	Sounds	Smells	Tastes	Textures
– faded paint, tomato soup color – huge dent in driver's door	– roaring motor – rattle in door – buzzing speakers	– dirty oil – pine cleaner – stale cheese	– none	– "dusty" paint – cracked upholstery

Gather   On a sensory chart, write down key sensory details about the object you have chosen.

Organizing Details

It's important to present your details in an order that makes your description easy to follow. The student from the above example decided to use chronological order in describing her first car, starting when she first saw it.

1. Dent in driver's door

2. Pale "tomato soup" paint

3. Cracked upholstery inside

4. Inside smelled like 1. oil, 2. pine, and 3. stale cheese

5. The engine roared

Organize   List the details you plan to include in an appropriate order. (See page 96 for help.)

_____

_____

_____

_____

LO7 Writing the First Draft

A first draft is a chance to get your thoughts down on paper without worrying about perfect grammar or spelling. Even your organization and details can be changed later, during revision.

Read Read and enjoy the following descriptive paragraph.

Tomato Can

Topic Sentence

It was a Saturday morning when my uncle Elijah took me   *1*
to buy my first car. He had discovered it on Craigslist. Outside,
the car was depressing. Its red paint had faded to a dusty
tomato soup color that came off on your fingers. The driver's
side door was one big dent, and it rattled when I opened it.   *5*
Inside, the fake leather seats were cracked, and crumbly
orange foam padding showed through. The interior stank of
dirty motor oil and what smelled like old cheese, even through
the stench of a new pine freshener the seller had hung on the
rearview mirror. When my uncle said, "Start it up," I turned   *10*
the key to the roar of a broken exhaust. I shut it off and next

Body Sentences

tried the radio. The speakers buzzed like angry hornets. When
Elijah said, "We'll take it," I almost felt like crying. I drove his
car home, while he drove the junk heap to his house to work
on. Later that night, he brought the "Tomato Can" back to my   *15*
house to switch vehicles. I couldn't believe it was the same car.
He had used a restoring wax, and the paint was now a deep,
shiny red. A new exhaust pipe made the engine purr. Polka
dot seat covers hid the old upholstery, and new speakers were
playing one of my favorite songs. The driver's door was still   *20*
one big dent, but it didn't rattle when I opened it. "I found a
coat hanger inside," he said. I could still smell cheese, but that
would fade with time. I had my first set of wheels.

Closing Sentence

Consider the Craft

1. What do you like best about this paragraph?

2. What are two of your favorite details?

3. How much time does the event cover?

4. Does the writer say just enough about the experience, too much, or too little?

The Working Parts of a Paragraph

As shown on the previous page, a paragraph has three main parts, each with its own purpose.

Paragraph Outline

Topic Sentence: A topic sentence introduces your topic and gets your reader's interest.

Body Sentences: The sentences in the middle part describe the topic with sensory details.

Closing Sentence: A closing sentence (or two) often summarizes the topic. Or it may leave the reader with something to think about.

Drafting Tips

When writing a descriptive paragraph, you are trying to capture the sights, sounds, and other details related to your topic. To do this, consider the following strategies.

In the opening sentence . . .

- Identify the topic to be described.
- Get your reader's interest.

In the middle sentences . . .

- Include specific sensory details.
- Use chronological order, order of location, or logical order to organize your details.

In the closing sentence . . .

- Sum up your own feelings about the subject (either directly or by suggestion).
- Or leave the reader with something to think about.

CONSIDER THE TRAITS

Voice is very important in descriptive writing. Choose words that show your own interest in the topic and are appropriate for the assignment.

Write Prepare your first draft using the information above and your planning on pages 119–120 as a guide.

Daniel Ochoa IFOTOCHOA, 2011 / Used under license from Shutterstock.com

LO8 Revising the Writing

Start the revising process by reading your first draft two or three times to get a feel for your work so far. Then have one of your classmates read and react to your work using a response sheet as a guide. (See page 353.)

Using Transitions

Transitions are words and phrases that link ideas in writing so that the reader can clearly follow your ideas. Transitional words and phrases that show time include *first, next, then, when, after that,* and so on. Transitions that indicate location include *above, below, at the bottom*, and so on. When describing, you may need to use both types of transitions.

Revising in Action

Read aloud the unrevised and then the revised version of the following passage. The revised version includes the transitions.

> It was Saturday morning when my uncle Elijah took me to buy my first car. He had discovered it on Craigslist. *Outside,* The car was depressing. Its red paint had faded to a dusty tomato soup color that came off on your fingers. The driver's side door was one big dent, and it rattled when I opened it. *Inside,* The fake leather seats were cracked, and crumbly orange foam padding showed through. The interior stank of dirty motor oil. . . . *When* My uncle said, "Start it up.", I turned the key to the roar of a broken exhaust. I shut it off and *next* tried the radio.

Revise Improve your writing, using the checklist below and your classmate's comments on the response sheet.

Revising Checklist
Words
☐ 1. Do I focus on a specific topic to describe?
☐ 2. Do I include enough sensory details?
Organization
☐ 3. Have I included a topic sentence, body sentences, and a closing sentence?
☐ 4. Have I organized my details in the best way?
☐ 5. Do I use transitions to connect my ideas?
Voice
☐ 6. Do I sound interested and knowledgeable?

LO9 Editing the Writing

When you edit, you check your revised writing for the proper use of capitalization, punctuation, grammar, usage, and spelling. This should be one of the last things that you do during the writing process.

Basic Capitalization

Correct capitalization will be one of the most basic things to check for. In your description, there are essentially two basic capitalization rules that you will need to check for: (1) first words of sentences, and (2) proper nouns and adjectives. Proper nouns and adjectives are the specific names of people, places, things, and so on.

First Word in a Sentence

- **T**he driver's door was one big dent, but it rattled when I opened it.
- **I**nside, the fake leather seats were cracked, . . .

First Word of a Direct Quotation *(what someone says)*

- When my uncle said, "**S**tart it up," I turned the key to the roar of a broken exhaust.

Proper Nouns and Adjectives

- It was a **S**aturday morning when my uncle **E**lijah took me to buy my first car.
- He had discovered it on **C**raigslist. *(the specific name of a Web site)*

Capitalization Practice   Read the sentences below. Correct any capitalization errors that you find. Use the information above as a guide. The first one is done for you.

1. I stood in the parking lot of the New York mets during their spring training.
2. all of a sudden david wright pulled up in his car.
3. I walked over to him with his card and said, "could you please sign this?"
4. without hesitation, he said, "no problem" and signed it for me.
5. A few minutes later, another player pulled up in a black corvette.
6. he was one of the coaches, and I wasn't interested in him.
7. Then I walked toward digital domain park, the team's spring stadium.
8. just to my right, I saw r. a. dickey, one of the mets' main pitchers.

Additional Practice: For additional practice, see pages 504–505.

Apply   Check your revised paragraph for capitalization using the information above as a guide.

Basic Punctuation

Be sure that you use proper end punctuation—periods, question marks, or exclamation points—at the end of your sentences. Also be sure that you use a comma in compound sentences,. A compound sentence is two or more simple sentences connected by *and, but, or,* and so on.

End Punctuation

- Rock climbing is popular at Devils Lake State Park. *(statement)*
- Does rock climbing interest you? *(question)*
- Signs in the park say: Watch for snakes! *(exclamation mark)*

Practice   Read the following passage, and add the correct end punctuation.

What does the future hold for our energy needs? Will we rely mostly on wind power and solar power. Some people feel biodegradable sources of energy like corn and seaweed have potential. In the near future, we might discover even more exciting sources of energy. In other words, the best may be yet to come!

Commas in Compound Sentences

- Todd works out and runs all of the time, **but** I am woefully out of shape.
- He likes to keep active all of the time, **and** I enjoy sedentary, restful activities.

Punctuation Practice   Read the sentences below. Insert commas as needed in any compound sentences.

1. The initial explosion from the bomb injured people, and many cars and buildings were destroyed.
2. The explosion also created tremendous amounts of smoke, dust, and heat.
3. The smoke and dust immediately turned day into night, but the darkness eventually gave way to light as many fires started.
4. Buildings near the center of the city went up in flames first, and the surrounding structures caught fire from exposed wires and damaged gas lines.
5. People did what they could to escape the heat, yet their efforts were futile.

Additional Practice: For additional practice, see pages 574–575.

Apply   Check your revised writing for end punctuation and commas in compound sentences.

Marking a Paragraph

The model that follows has a number of errors.

Editing Practice   Correct the following paragraph, using the correction marks below. One correction has been done for you.

Easter Island Mystery

Unknown sculptors carved huge stone statues in an old volcano on *1*
easter island. The statues were carved in a quarry within the crater of
an old volcano, and they were somehow moved to their present locations
around the island. The sculptors worked with stone tools. It is not believed
that they had wood for lifting, ropes for pulling, or wheels for moving. More *5*
than 250 of these statues stand guard on the volcano's slopes, and 300
additional statues lie scattered around the island. The statues are different
heights—the average being between 17 and 26 feet. The tallest towers
are 72 feet, and the shortest measures 10 feet. The statues are known for
their large, broad noses and jutting chins. they are thought to be modeled *10*
after the faces of primitive Polynesians, immigrant peoples from peru, or
early Caucasian visitors. These works of art are one of the world's wonderful
mysteries.

Correction Marks

⌐ delete	⋏ add comma	∧ word add word
d capitalize	? add question mark	⊙ add period
ø lowercase		⬭ spelling
∧ insert	∨ insert an apostrophe	⌮ switch

INSIGHT ——

Remember that editing should be one of the last things that you do during the writing process. If you attempt to edit too early in the process, you may not make the necessary revisions or changes in your thoughts and ideas.

Correcting Your Paragraph

With your paragraph revised, it is now time to edit it for correctness.

Edit   Prepare a clean copy of your paragraph and use the following checklist to look for errors. Continue working until you can check off each item in the list.

Editing Checklist

Words

☐ **1.** Have I used the right word *(their, they're, there)*?

☐ **2.** Have I used more action verbs than "be" verbs? (See page 458.)

Sentences

☐ **3.** Have I varied the beginnings and lengths of sentences? (See pages 104–105.)

☐ **4.** Have I avoided fragments and run-ons? (See pages 410–413, 416–417.)

Conventions

☐ **5.** Do I use correct verb forms *(he saw,* not *he seen)*? (See pages 464, 466.)

☐ **6.** Do my subjects and verbs agree *(she speaks,* not *she speak)*? (See pages 394–403.)

☐ **7.** Have I capitalized first words and proper nouns and adjectives? (See page 504.)

☐ **8.** Have I checked for end punctuation? (See page 125.)

☐ **9.** Have I used commas in compound sentences? (See page 514.)

☐ **10.** Have I carefully checked my spelling?

Adding a Title

A title should grab a reader's attention and generate curiosity about the paragraph. To make an attention-grabbing title, you can use one of these strategies.

- Use an interesting phrase or idea from the paragraph.

  Easter Island Mystery

- Use repetition of similar vowel sounds.

  Island Art

- Capture the main idea of the paragraph.

  Primitive Stone Art

Create   Invent an attention-grabbing title for your own descriptive paragraph.

> "When your writing is filled with details, it has a lot more impact."
> —Ivan Levison

Review and Enrichment

On the next four pages, you will find a descriptive essay to read and respond to. This essay is followed by a number of writing ideas to choose from to write a descriptive paragraph or essay of your own. The reading and writing that you do in this section will reinforce and enrich the work you have already completed in this chapter.

Prereading

The way you describe something can reveal as much about yourself as it about the topic itself. The details you include, the order in which you present them, your choice of words—all of these decisions say something about who you are. No two people examining the same topic will describe it quite the same.

This is part of the fun of reading and writing descriptions. In reading, you get a chance to learn about a topic, but also to meet the author. In writing, you are able to describe topics on your own terms and share a little bit of yourself in the process.

CONSIDER THE TRAITS

As you read the descriptive selection that follows, consider how the **voice** affects your understanding of what is being described. What mood does that voice generate in you? When finished reading, ask yourself what lasting effect the writing has had on you.

Identify   Name an event or experience that you could describe. Explain your choice.

_____

_____

List sensory details about the event. Consider using a sensory chart. (See page 113.)

_____

_____

What do you think?

Consider the quotation above. Why do details increase the impact or value of a piece of writing?

Reading and Reacting

Read   Read the following essay by Joseph T. O'Connor, originally published in *Newsweek*. Notice the way the author uses specific details throughout the essay, which is part description and part narration or story. Use the reading process to help you gain a full understanding of the essay. (See pages 14–15.)

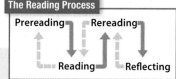

About the Author

Joseph T. O'Connor was eighteen years old when *Newsweek* published his essay about a hiking trip in the Sierra Nevadas. The experience he describes "woke him up," changing his thinking and converting him into an honors scholar. He is now pursuing an M.A. at Harvard Graduate School of Journalism.

A View from Mount Ritter

"I hate this," I thought. We were on our way to the top of Mount Ritter   *1*
in northeastern California. You would think everyone, near one of the
tallest ridges in the Sierra Nevadas, would be in high spirits. But on this
particular day the rain fell in torrents. Quarter-size hailstones pelted our
protective helmets as thunder echoed through the canyons.   *5*

It was the second week of my mountain expedition in California. The
first week there had not been a cloud in the sky, but on Tuesday of week
two, a dark cover crept in from the west, painting the sunlit, blue sky
black. The storm came in so fast we didn't even notice it until our shadows
suddenly disappeared.   *10*

"Here it comes," our guide warned. As if God himself had given the
order, the heavens opened, just a crack. Huge drops began falling but
abruptly stopped, as if to say, "You know what's coming; here's a taste." As
we began searching for shelter, a bolt of lightning ripped open the blackish
clouds overhead and in **unison** thunder cracked, leaving everyone's ears   *15*
ringing. We were in the midst of a huge July thunderstorm. Ethan, our
guide, had said that during the summer in the high Sierras it might rain
twice, but when it does, it's best not to be there. Suddenly lightning struck
a tree not 20 feet from where I was standing.

"Lightning positions!" Ethan yelled frantically. A little too frantically   *20*
for my taste. I thought he was used to this kind of thing. As scared as
I was, squatting in a giant puddle of water and hailstones, with forks
of lightning bouncing off the canyon walls around me, I couldn't help
chuckling to myself at the sight of Ethan's dinner-plate-sized eyeballs

as he panicked like an **amateur**. Soon after the lighting died down some, we hiked to the shelter of nearby redwoods to put on rain gear. While we prayed for the rain to subside, I watched the stream we stood beside grow into a raging white water river. Another expeditioner, Mike, and I were under a full redwood donning our not-so-waterproof equipment when I realized we were standing on a small island. 30

"Mike! Let's go!" I yelled, my exclamation nearly drowned out by the roar of water surrounding us and another roll of thunder.

"I'm way ahead o' ya!" he screamed in his thick New York accent, and his goofy smile broke through the torrents. "Ya ready?"

"Yeah!" I yelled back, and jumped from our island into the knee-deep water. He followed as we slopped through the storm, losing our footing every few feet.

The unforgiving downpour lasted all day and into the night as we stumbled down the rocky cliffs seeking the driest place to set up camp. It was dusk before we found a small clearing in a pine forest and began what was to be the worst night of my life. We constructed our tents in the dark, fumbling with the ropes with frozen hands and finishing just as a stiffness like **rigor mortis** set in. We lay awake all night, shivering in our wet sleeping bags while rain poured down and a small stream made its way through our tent.

It's funny how these memories keep coming back to me as if it were just yesterday. All this happened last summer, after my junior year in high school. I had decided to attend a mountaineering program in the Sierras. Two weeks in the back country with no sign of civilization. It sounded exciting and slightly dangerous, and I've always been up for a good adventure. I found out on that trip that nature is underestimated. The experience was the most invigorating, fulfilling, stimulating two weeks of my life. For the first time since I could remember, my head was crystal clear. I felt born again, only two weeks old. On top of Mount Ritter, 13,000 feet above sea level, I was **entranced** at the sight of the orange-red sun as it peeked over the glistening peaks far off in the east. Cumulous clouds appeared transparent as they glowed bright red in the morning glory. . . .

Vocabulary

unison
in agreement, at the same time

amateur
inexperienced, nonprofessional

rigor mortis
muscle stiffening after death

entranced
filled with delight

React Answer the questions below about the selection on pages 129–130. Then discuss your responses with your classmates.

1. What sensory details does O'Connor use to bring the experience to life? List at least seven in the sensory chart below.

Sensory Details

Sights	Sounds	Smells	Tastes	Textures

2. How is the essay organized—spatially, chronologically, or logically? Explain.

The writer organizes the details in the order they occurred, so the essay is organized

chronologically.

3. What are two examples of personal reflections in the essay? (See page 117.)

4. How would you rate this essay and why?

Weak ★ ★ ★ ★ ★ Strong

Drawing Inferences

An *inference* is a logical conclusion that you can make about something that is not actually said or stated in a text. A worthy inference does, however, result from a clear and careful understanding of what *is* said. To practice drawing inferences, answer the following questions about the narrative on pages 129–130. Afterward, share your responses with your classmates.

1. What conclusions can you draw about the writer's level of confidence?

2. Why do you think the experience made him feel "born again"?

Writing

Write a descriptive paragraph or descriptive essay, using the guidelines on the next two pages. Check with your instructor about any specific requirements he or she may have for this writing. Use the writing process to help you complete your work. (See pages 68–73.)

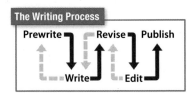

Prewriting

Choose one of the following ideas for your descriptive writing. Or decide upon another idea of your own.

Writing Ideas

1. Write about one of the descriptive topics you identified in the "Person, Place, Thing" prewriting activity on page 119.

2. Write about a significant event in your life from page 128.

3. Write about one of the photographs in *Fusion 1*.

4. Write about a favorite work of art.

5. Write about your favorite restaurant.

When planning . . .

Refer to pages 119–120 to help with your prewriting and planning. Also use the tips below.

- Choose a topic you care deeply about. Writing about something you find interesting is always easiest.
- Gather as many sensory details as possible.
- From those details, select the ones that will most effectively capture the subject.
- Choose a pattern of organization that immediately draws your readers in and carries them along to the end.
- When revising, make sure your tone is appropriate for the topic. For example, your tone should sound exciting if the topic is exciting, and sound serious if the topic is serious.

Writing and Revising

Refer to pages 121–123 to help you write and revise your first draft. Also use the tips below to help with your drafting and revising.

When writing . . .

- Include an effective beginning, middle, and ending in your descriptive piece. Each part has its own role to play. (See page 122.)
- Write your first draft freely, allowing yourself to be immersed in the experience again.
- Add new ideas as they come to mind during your writing, but only if they seem important to include.

When revising . . .

- Let your first draft sit unread for a while. Then read it carefully, with fresh eyes. Reading a printed copy can help you see it differently.
- Consider where sensory details seem missing and fill them in.
- Also consider where sensory details seem unnecessary or slow the reading and cut them.
- Make sure your chosen organization works well and helps your reader follow your ideas.
- Ask a classmate or another writer to review and critique your writing. Use a Peer Review Sheet to guide the critique. (See page 547.)

Editing

Refer to the checklist on page 127 when you are ready to edit your descriptive writing for style and correctness.

Reflecting on Description Writing

Answer the following questions about your descriptive reading and writing experience in this chapter.

1. Why is description so common in essays and articles?

   Descriptive writing helps readers to feel they have experienced the subject for themselves.

2. What is your favorite descriptive writing in this chapter? Why?

3. What reading strategy in this chapter do you find most helpful? Explain.

4. What is the most important thing you learned about reading a descriptive paragraph or essay?

5. What do you like most about the descriptive paragraph you wrote for this chapter? Why?

6. What is one thing you would like to change in your paragraph?

7. What is the most important thing you have learned about writing descriptive paragraphs and essays?

Key Terms to Remember

When you read and write description essays, it's important to understand the following terms.

- **Sensory details**—the sights, sounds, smells, tastes, and touch sensations of a descriptive subject.
- **Chronological order**—details arranged by time of occurrence.
- **Spatial order**—details arranged by their location in a setting.
- **Logical order**—details arranged from most important to least, or from least important to most.

7

> "We write to taste life twice, in the moment, and in retrospection."
> —Anaïs Nin

Narration

Early on, you may have been lucky enough to have had someone read you bedtime stories. If so, then you know "in your bones" the elements of a good story. Storytellers hold a young child's interest by building drama and suspense. At least, this is the opinion of William Zinsser, who has skillfully written about the craft of writing in his famous book *On Writing Well.*

This chapter deals with narrative writing, the sharing of personal stories. To narrate is "to give an account of an event." First you will learn about the importance and popularity of the narrative form. Then you will read and react to both a professional and a student narrative paragraph before developing one of your own. And along the way, you will experience the power of storytelling.

Learning Outcomes

LO1 Understand narration.

LO2 Learn about reading strategies.

LO3 Read and react to a professional paragraph.

LO4 Read and react to a student paragraph.

LO5 Practice reading skills.

LO6 Plan a narrative paragraph.

LO7 Write the first draft.

LO8 Revise the writing.

LO9 Edit the writing.

What do you think?

According to the quotation, writing allows you "to taste life twice." What does this mean to you? How does this idea relate to narrative writing?

Glenda M. Powers, 2011 / Used under license from Shutterstock.com

LO1 Understanding Narration

American author William Faulkner said, "The past is never dead; it's not even past." If you think about your own life, you can understand this idea. You hold many memories about growing up and reaching adulthood, so your past is in no way dead. Neither is it over, because your experiences continue to help shape who you are and what you will become.

Importance of the Past

If you were to review the autobiography section in a local bookstore, you would see how important the past is to writers. Their past experiences are in their bones, and they need to write about them. And the popularity of these books shows that readers are definitely interested in the lives of others, from the rich and famous to ordinary people much like you and your classmates.

> "Story is everything. All writing of whatever kind begins with narrative."
> —John Rouse

Writing about their past experiences helps writers make sense of life, the world, and their place in it. Their personal writing says, "For better or worse, here's what I've experienced and how I feel about it. I'd like to share my story with you." Autobiographies share interesting details about the writer's life and reveal important truths about life in general.

Autobiography Versus Personal Narrative

An autobiography shares the story of a writer's life; a personal narrative focuses on one specific event or experience. In a sense, an autobiography is a collection of personal narratives, because it covers key events in the writer's life. A single narrative highlights a memorable moment or a life-changing event.

INSIGHT
What motivates an autobiographical writer? Just about anything, including successes, setbacks, self-discovery, pride, and recovery.

Identify Suppose you were assigned to read or watch an autobiography about one of the following individuals. Circle the one you would pick; then explain your choice. (A quick check online will identify any of these people.)

Michelle Obama   Spike Lee

Mark Zuckerberg   Oprah Winfrey

Beyoncé   Michael Moore

Mariano Rivera

_____

_____

_____

_____

_____

Reading

Reading narratives can be an extremely enjoyable experience. After all, who doesn't enjoy a good story? You can also learn a lot about life from narratives.

LO2 Learning About Reading Strategies

These two strategies—following the key actions and answering the 5 W's and H—will help you read narrative texts.

Strategy 1:
Following the Key Actions

When reading a narrative, it's important that you follow the key actions in the order they occur. A graphic organizer called a time line works well for this purpose. On it, you can identify the main actions of a story chronologically, or by time.

Time Line

1.	(Key actions in order)
2.	
3.	
4.	
5.	

Strategy 2:
Answering the 5 W's and H

In one way, you can simply enjoy a narrative that holds your interest from beginning to end as a good story. But to truly understand a narrative, you need to identify the key actions. To do this, you can answer the 5 W's and H about the story. (This is a strategy used by reporters when they gather details for a news story.)

5W's and H

Who was involved in the experience?

What happened?

When did it happen?

Where did it happen?

Why did it happen?

How did it happened?

> **Tip**
> Sometimes you will not find answers to all of these questions, but stories usually reveal most of the 5 W's and H details.

Evangelos, 2011 / Used under license from Shutterstock.com

LO3 Reading and Reacting to a Professional Paragraph

Read The following narrative paragraph comes from Tim Kemper, a writer and an editor at an educational publishing house. The paragraph tells about the final moments leading up to his first skydiving experience. Remember to use the reading process to help you fully appreciate the text.

The Reading Process

Prereading ⤵ Rereading

Reading ⤴ Reflecting

The Earth Below Us

Some 9,000 feet off the ground, I peered down at the clouds below me   1
and realized I had reached a point of no return. I was about to jump out of
an airplane. Earlier that day, when I asked my brother about his first time
skydiving, he singled out this moment as his most frightening. "Dude, I'm
telling you—I almost blacked out," he offered, only half-jokingly. Those   5
words were imbedded in my mind as my tandem partner, Dale, tightened
the harness that held us together and guided us to the open exit door. With
half of my body dangling outside of the plane, I reached out and gripped
a support bar under the right wing. I had to tighten my grip to fight the
wind, which pushed with the force of a charging linebacker. Below me   10
I could see perfectly square plots of farmland in between breaks in the
clouds, and I almost missed Dale's final instructions over the buzz of the
Cessna's twin engines. "When you are ready, cross your arms over your
chest, and we'll jump," he yelled. Surprisingly, I didn't black out. I was
ready. So I crossed my arms, and we jumped.   15

React Answer the following questions about the paragraph. Then discuss your responses with your classmates.

1. What are the 5 W's and H of this experience? _____

2. What is the main point of this narrative paragraph? (See pages 30–31.)

   _____

3. How are the details organized—logically, chronologically, by order of importance? (See pages 96–97.) _chronologically_____

4. How would you rate this narrative paragraph and why?

   Weak ★ ★ ★ ★ ★ Strong

   _____

5. What idea or part seems to be the most important to you? _____

A CLOSER LOOK   at Reading Narratives

Considering the Author and Setting

Knowing about the author and the setting of a narrative will enrich your reading experience. (Setting refers to the time and place of the action.) There are three basic ways that you can learn this information.

1. The introduction to the text may highlight key facts about the author and the setting.
2. The text itself may provide some of this information.
3. The Internet may provide information about the author and his or her work.

Identify Learn as much as you can about the author and setting of the professional narratives that you read.

Showing Versus Telling

The writer on the previous page uses a mixture of showing and telling to recreate his experience. Telling involves reporting what happened; showing involves re-creating the experience. The following techniques help writers to show what happens in their narratives.

Showing Details

- **Sensory details** share sights, sounds, smells, tastes, and textures.
  The smell of old cigarettes and expired perfume turns my stomach.
  The weight of my backpack thrusts me forward in the rush-hour crowd.
- **Dialogue shares** the conversation between people.
  "So where are you from?" I asked.
  "Sudbury. My boyfriend is in jail, and they're letting him go today."
- **Personal thoughts and feelings** reveal the writer's state of mind.
  I have no idea how to talk to this woman, but she seems to like me.

Select Identify two or three details from the paragraph on page 138 that you especially like.

1. _____

2. _____

LO4 Reading and Reacting to a Student Paragraph

Read Read the following narrative paragraph. Remember to use the steps in the reading process. (See pages 14–15.)

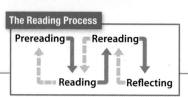

The Reading Process

Prereading   Rereading

Reading   Reflecting

Taking a Bow

My final moments on stage during the musical *Grease* are ones I'll   *1*
never forget. It was a Saturday night, and my high school's matchbox-
sized theater was filled to capacity, only no one was sitting. The cast,
crew, and I stood hand in hand, soaking in a standing ovation. The cheers
and clapping made me feel a supreme sense of satisfaction. This was the   *5*
culmination of three months of hard work. And this show, our last one, was
our best. My voice was shot. My hair was frizzy. And sweat beads trickled
down my brow, streaking globs of black mascara under my eyes. I looked
like a mess, but I didn't care. I turned to my friend Stacie and yelled, "I
don't ever want to forget this!" She squeezed my hand and replied, "A   *10*
standing O takes care of all the hurts." Meanwhile, my family was going
bonkers in the fourth row. Dad pumped his fist as if the Steelers had won
the Super Bowl, while my mom waved her hands in the air wildly. Usually,
these actions would make me run for cover, but not tonight. I never did
pursue a career in theater, but on that night Broadway didn't seem so far   *15*
away.

React Answer the following questions about the paragraph. Then discuss your answers with your classmates.

1. What are the key actions in this paragraph? Identify them on a time line.

   _____

2. What are the 5 W's and the H of this experience? _____

3. How much time is covered in this narrative? Explain.

   _____

4. How would you rate this paragraph and why?

   Weak ★ ★ ★ ★ ★ Strong

   _____

5. What idea or part stands out for you?

   _____

A CLOSER LOOK at Analyzing the Details

As you learned on page 139, strong narratives often include sensory details, dialogue, and the writer's personal thoughts and feelings. The writer of the paragraph on page 140 used all three types of details in her paragraph.

Identify On your own paper, make a chart like the one below. Then fill it in with examples of sensory details, dialogue, and personal thoughts from "Taking a Bow" on page 140.

Showing Chart

Sensory Details	Dialogue	Personal Thoughts and Feelings
• matchbox-sized theater • frizzy hair • sweat beads • globs of black mascara	• "I don't ever want to forget this!" • "A standing O takes care of all the hurts."	• Supreme sense of satisfaction • Broadway didn't seem so far away

Practice What details (sensory details, dialogue, personal thoughts and feelings) are the most memorable in this narrative? Explain.

_____

_____

_____

_____

LO5 Practicing Reading Skills

Reading is a great way to build your vocabulary and practice important thinking skills. The activities below will help you work on both.

Vocabulary: Using Context

Page 24 explains one strategy—using context clues—that will help you understand new words in your reading. Context clues are clues provided by the words and ideas around unfamiliar words.

> **Using context:** In the paragraph on page 138, the writer refers to his "tandem partner." The second half of the sentence explains "tandem partner" in this context.
>
> "My tandem partner, Dale, tightened the harness that held us together and guided us to the open exit door." *(A "tandem partner" in the context of skydiving is someone, presumably an expert, who is connected to another diver by a harness.)*

Identify Use context clues to define or explain the italicized words from the paragraph on page 140.

1. "The cast, crew, and I stood hand in hand, soaking in a standing *ovation*. The cheers and clapping made me feel a supreme sense of satisfaction. . . ."

   Context clues (words or ideas that help explain "ovation"): _____

   Meaning: _____

2. "This was the *culmination* of three months of hard work. And this show, our last one, was our best. . . ."

   Context clues (words or ideas that help explain "culmination"): _____

   Meaning: _____

Thinking Critically: Drawing Inferences

An *inference* is a logical conclusion that you can make about something that is not actually stated in a text.

> **Drawing Inferences:** In the paragraph on page 138, you could draw the conclusion that the writer is adventurous. He had never gone skydiving before, but he seems in control of his emotions. That isn't to say the experience wasn't frightening. The details he shares in the first half of the paragraph are evidence that he was nervous up until the final moments before he jumped.

Explain To practice drawing inferences, answer the following questions about the narrative paragraph on page 140.

1. What conclusions about Rochelle can you draw? _____

2. What value or meaning did the musical hold for her? _____

Writing

Starting on this page, you will plan and write a narrative paragraph about a special moment in your life. Be sure to use the writing process to help you do your best work. (See pages 68–73.)

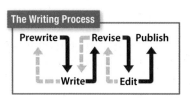

LO6 Planning a Narrative Paragraph

Remember that special moments are different for different people. Not everyone has bumped into a famous person, won the lottery, or survived a tsunami.

> "I've never tried to block out the memories of the past, even though some are painful. . . . Everything you live through helps to make you the person you are now."
> —Sophia Loren

Selecting a Topic

Below, a writer listed four experiences that he clearly remembers. He decided to write about his backpacking trip with his brother.

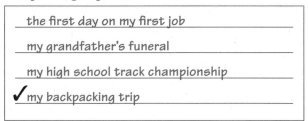

the first day on my first job

my grandfather's funeral

my high school track championship

✓ my backpacking trip

Select List four important memories from your life. Then put a check next to one memory you would like to write about in a personal narrative paragraph.

Using Chronological Order

Once you have selected a topic, think carefully about the order of events as you remember them. In most cases, narrative paragraphs are arranged chronologically (by time).

Identify Use a time line like the one to the right to list the main events of your experience in time order.

Time Line	
1.	pedaling with brother on a mountain trail
2.	loses track of brother because of fog
3.	fog lifts and stop to rest on a ridge
4.	I and my brother share feelings

Gathering Sensory Details

The most vivid narrative paragraphs use plenty of sensory details. Such details allow the reader to picture, hear, and touch what you describe. You can use a sensory chart to list specific sensory details about an experience.

Sensory Chart

Sights	Sounds	Smells	Tastes	Feelings/Textures
-forests of evergreens -dirt path -mountain ranges -thick fog	-talk with brother -birds chirping -crunching leaves	-fresh air -smell of rain	-peanut butter granola bar	-achy thighs -burning lungs

INSIGHT —

To gather the best details, try talking about the experience with someone or writing freely and rapidly about it.

Kayros Studio "Be Happy!", 2011 / Used under license from Shutterstock.com

Collect   Complete a sensory chart like the one below. Collect any sights, sounds, smells, tastes, feelings, or textures that you may want to include in your narrative. (Not all senses will necessarily pertain to your experience.)

Sights	Sounds	Smells	Tastes	Feelings/Textures

LO7 Writing the First Draft

Writing a first draft is your first attempt to connect the thoughts you have gathered about your topic. Don't try to make everything perfect. Instead, simply get all of your ideas on paper.

Read Carefully read and enjoy this writer's paragraph about a special time in his life.

A Rugged Ride

Topic Sentence

Riding up the mountain trail, my thighs ached and my lungs burned, but I couldn't be happier. Fifty feet in front of me pedaled my brother, Keith, fresh off his tour with the Marines. This mountain biking adventure was his idea. The green, forest-lined trail was rugged, with sharp turns and steep descents. At one point we hit a patch of fog and I lost sight of Keith. It felt as if we were riding through clouds. The ghostly air was damp and smelled like rain. I slowed down and called for my brother, "Are you still up there?" "Would I be anywhere else?" he yelled back. When the fog disappeared, we stopped for a breather on a ridge that overlooked a vast valley. A sea of pointy evergreens stretched for miles, ending near the peak of a distant mountain. While I snacked on a peanut butter granola bar, Keith glanced over at me and said, "This is fun, isn't it?" "It's good having you back, man," I responded. With that, we hopped on our bikes and continued our adventure.

Body Sentences

Closing Sentence

Consider the Craft

1. What do you like best about this paragraph?

2. What are two of your favorite details?

3. How much time does the event cover?

4. Does the writer say just enough about the experience, too much, or too little?

The Working Parts of a Paragraph

A paragraph consists of three main parts, and each has a special function. The information that follows explains each part.

Paragraph Outline

Topic Sentence: A topic sentence sets the stage for the paragraph. It identifies your topic and puts it in perspective in an interesting way.

Body Sentences: The body sentences support the topic sentence. Specific details are included to make each main point clear to the reader.

Closing Sentence: A closing sentence (or two) captures the importance of the experience.

Drafting Tips

When you write a narrative paragraph, you are essentially sharing a story. Consider these storytelling techniques to interest your readers.

READING-WRITING CONNECTION

Review the model narratives in this chapter for approaches or techniques that may help you with your writing.

- **To make your beginning special,** start right in the middle of the action (rather than starting with a more traditional topic sentence).

- **To keep your reader in suspense,** leave out certain details that give the ending away. Instead, offer clues about what might happen, or give false clues so that the real outcome is truly a surprise. Make a mystery out of your personal story.

- **To give your story impact,** include dialogue, but be selective. Make sure the conversation enhances or adds to the story.

- **To bring your writing to an effective end,** look around you. Cars screech to a halt. A jet trail eventually drifts away. Bathtubs swirl for a while, then gurgle. What will your ending do?

INSIGHT

How you develop your story depends on what you want it to do—inform, entertain, amuse, surprise, or shock.

Write Develop your first draft using the information on this page and your planning on pages 143–144 as a guide.

LO8 Revising the Writing

Start the revising process by reading your first draft two or three times to get a feel for your work so far. Then have one of your classmates read and react to your work using a response sheet as a guide. (See page 547.)

Adding Specific Verbs and Modifiers

You can improve your paragraph by adding specific nouns and modifiers.

General Noun	**Specific Noun**
The **place** was beautiful.	The **valley** was beautiful.

General Verb	**Specific Verb**
My thighs **hurt**.	My thighs **ached**.
My brother **rode** in front of me.	My brother **pedaled** in front of me.

Revising in Action

Read aloud the unrevised and then the revised version of the following excerpt. Note how the specific words energize the writing.

> . . . we stopped for a ~~rest~~ *breather* on a ridge that overlooked ~~a large opening~~ *a vast valley*. ~~There were evergreens everywhere,~~ *A sea of pointy evergreens stretched for miles,* ending near the peak of a distant mountain. While I ~~ate~~ *snacked on* a peanut butter granola bar...

Revise Improve your writing, using the checklist below and your classmate's comments on the response sheet. Continue working until you can check off each item in the list.

Ideas

☐ **1.** Do I focus on one specific experience or memory?

☐ **2.** Do I include enough sensory details?

☐ **3.** Do I include dialogue or personal thoughts if appropriate?

Organization

☐ **4.** Have I included a topic sentence, body sentences, and a closing sentence?

☐ **5.** Is the paragraph organized chronologically?

Voice

☐ **6.** Do I sound interested and sincere?

LO9 Editing the Writing

In some narrative paragraphs, dialogue may be used to reveal the personalities of the people involved in the story. When you include conversations between people, use quotation marks before and after their exact words, also called direct quotations. However, when you share what people say without using their exact words, also called indirect quotations, do not use quotation marks. See the examples that follow.

INSIGHT

Direct quotations should sound natural, as if the person is speaking. Read direct quotations out loud to check the way they sound.

Direct Quotation

Sitting in my one-room apartment, I remember Mom saying, **"Don't go to the party with him."**

Indirect Quotation

I remember Mom saying **that I should not go to the party with him.**

Note: The words *if* and *that* often indicate an indirect quotation.

Punctuation Practice Read the sentences below. Place quotation marks ("") before and after the exact words in direct quotations. If the sentence is correctly punctuated, write *correct* next to it.

1. "Christina, could you give me a ride to the airport?" I asked. _____
2. "You are one lucky guy," said Reid. _____
3. The tour guide said that we should get our cameras out. ____correct____
4. "There's little chance I'll ever eat octopus," joked Hailey. _____
5. Before we left, I said, "Don't forget your wallet and cell phone!" _____
6. Kyle said if he goes to the movie tonight, he will miss the party. correct
7. "Where did you get that dress?" asked Brianna. _____
8. Derrick says that he thinks your sweater shrunk in the dryer. __correct__

Additional Practice: For more practice see pages 524–525.

Apply Read your narrative paragraph. If it contains any direct quotations, make sure they are properly marked with quotation marks. If you did not use any direct quotations, consider adding one or two to enliven your writing.

Punctuation Used with Quotation Marks

As you edit your narrative paragraph, pay special attention to the punctuation marks used with quotation marks. Here are three rules to follow:

- When periods or commas follow the quotation, place them before the closing quotation mark.

  "Never be afraid to ask for help," advised Mr. Lee.

  "With the evidence we now have," Professor Howard said, "many scientists believe there could be life on Mars."

- When question marks or exclamation points follow the quotation, place them before the closing quotation mark if they belong with the quoted words. Otherwise, place them after the quotation mark.

  "Bill, do you want to go to the gym with me?" I asked.

  Were you telling the truth when you said, "Let's go home"?

- When semicolons or colons follow the quotation, place them after the quotation mark.

  He said, "Absolutely not"; however, he relented and left work early.

Punctuation Practice In each sentence, correct the misplaced punctuation marks. (Use the transpose sign ◠.) Refer to the rules above for help.

1. "Please hand your papers in by the end of the week", advised Professor Hopkins.

2. Mark said, "See you soon;" however, he missed his flight.

3. "With everything that happened", my boss said, "it might be best to take Friday off."

4. "Don't be late"! exclaimed Lisa.

5. "Should we meet tomorrow"? asked Renee.

6. Did you really mean it when you said, "We are just looking?"

7. "Remember, you have a doctor's appointment on Thursday", my mom reminded me.

8. "Can you pass me the ketchup"? I asked.

Additional Practice: For more practice see pages 524–525.

Apply Read your narrative paragraph. Check the punctuation of dialogue closely.

Marking a Paragraph

The model that follows has a number of errors.

Editing Practice Correct the following paragraph, using the correction marks below.

Creature of Habit?

People say I'm a creature of habit, but that's not entirely true. For
instance, I like to try new foods. When I was in New hampshire, I ate raw
oysters. People say they taste like the ocean. Indeed, they are very salty.
I do enjoy the thrill of a new food, but oysters will not become a staple of my
diet. Besides eating bizarre foods, I also enjoy going on weeknd (weekend) adventures.
Last saturday, my friends and I went camping outside of the city. We
didn't even set up tents, deciding to sleep under the stars. Unfortunately,
the rising sun woke us up at about 6:00 a.m. I only got about four (for) hours of
sleep, so I was tired and crabby for the rest of the day. I guess that's one (won) way I
am a creature of habit. I like my sleep. Another unusual activity I enjoy is
Pilates. For some reason my friends think this makes me a wimp, but I bet
they couldn't make it through (threw) one class. I would love to see them try.

1

5

10

Correction Marks

℈ delete	⌃ add comma	word ∧ add word
d̲̲ capitalize	? add question mark	⊙ add period
ø̲ lowercase	∧	⬭ spelling
∧ insert	⌄ insert an apostrophe	⊓⊔ switch

Additional Practice: For more practice see pages 524–525.

Correcting Your Paragraph

Now it's time to correct your own paragraph.

Edit Create a clean copy of your revised writing and use the following list to check for errors. Continue working until you can check off each item in the list.

Words
- [ ] 1. Have I used specific nouns and verbs? (See page 102.)
- [ ] 2. Have I used more action verbs than "be" verbs? (See page 458.)

Sentences
- [ ] 3. Have I varied the beginnings and lengths of my sentences? (See pages 104–105.)
- [ ] 4. Have I combined short choppy sentences? (See page 105.)
- [ ] 5. Have I avoided shifts in sentences? (See page 422.)
- [ ] 6. Have I avoided fragments and run-ons? (See pages 104, 410–413, 416–417.)

Conventions
- [ ] 7. Do I use correct verb forms (*he saw*, not *he seen*)? (See pages 464, 466.)
- [ ] 8. Do my subjects and verbs agree (*she speaks*, not *she speak*)? (See pages 394–403.)
- [ ] 9. Have I used the right words (*their, there, they're*)?
- [ ] 10. Have I capitalized first words and proper nouns and adjectives? (See page 504.)
- [ ] 11. Have I punctuated dialogue correctly? (See pages 524–525.)
- [ ] 12. Have I carefully checked my spelling?

Adding a Title

Make sure to add an attention-getting title. Here are three simple strategies for creating one.

- Use a phrase from the paragraph:

  Creature of Habit?

- Use a main idea from the paragraph:

  Taking a Bow

- Use strong, colorful words from the paragraph:

  A Rugged Ride

Create Prepare a clean final copy of your paragraph and proofread it before you share it.

Review and Enrichment

On the next four pages you will find a multi-paragraph personal narrative to read and respond to followed by a number of narrative writing ideas to choose from. Completing these activities will help you form a better understanding of narration.

"Experience is a hard teacher because she gives you the test first, the lesson afterwards."
—Vernon Saunders Law

Prereading

Many of your most memorable experiences involve family members. You may have become reacquainted with a brother or a sister. You may have had to deal with the passing of a beloved family member, or you may find yourself in conflict with someone in your immediate or extended family.

Identify Think of two family members (immediate or extended) who have influenced you in a significant way. Then list one or two experiences with that person that stand out in your mind. Share your thoughts with your classmates.

CONSIDER THE TRAITS

As you read the narrative that follows, focus first on the **ideas**—the main point and supporting details in the story. Then consider the **organization**—the way the opening, the middle, and closing parts are constructed. Also think about the author's **voice**—the overall tone of the writing. And finally, ask yourself if these traits combine to produce an effective reading experience.

Person: _____

        Experiences: _____

Person: _____

        Experiences: _____

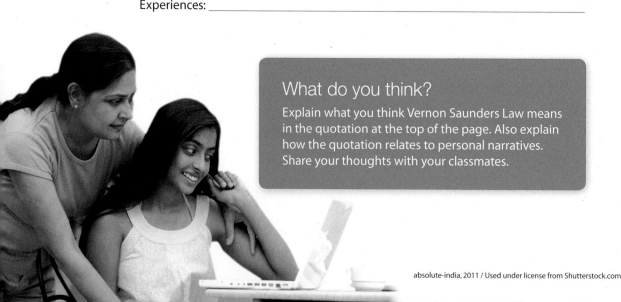

What do you think?

Explain what you think Vernon Saunders Law means in the quotation at the top of the page. Also explain how the quotation relates to personal narratives. Share your thoughts with your classmates.

Reading and Reacting

Read   This narrative focuses on a tragic experience—the murder of the writer's brother. Use the reading process to help you gain a full appreciation of the narrative. (See pages 14–15.) And keep your class notebook handy for notes and personal thoughts at different points during your reading.

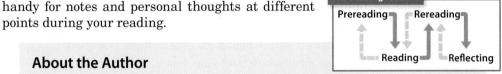

About the Author

After receiving a Ph.D. from the University of Chicago, Brent Staples worked as an adjunct professor of psychology at colleges in Pennsylvania and Chicago, then as a reporter for the *Chicago Sun-Times,* and most recently as an editorial writer for the *New York Times.*

A Brother's Murder

It has been more than two years since my telephone rang with the news that my younger brother Blake—just 22 years old—had been murdered. The young man who killed him was only 24. Wearing a ski mask, he emerged from a car, fired six times at close range with a massive .44 Magnum, then fled. The two had once been inseparable friends. A senseless rivalry—beginning, I think, with an argument over a girlfriend—escalated from posturing, to threats, to violence, to murder. . . .   5

As I wept for Blake I felt wrenched backward into events and circumstances that had seemed **light-years** gone. Though a decade apart, we both were raised in Chester, Pennsylvania, an angry, heavily black,   10 heavily poor, industrial city southwest of Philadelphia. There, in the 1960s, I was introduced to **mortality**, not by the old and failing, but by beautiful young men who lay wrecked after sudden explosions of violence. . . .

As I fled the past, so Blake embraced it. On Christmas of 1983, I traveled from Chicago to a black section of Roanoke, Virginia, where he   15 then lived. . . . One evening . . . standing in some Roanoke dive among drug dealers and grim, hair-trigger losers, I told him I feared for his life. He had **affected** the image of the tough he wanted to be. But behind the dark glasses and the swagger, I glimpsed the baby-faced toddler I'd once watched over. I nearly wept. I wanted desperately for him to live. The   20 young think themselves immortal, and a dangerous light shone in his eyes as he spoke laughingly of making fools of the policemen who had raided his apartment looking for drugs. He cried out as I took his right hand. A line of stitches lay between the thumb and index finger. Kickback from a shotgun, he explained, nothing serious. Gunplay had become part of his life.   *25*

I lacked the language simply to say: Thousands have lived this for you and died. I fought the urge to lift him bodily and shake him. This place and the way you are living smells of death to me, I said. Take some time away, I said. Let's go downtown tomorrow and buy a plane ticket anywhere, take a bus trip, anything to get away and cool things off.   *30*

He took my alarm casually. We arranged to meet the following night— an appointment he would not keep. . . .

As I stood in my apartment in Chicago holding the receiver . . . I felt as though part of my soul had been cut away. I questioned myself then, and I still do.   *35*

Did I not reach back soon or **earnestly** enough for him? For weeks I awoke crying from a **recurrent** dream in which I chased him, urgently trying to get him to read a document I had, as though reading it would protect him from what had happened in his waking life.

His eyes shining like black diamonds, he smiled and danced just   *40*
beyond my grasp. When I reached for him, I caught only the space where he had been.

Vocabulary

light-year
the distance light can travel in one year's time: about 6 trillion miles

mortality
the inevitability of dying

affect
to adopt or pretend

earnest
sincere

recurrent
repeated

Katrina Brown, 2011 / Used under license from Shutterstock.com

React Answer the following questions about the narrative. Share your responses with your classmates.

1. What are the 5 W's and H of this experience?

   Who? Author and his brother *What?* Author recalls brother's murder *Why?* A silly argument

   When? Two years ago *Where?* Roanoke, Virginia *How?* Gun violence

2. What is the writer's main point in this narrative? Is it simply to share the tragic details of his brother's death, or is it more than that? Explain.

   _____

3. What types of details does the writer use—sensory details, dialogue, personal thoughts and feelings?

   sensory details, dialogue, and personal thoughts and feelings
   _____

4. What does the writer do in each part of the narrative? (Name one or two things.)

   Opening: Introduces the tragic circumstances of the murder
   _____

   Middle: Details how the author intervenes with the brother's dangerous lifestyle
   _____

   Closing: Gives a final thought about the personal narrative
   _____

5. How would you rate this narrative and why?

   Weak ★ ★ ★ ★ ★ Strong

   _____

Drawing Inferences

An *inference* is a logical conclusion that you can make about something that is not actually said or stated in a text. A worthy inference does, however, result from a clear and careful understanding of what *is* said. To practice drawing inferences, answer the following questions about the narrative on pages 153–154. Afterward, share your responses with your classmates.

1. What is meant in lines 26–27: "Thousands have lived this for you and died"?

2. What conclusions about the writer can you draw from this narrative?

Writing

Write a narrative paragraph or narrative essay following the guidelines on the next two pages. Check with your instructor about any specific requirements that she or he may have. Use the writing process to help you to do your best work. (See pages 68–73.)

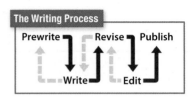

Prewriting

Choose one of the following or another appropriate writing idea for your narrative.

Writing Ideas

1. Write about one of the experiences that you identified in the planning activity on page 143.

2. Write about a time in your own life when you wished that a particular experience involving a sibling had never happened.

3. Do you consider yourself a creature of habit? If so, write about your habits or about one in particular.

4. Write about a humorous experience in your life, and challenge yourself to show rather than simply tell about the humor. (See page 139.)

5. Expand your narrative paragraph from pages 143–151, turning it into a more complete and detailed personal narrative.

6. Write a narrative based on a favorite photograph from your childhood.

When planning . . .

Use the tips that follow and the information on pages 143–144 to help you with your prewriting and planning.

- Choose a specific personal experience to write about.
- Consider your purpose (*to inform, to entertain,* and so on), your audience (*peers, family members,* and so on), and the main point you would like to share.
- Collect plenty of details (*sensory details, dialogue, personal thoughts*).
- Review the narratives in this chapter to see how they are developed.

Writing and Revising

Use the tips that follow and the information on pages 145–147 to help you with your drafting and revising.

When writing . . .

- Include an opening, a middle, and a closing in your narrative. Each part has a specific role. (See page 146.)
- Follow your planning notes, but feel free to include new ideas that pop into your mind as you write. Some of these new ideas may be your best ones.
- Remember that sensory details include more than what you see. Also consider sounds, smells, tastes, and feelings/textures.
- Include dialogue and personal thoughts to re-create the experience for your reader.

When revising . . .

- Determine if you've done too much telling and not enough showing.
- Also ask yourself if your story will interest and engage your reader. If it doesn't, determine what changes need to be made.
- Have at least one trusted peer react to your narrative. Ask for his or her honest reaction.

Editing

Refer to the checklist on page 151 when you are ready to edit your narrative for style and correctness.

Diego Cervo, 2011 / Used under license from Shutterstock.com

Reflecting on Narrative Writing

Answer the following questions about your narrative reading and writing experiences in this chapter.

1. What makes a personal narrative enjoyable to read?

   _____

2. What is your favorite narrative in this chapter? Explain.

   _____

3. What reading strategy highlighted in this chapter seems most helpful? Explain.

   _____

4. What do you like the most about the narrative paragraph that you wrote in this chapter? Explain.

   _____

5. What is one thing that you would like to change in this paragraph?

   _____

6. What is the most important thing that you have learned about writing a narrative?

   _____

Key Terms to Remember

When you read and write narratives, it's important to understand the following terms.

- **Autobiography**—the story of a person written by that person
- **Personal narrative**—an account of one specific experience in the writer's life
- **Sensory details**—specific sights, sounds, smells, tastes, and feelings/textures
- **Dialogue**—conversation between characters
- **Chronological order**—organized according to time
- **5 W's and H strategy**—answering *who? what? when? where? why?* and *how?* about an experience

8

Illustration

> "Good writing is clear thinking made visible."
> —Bill Wheeler

The backbone of any good piece of writing is the details that support the main idea. Without them, the writing simply won't hold up. This fact holds true for newspaper stories, magazine articles, text chapters, and blog posts. A newspaper columnist stating that violence in a city has reached unacceptable proportions will provide examples to make the statement credible. A fashion writer's positive review of a new clothing line will include reasons for her approval.

An illustration paragraph supports a general idea with specific examples. Recognizing key examples in reading will help you analyze texts and remember important information. Meanwhile, offering key examples in your writing will help you communicate your ideas more convincingly.

In the first part of this chapter, you will read and react to examples of illustration paragraphs. In the second part, you will write one of your own.

Learning Outcomes

LO1 Understand illustration.

LO2 Learn about reading strategies.

LO3 Read and react to a professional paragraph.

LO4 Read and react to a student paragraph.

LO5 Practicing reading skills.

LO6 Plan an illustration paragraph.

LO7 Write the first draft.

LO8 Revise the writing.

LO9 Edit the writing.

What do you think?

According to the quotation, good writing demonstrates clear thinking. What do you think is the connection between the two?

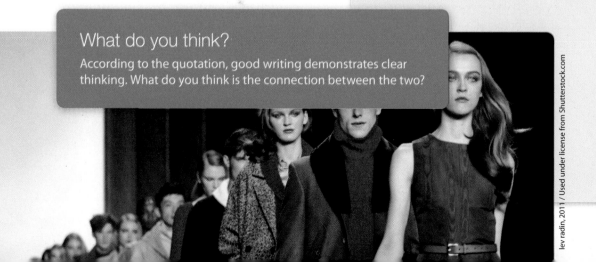

lev radin, 2011 / Used under license from Shutterstock.com

LO1 Understanding Illustration

What comes to mind when you think about the word *illustration?* If it is something art-related, you are not wrong. After all, drawings, sketches, and paintings are all considered illustrations. How then does illustration relate to writing? To answer this question, consider that *illustration* is defined in one sense as "the act of clarifying or explaining." Artists provide clarity by offering a visual representation of things. Writers clarify ideas by offering written explanations. Illustration paragraphs, in particular, clarify and explain ideas by offering examples.

> "No man with a conscience can just bat out illustrations. He's got to put all his talent and feeling into them!"
> —Norman Rockwell

A Familiar Structure

In most cases, illustration paragraphs generally follow a similar organizational pattern. They begin with a main idea, followed by examples and other types of details that support the idea. The following passage demonstrates this pattern.

> *(Main idea)* Global warming is already having a serious impact on the world around us. *(First example)* According to NASA, average temperatures have climbed 1.4 degrees Fahrenheit around the world since 1880, with most of the warm-up occurring in the last few decades. *(Second example)* Arctic ice is rapidly disappearing, and the loss of habitat is endangering polar bears. *(Third example)* Glaciers and mountain snows are rapidly melting. . . .

This pattern—main point, followed with examples—is a main feature in almost all forms of informational writing.

INSIGHT

Examples help a writer illustrate or support a main point. Other common types of supporting details in informational writing include facts, statistics, reasons, quotations, and definitions. (See pages 39–40.)

Identify Find a passage (similar to the one above) in one of your textbooks or on a Web site in which the writer illustrates a main idea. Identify the main idea and supporting examples in the text. Share the passage with your classmates.

Reading

Illustrating a main idea is the most common arrangement of ideas in academic writing. The strategies that follow will help you read texts that follow this arrangement.

LO2 Learning About Reading Strategies

Strategy 1: Identifying the Main Idea and Support

The main idea in an illustration paragraph is generally located in the first sentence—the topic sentence. It expresses a point about the topic that the writer illustrates throughout the rest of the paragraph. Once you determine the main idea, look for examples that support it. The examples and other details should be provided in the sentences that follow.

The number of supporting examples and details in a paragraph depends on the main idea. One writer may share a single example or story in great detail to support the main idea. Another writer may use three, four, or five brief examples. It all depends on what the writer feels is the best way to develop her or his main idea.

Strategy 2: Using a Line Diagram

To keep track of the key components, consider using a line diagram. Identify the main idea along the top of the diagram, and the supporting examples on the legs. If the paragraph includes additional details about any of the examples, add support legs to the example.

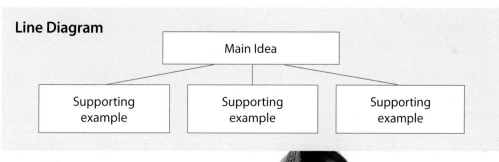

Line Diagram

Main Idea

Supporting example · Supporting example · Supporting example

funflow, 2011 / Used under license from Shutterstock.com

Practice Use these strategies for your next illustration reading assignment. Afterward, discuss your work with a classmate.

LO3 Reading and Reacting to a Professional Paragraph

Read   Read the following illustration paragraph from *Sociology: Your Compass for a New World,* an introductory-level sociology textbook by Robert J. Brym and John Lie. The paragraph illustrates a point about the power of teamwork. Remember to use the reading process to help you complete the reading. (See pages 14–15.)

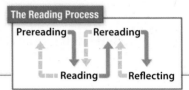

The Reading Process
Prereading Rereading
Reading Reflecting

Groupthink

    The power of groups to ensure conformity is often a valuable asset.   *1*
Sports teams could not excel without the willingness of players to undergo
personal sacrifice for the good of the group, nor could armies function.
In fact, sociologists have demonstrated, and as high-ranking military
officers have observed, group cohesion—not patriotism or bravery—is the   *5*
main factor motivating soldiers to engage in combat (Stouffer et al., 1949;
Marshall, 1947: 160-1). As one soldier says in the 2001 movie *Black Hawk
Down*: "When I go home people will ask me: 'Hey, Hoot, why do you do it,
man? Why? Are you some kinda war junkie?' I won't say a goddamn word.
Why? They won't understand. They won't understand why we do it. They   *10*
won't understand it's about the men next to you. And that's it. That's all
it is."

Works Cited

Stouffer, Samuel A., et al. 1949. *The American Soldier,* 4 vols. Princeton, NJ: Princeton
    University Press.
Marshall, S.L.A. 1947 *Men Against Fire: The Problem of Battle Command in Future
    War.* New York: Morrow.

"Groupthink" from BRYM/LIE. *Sociology: Your Compass for a New World,* 2E. © 2006 Thompson, a
part of Cengage Learning, Inc.

React   Answer the following questions about the paragraph "Groupthink." Then discuss your responses with your classmates.

1. What is the main idea of this paragraph?   Group conformity is a valuable asset.

2. What examples or other details illustrate the main ideas?   Sports teams and
    military groups

3. What supporting idea stands out for you? Explain. _____

4. What, if anything, could the writer have added to make the paragraph
    more complete? _____

A CLOSER LOOK at Illustration

Recognizing Signal Words

In illustration paragraphs, look for signal words or transitions to indicate that an example is being identified. Common ones include "for example" and "in addition." As you read illustration paragraphs, look for words like the ones in the chart below. Whenever you see one of these words or phrases, expect an example to follow it.

THE READING-WRITING CONNECTION

Use the signal words listed below to help you identify, or introduce examples in your own illustrative paragraphs.

Words that can be used to add examples:

for example	another	for instance
also	moreover	additionally
next	in addition	along with

Practice Note the signal words used in all of your academic reading assignments.

Considering Different Types of Supporting Details

While *examples* are the most common type of supporting detail in illustration paragraphs, some other types of supporting details may help writers illustrate ideas or explain the examples. Here are five other types of supporting details to be aware of as you read illustration paragraphs:

- **Reasons** offer a cause, an explanation, or a justification for an action or event.
- **Facts** offer statements or claims that can clearly be proven.
- **Statistics** offer concrete numbers about a topic.
- **Quotations** are the exact words of someone that offer insight on a topic.
- **Definitions** give the meanings of terms.

Evaluate Evaluate the illustration paragraph on the preceding page. What types of supporting details does the paragraph use to illustrate the main idea? Discuss your answers with a classmate.

LO4 Reading and Reacting to a Student Paragraph

Read Read the following paragraph that illustrates why today's youth is called the "Elsewhere Generation." Use the reading process to help you complete your reading. (See pages 14–15.)

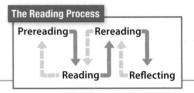

The Reading Process

Prereading Rereading

Reading Reflecting

The Elsewhere Generation

With their immersion in social media, **millennials** are being called the   *1*
"Elsewhere Generation." Quite often, a millennial will ignore people in the
same room while virtually interacting with people elsewhere. A teenage
boy plays a multiplayer online role-playing game with people in a different
country while his brothers beg him to play basketball outside. A group of   *5*
friends sits in a cafe, but instead of talking to each other, they are texting
people who are miles away. A student is listening to a lecture while typing
a status update on Facebook. Two joggers run side by side, but each is
talking on a headset to someone elsewhere. This constant multitasking
means that millennials can interact with many people in many places at   *10*
once. Sometimes, though, millennials seem to be everywhere and nowhere
at the same time.

Vocabulary

millennial
a person born between the
mid 1970s and the early
2000s

React Answer the questions below about the paragraph "The Elsewhere Generation." Then discuss your responses with your classmates.

1. What is the main idea of the paragraph? Millennials are being called the "Elsewhere generation" because they multi-task so often that they fail to interact with the people closest to them.

2. What examples does the writer use to illustrate the main idea? _____

3. What is the purpose of the paragraph—to inform, to persuade, to entertain? Explain. to inform _____

4. What questions, if any, do you still have about the topic?

_____

A CLOSER LOOK   at Illustration

Creating the Organization

Knowing how the details are organized can help you recognize the type of paragraph you are reading. Unlike paragraphs that describe a process or share a story, the details of an illustration paragraph often have equal value, meaning they can be reordered and the paragraph will still seem clean and coherent.

Notice how the content of the next two paragraphs is the same, but the order is not.

Paragraph 1

Since the 1970s, the culinary world has experienced an explosion of fusion food, which blends elements of different cuisines. For example, Chinese potstickers may be filled with European ingredients. Japanese sushi rolls may include California staples like smoked salmon and avocado. A Mexican-South Korean eatery may combine traditional Mexican offerings (chicken, cilantro, and cheese) with South Korean offerings (fried egg, tofu, and soy sauce) to make a single burrito. As global cultures continue to blend together, so too will the cuisines.

Paragraph 2

As our world's cultures have blended in the 21st century, so too has our cuisine. Since the 1970s, the concept of fusion food has exploded in popularity. It's now not uncommon to find an eatery that combines traditional Mexican and South American offerings to make a tofu burrito. Yet another restaurant may feature Chinese potstickers with European fillings. Even the popular California roll is an example of fusion food, combining the idea of Japanese sushi rolls with smoked salmon and avocado—two California staples. As you can see, globalization is reshaping culinary traditions.

Evaluate   Study the supporting details in the two paragraphs you have read in this chapter. Would the paragraph still make sense if the examples were in a different order? Share your thoughts with your classmates.

Special Challenge   Rewrite the paragraph on page 162 with the support details in a different order. Make any other changes in the paragraph to ensure that it reads smoothly.

LO5 Practicing Reading Skills

When reading, you will naturally come across new words and new ideas. The strategies below will help you understand new words.

Vocabulary: Understanding New Words

Many words in our language are made up of word parts—prefixes, suffixes, and base words or roots. Base words are the starting point for most words. Prefixes are word parts that come before base words, and suffixes are word parts that come after base words. (See pages 25, 549–557 for more.)

- **Base word:** *Oper* meaning "work" is the base word or root in *operate*.
- **Prefix:** *Co* is a prefix meaning "together, with" that comes before *pilot* in *copilot*.
- **Suffix:** *Ist* is a suffix meaning "one who" that comes after *art* in *artist*.

Identify   Define or explain each word part for the following words. Refer to the glossary of common prefixes, suffixes, and roots in the Appendix for help. (See pages 549–557.) Then write a complete definition of the word.

1. **interact**

   inter _____

   act _____

   So *interact* means . . . _____

2. **conformity**

   con _____

   form _____

   ity _____

   So *conformity* means . . . _____

Reading Critically: Levels of Knowing

On page 22, you will find a chart that lists the different levels of thinking from the most basic (*remembering* and *understanding*) to the most challenging (*evaluating* and *creating*). A brief explanation follows each level of thinking. For example, remembering involves identifying key terms or points in the reading.

Practice   Apply the following levels of thinking to the illustration paragraph on page 162 by following the direction in parentheses.

- **Remember:** *(List the key points.)*
- **Understand:** *(Explain what you have learned.)*
- **Evaluate:** *(Judge the value of the information.)*

Writing

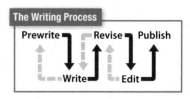

In your own paragraph, you will illustrate something about modern culture or life. Be sure to use the writing process to help you do your best work. (See pages 68–73.)

LO6 Planning an Illustration Paragraph

Selecting a Topic

The topic for your paragraph should be related to modern culture—a type of television show, a type of technology, a brand of clothing, and so on. You should be able to think of any number of interesting topics to illustrate your main idea.

Select List possible topics under at least three of the categories below. (One example is provided for you.) Then circle the one that you want to write about in an illustration paragraph.

Favorite type of . . .				
books	movie/ television	music	sports	other
			football	

Deciding on a Focus

Once you choose a topic, decide on a feature of this topic that you could illustrate in your paragraph. For example, in the student paragraph on page 164, the writer focuses on situations where people are disconnected from the immediate world around them to illustrate why today's youth is known as the "elsewhere generation." To write about a feature of football, a writer might illustrate changes that are being made because of head injuries.

Explain In the space below, explain the feature or part of this topic that you will illustrate in your paragraph.

_____

_____

> **INSIGHT** _____
> Finding a focus for your writing is a crucial part of prewriting. It gives you direction to move forward with your planning and writing. Make sure the topic is not so broad that it will not fit in a paragraph.

Identifying Your Examples

Once you have established a focus, you need to identify the examples that will help illustrate this feature.

Identify   List three or four examples that you could use to illustrate your focus. The writer of a paragraph that illustrates the measures taken to prevent head injuries in football listed these three examples.

Better in-game concussion testing

Limits on full-contact and off-season practice time

Stricter fines and penalties for illegal "head" hits

Gathering Details

After you think of examples, you may have to come up with additional details to clarify each example. For example, the writer of the paragraph about football safety would need to explain how players are tested during games for concussions.

Collect   Identify details that are necessary to clarify any of your examples. You may have to do some research to complete this part.

Forming Your Topic Sentence

Your topic sentence should state your topic and identify your focus. The following formula can help you write your sentence.

The topic	a feature or part of the topic		topic sentence.
Head injuries in the NFL	**+** additional safety measures	**=**	Numerous head injuries in the NFL have led to additional safety measures.

Create   Write your topic sentence using the formula above as a guide. If necessary, write two or three versions and then choose the best one.

[ ]   **+**   [ ]   **=**   [ ]

LO7 Writing the First Draft

After you have completed your prewriting and planning, you are ready to write your paragraph. Provided below is another sample illustration paragraph to consider before you write.

Read Read the paragraph, noting the distinct beginning, middle, and ending parts.

Heading in the Right Direction

Topic Sentence

Numerous head injuries in the NFL have led to additional *1* safety measures. New studies conclude that concussions can lead to long-term, crippling brain damage. As a result, the league has beefed up its baseline testing for players who suffer head injuries during a game. Before gaining permission to *5* reenter the game, a player in question must now pass a six- to eight-minute test that measures things such as memory, balance, and concentration. The NFL is also cutting back on practice time and off-season programs, as well as limiting full-contact practices in the pre-season and regular season. With *10* less time to bang heads, fewer concussions should happen. In addition, the league is enforcing stricter fines and penalties for illegal helmet-to-helmet hits—those hits where a player launches himself headfirst to strike an opposing player's helmet. The measures listed above are just a few of the steps *15* the NFL is taking to make the game safer. Still, the media, lawmakers, and former players say the league is failing to do enough to protect players. It will be interesting to see what additional safety measures will come in the future. The game may soon look much different than it does today. *20*

Example 1

Example 2

Example 3

Closing Sentence

Consider the Craft

1. What do you like best about the paragraph?
2. What are your two favorite details?
3. Do the examples help clarify the main idea?
4. Does the writer sound knowledgeable?

Mike Flippo, 2011 / Used under license from Shutterstock.com

The Working Parts of a Paragraph

A paragraph consists of three main parts, each of which has a special function. The information that follows explains each part.

Paragraph Outline

Topic Sentence: The topic sentence states the topic and the focus of the paragraph.

Body Sentences: The body sentences provide examples and other details that illustrate the main idea, which was established in the topic sentence.

Closing Sentence: The closing sentence sums up the main point or recasts it in a new or interesting way.

Tip

Remember the transitional words used to add information: *additionally, along with, also, another, as well, finally, for example, for instance, in addition, next, other,* and so on.

Drafting Tips

When you write an illustration paragraph, you are clarifying an idea by providing examples. Consider the following techniques to give your reader a clear understanding of your main idea.

- Use at least three strong examples or other types of support to illustrate your main idea.

- Arrange the examples in an order that makes the best sense. (Remember that examples in illustration paragraphs may work in more than one order.)

- Clearly explain each example so it is clear to the reader.

- Review the models you have read in this chapter for ideas for your own paragraph.

Write Develop your first draft using the information on this page and your planning on pages 167–168 as a guide.

Jaimie Duplass, 2011 / Used under license from Shutterstock.com

LO8 Revising the Writing

Start the revising process by reading your first draft two or three times to get a feel for your work so far. Then have one of your classmates read and react to your work using a response sheet as a guide. (See page 547.)

Cutting Unnecessary Ideas

Unnecessary ideas repeat what was already said or include unrelated or inaccurate information. They should be cut or deleted.

Repeated Idea: The power of groups to ensure conformity is often a valuable asset. ~~It can be very useful.~~

Unrelated Idea: With their immersion in social media, millennials are being called the "Elsewhere Generation." ~~Young people don't understand the value of hard work.~~

Inaccurate Information: The NFL is enforcing stricter fines and penalties for illegal helmet-to-helmet hits. ~~If a referee judges a tackle as a helmet-to-helmet, he can penalize the guilty player five yards.~~ *(The penalty is 15 yards.)*

Revising in Action

Read aloud the unrevised and then the revised version of the following passage. Notice that an unrelated and a repeated idea have been cut.

Hurricane Katrina led to the largest displacement of Americans since the Civil War. More than a half-million people sought shelter outside their homes ~~elsewhere.~~ The New Orleans area was hit hardest, with more than 90 percent of its residents evacuated. ~~New Orleans is known as "The Big Easy" because of its easy-going, laid back attitude.~~

Revise Improve your writing, using the following checklist and your classmate's comments on the response sheet. Continue working until you can check off each item.

Revising Checklist

Ideas
- ☐ 1. Have I created a strong topic sentence for my paragraph?
- ☐ 2. Do I include at least three examples to illustrate my main idea?

Organization
- ☐ 3. Does my paragraph have effective opening, middle, and closing parts?
- ☐ 4. Do I use transitions, if necessary, between examples? (See page 163.)

Voice
- ☐ 5. Do I sound knowledgeable and interested?

LO9 Editing the Writing

The main work of editing is to check the effectiveness of individual words and sentences and correct any errors in your revised writing.

Capitalizing Proper Nouns and Adjectives

You know most of the basic rules related to capitalization, but it is useful to review them before you edit your writing. In addition to capitalizing the first word in a sentence, here are three other rules to remember.

- **Sections of the country** are capitalized, but words that indicate direction are not: Paul moved to the **Northwest** last year. He lives **south** of Seattle.

- **Titles used with the name of a person** are capitalized, but titles used by themselves are not: **Mayor Henderson** solved the city's sewage problem, a problem that the former **mayor** failed to address.

- **The first word in a direct quotation** is capitalized, but only if it begins a full sentence: Shawna asked, **"Does** anyone want to meet at the coffee shop?" I would have said **"yes,"** but I was busy.

Capitalization Practice Rewrite the following sentences, adding capitalization where needed and lowercasing any letters that should not be capitalized.

1. The midwest in the United States is made up of 12 states.
2. The Southern half the midwest is comprised of kansas, Missouri, Illinois, Indiana, and Ohio.
3. Before becoming President, Barack Obama worked as a Senator in Illinois.
4. The Midwest is East of president Obama's birthplace—Honolulu, Hawaii.
5. Bill Bryson said, "you can always tell a midwestern couple in Europe because they will be standing in the middle of a busy intersection looking at a wind-blown map and arguing over which way is west."
6. Many people from other regions, especially the northeast, are used to busy intersections.

Additional Practice: For additional practice, see pages 504–507.

Apply Check your illustration paragraph for the capitalization rules above. (For more information, see pages 504–507.)

Additional Capitalization

Here are three additional rules about capitalization that are important to understand when you edit your writing.

- **Specific names of special events** (historic events, holidays, sporting events, and so on) are capitalized, but general terms for the events are not: Americans celebrate **Veterans Day** every November 11. The **day** honors living and dead **veterans** of war.
- **Specific names of places** (mountains, rivers, buildings, bridges, and so on) are capitalized, but general references to them are not: Chicago's **Sears Tower** was officially renamed the **Willis Tower** in 2009. With 108 stories and standing 1,451 feet high, the **tower** was the tallest in the world from 1973 to 1998.
- **Specific names of organizations** (military groups, sports teams, political parties, and so on) are capitalized, but general references to them are not: The **New York Rangers** played the **New Jersey Devils** in hockey. The proximity of both **teams** makes them natural rivals.

NOTE: Capitalize the first and last word and other important words for a specific name of something. Do not capitalize words such as *of, on, for, the,* or *a* if they are within the name.

United States of America   Susan G. Koman for the Cure

Practice   Rewrite the following sentences, adding capitalization where needed and lowercasing any letters that should not be capitalized.

1. My favorite holiday is thanksgiving because our family dines at leroy's cafe.
2. Each labor day, my family drives along the Mississippi river to my aunt's house in st. louis.
3. My uncle belongs to the Republican party, my mom belongs to the democratic party, but I am independent of any party affiliation.
4. Many tourists visit the empire State Building in New York; the Plaza hotel is a favorite tourist stop as well.
5. A restaurant called tavern on the green has closed, but it was once a popular eating place in Central park.
6. Rescue missions are common in most large cities; the unity rescue mission in Quincy helps many people.

Additional Practice: For additional practice, see pages 504–509.

Apply   Check your illustration paragraph to make sure that you have followed the capitalization rules above.

Marking a Paragraph

The model that follows has a number of errors.

Editing Practice   Correct the following paragraph, using the correction marks below. One correction has been done for you.

Forged by Pain

Frida Kahlos path toward political and artistic fame was paved by   1

pain. As a child, Kahlo were bedridden for nine months with polio. Then,

at age 18, she was critically injured in an autobus <u>acident</u>. During the

accident

collision Kahlo was impaled by a handrail and ~~suffer~~ fractures in her spine

suffered

and pelvis. it took months of painful rehab to walk again, and the pain   5

and injuries lingered throughout her lifetime. But during the months of

agonizing rehab, kahlo took up painting. It was during this period when

Kahlo started working on her first of many famous self-portraits. The

physical pain she <u>epxerienced</u> as a youth and the emotional pain from her

experienced

unsteady marriage is reflected in her self-portraits many people belief that   10

is what makes them so powerful.

Correction Marks

⤳ delete	⋀ add comma	*word* ∧ add word
d̲ capitalize	? add question	⊙ add period
d̸ lowercase	∧ mark	⬯ spelling
∧ insert	⌄ insert an apostrophe	⬯ switch

Correcting Your Paragraph

Now it's time to correct your own paragraph.

Apply   Create a clean copy of your revised paragraph and use the following checklist to check for errors. Continue working until you can check off each item in the list.

Editing Checklist

Words

☐ 1. Have I used specific nouns and verbs? (See page 102.)

☐ 2. Have I used more action verbs than "be" verbs? "Be" verbs include words like *is, are, was, were*. (See page 458.)

Sentences

☐ 3. Have I avoided sentence errors such as fragments and run-ons? (See pages 410–413, 416–417.)

Conventions

☐ 4. Do I use correct verb forms (*he saw*, not *he seen*)? (See pages 464, 466.)

☐ 5. Do my subjects and verbs agree (*she speaks*, not *she speak*)? (See pages 394–403.)

☐ 6. Have I used the right words (*their, there, they're*)?

☐ 7. Have I capitalized first words and proper nouns and adjectives? (See page 504.)

☐ 8. Have I used the proper punctuation marks at the end of my sentences?

☐ 9. Have I used commas after long introductory word groups? (See pages 514–517.)

☐ 10. Have I used apostrophes correctly in contractions and to show possession? (See pages 530–531.)

Adding a Title

Make sure to add an appropriate title for your essay. Here are three strategies to try.

- Highlight the main idea:

   Groupthink

- Think creatively:

   The Elsewhere Generation

- Make a bold statement:

   Forged by Pain

> "Example is not the main thing in influencing others, it is the only thing."
> —Albert Schweitzer

Review and Enrichment

The first part of this chapter introduced you to reading and writing illustration paragraphs. This section reviews and expands on that information by providing an illustration essay to read and respond to. You will also be given a number of writing ideas to choose from to develop into an illustration paragraph or essay. These activities will broaden your understanding of this form of writing.

CONSIDER THE TRAITS

As you read the essay that begins on the next page, focus first on the **ideas**—the thesis (main idea) of the essay and the examples that are used to illustrate it. Then consider **organization**—the way that the opening, middle, and closing parts are constructed. Also note the author's **voice**—his special way of speaking to the reader. Finally, ask yourself if these traits combine to produce a satisfying reading experience.

Prereading

Earlier in this chapter, you read a paragraph entitled "The Elsewhere Generation" (page 164). It illustrated the idea that technology has increasingly caused millenials—the generation born between the mid 1970s and the early 2000s—to become detached from face-to-face interaction. Whether that idea is true or not is debatable, but stereotypes about specific generations of people often stick. The "Baby Boomer" generation, for instance, is known for being more rebellious and independent than the generation preceding it. No doubt today's children will be given a new label. Perhaps they will be the "Save the Earth" generation or the "Social Justice" generation.

Reflect Write freely for 5 minutes about your generation. Think about some examples of stereotypes that will follow your generation. Do you agree with them? Why or why not?

_____

_____

_____

What do you think?

The quotation above refers to "example" as having great influence. How can examples be influential or important? Discuss this idea with your classmates.

Reading and Reacting

Read Use the reading process to understand the four amazing inventions featured in this illustration article.

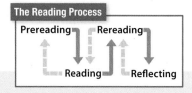

The Reading Process

Prereading   Rereading

Reading   Reflecting

About the Author

Robert King is coauthor of *Inquire: A Guide to 21st Century Learning* as well as two dozen novels.

A Penny for Your World-Saving Thoughts

Most people in the developed world think of technology as the newest $300 cell phone, or the best $50,000 hybrid vehicle, or one of our many $40,000,000 predator drones. In the developing world, however, a whole different breed of entrepreneurs is working on technologies that cost very little and use materials as simple as corncobs and discarded 2-liter bottles. These inventors don't care so much about the future as about the present, in which over a billion people live without access to safe drinking water (World). With a rare combination of ingenuity and compassion, a generation of inventors is fixing the world's worst problems with the simplest solutions.

For example, Amy Smith, an instructor at MIT, works in the Peruvian Andes to turn corncobs into charcoal. Like 800 million others in the world, the locals of El Valle Sagrado de los Incas currently heat their homes with agricultural waste products such as dung, straw, and corncobs. These fuels produce a great deal of smoke, which causes respiratory infections, the leading cause of death for those under five in such homes. By turning corncobs into charcoal, Smith converts a high-smoke fuel to a low-smoke one, not only heating homes but saving lives. Her process involves corncobs, matches, a 55-gallon drum with a lid, and patience. She jokingly calls her creations "carbon macro-tubes" (Ward).

While Smith works in Peru to bring clean heat to family homes, a man called "Solar Demi" is working to bring light to the slums of Manila, Philippines. In these tight-packed quarters, electricity is scarce, and most people live in total darkness. Demi takes discarded two-liter bottles, strips off their labels, cleans them, and fills them with a mixture of distilled water and bleach. He then cuts a hole in the roof of a home and fits the bottle in place with a watertight flange. This simple arrangement costs $1 per installation and produces 55 watts of free solar lighting. The Liter of Light Project aims to bring solar bottle lighting into one million homes in the Philippines (Ambani).

In South Africa, the problem is not lack of light but lack of water.

Traditionally in many tribes, women and girls carry water in containers   *32*
on their heads, a technique that requires numerous trips (keeping girls
out of school) and causes stress injuries to necks. To solve this problem,
architect Hans Hendrikse and his brother Piet have developed a wheel-   *35*
shaped plastic drum that can hold up to 50 liters and is durable enough
to roll across the ground behind a person. Four trips for water turn into
one, and backbreaking loads turn into an easy stroll with a sloshing drum
behind. By working with global partners, the Hendrikses are providing the
Q-drum cheaply to those who need it most (Hendrikse).   *40*

It's become fashionable to talk about how the future belongs to the
Throughout the developing world, unsafe drinking water is a huge
problem. It causes diarrhea, which kills 1.5 million children every
year—more than AIDS and malaria combined. The company Vestergaard
Frandsen wants to put a stop to it, so it has developed the LifeStraw—a
compact filtering device that is about the size of a fat ballpoint pen.   *45*
Children can carry this straw with them and drink surface water without
fear of getting waterborne diseases. The straw costs about $20 in the
developed world, but Vestergaard Frandsen is working with international
partners to provide the straw affordably to those elsewhere who do not
have safe supplies of water ("LifeStraw").   *50*

It's become fashionable to talk about how the future belongs to the
innovators, and people who say such things are often thinking about space
elevators and the like. But the present also belongs to the innovators—
those who make corncob coal and soda-bottle lights, and drums and straws
that deliver water. All of these inventions are simple, elegant solutions to   *55*
the world's oldest problems. With thinking like this, not only is our future
bright, but our present can be as well.

Works Cited

Ambani, Priti. "An Innovative and Cheap 'Solar Bottle Bulb' Solution Lights Homes in
    Manilla." *Ecoprenurist.* N.p. Web. 14 Sept. 2011. 21 October 2011.
Hendrikse, Piet. "The rolling water container for developing countries." *WHCC Health
    Innovations.* WHCC. Web. N.d. 21 October 2011.
"LifeStraw Introduction." *Vestergaard Frandsen.* VF. N.d. Web. October 2011.
Ward, Logan. "MIT's Guru of Low-Tech Engineering Fixes the World on $2 a Day."
    Popular Mechanics 1 Aug. 2008: 68-72. Print.
World Health Organization. "Access to safe drinking water improving; sanitation needs
    greater efforts." *World Health Organization.* 15 March 2010. Web. 21 October 2011.

React   Answer the following questions about the illustration essay. Share your responses with your classmates.

1. What single idea do all four of the examples illustrate?

    Each example examines a simple invention that targets a worldly problem.

    _____

2. Which of the solutions seems the most powerful to you? Why?

    _____

3. What details does the writer use to make the illustrations clear and interesting?

    _____

    _____

4. How does the writer get your attention in the opening?

    The author uses striking contrasts to gain the reader's attention.

    _____

5. How does the writer use the conclusion to connect to life in general?

    The conclusion shows how innovation is as much a part of the present as it will be in the

    future.

6. How would you rate this illustration, and why?

    Weak ★ ★ ★ ★ ★ Strong

    _____

    _____

Drawing Inferences

An *inference* is an idea that a reader logically assumes even though it is not stated outright by the author. In the article, King often mentions how international partners are working with inventors and companies to provide these solutions cheaply to those who need them. Write two inferences you could draw from these repeated statements. Answers will vary.

_____

_____

Writing

Write an illustration paragraph or essay following the guidelines on the next two pages. Check with your instructor about any specific requirements she or he may have for this writing. And be sure to use the writing process to help you do your best work. (See pages 68–73.)

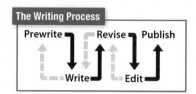

Prewriting

Choose one of the following ideas for your descriptive writing. Or decide upon another idea of your own.

Writing Ideas

1. Write about one of the modern culture topics you identified in the prewriting activity on page 167.

2. Write about the generation you wrote about in the freewriting exercise on page 176.

3. Write about a topic related to your major or academic concentration.

4. Write about a topic that impacts your home or academic community.

5. Write about a topic related to a photograph or model in this chapter.

When planning . . .

Refer to pages 167–168 to help you with your prewriting and planning. Also use the tips below.

- Choose a topic that you care about. Writing about something you like helps you put more effort into your work.
- Decide on an interesting focus or feature of the topic to illustrate.
- Be able to identify at least three examples to illustrate your topic. Make sure the examples clearly illustrate the main idea for your readers.
- Consider different types of supporting details to further illustrate your examples (see page 163).
- Review the illustration writing in this chapter to see how they are developed. Some of the techniques those writers used may help you shape your own thoughts and ideas.

Writing and Revising

Refer to pages 169–171 to help you write and review your first draft. Also use the tips below to help you with your drafting and revising.

When writing . . .

- Write your first draft freely, generally following your planning. But also be open to new ideas.
- Don't worry about getting anything just right in this writing.
- Include an effective beginning, middle, and ending in your illustration piece. Each part plays its own role. (See page 170.)
- Clearly explain each one of the examples.
- When necessary, use transitional words to connect the examples in the paragraph.

When revising . . .

- Let your first draft sit unread for a bit. Then reread it carefully, with fresh eyes.
- Determine if your writing answered key questions readers might have about your topic.
- Decide if all of your ideas are necessary—or directly related to your topic and focus.
- Be prepared to do further research if you need more examples or details.
- Ask a classmate to review your writing, using a peer review sheet. (See page 547.)

Editing

Refer to the checklist on page 175 when you are ready to edit your illustration piece for style and correctness.

Reflecting on Illustration Writing

Answer the following questions about your illustration reading and writing experiences in this chapter.

1. What are the two key parts of illustration writing?

   (1) A main idea and (2) examples that illustrate that idea

2. Why are examples so important in this type of writing?

   The main idea loses its authority without examples to support it.

3. Which reading strategy in this chapter seems the most helpful?

4. What is your favorite model in this chapter? Explain.

5. How will your understanding of illustrating a topic help you with your academic reading?

6. What is the easiest thing about writing an illustration essay? The hardest?

7. What do you like best about your essay?

8. What is one thing you would like to change in it?

Key Terms to Remember

When you read and write illustration essays, it's important to understand the following terms.

- **Illustration**—the act of clarifying or explaining in writing
- **Example**—something that represents the whole group
- **Line diagram**—a graphic organizer used to identify the main idea and examples in writing

9

"Words mean more than what is set down on paper. . . ."
—Maya Angelou

Definition

Read any word in a dictionary, and you'll find other words to define it. Each one of these words has its own definition. This web of words creates the enormous network that is our language.

A paragraph of definition may start with a dictionary definition, but then it includes other types of information such as synonyms for the word, examples of the word in use, and its history. In other words, a dictionary definition is only a launching point for a fuller explanation.

In this chapter, you will learn about this form of writing. First you will read and react to a professional paragraph of definition. Then you will do the same for a student paragraph. Finally, you will write a definition paragraph of your own. During your work, you will begin to appreciate what it means to define a term.

Learning Outcomes

LO1 Understand definition.

LO2 Learn about reading strategies.

LO3 Read and react to a professional paragraph.

LO4 Read and react to a student paragraph.

LO5 Practice reading skills.

LO6 Plan a definition paragraph.

LO7 Write the first draft.

LO8 Revise the writing.

LO9 Edit the writing.

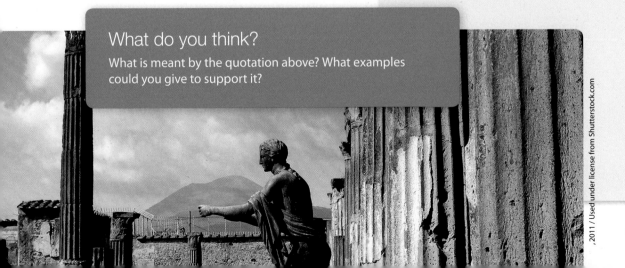

What do you think?
What is meant by the quotation above? What examples could you give to support it?

LO1 Understanding Definition

On the surface, a definition paragraph looks like a basic form of informational writing—sharing the meaning of a word. Many times, however, definition paragraphs go into much greater detail about a word, requiring research from a number of primary and secondary sources. In such cases, writing a definition paragraph becomes a practice in research writing.

> "We do not see first, then define. We define first and then see."
> —Walter Lippman

The paragraphs that you will read in this chapter involved quite a bit of research. So too will the definition paragraphs you encounter in your college reading and writing.

Professional Versus Student Paragraphs

Professional paragraphs of definition are generally written for one of two reasons. First, they are directed at the reader, to present information (as is usually the case in your textbooks). Second, they are directed more to the writer, to explore a term in order to better understand it. Often you may see this second sort of writing in personal essays and opinion pieces.

For your own writing in this chapter, you will focus on the second approach: writing to explore a word. Your task will be to consider a term that interests you, and then write about it in a way that increases your understanding of the word. At the same time, you will be sharing what you've learned with your readers.

INSIGHT ──

When writing a definition paragraph, you must make sure that you understand the term and its background. You must also gather your own thoughts about the term.

Identify   Identify two possible topics for definition in each of the following categories. (One idea is provided.) Then discuss your responses with your classmates.

History: _democracy_____

Technology: _____

Health: _____

The arts: _____

Environment: _____

Reading

Reading a definition paragraph involves connecting new information to what you already know about the topic.

LO2 Learning About Reading Strategies

The following reading strategies can help you get the most from definition paragraphs.

Strategy 1: Considering the Term

Before reading the definition, consider the following questions.

- **What do I already know about the term?** Have you encountered it before? If not, do you recognize the root word and any prefixes or suffixes?
- **What is the context of this definition?** Is it presented within a particular course of study? What do you know about the author that might affect the definition? Is the definition intended to inform or to explore? (See "Professional Versus Student Paragraphs" on page 184.)
- **What do I expect to learn from the definition?** With the previous questions in mind, what might you predict about the definition? What do you hope to learn, and what do you expect the author may have to say?

Strategy 2: Understanding the Support

Support for a definition paragraph may include dictionary definitions, personal definitions, word histories, encyclopedia information, synonyms and antonyms, comparisons, quotations, examples, and so on. It may help to chart the different types of support when you read a definition paragraph. Here is the start of a support chart:

Support Chart

Term defined: _____

- Dictionary definition: _____

- Personal definitions: _____

- Word history: _____

LO3 Reading and Reacting to a Professional Paragraph

Read This paragraph first appeared in *An Invitation to Health*, a health textbook. To gain a full understanding of the paragraph, follow the reading process.

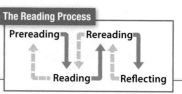

The Reading Process

Prereading → Rereading

Reading → Reflecting

The Three Most Difficult Words

  While "I forgive you" may be three of the most difficult words to say,   *1*
they are also three of the most powerful—and the most beneficial for the
body as well as the soul. Being angry, harboring resentments, or reliving
hurts over and over again is bad for your health in general and your
heart in particular. The word *forgive* comes from the Greek for letting   *5*
go, and that's what happens when you forgive: You let go of all the anger
and pain that have been demanding your time and wasting your energy.
To some people, forgiveness seems a sign of weakness or submission.
People may feel more in control, more powerful, when they're filled with
anger, but forgiving instills a much greater sense of power. Forgiving a   *10*
friend or family member may be more difficult than forgiving a stranger
because the hurt occurs in a context in which people deliberately make
themselves vulnerable. When you forgive, you reclaim the power to choose.
It doesn't matter whether someone deserves to be forgiven; you deserve
to be free. However, forgiveness isn't easy. It's not a time-time thing but a   *15*
process that takes a lot of time and work involving both the conscious and
unconscious mind. . . .

"The Three Most Difficult Words" from HALES. *An Invitation to Health,* 7E. © 2012 Brooks/Cole, a part of Cengage Learning, Inc. Reproduced by permission. www.cengage.com/permissions

---

React Answer the following questions about the paragraph. Then discuss your responses with your classmates.

1. What is the main idea of this paragraph?

   Forgiving is a powerful action, which can help the body as well as the soul.

2. What was your understanding of this term before your reading?

3. What different types of explanations or support are provided? Consider completing a support chart to help answer this question. (See page 185.)

4. How would you rate this paragraph and why?

   Weak ★ ★ ★ ★ ★ **Strong**

A CLOSER LOOK at Definition

Considering Specific Terminology

A dictionary definition focuses primarily on "terminology," which is to say the study of a word's usage, its parts, its synonyms, and its antonyms. Those same tools can be used in a definition paragraph.

- **Usage:** An explanation of how a word is used (noun, verb, etc.) can pretty much define that word. Still, usage changes over time, and other tools can be helpful in revealing additional shades of meaning.
- **Parts:** Nearly every word is a combination of word parts. Consider *multisyllabic,* from the Latin *multus* (meaning "many"), the Greek *syllablē* (meaning "to gather together"), and *ic* (a suffix meaning "of" or "related to"). Evaluating those parts can help define words. (See pages 25, 549–557.)
- **Synonyms:** These are words that are similar to one another. By comparing a word to synonyms, a definition shows what a word is like.
- **Antonyms:** These are words with opposite meanings. By contrasting a word to antonyms, a definition refines understanding of meaning.

Identify As you read a definition paragraph or essay, look for examples of the main word's usage, parts, synonyms, and antonyms.

Considering General Use

Besides terminology, a dictionary definition often includes a word's context—its history, and example sentences showing its use. Some dictionaries may even include notable quotations that employ the word and anecdotes (personal stories) about it.

- **History:** Many words in English are borrowed from other languages. You can find the history of a word by looking in the brackets [ ] for the entry. Knowing these sources can make a word more memorable.
- **Examples:** Often, a sentence placing the term in context is all that is needed to make that term's meaning clear.
- **Quotations:** Quotations share the thoughts of others about the term.
- **Anecdotes:** Like quotations, anecdotes help to explain a word by giving it a larger context. An anecdote shares a story about the word. An anecdote can add insight perhaps not possible from a quotation.

Identify As you read a dictionary definition or a definition paragraph, look for examples of these types of support.

LO4 Reading and Reacting to a Student Paragraph

Read   Read the following paragraph about social media. Remember to use the reading process to help you gain a full understanding of the text. (See pages 14–15.)

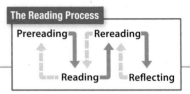

The Reading Process

Prereading   Rereading

Reading   Reflecting

What Is Social Media?

Social media is not an easy concept to define. Like a cloud, the   1
more closely you look at it, the foggier it becomes. The word *social* has
to do with human interaction, and the word *media* means "systems of
communication." Together, they seem easy enough to understand as
"human systems of communications." But social media is most often used   5
for electronic communications on the Internet. Usually that consists of
posting text messages, photos, and maybe short videos online for friends.
People use it to stay in touch with friends. People also use social media as
a form of self-expression. A person who is having a bad day can mention
it online, and friends can sympathize. Or when something great happens,   10
a person can post it, and friends can help celebrate. In addition, as Lee
Rainie of the Pew Research Center says, "If it's set up right, it's a rich
environment of lots of learning and sharing of important material." In
the end, the best definition of social media may be "a special form of
conversation."   15

React   Answer the following questions about the paragraph. Then discuss your answers with your classmates.

1. What is the main idea of this paragraph?

   Social media is a difficult word to define, because it has many broad meanings.

2. What was your understanding of the topic before your reading?

3. What types of support does the writer include? Consider completing a support chart to help you answer this question. (See page 185.)

4. How would you rate this paragraph and why?

   Weak ★ ★ ★ ★ ★ Strong

A CLOSER LOOK at Reflecting on Your Reading

On page 185, you learned about an important strategy, thinking about the term before reading about it. You can, of course, think about the topic after you read about it, too. Answering these questions will help you do this:

- What new information did you learn about the term?
- How might you use this information?
- What questions do you still have about it?

Identify   Answer the above questions for each of the reading models.

"The Three Most Difficult Words"

_____

_____

_____

_____

"What Is Social Media?"

_____

_____

_____

_____

Reflect   If you had written each of these paragraphs, what would you have added or changed to make each one even more effective?

_____

_____

_____

_____

_____

_____

LO5 Practicing Reading Skills

Reading is a great way to build your vocabulary and practice important thinking skills. The activities below will help you work on both.

Vocabulary: Understanding Word Parts

Page 25 explains one strategy—understanding word parts—that will help you understand new words in your reading. Word parts include roots or base words, which are the starting point for most words. Prefixes are word parts that come before roots to form new words. Suffixes are word parts that come after roots to form new words.

- **Base Word:** *Free* is the root or base word in *freedom*.
- **Prefix:** *Bi* is a prefix meaning "two" that comes before the root *cycle* in *bicycle*.
- **Suffix:** *Ity* is a suffix meaning "state of" that comes after the root *brev* in *brevity* (meaning the "state of being brief").

Identify   Define or explain each word part for the following words. Some of the word parts you will know just by sight. For the others, refer to the glossary of common prefixes, suffixes, and roots in the Appendix (see pages 549–557). Then try to write a complete definition of the word.

NOTE: These words come from the paragraphs you have read in this chapter.

1. *reclaim*
   re _back, again_
   claim _cry out_
   So *reclaim*
   means . . . _____

2. *interaction*
   inter _between_
   act _do_
   ion _act of, state of, result of_
   So *interaction*
   means . . . _____

3. *conscious*
   con _together, with_
   sci _know_
   ous _ful of, having_
   So *conscious*
   means . . . _____

Thinking Creatively: Working with Metaphors

One way to deepen your understanding of your reading is to compare the topic to something else. When you make comparisons of two unlike objects or ideas you are thinking metaphorically.

Complete   To help you think in this way, complete the following open-ended statements related to the two definition paragraphs you have just read.

- If *forgiveness* were a piece of clothing, it would be _____ because . . .
- If *forgiveness* were a color, it would be _____ because . . .
- If *social media* were a game it would be _____ because . . .
- If *social media* were a food it would be _____ because . . .

Writing

It is time now to begin planning and writing your own definition paragraph about a term you wish to better understand. Remember to use the writing process to help you do your best work. (See pages 68–73.)

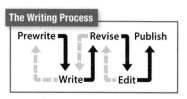

LO6 Planning a Definition Paragraph

As you've seen, a word can mean different things to different people. Part of the enjoyment of writing a definition paragraph is in discovering just what a particular term means to you and other people.

> "Nothing in life is to be feared. It is only to be understood."
> —Marie Curie

Selecting a Topic

To decide upon a topic, think of a term that either . . .

- means something important to you, or
- you would like to better understand.

Here are the terms that a student might list for consideration.

Terms that are important to me	Terms that I'd like to better understand
– loyalty	– faith
– independence	– pandemic ✔
– hipness	– willingness

The student chose to write about "pandemic" after hearing the word on a news report.

List Make a list of at least three terms that are important to you and three that you would like to better understand. Check the term that you would like to define in a paragraph.

Terms that are important to me	Terms that I'd like to better understand

Gathering Details: Terminology and Context

Once you have selected a term, gather details about it to use in your definition paragraph. In the example below, a student used a support chart to keep track of his details.

Support Chart

Term defined: *pandemic*

Dictionary definition	an "infectious disease covering a wide geographic area and affecting a large proportion of the population"
Comparison	Pandemic and epidemic
History	Pandemic comes from the Greek *pandemos*. The greek root *pan* means "every" or "all" and *demos* means "common people."
Examples	Black Death during the Dark Ages; flu pandemic in 1918 (killed 40 to 50 million); H1N1; and HIV

Collect Gather details for your paragraph, and use a support chart to keep track of your supporting ideas. Try to collect at least three types of support.

Term defined:

Dictionary definition	
Comparison	
History	
Examples	

Forming a Topic Sentence

Once you have collected your support, write a topic sentence for your paragraph. The formula below shows the two main parts in a topic sentence.

Specific topic	an important feeling or part		topic sentence.
Pandemic	**+** strikes fear into people everywhere	**=**	Pandemic is a term that strikes fear into people everywhere.

Create Write a topic sentence for your paragraph using the formula above. If necessary, write two or three versions until your thesis says what you want it to say.

Specific topic	an important feeling or part		topic sentence.
	+	**=**	

LO7 Writing the First Draft

Writing a first draft is your first attempt to connect all of the thoughts you have gathered about your topic. Don't try to make everything perfect. Instead, simply get all your ideas on paper.

Read Carefully read the following paragraph about the word *pandemic*.

Spreading the Word

Topic Sentence

Pandemic is a medical term that strikes fear into people everywhere. One news report might say, "The threat of a pandemic flu hitting the United States exists"; another one might say, "The World Health Organization has raised the level of the influenza pandemic alert." Who wouldn't be scared by threats such as these? So what exactly is a pandemic and where did this word come from? A pandemic is an "infectious disease covering a wide geographic area and affecting a large proportion of the population." Being "infectious" is a key feature because a disease cannot be a pandemic unless it can be spread by humans over a very wide area. So influenza can be pandemic, but cancer cannot. Some people use *pandemic* interchangeably with *epidemic*. But an epidemic doesn't become pandemic until it covers an extremely widespread area, such as a series of countries. *Pandemic* comes from the Greek *pandemos*: The Greek root *pan* means "every" or "all" and *demos* means "common people." Thus, *pandemos* means "all the people," so the connection with pandemic is clear. Two pandemics that are often cited are the Black Death during the Dark Ages and the flu pandemic in 1918 that killed from 40 to 50 million people. Current pandemics include H1N1, an infectious flu virus, and HIV. Here's a scary final thought: Globetrotting provides an easy way for pandemics to occur.

Body Sentences

Closing Sentence

1

5

10

15

20

Consider the Craft

1. What do you like best about this paragraph?
2. What types of details does the writer include about the main word?
3. Does the writer say just enough about the word, too much, or too little?
4. What did you learn about the word *pandemic*?

The Working Parts of a Paragraph

A paragraph consists of three main parts, and each has a special function. The information that follows explains each part.

Paragraph Outline

Topic Sentence:	A topic sentence names the term and a focus for your paragraph. (See page 192.)
Body Sentences:	The body sentences present your support. (See your support chart from page 192.)
Closing Sentence:	A closing sentence leaves the reader with a final thought about the term.

Drafting Tips

When you write a definition paragraph, you should give your readers a broad understanding of a word. Consider these tips for drafting a well-rounded paragraph.

- **To capture your reader's attention,** offer a surprising detail near the beginning of the paragraph, if possible in the topic sentence.

- **To add to your reader's understanding,** remember to offer historical information, example sentences using the word, and a quotation using the word.

- **To develop your definition fully,** add your own explanations and analogies to tie everything together. (The model on page 193 gives possible report headlines early on, and later it offers analogies of the definition.)

- **To help the paragraph move smoothly,** use transitional words to connect one point or detail to the next.

- **To bring your writing to an effective end,** focus on a key point about the term or stress the term's importance.

INSIGHT ————————————————————————————

Every academic and professional discipline has a different vocabulary. Defining terms is an important starting point for any discussion about any text.

Write Develop your first draft using the information on this page and your planning on pages 191–192 as a guide.

LO8 Revising the Writing

Start the revising process by reading your first draft two or three times to get a feel for your work so far. Then have one of your classmates read and react to your work using a response sheet as a guide. (See page 547.)

Rewriting Confusing Sentences

Any time you come across a sentence in your first draft that doesn't sound right or causes you to stumble, you should rewrite it.

Confusing sentence: When people write *pandemic,* they think *epidemic* all over again.

Rewritten for clarity: Some people use *pandemic* interchangeably with *epidemic.*

Revising in Action

Read aloud the unrevised and then revised version of the following passage. Note that the second sentence has been rewritten because it was confusing.

> Ever since Carl Sagan's PBS special first aired, people have known that the word *comos* means "universe." ~~A different definition was once used for it to give it a different meaning.~~ The word comes from the Greek *kosmos,* which means "order." When the word is added to the Greek word *polis,* meaning "city," terms like *cosmopolitan* result. This term began, however, with a more down-to-earth definition.

Revise Improve your writing, using the following checklist and your partner's comments on the response sheet.

Revising Checklist
Ideas

☐ 1. Do I state the topic and focus of my paragraph in the topic sentence?

☐ 2. Do I include different types of support (definitions, examples, and so on)?

☐ 3. Do I state all of my ideas clearly?

Organization

☐ 4. Does my paragraph have effective opening, body, and closing sentences?

☐ 5. Have I arranged the supporting details in an effective way?

Voice

☐ 6. Do I sound knowledgeable and interested?

LO9 Editing the Writing

The main work of editing is correcting your revised first draft. These next two pages cover the correct usage of apostrophes.

Using Apostrophes in Contractions

A contraction is a shortened form of a word or group of words with the missing letters replaced by an apostrophe. Here are some examples.

Common Contractions

I'm (I + am; the *a* is left out)
don't (do + not; the *o* is left out)
they're (they + are; the *a* is left out)
it's (it + is; the *i* is left out)
should've (should + have; the *h* and *a* are left out)

wouldn't (would + not; the *o* is left out)
they'd (they + had; the *h* and *a* are left out)
must've (must + have; the *h* and *a* are left out)

Missing Letters or Numbers

Letters or numbers are left out in the following types of words and phrases. Apostrophes indicate where the omissions occur.

class of '10 (the number *20* is left out)
stop 'n' go traffic (the letters *a* and *d* are omitted)

Apostrophe Practice Place an apostrophe as needed in the following sentences. If no apostrophe is needed, write "correct" on the blank next to the sentence.

1. Im sure that Jackson wouldve wanted to attend. _____

2. The menu listed "mac'n'cheese" and "ham'n'eggs." _____

3. The band was rockin' way past midnight. _____

4. Its unfortunate that my phone lost its protective case. _____

5. We're looking forward to the reunion of the class of 09. _____

6. You shouldnt stay up all night. I wouldnt. _____

7. Their flight might depart before theyre at the airport. _____

Additional Practice: For more practice see pages 530–531.

Apply Read the sentences in your definition paragraph, watching for contractions and special words with missing characters. Make sure these words have apostrophes in place to mark the missing letters or numbers.

Using Apostrophes to Show Basic Possession

Use apostrophes to show possession. Possession means "the act of having ownership." The placement of the apostrophe depends on whether the noun is singular or plural. Study the following examples.

Singular Possessives

■ The possessive form of singular nouns is usually made by adding an apostrophe and an *s*.

> my computer**'s** virus   Elena**'s** latest hairstyle   last night**'s** storm

■ When a singular noun of more than one syllable ends with an *s* or *z* sound, the possessive may be formed by adding just an apostrophe, or an apostrophe and an *s*.

> St. Louis**'** best park   or   St. Louis**'s** best park

Plural Possessives

■ The possessive form of plural nouns ending in *s* is made by adding just an apostrophe.

> the instructors**'** offices   the Smiths**'** damaged car

■ For plural nouns not ending in *s*, add an apostrophe and *s*.

> The men**'s** locker room   the children**'s** section of the library

Apostrophe Practice   Indicate where apostrophes are needed in the following sentences. If no apostrophe is needed, write "c" for "correct" on the blank line.

1. Carl car looks the same as Lois car. _____
2. The Kings house is smaller than the Davises house. _____
3. I like Wisconsin weather better than Texas weather.   *correct* _____
4. The women organization donated to the children toy fund. _____
5. The alumni donation helped the children fund most. _____
6. The men suits use Sharissa design. _____

Additional Practice: For more practice see pages 530–531.

Apply   Read the sentences in your definition paragraph, paying special attention to nouns that show possession. Be sure that you have correctly placed apostrophes in these words.

Marking an Essay

Edit the following model before you edit a revised version of your own paragraph.

Editing Practice Carefully read the following paragraph, looking for problems listed in the checklist on the next page. Correct the model using the marks listed below. The first correction has been done for you.

A Cosmic Word

Ever since Carl Sagan's PBS special first aired, people have known   *1*
that the word *cosmos* means "universe." This term began, however, with a
more down-to-earth definition. The word comes from the Greek *kosmos*,
which means "order." When this word is added to the Greek word *polis*,
meaning "city," Terms like *cosmopolitan* result. Even so, readers who pick   *5*
up the latest edition of *Cosmopolitan* isn't looking to find out about orderly
cities, but about fashion and fragrance—parts of the life of a cosmopolitan
woman. They certainly aren't looking for stories about asteroids and other
cosmic phenomena. Knowing that, how is it that a word for "order" came to
be synonymous with the word four universe. Since the time of the ancient   *10*
Greeks, many philosophers and theologians has noted that the universe is
orderly instead of chaotic. It follows certain laws. In fact, modern scientists
who seek to understand this orderly universe are called *cosmologists*.
Every resident of the cosmos can take comfort from the fact that such
thinkers aren't called *chaos-ologists*.   *15*

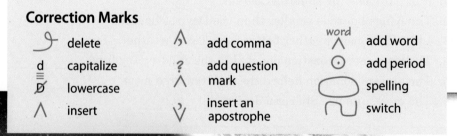

Correction Marks

✂ delete	⌂ add comma	⌄ᵂᵒʳᵈ add word
d̲ capitalize	? add question	⊙ add period
ᴅ̸ lowercase	∧ mark	⬭ spelling
∧ insert	ᵛ insert an apostrophe	⤮ switch

Correcting Your Paragraph

Now it's time to correct your own definition paragraph.

Edit Prepare a clean copy of your revised essay and use the following checklist to edit it. Continue working until you can check off each item in the list.

Editing Checklist

Words

☐ **1.** Have I used specific nouns and verbs? (See page 102.)

☐ **2.** Have I used more action verbs than "be" verbs? (See page 458.)

Sentences

☐ **3.** Have I used sentences with varying beginnings and lengths? (See pages 104–105.)

☐ **4.** Have I avoided improper shifts in sentences? (See page 422.)

☐ **5.** Have I avoided fragments and run-ons? (See pages 410–413, 416–417.)

Conventions

☐ **6.** Do I use correct verb forms (*he saw,* not *he seen*)? (See pages 464, 466.)

☐ **7.** Do my subjects and verbs agree (*she speaks,* not *she speak*)? (See pages 394–403.)

☐ **8.** Have I used the right words (*their, there, they're*)?

☐ **9.** Have I capitalized first words and proper nouns and adjectives? (See page 504.)

☐ **10.** Have I used commas after long introductory word groups and to separate items in a series? (See pages 516, 518.)

☐ **11.** Have I correctly punctuated any dialogue? (See pages 524–525.)

☐ **12.** Have I used apostrophes correctly in contractions and to show possession? (See pages 530–531.)

Adding a Title

Make sure to add an attention-getting title. Here are three strategies to try.

- Highlight the main idea:

  A Cosmic Word

- Think creatively:

  Spreading the Word

"Philosophy, rightly defined, is simply the love of
wisdom."
—Marcus Tullius Cicero

Review and Enrichment

You have been introduced to reading and writing the definition paragraph. This section reviews and expands on that information by providing a multiparagraph definition essay to read and respond to. You will also be given a number of writing ideas to choose from to develop into another definition paragraph or a definition essay. These activities will broaden your understanding of definition writing.

Prereading

College instructors often say that studying at the university level allows you to participate in the ongoing dialogue about important issues. Reading helps you build a solid working knowledge of the issues to be able to discuss them intelligently. That knowledge starts with an understanding of key terms associated with each issue.

> ### CONSIDER THE TRAITS
>
> As you read the essay that begins on the next page, focus first on the **ideas**—the word that is being defined and the types of details that are used to define and explain it. Then consider the **organization**—the way that the opening, middle, and closing parts are constructed. Also note the authors' **voice**—their special way of speaking to the reader. Finally, ask yourself if these traits combine to produce a satisfying reading experience.

Identify   List two or three important issues (*social justice, environmental footprint,* and so on) that you have heard or read about in your college courses or in the media. Afterward, share your lists with your classmates.

_____

_____

_____

_____

What do you think?

Compare Cicero's definition of *philosophy* in the quote at the top of the page with a dictionary definition. How are they similar? How are they different? Share your thoughts with your classmates.

Reading and Reacting

Read   The following essay, which comes from the introductory chapter in a psychology textbook entitled *Psychology: A Journey,* provides an extended definition of the term *psychology.* Use the reading process to help you carry out your reading (see pages 14–15), and keep your notebook handy for writing responses during your reading.

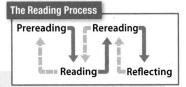

About the Authors

Dr. Dennis Coon has a doctorate in psychology from the University of Arizona. He taught for 22 years at Santa Barbara City College in California. Currently, he lives in Tucson, teaching, writing, editing, and consulting. He also builds and plays acoustic guitars and has written and lectured on this subject.

Dr. John Mitterer received his doctorate in cognitive psychology from McMaster University and currently teaches at Brock University, both in Ontario, Canada. He has received numerous awards for distinguished teaching and contributions to education. His hobbies include golfing and bird-watching, the latter having taken him to the Galapagos Islands; Papua, New Guinea; and Uganda.

What is psychology and what are its goals?

People have always been curious about human behavior. The word *1* psychology itself is thousands of years old, coming from the ancient Greek roots *psyche*, which means "mind," and *logos*, meaning "knowledge or study." However, have you ever actually seen or touched a "mind"? Because the mind can't be studied directly, **psychology** is now defined as the *5* scientific study of behavior and mental processes.

To what does behavior refer in the definition of psychology? Anything you do—eating, hanging out, sleeping, talking, or sneezing—is a behavior. So are studying, snowboarding, gambling, watching television, tying your shoelaces, giving someone a gift, learning Spanish, and reading this book. *10* Naturally, we are interested in *overt behaviors* (directly observable actions and responses). But psychologists also study *covert behaviors*. These are private, internal activities, such as thinking, dreaming, remembering, and other mental events (Jackson, 2008).

Today, psychology is both a science and a profession. As scientists,   *15*
some psychologists do research to discover new knowledge. Others are
teachers who share their knowledge with students. Still others apply
psychology to solve problems in mental health, education, business, sports,
law, and medicine (Coolican et al., 2007). Later we will return to the
profession of psychology. For now, let's focus on how knowledge is created.   *20*
Whether they work in a classroom, lab, or a clinic, all psychologists rely on
critical thinking and information gained from scientific research.

Works Cited

Coolican, H., Cassidy, T., Dunn, O., Sharp, R. et al. (2007). *Applied psychology* (2nd ed.).
    London: Hodder Education.
Jackson, S.L. (2008). *Research methods: A modular approach.* Belmont, CA: Cengage
    Learning/Wadsworth.

Vocabulary Practice

Explain or define the following words or concepts by using your understanding of context clues and your understanding of word parts. (See pages 24–25.)

- psychology (line 5)
- overt behaviors (line 11)
- covert behaviors (line 12)

React Answer the following questions about the essay defining *psychology*. Then share your responses with your classmates.

1. What is the main idea of this essay?

   The main idea defines psychology.
   _____

2. What was your understanding of the topic before reading this essay?

   _____

   _____

3. What types of support do the writers include? Consider completing a support chart. (See page 185.)

Support Chart	
Term defined:	
Dictionary definition	
History	
Examples	

4. How effective is the essay and why?

   Weak ★ ★ ★ ★ ★ Strong

   _____

   _____

5. What questions do you still have about this topic?

   _____

   _____

Drawing Inferences

An *inference* is a logical conclusion that you can make about something that is not actually said or stated in a text. A worthy inference does, however, result from a clear and careful understanding of what *is* said. To practice drawing inferences, answer the following questions about the essay on pages 201–202. Afterward, share your responses with your classmates.

1. From this introductory essay, what can you conclude about the study of psychology? Would it be very predictable like mathematics, very unpredictable like art, or like something else? Explain.

2. What conclusions can you draw from this brief essay about the value of psychology?

Writing

Write a definition paragraph or definition essay following the guidelines on the next two pages. Check with your instructor about any specific requirements that he or she may have. Also be sure to use the writing process to help you do your best work. (See pages 68–73.)

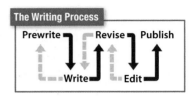

Prewriting

Choose one of the following or another appropriate writing idea for your definition paper.

Writing Ideas

1. Write about another one of the definition topics you brainstormed on page 184 or in the planning activity on page 191.

2. Write about a word that relates to your major or academic concentration.

3. Write about a word that is currently in the news.

4. Write about a word that is overused or misused.

5. Write about a word that is related to an art or a sport.

6. Write about a word that does or does not describe you.

When planning . . .

Refer to pages 191–192 to help you with your prewriting and planning. Also use the tips that follow.

- Choose a word that truly interests you.
- Explore the word from a number of different angles. (See page 192.)
- If necessary, check primary and secondary sources to learn more about the word.
- Review the examples of definition writing in this chapter to see how they are developed.

Writing and Revising

Refer to pages 193–194 to help you write and revise your first draft. Also use the tips that follow.

When writing . . .

- Include opening, middle, and closing parts in your definition piece. Each part has a specific role. (See page 194.)
- Use different levels of detail to make your ideas clear. (See page 93.)
- Use transitions (*ever since, then, now, today,* and so on) to help smoothen the flow of ideas.

When revising . . .

- Determine if your definition piece answers key questions readers might have about the word.
- Be prepared to do some additional research if necessary.
- If you're dissatisfied with any parts of your writing, be sure to rethink/ rewrite them.
- Have at least one trusted peer react to your writing.

Editing

Refer to the checklist on page 199 when you are ready to edit your work for style and correctness. Pay special attention to your use of apostrophes. (See pages 196–199.)

Jenkedco, 2011 / Used under license from Shutterstock.com

Reflecting on Definition Writing

Answer the following questions about your reading and writing experiences with the definition form in this chapter.

1. What value do definition paragraphs have for the reader?

   _____

   _____

2. Which reading strategy in this chapter seems the most helpful? Explain.

   _____

   _____

3. What is your favorite paragraph in this chapter? Explain.

   _____

   _____

4. Besides a dictionary definition, what are some other ways you can define a word in your writing?

   _____

   _____

5. What do you like best about your definition paragraph?

   _____

6. What is one thing you would like to change in it?

   _____

Key Terms to Remember

When you read and write definition paragraphs, it's important to understand the following terms.

- **Definition**—the formal statement or explanation of a meaning of a word
- **Word terminology**—the study of a word's usage, its parts, its synonyms, and its antonyms
- **Word context**—the history of a word, example sentences using the word, notable quotations that employ the word, or anecdotes (personal stories) about it
- **Support chart**—a graphic organizer used to identify or gather different types of details in a definition paragraph or essay

10

Process

"This is a world of process,
not a world of things."
—Margaret J. Wheatkey

> "This is a world of process,
> not a world of things."
> —Margaret J. Wheatkey

Much of the information you will encounter in college will deal with processes. In this textbook, for instance, you have learned that successful reading and writing is not a product of a single action but rather a series of steps. The reading process involves prereading, reading, rereading, and reflecting. The writing process involves prewriting, writing, revising, editing, and publishing. By following the steps, you can improve your reading and writing.

Some processes deal with complicated subjects like cellular respiration or health-care reform. Recognizing and knowing how to read process paragraphs will help you understand these difficult topics. Likewise, the ability to clearly explain a process in writing can help you greatly as a college student.

In this chapter you will read and react to different types of process paragraphs. Then you will write a process paragraph of your own.

Learning Outcomes

LO1 Understand the process form.

LO2 Learn about reading strategies.

LO3 Read and react to a professional paragraph.

LO4 Read and react to a student paragraph.

LO5 Practice reading skills.

LO6 Plan a process paragraph.

LO7 Write the first draft.

LO8 Revise the writing.

LO9 Edit the writing.

What do you think?

Read the quote at the top of the page. How is our world a "world of process"?

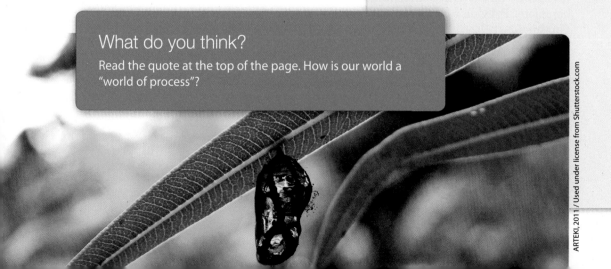

ARTEKI, 2011 / Used under license from Shutterstock.com

LO1 Understanding the Process Form

The story behind the title of author Anne Lamott's *Bird by Bird: Some Instructions on Writing and Life* comes from a valuable lesson about taking things one step at a time. One night, as a child, Lamott observed her 10-year-old brother at the point of tears. His lengthy report about birds was due the next morning, and even though he had been given three months to write it, he had not yet started. To calm him, Lamott's father offered a bit of advice: "Bird by bird buddy. Just take it bird by bird."

Working step by step is a common theme in all walks of life. Scientists use the scientific method to increase their understanding of different things. This method involves following certain steps. Athletes use a step-by-step approach to analyze and improve their skills. For example, basketball players will follow certain steps to master free throws. As a college student, you should follow the steps in the reading and writing processes to help you complete your assignments.

> "The older I get the more wisdom I find in the ancient rule of taking first things first. A process which often reduces the most complex human problem to a manageable proportion."
> —Dwight D. Eisenhower

For any type of process, you should think in terms of chronological order or time order. By its very nature, following a process step by step means that you are working chronologically. Keep this basic point in mind as you read the process models in this chapter and as you develop your own process paragraph.

Types of Process Writing

Many process paragraphs explain how something works or occurs. For example, a science text may explain the water cycle, or an anthropology text may explain the industrialization of an agrarian (farming) society. Other process paragraphs explain how to do or make something—how to design a Web site or how to make an electromagnet.

Identify List two accomplishments in your life that required a series of steps to complete. Provide a brief explanation of each one. Share your responses with your classmates.

_____

_____

INSIGHT ————————————————————————————————

Observing a process is one of the best ways to research it, but sometimes your eyes can't catch every step.

Reading

Process paragraphs offer practical advice. Often they can help you learn how to do something or how something works. The key is to closely analyze the steps in the process. These strategies will help you read process paragraphs.

LO2 Learning About Reading Strategies

Strategy 1: Recognizing Ordering Formats

When reading a process, it is important to pay attention to the order—how one step follows another. Clue words or transitions will often introduce the various steps so that they are easy to identify and follow. To the right are a few common ordering formats that you might encounter.

Strategy 2: Keeping Track of the Steps

Since process paragraphs are most often written in chronological (time) order, you can use a cycle diagram or a time line to keep track of the steps. A cycle diagram is helpful for continuous processes, such as the water cycle. A time line is helpful for processes that have a beginning and an end, with steps in between.

Common Ordering Formats

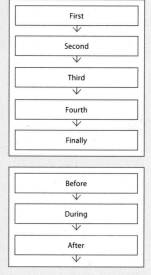

Cycle Diagram

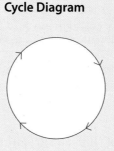

Time Line

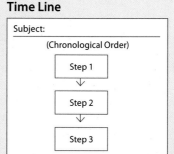

Piti Tan, 2011 / Used under license from Shutterstock.com

Tip

Either of these graphic organizers—a cycle diagram or a time line—works well as a studying strategy, especially in science classes. Seeing the steps in a process graphically displayed will help you remember them.

LO3 Reading and Reacting to a Professional Paragraph

Read Read the following process paragraph explaining how forensic scientists inspect a bloodstain. It comes from *Forensic Science: Fundamentals and Investigations,* a textbook that covers the basic principles of forensic science. Use the reading process to help you gain a full understanding of the text. (See pages 14–15.)

The Reading Process

Prereading → Rereading

↓ ↑

Reading → Reflecting

About the Author

Anthony J. Bertino is an author and educator who taught biology for more than 39 years, with a special interest in *forensics*. He taught at Canandaigua Academy in New York for 34 years before retiring in 2001. Bertino is now a supervisor at the University of Albany Graduate School of Education in New York and is an active national and state workshop presenter on forensic science instruction. He has also written articles for *The Science Teacher* magazine.

Crime-Scene Investigation of Blood

There are several steps used in processing a bloodstain, and each can provide a different kind of critical information. The first step is to confirm the stain is blood. Could ketchup, ink, or any other red substance cause the red stain? Before trying to collect the blood, it is necessary to confirm that the evidence is blood, either by using the Kastle-Meyer test or the Leucomalachite green test. If the substance proves to be blood, the second step is to confirm that the blood is human. One test that can be used to determine this is the ELISA test. The third step is to determine the blood type. Depending on the circumstances, blood typing may not be done at all, just DNA analysis.   *1*

5

10

"Crime-Scene Investigation of Blood" from BERTINO. *Forensic Science: Fundamentals and Investigations,* Copyright 2012 Wadsworth, a part Cengage Learning, Inc.

React Answer the following questions about the paragraph. Then discuss your responses with your classmates.

1. What is the main idea of this paragraph? (See pages 30–31.) <u>How to process a bloodstain</u>

2. What three steps are involved in the process? <u>(1) confirmation of blood; (2) confirmation of human blood; (3) determine blood type</u>

3. What is the purpose of this paragraph—to explain, to persuade, to entertain? Explain. <u>to explain</u>

4. How would you rate this paragraph and why?

   Weak ★ ★ ★ ★ ★ Strong _____

5. What questions, if any, do you still have about the topic? _____

A CLOSER LOOK at Word Clues

As you read, stay alert for key words that signal a process. Writers often indicate a new step by using transitional phrases like *first step, second phase, next stage,* or *final event.* Such words tell the order in which the steps occur. Here is a longer list of word clues that signal time order in process writing.

■ First	■ Next	■ Last
■ Start	■ Then	■ Final
■ Begin	■ Third	■ End
■ Second	■ Eventually	

In some process writing, dates (December 4, 1941), centuries (4th century), decades (1980s), months (March), and days (Monday) are used to tell when a phase in a process begins or ends.

Identify the First Step

Since processes are explained in time order, it is critical that you identify the first step in the process before moving on to the rest of the paragraph. Here are the specific word clues that indicate the beginning of a process.

■ First step	■ Begins with
■ First phase	■ To start
■ First	■ Starts with
■ To begin	

NOTE: Stay alert for two-part sentences that include more than one step, like the following example:

Once you jack up the car, loosen the flat tire.

Step 1   Step 2

LO4 Reading and Reacting to a Student Paragraph

Read Read this student paragraph about applying for a passport. Remember to use the steps in the reading process to help you gain a full understanding of the text. (See pages 14–15.)

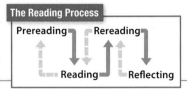

Two Steps Forward, One Step Back

Walking the streets of Rome requires patience and a sense of   1
adventure. Before you set out, be sure to wear a comfortable pair of shoes.
Roman streets, at least the most interesting ones, are cobbled. Also
dress in light layers, even if you see most of the natives dressed in heavy
coats. Next, plan a route on a street map by circling the sites you want   5
to visit and the streets you need to follow. As you start, enjoy all that the
cityscape has to offer. Then, within the first 10 or 15 minutes, expect to get
lost. Roman streets, other than main thoroughfares, are never straight,
seldom marked, and rarely labeled on the street map you have in hand.
When this happens, you can try to retrace your steps. But if you are at   10
all adventurous, just keep going and enjoy what that part of the city has
to offer. You won't be disappointed, and sooner or later, you'll come across
a plaza or church square that will be marked on your map. Once you get
your bearings, proceed, but again, expect to get lost in no time at all. You
can continue in this way from plaza to plaza, enjoying the sites that you   15
come across as well as stopping for some refreshments or a meal. When
you've had enough, find a taxi or tram for the return trip because you'll
never find your way back by foot.

React Answer the following questions about the paragraph. Then discuss your answers with classmates.

1. What main idea is expressed in the first sentence?
   Walking the streets of Rome requires patience and a sense of adventure.

2. What steps are offered for the walking tourist in Rome?

3. Does the writer use transitions? Explain your answer.
   before, next, then, when, but, once, also

4. How would you rate this paragraph and why?

   Weak ★ ★ ★ ★ ★ Strong

A CLOSER LOOK at Analyzing the Details

As you learned on page 209, the details of a process can be analyzed graphically. To keep the order of events, steps, or instructions clear in your mind, fill in a time line like the one below.

Time Line

Subject: _____

Materials: _____

_____

_____

Step 1

↓

Step 2

↓

Step 3

↓

Outcome

INSIGHT

When you encounter process paragraphs that explain how to do something (change a tire), it is important to note any materials that are needed to complete the process.

Identify Fill in a process analysis chart about the paragraph "Two Steps Forward, One Step Back." Also identify any materials mentioned in the paragraph. Afterward, compare charts with your classmates.

Considering the Approach

Process paragraphs in textbooks will sound academic and serious. Process paragraphs based on personal experience will generally sound friendly and more relaxed.

Identify Find one sentence in the paragraph on page 210 that sounds especially academic to you, and one sentence in the paragraph on page 212 that sounds friendly and conversational.

LO5 Practicing Reading Skills

Reading is a great way to build your vocabulary and practice important thinking skills. The activities below will help you work on both.

Vocabulary: Using a Dictionary

You know the main role of a dictionary—to provide definitions for words. But dictionaries also provide many other types of information. For each entry, you can learn how to pronounce a word, how it is used (as a *noun, verb,* and so forth), its history, and so on. Here is a sample entry:

Pronunciation ┐   Part of Speech   ┌ History
 ┌ **futile** \fyoo til\ *adj.* [Lat. *futilis*] 1. Having no useful result. 2. Trifling
 │   and frivolous, idle. —**futility** *adv.* —**futileness** *n.*   │
Word   Usage   Meaning

Look Up   The words below come from the process paragraphs that you have just read. For each one, write down the meaning and one other piece of information that you find about it in a dictionary.

1. substance _____   3. tram _____

2. evidence _____   4. plaza _____

Reading Critically: Understanding Patterns of Reasoning

Most of the paragraphs and essays that you read in your classes will follow either deductive or inductive reasoning. Deductive thinking moves from a topic sentence or thesis statement expressing a main idea to specific supporting details. Inductive thinking moves in the other direction, from specific facts to a general conclusion.

Use these questions to check for deductive thinking.

- Does the paragraph or essay start with a topic sentence (or thesis) that expresses the main idea of the writing?
- Do the details support or follow the topic sentence?
- Does the conclusion logically follow the ideas that come before it?

Use these questions to check for inductive thinking.

- Does the text start with a series of facts, examples, and explanations?
- Do they logically lead up to a general conclusion?
- Does the general conclusion support the evidence before it?

Apply   Use the "critical questions" above to determine if the paragraphs on pages 210 and 212 follow deductive or inductive thinking.

Writing

In your own process paragraph, you will explain how something works or occurs, or how to do or make something. Be sure to use the writing process to guide your work. (See pages 68–73.)

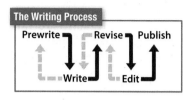

LO6 Planning a Process Paragraph

The information on these two pages will help you complete the important first step—prewriting—before you start writing.

Selecting a Topic

Use the following ideas to generate possible process-paragraph topics.

Consider a process that . . .

- relates to your major or academic concentration.
- demonstrates something you do well or want to learn more about.
- has made the news recently.
- impacts the world around you.
- relates to your favorite entertainment—sports, music, the arts.

Select List four process topics that can be covered in one paragraph. They may be something you know a lot about or something you need to research.

1. _____
2. _____
3. _____
4. _____

Reviewing the Process

Once you have selected a process topic, review what you know about it, and if necessary, do some additional research.

Reflect Carefully consider these questions to plan your research and collecting of details.

1. How well do I know this process? _____
2. If needed, how can I learn more about it? _____
3. Do I have time to conduct enough research? _____

Gathering Details

Use a process analysis chart to organize the steps for your process paragraph. The example below lists the steps of tree decay.

Gather To complete a process analysis chart, first write down your subject and, if applicable, any materials needed. Then fill in the steps involved in the process.

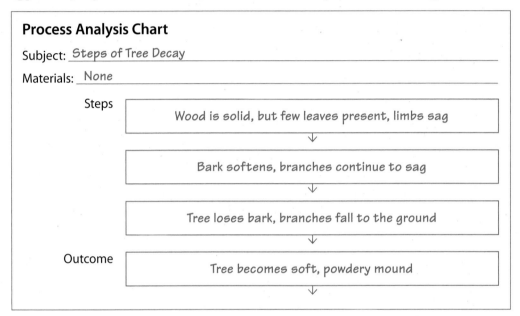

Process Analysis Chart

Subject: *Steps of Tree Decay*

Materials: *None*

Steps

Wood is solid, but few leaves present, limbs sag

↓

Bark softens, branches continue to sag

↓

Tree loses bark, branches fall to the ground

↓

Outcome

Tree becomes soft, powdery mound

↓

Using Transitions

Remember that transitions or linking words connect ideas by showing the relationship between them. In process paragraphs, time-order transitional words link the steps and add clarity to the writing. Refer to the following list as you write your paragraph. (Also see page 211.)

Transitions that show time order

before	during	after	next	finally
first	second	third	then	later
when	once	while	at	meanwhile

READING/WRITING CONNECTION

Transition words act as clue words for readers, signaling different steps in the process.

LO7 Writing the First Draft

Writing a first draft is your first attempt to connect all your ideas about a topic. While you write your first draft, don't worry about making everything right. Instead, focus on getting all your ideas on paper.

Read Carefully read and enjoy this student's paragraph about jump-starting a dead car battery.

Back from the Dead

Topic Sentence

One of the most frustrating situations to deal with is a car   1
with a dead battery. Fortunately, with a set of jumper cables and a little help, you can get back on the road in no time. To jump-start a car battery, you will need a set of jumper cables and a second car with a fully charged battery. First, line both cars up so the   5
batteries are as close as they can be. Make sure both cars are turned completely off. Next, familiarize yourself with the positive (+) and negative (-) terminals of both car batteries. After you have done so, connect one end of the positive jumper cable (usually red or orange) to the positive terminal of the dead battery. Then   10
Body Sentences connect the other end of the positive cable to the positive terminal of the live battery. Next, connect the negative cable (usually black) to the negative terminal of the live battery. Finally, clamp the other end of the negative cable to a solid nonpainted metal part of the engine of the dead car. From there, stand back and start the   15
car that's providing the jump. Wait about five minutes, and then try to start the car with the dead battery. If it starts up, your last
Closing Sentence step is to remove the cables in the reverse order in which you put them on. And then you can hit the road.

Consider the Craft

1. What do you like best about this paragraph?

2. Is the process easy to follow?

3. Does the writer use transitions to connect ideas? Which ones?

4. Could you complete the process by following the steps given in this paragraph?

The Working Parts of a Paragraph

A paragraph consists of three main parts, each one of which has a special function. The information that follows explains each part.

Paragraph Outline

Topic Sentence: The topic sentence introduces the process you will discuss.

Body Sentences: The body sentences explain the steps in the process in the correct order, usually time order.

Closing Sentence: The closing sentence sums up the paragraph and describes the outcome of the process.

Drafting Tips

When you are writing about a process, you want to explain it in a way that your reader will understand. Consider the following techniques.

- **Define any complicated words or technical terms.** If you are writing about a process not everyone knows about, make sure you use language that the reader will understand. Always define any terms that are special to a particular field or topic.
- **Use transitions that show time to connect the steps.** See page 216 for examples.
- **Present clear descriptions using sensory details.** Details that relate to the senses (sight, taste, sound, and so on) can clarify a process for the reader. Note how the paragraph on page 217 includes the color of the specific ends of the jumper cables.
- **Add a visual representation of the process** to accompany the paragraph. Pictures, graphics, and charts are all possibilities.
- **Test the writing.** Read the draft for organization and completeness. If possible, perform the process yourself, using your paragraph as a guide. Note where the writing is incomplete or out of order.

Write Develop your first draft using the information on this page, and your planning on pages 215–216 as a guide.

Rido, 2011 / Used under license from Shutterstock.com

LO8 Revising the Writing

Start the revising process by reading your first draft two or three times to get a feel for your work so far. Then have one of your classmates read and react to your work using a response sheet as a guide. (See page 547.)

Giving Commands

Since process paragraphs often offer instructions, consider using imperative sentences to improve your writing. Imperative sentences speak directly to the reader. Notice the imperative sentences that follow.

Imperative Sentences

- **Line up** both cars so the batteries are as close as they can be.
- **Connect** the negative cable to the negative terminal.

Revising in Action

Read aloud the unrevised and then revised version of the following excerpt. Note how the imperative sentences prevent wordiness and improve the instructional voice of the writing.

> . . . Then ~~you should~~ connect the other end of the positive cable to the positive terminal of the live battery. Next, ~~you will have to~~ connect the negative cable (usually black) to the negative terminal of the live battery. Finally, ~~you must~~ clamp the other end of the negative cable . . .

Revise Improve your writing, using the following checklist and your partner's comments on the response sheet. Continue working until you can check off each item.

Revising Checklist

Ideas

☐ 1. Do I explain an interesting process?

☐ 2. Do I include all the steps in the process?

Organization

☐ 3. Do I have an effective topic sentence and closing sentence?

☐ 4. Are the steps in a logical or time order?

☐ 5. Have I used transitions to connect my ideas?

Voice

☐ 6. Do I use command sentences to give instructions?

LO9 Editing the Writing

Some of the most common sentence errors writers make are fragments, comma splices, and run-ons.

Fragments and Run-Ons

Fragments and run-ons are errors that can derail the clarity of writing. A fragment is a word group that lacks a subject, verb, or some other essential part, making the thought incomplete. A run-on sentence is two sentences joined without adequate punctuation or a connecting word. See the fragment and run-on examples that follow and note how each is corrected.

Fragment:	Raymond left his house. Forgetting the present for his mother.
Corrected:	Raymond left his house, forgetting the present for his mother.
Run-On Sentence:	Kate decided to wear shorts the weather was beautiful.
Corrected:	Kate decided to wear shorts because the weather was beautiful.

Sentence Practice   On the short blank next to each example, identify the word group as a fragment (F), run-on (R), or complete sentence (C). Then rewrite the fragments and run-ons to make them correct, complete sentences.

1. Left the door open. _____F_____

   Correction: Frank left the door open. _____

2. The water park was a blast the water was extremely cold. _____R_____

   Correction: The water park was a blast. The water was extremely cold. _____

3. The dog spun in circles. While he was chasing his tail. _____F_____

   Correction: The dog span in circles, while he was chasing his tail. _____

4. I was late for the movie because my car ran out of gas. _____C_____

   Correction: _____

Additional Practice: For additional practice, see pages 410–413, 416–417.

Apply   Read your process paragraph, making sure all your sentences are complete and clear.

Comma Splices

Another common sentence error is the comma splice. Comma splices occur when two independent clauses are connected ("spliced") with only a comma. To correct the error, replace the comma with a period or a semicolon, or add a coordinating conjunction (*and, but, or, nor, for, so, yet*) after the comma. Consider the examples that follow.

Comma Splice:	People speak of sporting events in the same way they discuss war, that's not a fair comparison.
Corrected with a period:	People speak of sporting events in the same way they discuss war. **That's** not a fair comparison.
Corrected with a semicolon:	People speak of sporting events in the same way they discuss war**; that's** not a fair comparison.
Corrected with a coordinating conjunction:	People speak of sporting events in the same way they discuss war, **but** that's not a fair comparison.

Sentence Practice   Rewrite these examples to correct the comma splices.

1. Shelly compared her haircut to a natural disaster, I thought it looked good.

   Shelly compared her haircut to a natural disaster, though I thought it looked good.

2. My roommate won't stop talking, I don't understand why he says this stuff.

   My roommate won't stop talking. I don't understand why he says this stuff.

3. I hate it when the dryer fails to fully dry my clothes, I need to find more quarters.

   I hate it when the dryer fails to fully dry my clothes; I need to find more quarters.

4. I'm anxious for my test scores to arrive, my future depends on the outcome.

   I'm anxious for my test scores to arrive, because my future depends on the outcome.

Additional Practice: For additional practice, see pages 414–415.

Apply   Read your process paragraph, checking for any comma splices. Correct any that you find.

Marking an Essay

The model that follows has a number of errors.

Punctuation Practice   Correct the following paragraph, using the corrections marks below.

Proposing a New Amendment

    Did you know ~~their~~ *there* are two ways to propose a new amendment to the   *1*
Constitution? The first method is the path each current amendment has
taken. For this process to work an amendment must be proposed by a
two-thirds ~~thrids~~ vote in each house of Congress. Next, the proposed amendment
must be ratified by three-fourths of the states. Before it officially becomes   *5*
an amendment. The second way to amend the Constitution ~~are~~ *is* to call for
a Constitutional Convention. For this to happen, two-thirds of the states
would have to demand that the convention take place. similar to the first
method, the proposed amendment would then have to be ratified by a
three-fourths vote of the states. To date, this method has never been used   *10*
it is unlikely we will see a constitutional Convention anytime soon.

Correction Marks

℘ delete	℈\ add comma	⌃ add word	
d capitalize	? add question mark	⊙ add period	
∅ lowercase	⌄ insert an apostrophe	⌒ spelling	
⌃ insert		� switch	

INSIGHT

Avoid using two negative words to express a single negative idea. Double negatives are not acceptable in academic writing.

Double Negative: I don't have no change for a $20 bill.

    Standard: I don't have any change for a $20 bill.

        I have no change for a $20 bill.

Correcting Your Paragraph

Now it's time to correct your own paragraph.

Apply   Create a clean copy of your revised paragraph and use the following checklist to check for errors. Continue working until you can check off each item in the list.

Editing Checklist

Words

☐ 1. Have I used specific nouns and verbs? (See page 102.)

☐ 2. Have I used more action verbs than "be" verbs? *Is, are, was,* and *were* are examples of "be" verbs. (See page 458.)

Sentences

☐ 3. Have I varied the beginnings and lengths of sentences? (See pages 104–105.)

☐ 4. Have I combined short choppy sentences? (See page 105.)

☐ 5. Have I avoided fragments, run-ons and comma splices? (See pages 410–417.)

Conventions

☐ 6. Do I use correct verb forms (*he saw,* not *he seen*)? (See pages 464, 466.)

☐ 7. Do my subjects and verbs agree (*she speaks,* not *she speak*)? (See pages 394–403.)

☐ 8. Have I used the right words (*their, there, they're*)?

☐ 9. Have I capitalized first words and proper nouns and adjectives?

☐ 10. Have I used commas after long introductory word groups? (See pages 514–517.)

☐ 11. Have I carefully checked my spelling?

Adding a Title

Make sure to add a title that calls attention to the topic. Here are two simple strategies for creating one.

- State the topic:

  Proposing a New Amendment

- Think creatively:

  Back from the Dead

Create   Prepare a clean final copy of your paragraph and proofread it before you share it.

Review and Enrichment

You have been introduced to reading and writing the process paragraph. This section reviews and expands on that information by providing a multiparagraph process essay to read and respond to. You will also be given a number of writing ideas to choose from and develop in a paragraph or an essay. These activities will broaden your understanding of process writing.

> "Life is a lively process of becoming."
> —Douglas MacArthur

Prereading

Process writing covers a wide range of topics. Reading process essays can answer complicated questions: *How does a nuclear fission reactor work? How do bacteria reproduce?* Other times it helps solve practical questions: *What's the best way to cook an omelet? What steps should I follow to tie a half-Windsor tie knot?* No matter the topic, reading a paragraph or longer piece of writing about a process requires concentration, reflection, and analysis.

CONSIDER THE TRAITS

As your read the essay on the next page, focus first on the **ideas**—the subject and steps in the process. Then consider the **organization**—the way that the opening, middle, and closing parts are put together. Also note the authors' **voice**—how they present the ideas. And finally, ask yourself if these traits combine to produce a satisfying reading experience.

Identify   What practical processes do you wonder about? What more-involved processes have you always wanted to understand better? List two of each. Then share your ideas with your classmates.

- Practical processes:

  How do you ride a wave on a surfboard?

  _____

- Complicated processes:

  How do automated Internet radio services like Pandora work?

  _____

What do you think?

Explain what you think Douglas MacArthur means in the quotation at the top of the page. (The key word is *becoming*, meaning "growing" or "coming to be.") Share your thoughts with your classmates.

Reading and Reacting

Read The following example comes from a chapter in *Becoming a Master Student* by Dave Ellis. This part focuses on the basic steps to follow to begin any test, plus the steps to follow to answer a specific type of test question. Use the reading process to help you gain a full understanding of the text. Also have your notebook handy in case you want to respond to the text as you read.

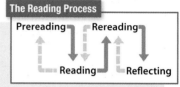

The Reading Process

About the Author

Dave Ellis is an author, an educator, a workshop leader, and a lecturer. His book *Becoming a Master Student* is a best seller in its 13th edition, and it is used by students in the United States and in several other countries. He has co-authored other books on subjects such as human effectiveness and career planning.

What to Do During the Test

Prepare yourself for the test by arriving early. Being early often leaves time to do a relaxation exercise. While you're waiting for the test to begin and talking with classmates, avoid asking the question, "How much did you study for the test?" This question might fuel anxious thoughts that you didn't study enough.   *1*

     5

As you begin

Ask the teacher or test administrator if you can use scratch paper during the test. (If you use a separate piece of paper without permission, you might appear to be cheating.) If you *do* get permission, use this paper to jot down memory aides, formulas, equations, definitions, facts, or other material you know you'll need and might forget. An alternative is to make quick notes in the margins of the test sheet.   *10*

Pay attention to verbal directions given as a test is distributed. Then scan the whole test immediately. Evaluate the importance of each section. Notice how many points each part of the test is worth; then estimate how much time you'll need for each section, using its point value as your guide. For example, don't budget 20 percent of your time for a section that is worth only 10 percent of the points.   *15*

Read the directions slowly. Then reread them. It can be agonizing to discover that you lost points on a test merely because you failed to follow the directions. When the directions are confusing, ask to have them clarified.   *20*

Now you are ready to begin the test. If necessary, allow yourself a minute or two of "panic" time. Notice any tension you feel, and apply one   *25* of the techniques explained in the article "Let Go of Test Anxiety" later in this chapter.

Answer the easiest, shortest questions first. This gives you the experience of success. It also stimulates associations and prepares you for more difficult questions. Pace yourself, and watch the time. If you can't   *30* think of an answer, move on. Follow your time plan.

If you are unable to determine the answer to a test question, keep an eye out throughout the test for context clues that may remind you of the correct answer or provide you with evidence to eliminate wrong answers.

35

Multiple-choice questions
- *Answer each question in your head first.* Do this step before you look at the possible answers. If you come up with an answer that you're confident is right, look for that answer in the list of choices.
- *Read all possible answers before selecting one.* Sometimes two   *40* answers will be similar and only one will be correct.
- *Test each possible answer.* Remember that multiple-choice questions consist of two parts: the stem (an incomplete statement or question at the beginning) and a list of possible answers. Each answer, when combined with the stem, makes a complete statement or question-   *45* and-answer pair that is either true or false. When you combine the stem with each possible answer, you are turning each multiple-choice question into a small series of true/false questions. Choose the answer that makes a true statement.
- *Eliminate incorrect answers.* Cross off the answers that are clearly   *50* not correct. The one you cannot eliminate is probably the best choice.

"What to Do During the Test" from ELLIS. *Becoming a Master Student,* 13E. ©2011 Wadsworth, a part of Cengage Learning, Inc. Reproduced by permission. www.cengage.com/permissions

Vocabulary Practice
Define the following words by using clues from the article. (See page 24.) Also list the words or phrases that help you define each term.
- alternative (line 12)
- clarified (line 23)
- context clues (line 33)
- eliminate (line 50)

React   Answer the following questions about the reading on pages 225–226. Then share your responses with your classmates.

1. What is the purpose of this reading (to inform, to entertain, to persuade)?

    To inform

2. Who is the intended audience (general readers, students, professionals)?

    students

3. What is the main topic or process that is explained in the model? Where in the reading is it identified?

    How to properly take a test is described in the middle paragraphs.

4. What are the main steps to follow in the main process? Consider using a time line to chart these steps. (Don't include very specific details in your time line.)

    Subject: _____

    ↓

    ↓

5   What other process is described in the last part of the text?

    How to answer multiple-choice test questions

6. How many steps are listed for this process?

    Four

7. Does the author use imperative sentences ? (See page 219.) If so, record two of them.

    Yes

8. How would you rate this example of process writing?

    Weak ★ ★ ★ ★ ★ Strong

    _____

8. What are two things that you learned in this reading?

    _____

9. What questions, if any, do you still have about either of the processes?

    _____

    _____

Writing

Write a process paragraph or process essay following the guidelines on the next two pages. Check with your instructor about any specific requirements that she or he may have. And be sure to use the writing process to help you do your best work. (See pages 68–73.)

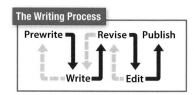

Prewriting

Choose one of the following topics or another appropriate writing idea for your process paper.

Writing Ideas

1. Write about another one of the process topics you identified in the planning activity on page 215.

2. Write about a process that relates to your major or academic concentration.

3. Write about how to do something that you can do very well.

4. Write about a process that impacts the way we live.

5. Write about how to deal with someone you don't get along with.

6. Write a process paragraph or essay related to a photograph in this text.

When planning . . .

Refer to pages 215–216 to help you with your prewriting and planning. Also use the tips that follow.

■ Make sure that you know the process well before you try to explain it.

■ If necessary, carry out research to learn about the process.

■ Create a visual representation of the steps in the process and decide if they are all there and in the correct order.

■ Review the examples of process writing in this chapter to see what types of information they include.

Tip

Remember that process papers can be academic and serious or more informal and relaxed depending on the topic and your familiarity with it.

Writing and Revising

Refer to pages 217–219 to help you write and revise your first draft. Also use the tips that follow.

When writing . . .

- Include opening, middle, and closing parts in your process writing. Each part has a specific role. (See page 218.)
- Follow your planning notes as you discuss the steps of the process, but also be sure to add specific details to help explain each step.
- Use transitions to help identify different steps in the process. (See page 216.)
- Consider adding a visual representation of the process.

When revising . . .

- Ask yourself if your explanation is clear and complete.
- Decide if you need to do any additional research on your topic.
- Make sure all the steps are accounted for and that they are in the correct order.
- Have at least one trusted peer react to your writing.

Editing

Refer to the checklist on page 223 when you are ready to edit your work for style and correctness.

Reflecting on Process Writing

Answer the following questions about your reading and writing experiences with the process form in this chapter.

1. What is the purpose of the process form?

   Process writing explains how something works or occurs.
   _____

2. What reading strategy in this chapter seems most helpful?

   _____

3. What is your favorite process paragraph from this chapter?

   _____

4. What words or phrases make a process paragraph easy to recognize and follow?

   _____

5. What do you like most about the process paragraph that you wrote in this chapter? Explain.

   _____

6. What is one thing that you would like to change in it?

   _____

7. What is the most important thing that you have learned about writing a process paragraph?

   _____

Key Terms to Remember

When you read and write process paragraphs, it's important to understand the following terms.

- **Process**—a series of actions, steps, or changes bringing about a result
- **Ordering**—the following of one thing after another
- **Chronological order**—time order, commonly used in process paragraphs
- **Cycle chart**—a graphic organizer that identifies the steps in a recurring process
- **Process time line**—a graphic organizer that identifies the steps of a process; may also include any materials needed, and the outcome

11

> "You ask what is the use of classification . . . ?
> I answer you: order and simplification are the
> first steps toward the mastery of a subject."
> —Thomas Mann

Classification

Music is a popular subject. It is loved and enjoyed around the world. However, *music* covers a lot of territory. Think of the many styles, artists, and genres out there. It could take someone years to become an authority on a single era of classical music. At the same time, that music expert would probably know very little about the latest trends in hip-hop.

When you encounter a topic as large or as complex as music, it is helpful to break it down into manageable categories or parts. Then you can examine the parts separately. This organizational strategy is called classification. You will often encounter classification in your college reading and writing.

In this chapter, you will read a number of classification paragraphs and then develop one of your own. Doing so will help you better understand the individual parts of a topic and how they relate to one another.

Learning Outcomes

LO1 Understand classification.
LO2 Learn about reading strategies.
LO3 Read and react to a professional paragraph.
LO4 Read and react to a student paragraph.
LO5 Practice reading skills.
LO6 Plan a classification paragraph.
LO7 Write the first draft.
LO8 Revise the writing.
LO9 Edit the writing.

What do you think?
How might you use classification in your daily life?

LO1 Understanding Classification

Look up at the sky on a clear night, and you will realize how challenging it can be to classify a topic. At first glance the stars look alike, but a close examination reveals key differences in one star from the next. Through years of hard work, astronomers like Angelo Secchi have explored these differences using systems of classification.

> "Science is the systematic classification of experience."
> —George Henry Lewis

In 1863 Secchi studied 4,000 different star patterns and concluded that every star in the sky could be categorized into one of five classes based on unique patterns. At the time, such a classification was revolutionary. It formed a new understanding of the universe.

Today, Secchi's system of classification is considered out of date, and a more detailed classification system has emerged, grouping stars into seven classes based on surface temperature, color, and size.

Branching Out

As the star example shows, classifications are not always permanent. But not all classifications are as complicated as the one described above, nor do they need to be held to strict scientific analysis. Take something as ordinary as barbeque sauce. It can be grouped by taste, ingredient, brand, and price. Classifying, sorting, and arranging can be applied to many subjects in all walks of life, from barbeque sauces to baby carriages.

Identify For each topic below, identify four or five categories, or subgroups. This is basic classification. (If one of these topics doesn't work for you, substitute another one.) Afterward share your work with your classmates.

movies	soft drinks	exercise

Reading

Reading classification paragraphs helps you recognize the variety hidden in a complex topic.

LO2 Learning About Reading Strategies

Strategy 1: Analyzing the Categories

There are three basic questions to answer when reading a classification paragraph:

1. How does the writer break down the topic into categories?
2. How does the writer describe each category?
3. Are the categories equal?

> **INSIGHT**
>
> Certain phrases, like the ones below, signal a classification.
> - Four types
> - Separate classes
> - Different categories
> - Certain kinds

The Process in Action

Here is an analysis of a paragraph about basic taste sensations.

1. **How does the writer break down the topic into categories?**
   Salty, sweet, sour, and bitter

2. **How does the writer describe each category?**
   A salty taste comes from substances that include sodium, such as potato chips. The sweet sensation comes from sugars, both processed and natural. Sour tastes come from acidic foods such as lemons, and bitter tastes come from alkaline foods such as coffee.

3. **Are the categories equal?**
   All of the categories seem related, and they are explained with the same type of details.

Strategy 2: Diagramming the Key Parts

Classification paragraphs generally follow a similar pattern. The first sentence or two introduces the topic and categories. Then each category is addressed separately, including supporting details, which may involve a definition, examples, or traits.

To help you visualize the categories and supporting details, you can use a line diagram.

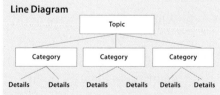

Practice Use these strategies for your next classification reading assignment. Afterward, discuss your work with a classmate.

LO3 Reading and Reacting to a Professional Paragraph

Read   Read the following classification paragraph from *Psychology: A Journey,* a psychology college textbook written by Dennis Coon and John O. Mitterer. The paragraph classifies different types of parental discipline. Remember to use the reading process to help you complete your reading. (See pages 14–15.)

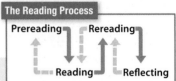

About the Authors

Dennis Coon is an author, instructor, and doctor of psychology. He joined with John O. Mitterer, a doctor of cognitive psychology and an instructor at Brock University, in Ontario, Canada, to author *Psychology: A Journey.*

Effective Discipline

Parents typically discipline children in one of three ways. Power assertion refers to physical punishment or a show of force, such as taking away toys or privileges. As an alternative, some parents use withdrawal of love (withholding affection) by refusing to speak to a child, threatening to leave, rejecting the child, or otherwise acting as if the child is temporarily unlovable. Management techniques combine praise, recognition, approval, rules, reasoning, and the like to encourage desirable behavior. Each of these approaches can control a child's behavior, but their side effects differ considerably.

1

5

"Effective Discipline" from COON/MITTERER. *Psychology: A Journey,* 4E. © 2011 Wadsworth, a part of Cengage Learning, Inc.

React   Answer the following questions about the paragraph "Effective Discipline." Then discuss your responses with your classmates.

1. What is the main idea of this paragraph?

   Parents discipline children in one of three ways.

2. What are the three main parts of this classification? Consider using a line diagram to identify them.

   Power assertion; withdrawal of love; management techniques

3. How do the writers describe each category?

   Power assertion: physical punishment or show of force; withdrawal of love: withholding affection; management: combines praise, recognition, approval, rules, and reasoning

4. What questions if any, do you still have about the topic?

A CLOSER LOOK at Classification

Consider the Factors for Classifying

Identifying the factors for classifying will help you understand and evaluate classification paragraphs. The writer of the paragraph on page 241, for example, considers factors such as *color, ingredients,* and *taste* to break the topic of mustard into separate categories.

Here are three tips for identifying classification factors.

1. **Read the text multiple times.** After you read through the entire paragraph, carefully reread the body sentences, where the author most often describes the categories.

> NOTE: In shorter pieces of writing, like paragraphs, a writer may use only one classification factor.

2. **Graph the main parts.** Use a line diagram (see page 233) to identify and display the main parts of the classification paragraph. This will help you identify the factor(s) behind the classification.

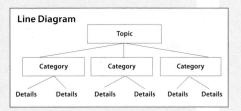
Line Diagram

3. **Look for a common factor(s).** Study the line diagram, especially the details for each category. Ask yourself what they have in common. The common factor in the paragraph on the previous page is the *actions* parents use to discipline their children.

> SPECIAL NOTE: Discuss the paragraph with a classmate if you have trouble identifying the common factor or factors. (It may be that the writer didn't effectively think through his or her classification.)

Consider the Audience and Purpose

To judge the quality of a classification text, consider its **audience** and **purpose**. The audience for "Effective Discipline" is students because it comes from a college textbook. As such, its purpose is to inform. The audience for the paragraph about mustard on page 241 is much more general, and its purpose is to attract and inform readers interested in food-related topics. A strong classification paragraph should effectively inform its audience.

Vocabulary

audience
the intended readers of a written text

purpose
an author's reason for writing

LO4 Reading and Reacting to a Student Paragraph

Read   Read the following paragraph that classifies types of solar energy. Use the reading process to help you complete your reading. (See pages 14–15.)

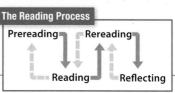

The Reading Process

Prereading   Rereading

Reading   Reflecting

Plugging into Sunlight

    With fossil fuels running out, people are discovering more and more *1* ways to use the free energy of the sun. The simplest form of solar energy is solar lighting, which means designing buildings to take advantage of natural light. A more advanced form is solar heating, or gathering the sun's warmth and using it to heat a building. A third use of solar energy *5* is solar cooking. Box cookers are insulated boxes with clear tops, and **parabolic** cookers use solar rays to boil water or cook food. A fourth use of solar energy provides drinkable water to millions of people. Solar water treatment devices can turn salt water into freshwater and can disinfect water using the sun's rays. Finally, **photovoltaic** cells convert sunlight into *10* electrical energy, which can power household devices and even electrical vehicles. Or course, the oldest type of solar power was not invented by people but by plants. Photosynthesis turns sunlight, water, and minerals into food for plants and the whole world!

React   Answer the questions below about the paragraph "Plugging into Sunlight." Then discuss your responses with your classmates.

1. What is the main idea of this paragraph?

    There are different uses of solar energy.

2. How many categories are included in this classification?

    Five

3. Does the writer describe or explain each category? Give an example.

    Yes

4. What is the intended purpose of this paragraph—to entertain, to inform, to persuade?

    To inform

5. What questions, if any, do you still have about the topic?

Vocabulary

parabolic
curve-shaped

photovoltaic
capable of producing voltage

A CLOSER LOOK   at Analyzing the Categories

As you evaluate the paragraph on the preceding page, pay special attention to the categories of solar energy. In effective classification writing, the categories, or subgroups, exhibit the following three qualities.

Categories should be . . .

- **exclusive,** meaning that one category does not overlap with other categories.
- **consistent,** meaning categories share the same classification factors. (See page 235.)
- **equal,** meaning categories are described with a similar number of details.

Evaluate   Analyze the categories by answering these three questions about them. (See page 233.)

1. How does the writer break down the topic into categories?

   _____

   _____

2. How does the writer describe each category?

   _____

   _____

3. Are the categories equal? Explain.

   _____

   _____

Considering the Factors

As you analyze the categories in a classification, consider the common factor or factors used to make the categories. (See page 235.)

Identify   On your own or with a classmate, identify the common factor or factors used to create the classification on page 236.

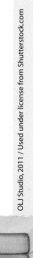

OLJ Studio, 2011 / Used under license from Shutterstock.com

LO5 Practicing Reading Skills

In a classification paragraph or essay, the author may provide examples of a category without specifically defining the category, or may provide a specific definition without examples. In either case, you must make inferences as you read.

Inferring Category Definitions

In the "Effective Discipline" paragraph, the authors sometimes provide examples of a category without a specific definition. As a reader, you must infer the definitions from the examples:

- **"Power assertion** refers to physical punishment or a show of force."
  (**Inferred definition:** Power assertion uses the parent's greater physical strength or authority to punish bad behavior.)
- **"Management techniques** combine praise, recognition, approval, rules . . ."
  (**Inferred definition:** Management techniques shape positive behaviors using positive reinforcement.)

Infer From each category and set of examples below, infer a specific category description.
  1. Marine mammals include polar bears, walruses, sea lions, and sea otters.
  2. Primates include lemurs, monkeys, baboons, great apes, and human beings.
  3. Marsupial animals include kangaroos, opossums, koalas, and sugar gliders.

Inferring Examples

In the "Plugging into Sunlight" paragraph, the author sometimes provides definitions of categories without specific examples. As a reader, you must infer the examples:

- **"Solar lighting** . . . means designing buildings to take advantage of natural light."
  (**Inferred examples:** Windows, skylights, and open floor plans provide solar lighting.)
- **"Solar heating** . . . [is] gathering the sun's warmth and using it to heat a building.)
  (**Inferred examples:** Water-filled solar collectors connected to radiators would be an example of solar heating.)

Infer From each category and definition, infer examples that would fit in the category.
  1. Reptiles are cold-blooded animals that lay eggs and have scaly skin.
  2. Amphibians are cold-blooded animals that often change from water- to air-breathing forms.

Writing

Writing a classification paragraph is a manageable assignment if you choose a topic that can easily be broken down into categories. The instructions below will help you discover a good topic and lead you through the writing process. (See pages 68–73.)

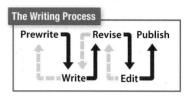

The Writing Process

Prewrite → Revise → Publish
Write → Edit

LO6 Planning a Classification Paragraph

You will explore the categories of a topic of your choice. To begin, choose four subject areas that interest you from the following list of the essentials of life.

Essentials of Life

food	intelligence	resources
clothing	personality	energy
shelter	senses	money
education	emotions	government
work	goals	laws
entertainment	health	rights
recreation	environment	science
religion	plants	measurement
family	animals	machines
friends	land	tools
community	literature	agriculture
communication	arts	business

1. **Subject area:** _____

2. **Subject area:** _____

3. **Subject area:** _____

4. **Subject area:** _____

Select Review the subjects that you have listed above. Select one that could lead to classification topics. Then identify possible topics as is done below. Circle the topic that seems most promising.

Subject area: _government_

Topics: _types of political systems, types of U.S. political parties, types of monarchies, levels of state government_

Researching Your Topic

After you choose a topic, you may need to do some research to learn more about it before you identify your categories. (Three or five is a good number for a classification paragraph.) Internet sites, reference books, and textbooks are good places to start. Remember, the categories must be exclusive, consistent, and equal (see page 237).

Identify Using a graphic organizer like the one below, list three to five categories for your topic. In the second column, describe each category. Make sure the description clarifies how the category is different from the rest.

INSIGHT ——————
Remember that you will need an equal amount of detail to describe the categories.

Categories or types of _____	Description Details

Creating Your Topic Sentence

Your topic sentence should name your topic and introduce the categories you will describe in your paragraph. Use the following formula to create this sentence.

The specific topic	**+**	an introduction to the categories	**=**	an effective topic sentence.
sleeping disorders		four basic types of disorders		Experts identify four basic types of sleeping disorders.

Create Write a topic sentence for your paragraph using the formula above. If necessary, write two or three versions until your topic sentence says what you want it to say.

LO7 Writing the First Draft

After you are done planning, you are ready to write the first draft of your paragraph. Provided below is another sample classification paragraph.

Read Read the paragraph, noting how the writer classified the topic, mustard, into four distinct subgroups.

My Condiments to the Chef

Topic Sentence

Category 1

   When most Americans talk about mustard, they mean   *1*
a type of bright-yellow goo that the rest of the world hardly
recognizes. Actually there are four basic types of mustard.
Yellow mustard is the most common in America, made from
finely ground mustard seeds, vinegar, and a bright yellow   *5*
coloring called turmeric. Yellow mustard is mild and is a

Category 2

common seasoning on hot dogs. For a spicier type of mustard,
people enjoy brown mustard, which is made from coarse-
ground mustard seeds and looks yellow and brown. For an
even stronger flavor, mustard lovers turn to the famous   *10*

Category 3

mustard called Dijon, named after the French city where it
was first processed. Dijon mustard is finely ground and is

Category 4

usually mixed with wine instead of vinegar. Finally, there
are many hybrid mustards categorized as specialty mustards,

Closing Sentence

including everything from honey to jalapeños. When it comes   *15*
to taste, there's a mustard for just about everybody.

Harris Shiffman, 2011 / Used under license from Shutterstock.com

Consider the Craft

1. What do you like best about this paragraph?

2. What are two of your favorite details?

3. What is the reason behind the arrangement of the categories?

The Working Parts of a Paragraph

A paragraph consists of three main parts, each of which has a special function. The information that follows explains each part.

Paragraph Outline

Topic Sentence: The topic sentence introduces the subject and refers to the types or categories. (See page 240.)

Body Sentences: The body sentences name and describe each category, and, if possible, provide examples.

Closing Sentence: The closing sentence leaves the reader with an interesting final thought.

Drafting Tips

When you write a classification, your goal is to share information in a clear, organized manner. To that end, consider the following tips as you write your first draft.

- **To make your beginning clear,** make sure that your topic sentence identifies your topic and introduces your categories.
- **To help your readers follow your classification,** decide on an effective and consistent (similar) way to introduce each category. Also decide on a logical arrangement of the categories.
- **To make sure that your writing has balance,** provide an equal number of details for each category.
- **To emphasize your purpose,** use language that reflects your goal—to inform, to entertain, and so on.

INSIGHT
Remember that a paragraph is a limited unit of writing, so restrict yourself to just a few supporting details for each category. (If you have a lot to say about each category, perhaps you should develop a classification essay. See pages 249–250.)

Write Develop your first draft using the information on this page and your planning on pages 239–240 as a guide.

LO8 Revising the Writing

Start the revising process by reading your first draft two or three times to get a feel for your work so far. Then have one of your classmates read and react to your work using a response sheet as a guide. (See page 353.)

Using Transitions

Transition words and phrases can help you identify each type or category and rank them, perhaps by age, importance, rarity, and so on.

One type	The simplest	The most common	The earliest
A second	A more complex	A less common	A later
A third	An advanced	A rare	A recent
↓ The last	↓ The most complex	↓ A very rare	↓ The newest

Revising in Action

Read aloud the unrevised and then revised version of the following excerpt. Note how the transition words identify and rank the categories.

> The simplest form of solar energy is
> . . . people are discovering more and more ways to use the free energy of the
>   , which
> sun. Solar lighting means designing buildings to take advantage of natural
> A more advanced form is
> light. Solar heating is; or gathering the sun's warmth and using it to heat a
> A third use of solar energy is ⊙
> building. Solar cooking, is a new reality for many. Box cookers are insulated
>
> boxes with clear tops, and parabolic cookers use solar rays to boil water or cook
>
> food. . . .

Revise Improve your writing, using the following checklist and your classmate's comments on the response sheet. Continue working until you can check off each item in the list.

Ideas
- [ ] 1. Do I identify my subject?
- [ ] 2. Do I name and describe the types or categories?

Organization
- [ ] 3. Do I have an effective topic sentence, body sentences, and a closing sentence?
- [ ] 4. Do I use transition words and phrases to identify and rank the types?

Voice
- [ ] 5. Does my voice sound knowledgeable and interested?

LO9 Editing the Writing

Subjects and verbs must agree in number. These two pages cover basic subject-verb agreement and agreement with compound subjects.

Basic Subject-Verb Agreement

A singular subject takes a singular verb, and a plural subject takes a plural verb:

One percussion instrument is the drums.
           singular subject   singular verb

Two percussion instruments are drums and cymbals
           plural subject   plural verb

In order to identify the actual subject, disregard any words that come between the subject and verb, such as words in a prepositional phrase:

One of the types of instruments is percussion.
singular subject   singular verb

(The words *types* and *instruments* are not subjects; both are objects of the prepositions.)

Agreement Practice   Correct the following sentences so that the subjects and verbs agree. The first sentence has been done for you.

1. Percussion instruments ~~makes~~ *make* noise by striking something.
2. Pianos, by that definition, ~~is~~ *are* percussion instruments.
3. The hammers inside a piano ~~strikes~~ *strike* the strings to make a sound.
4. Of course, drums ~~is~~ *are* also a type of percussion.
5. The drumsticks, made of hardwood, ~~hits~~ *hit* the skin of the drumhead to create the sound.
6. Another of the instrument types ~~are~~ *is* winds.
7. This family of instruments ~~include~~ *includes* flutes, clarinets, and even brass.
8. Wind ~~produce~~ *produces* the sound in these instruments.

Additional Practice: For additional practice, see pages 394–395.

Apply   Read your classification paragraph, making sure that your subjects and verbs agree.

Agreement with Compound Subjects

A compound subject is made of two or more subjects joined by *and* or *or*. When the subjects are joined by *and,* they are plural and require a plural verb:

A baritone and a trombone play the same range.
      plural subject   **plural verb**

When the subjects are joined by *or,* the verb must match the number of the last subject:

Either the woodwinds or the trumpet plays the main theme.
      singular subject singular verb

Either the trumpet or the woodwinds play the main theme.
      plural subject   plural verb

Agreement Practice   Correct the following sentences so that the subjects and verbs agree. The first sentence has been done for you.

1. Stringed instruments and their players ~~fills out~~ *fill out* the orchestra.
2. Violins and violas ~~plays~~ *play* the higher notes.
3. A cello or bass ~~handle~~ *handles* the lower notes.
4. The horsehair bow and the string ~~makes~~ *make* the sound.
5. Either music or screeches ~~emerges~~ *emerge* depending on the player's talent.
6. A soloist or all the violins ~~carries~~ *carry* the melody.
7. The conductor or the concertmaster ~~indicate~~ *indicates* when to bow.
8. The concertmaster and the strings ~~sits~~ *sit* closest to the audience.

Additional Practice: For additional practice, see pages 396–397.

Write   Write the end of each sentence, matching the verb to the compound subject.

1. The director and the orchestra _____

2. The orchestra or the director _____

Apply   Read your classification paragraph, making sure that your compound subjects agree with their verbs.

Marking a Paragraph

The model that follows has a number of errors.

Editing Practice   Correct the following paragraph, using the correction marks below. One correction has been done for you.

A Question of Taste

All the flavors that a person can taste is made up of a few basic taste   *1*
sensations. In the Western world, people are used to thinking about four
tastes: salty, sweet, sour, and bitter. The salty taste come from substances
that include sodium, such as snacks like potato chips or pretzels. The sweet
sensation comes from sugars, whether in processed foods like sweetened   *5*
cereals or naturally occurring in fruit or honey. Sour tastes come from
acidic foods (pH below 7) such as lemons and grapefruit, and bitter tastes
come from alkaline foods (pH above 7) such as coffee or dark chocolate. But
in the world Eastern, two other taste sensations are recognized. A savory
taste (umami) comes from amino acids, which are a basic part of meats   *10*
and proteins. And a spicy taste (piquancy) comes from substances like
the capsaicin in hot peppers. Given the savory and spicy nature of Indian,
Thai, chinese, and other Eastern foods, it's no wonder that these tastes are
recognized. With all the senses to consider, chefs can make every dish a
unique work of art.   *15*

Correction Marks

⌐ delete	⅄ add comma	∧ add word
d capitalize	? add question mark	⊙ add period
⅁ lowercase	ⱽ insert an apostrophe	⌒ spelling
∧ insert		⌒ switch

INSIGHT

In academic writing, the pronouns *I* and *you* have special rules for subject-verb agreement:

- *I* takes the verb *am* instead of *is*: I *am* (**not** I *is*).
- *I* also takes plural action verbs: I *sit* (**not** I *sits*).
- *You* always takes a plural verb: You *are*; you *sit* (**not** You *is*; you *sits*).

Correcting Your Paragraph

Now it's time to correct your own paragraph.

Apply   Create a clean copy of your revised paragraph and use the following checklist to check for errors. Continue working until you can check off each item in the list.

Words

☐   1. Have I used specific nouns and verbs? (See page 102.)

☐   2. Have I used more action verbs than "be" verbs? (See page 458.)

Sentences

☐   3. Have I combined short choppy sentences? (See page 105.)

☐   4. Have I avoided shifts in sentences? (See page 422.)

☐   5. Have I avoided fragments and run-ons? (See pages 410–413, 416–417.)

Conventions

☐   6. Do I use correct verb forms (*he saw,* not *he seen*)? (See pages 464, 466.)

☐   7. Do my subjects and verbs agree (*she speaks,* not *she speak*)? (See pages 394–403.)

☐   8. Have I used the right words (*their, there, they're*)?

☐   9. Have I capitalized first words and proper nouns and adjectives? (See page 504.)

☐   10. Have I used commas after long introductory word groups? (See pages 574–577.)

☐   11. Have I punctuated dialogue correctly? (See pages 524–525.)

☐   12. Have I carefully checked my spelling?

Adding a Title

Make sure to add a title to your paragraph. Here are some simple strategies for coming up with a catchy one.

■   Use a number:

   Four Types of Mustard

■   Use an expression:

   A Question of Taste

■   Think outside the box:

   Plugging into Sunlight

■   Be clever:

   My Condiments to the Chef

Create   Prepare a clean final copy of your paragraph and proofread it.

> "I find that different types of music are good
> for certain activities."
> —Peter Steele

Review and Enrichment

You have been working with the classification paragraph. This section reviews and expands on that information by providing a classification essay to read and respond to. You will also be given a number of writing ideas to choose from and develop in a paragraph or an essay of your own. These activities will broaden your understanding of classification.

Prereading

One of the more famous classification systems is the Myers-Briggs Type Indicator, or as it is more commonly called, the Myers-Briggs test. This extensive questionnaire divides the topic "personality type" into 16 exclusive categories. This test was created during World War II as a means of placing women in specific wartime jobs based on personality type. Now, the Myers-Briggs test has become the most widely used tool for personality assessment. It is still used extensively for team building, marketing, and relationship counseling.

CONSIDER THE TRAITS

As you read the classification essay on the next page, focus first on the **ideas**—the topic that is being classified, the categories, and the details that support and explain each category. Then consider the **organization**—the way that the opening, middle, and closing parts are constructed. Also notice the authors' **voice**—their special way of speaking to the reader. And finally, ask yourself if these traits combine to produce a satisfying reading experience.

Explore   The Myers-Briggs test classifies people as either extroverted or introverted. Extroverts are outgoing, action-orientated people, while introverts are shy, thought-orientated people. Do you consider yourself an extrovert or an introvert? Write down your answer. Then ask a classmate how they perceive you—either as introverted or extroverted. Compare your answers.

What do you think?

Do you agree with the quotation at the top of the page? How do certain activities influence the type of music you listen to? Can you classify your favorite music based on different activities, such as working, studying, exercising, and so on?

Reading and Reacting

Read This classification essay focuses on the four humors (liquids) that ruled western medical thought for over 2,000 years. Use the reading process to gain a full understanding of the reading.

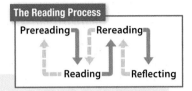

About the Author

Robert King is co-author of *Inquire: A Guide to 21st Century Learning* and two dozen novels.

The Humorous Humors

When we hear the word *humor*, we tend to think of a joke, but a person   *1*
in a *bad humor* is rarely suffering from a bad joke. The term *humor* used
in this way refers to its Greek origin, a word meaning "juice" or "sap." Way
back in 400 B.C., Hippocrates, the father of medicine, said that humans
were full of four basic types of sap—blood, yellow bile, black bile, and   *5*
phlegm. From that time until the mid-1800s, western medicine explained
and treated illness as an imbalance in these "humors."

The most recognizable humor is blood: "If you prick us do we not
bleed?" According to ancient doctors, this vital fluid came from the liver
and made a person red-cheeked and happy. For this reason, the word   *10*
sanguine meant both "bloody" and "happy." Blood was associated with
springtime, when young folks "got their blood up," becoming **amorous** and
foolhardy. In order to "bring down" all this hot, wet blood, doctors applied
cold, dry things. Given an extreme excess of blood, medieval physicians
solved the problem through **bloodletting**. As late as the American   *15*
Revolution, some army surgeons would let the blood from an ill soldier day
after day until the man recovered or died.

Another humor, yellow bile, did not apparently come from the liver
but from the gall bladder. This liquid somehow managed to be dry as well
as hot, making it associated with fire. As such, yellow bile produced a   *20*
fiery temper, with angry outbursts and roars of rage—making the person
choleric. Imbalances of this humor caused wars and riots—which spread
during the summer months until someone dowsed the sufferer with a
bucket of cold water. Excessive yellow bile could be drawn out as a vapor
through the application of large suction cups much like modern bathroom   *25*
plungers. The giant **hickeys** that remained, however, often made the
patient even angrier.

Black bile came from the **spleen**, which is why people often were
offended by someone's spleen (ill will). The Greek words for black bile,

melon chole, give us our modern word *melancholy*—which is depression. Black bile was cold and dry, the opposite of blood, so it naturally led to a condition opposite of happiness: **moroseness**. Autumn brought on the imbalance of melancholy, with trees turning to bare sticks against a sky that was losing birds and sun, both. Black bile was also associated with earth, the dust to which we all return. Yes, sad stuff. Still, unlike sanguine or choleric people—who were bled or dowsed back to health—the melancholic improved through hot, wet things such as warm brandy and steaming baths. Not surprisingly, many Romantic poets enjoyed being melancholy.

The last humor revealed itself repeatedly in handkerchiefs throughout time—the cold, wet stuff called phlegm. According to medieval doctors, an excess of phlegm caused colds and made a person slow and dull—or *phlegmatic*. Cold, wet winter was the season for this ailment. Associated with water, phlegm forever dripped and ran. To get rid of excess phlegm, people not only blew their noses but also used various medicines to purge themselves. In some senses, the phlegmatic person had the least appeal of any temperament type, being a slothful snuffler who seemed quite capable of passing the imbalance to anyone within sneezing distance.

All these humors are somewhat humorous to modern day readers. Lest we be too quick to judge our medical **forebears**, thought, let's remember that the human body is a complex thing. The liver does seem to be the source of a lot of blood, especially when you stab someone there. Consider, too, that though people were fond of stabbing each other, they were forbidden to take a look inside the dead man afterward—a hobby that da Vinci later popularized. And let's not be too high and mighty about our own medical knowledge. Most modern people don't even realize they have a spleen let alone know what to do with it. Many modern people are on some form of Prozac, though nobody knows why it works. Yes, we've come a long way since the theory of the humors, but it is likely that in a hundred years, our own medical knowledge will seem equally **barbarous** and humorous.

Vocabulary

humor
a juice or liquid; a mood or temperament

phlegm
snot

sanguine
bloody or happy

amorous
in love (amore)

foolhardy
reckless, stupidly unafraid

bloodletting
the practice of draining blood from a person to improve health

choleric
furious, given to snapping in anger

hickeys
a red welt caused by suction against the skin

spleen
an organ beneath the stomach, filters blood; ill will

moroseness
deep sadness

phlegmatic
sluggish and sleepy

forebears
those who went before

barbarous
uncivilized, savage

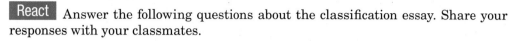 Answer the following questions about the classification essay. Share your responses with your classmates.

1. What four categories does the author describe?

   _____

2. What details do you find most interesting, surprising, or disturbing?

   _____

3. What tone does the author use in describing these categories? What evidence from the text shows the author's tone?

   _____

4. Often the author introduces terms and defines them in context—*humor, sanguine, choleric.* Write two other unfamiliar terms that the author introduces and tell what context clues helped you understand them.

   _____

5. In the final paragraph, the author turns a critical eye on modern medicine. What two facts does he mention to show that we aren't as advanced as we might think? How does his final sentence connect to the real world?

   _____

6. How would you rate this classification essay and why?

   Weak ★ ★ ★ ★ ★ Strong

   _____

Drawing Inferences

An *inference* is a logical conclusion that you draw from evidence in the text. To practice drawing inferences, answer the following questions about the essay you just read. Afterward, share your responses with your classmates.

1. What inferences can you draw from the line "Not surprisingly, many Romantic poets enjoyed their melancholy" (lines 38–39)?

2. Read the following statement: "Consider, too, that though people were fond of stabbing each other, they were forbidden to take a look inside the dead man afterward—a hobby that da Vinci later popularized." Judging from this statement, infer the author's opinion about violence against living people and dissection of dead people.

Writing

Write a classification paragraph or classification essay following the guidelines on the next two pages. Check with your instructor about any specific requirements that she or he may have. And be sure to use the writing process to help you do your best work. (See pages 68–73.)

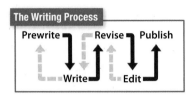

Prewriting

Choose one of the following or another appropriate writing idea for your classification writing.

Writing Ideas

1. Write about a topic that you identified in the planning activity on page 239.

2. Choose a topic based on one of your favorite interests (sports cars, clothing design, reality television, theater, and so on).

3. Write a classification based on your observations at a public place (park, library, bus stop, and so on).

4. Write a classification of attitudes toward politics, religion, or morality.

5. Write a classification about the wildlife or plant life in your neighborhood.

6. Write a classification of the ways to access news.

7. Write a classification based on one of the photographs in *Fusion 1*.

When planning . . .

Refer to pages 239–240 to help you with your prewriting and planning. Also use the tips that follow.

- Choose a topic that you understand well or can easily learn about.
- If necessary, research your topic to find all the major categories or parts.
- Collect similar types of details for each category.
- Decide on a logical way to order your categories.
- Review the classification writing examples in this chapter to see how they are developed.

Writing and Revising

Use the tips that follow and the information on pages 241–243 to help you with your drafting and revising.

When writing . . .

- Include an opening, a middle, and a closing part in your classification writing. Each part has a specific role. (See page 242.)
- Follow your planning notes, but also consider new ideas as they come to mind.
- Introduce each new category in the same basic way.
- Use transitions to shift from one category to the next.

When revising . . .

- Check that the order of your categories is logical and clear.
- Make sure the categories are exclusive, consistent, and equal (see pages 237).
- Decide if your classification will interest the reader. If not, improve your essay by adding new details, trying a different opening or closing strategy, and so on.
- Ask a trusted peer to react to your classification.

Editing

Refer to the checklist on page 247 when you are ready to edit your classification for style and correctness.

Reflecting on Classification Writing

Answer the following questions about your classification reading and writing experiences in this chapter.

1. Why do writers and researchers classify information?

   Classification helps make complex topics more manageable.

2. What is your favorite paragraph in this chapter? Explain.

3. What reading strategy in this chapter seems most helpful? Explain.

4. What is the main benefit of reading a classification paragraph?

5. What is the easiest thing about classification writing? The hardest?

6. What do you like best about your classification paragraph?

7. What is one thing you would like to change in it?

8. What are some transitional words or phrases that are common in a classification paragraph?

Key Terms to Remember

When you read and write classification writing, it's important to understand the following terms.

- **Classification**—the act of arranging or organizing according to categories, or subgroups
- **Categories**—specifically defined divisions; general types or classes of ideas
- **Line diagram**—a graphic organizer that can be used to show main categories and supporting details
- **Classification factors**—the qualities the writer uses to divide a topic into categories

12

"Shallow men believe in luck, believe in circumstances. Strong men believe in cause and effect."
—Ralph Waldo Emerson

Cause-Effect

Flip a switch; a light comes on. The relationship is obvious.

Make a joke; a friend laughs. The reason may be less obvious. *Was it the joke itself or your delivery? Is your friend just being polite or reacting to your attempt at humor?*

These are simple examples of cause-effect relationships. More complex examples include the causes and effects of a disease, the causes and effects of interest rates on consumer spending, and the causes and effects of solar flares.

This chapter deals with the cause-effect form of thinking and writing. First, you will learn about the basics related to this form. Then you will read and react to both a professional and a student cause-effect paragraph before writing one of your own. The strategies you learn in this chapter will apply to cause-effect assignments in all of your classes.

Learning Outcomes

LO1 Understand cause-effect.

LO2 Learn about reading strategies.

LO3 Read and react to a professional paragraph.

LO4 Read and react to a student paragraph.

LO5 Practice reading skills.

LO6 Plan a cause-effect paragraph.

LO7 Write the first draft.

LO8 Revise the writing.

LO9 Edit the writing.

What do you think?

Explain what the quotation above means to you. Share your thoughts with a classmate.

Vladislav Gajic, 2011 / Used under license from Shutterstock.com

LO1 Understanding Cause-Effect

In a chemistry class, you learn that combining certain chemicals results in a particular reaction. "Results in" is another way of saying "causes an effect." A history text may explain the reasons behind a particular event, and the consequences of that event. "Reasons" is another way of saying "causes," and "consequences" another way of saying "effects."

> " . . . no thought or action is without its effects, present or ultimate, seen or unseen, felt or unfelt."
> —Norman Cousins

These two examples indicate how central cause-effect analysis is in your classes. The body of knowledge in all disciplines is expanded largely by seeking to discover how things work, and that means finding out what causes what. This knowledge is then passed along by explaining the cause-effect relationship related to new situations and circumstances. Understanding this relationship can be more beneficial than memorizing facts.

Much of your college reading will involve cause-effect analysis. Often, the word "cause" or "effect" (or a similar term) will be mentioned in the text itself. Even if these words aren't used, you can recognize a cause-effect explanation by its two-part structure. The explanation will either introduce various causes and then conclude with the main effect, or it will begin with a single cause and then explain its many effects. In a few cases, cause-effect writing may begin with multiple causes and then discuss their many effects. Keep this two-part structure in mind as you read the cause-effect paragraphs in this chapter.

INSIGHT ————————————————————————————————

Finding cause-effect relationships is a way of analyzing a topic, as are classifying and comparing. Each type of analysis requires that you examine a topic closely, consider it deeply, and refine your understanding of it in the process.

Identify   Name two or three recent news stories that explain a cause-effect relationship. Provide a one- or two-sentence summary of each example. Share your summaries with your classmates.

1. _____

_____

2. _____

_____

3. _____

_____

Reading

Reading cause-effect paragraphs will introduce you to one of the more common tasks of college assignments—finding the reasons and results resting beneath the surface of complex topics.

LO2 Learning About Reading Strategies

These two strategies—studying the topic sentence and using a cause-effect organizer—will help you read cause-effect texts.

Strategy 1: Studying the Topic Sentence

By definition, a topic sentence introduces the reader to the topic of the paragraph and the key part of it that will be emphasized. So if you study the topic sentence in most cause-effect paragraphs, you should be able to learn a lot about the information that will follow. Here's an example:

> **Topic sentence:** Though the fighting ceased in 1953, the effects of the Korean War are still felt today.

Discussion: The topic of the paragraph is the Korean War. As the topic sentence states, the paragraph will focus on the remaining effects of the war. The causes will not be a major emphasis.

Remember that some paragraphs will not begin with a clearly defined topic sentence. So this strategy won't work for all cause-effect paragraphs.

Strategy 2: Using a Cause-Effect Organizer

Part of understanding a cause-effect paragraph is keeping track of the important details. Completing a cause-effect organizer will help you do so.

Subject	
Causes (Because of . . .)	Effects (. . . these conditions resulted.)
-	-
-	-
-	-

LO3 Reading and Reacting to a Professional Paragraph

Read This cause-effect paragraph comes from a science textbook called *Living in the Environment*. It explores the serious problem of the burning of tropical forests. Remember to use the reading process to help you gain a full understanding of the text. (See pages 14–15.)

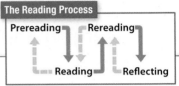

Burning Tropical Forests and Climate Change

The burning of tropical forests releases CO_2 into the atmosphere. Rising concentration of this gas can help warm the atmosphere, which is projected to change the global climate during this century. Scientists estimate that tropical forest fires account for at least 17 percent of all human-created greenhouse gas emissions, and that each year they emit twice as much CO_2 as all of the world's cars and trucks emit. The large-scale burning of the Amazon rain forest accounts for 75 percent of all Brazil's greenhouse gas emissions, making Brazil the world's fourth largest emitter of such gases, according to the National Inventory of Greenhouse Gases. And with these forests gone, even if savannah or second-growth forests replace them, far less CO_2 will be absorbed for photosynthesis, resulting in even more atmospheric warming.

1

5

10

"Burning Tropical Rainforests and Climate Change" from MILLER. *Living in the Environment*, 17E. © 2012 Brooks/Cole, a part of Cengage Learning, Inc.

React Answer the following questions about the paragraph. Then discuss your responses with your classmates.

1. What is the main idea of this paragraph?

   Burning tropical forests are one cause of global climate change.

2. Does the paragraph focus more attention on causes or effects? Consider using a cause-effect organizer to help you answer this question. (See page 257.)

   Effects

3. What are two things that you learned in this paragraph?

4. What questions do you still have about the topic?

A CLOSER LOOK at Cause-Effect

Considering the Evidence

People used to think that ice floats because it's thin. After all, needles and razor blades float, and they're made of metal, which is heavier than water. Then someone demonstrated that when you push a needle, a razor blade, and a thin piece of ice to the bottom of a basin of water, the ice will return to the top while the other two remain at the bottom.

This demonstration shows how important it is to be sure about a cause-effect relationship. Just because something seems to cause something else, doesn't mean it actually does.

Evaluate When studying the causes and effects in a paragraph, always judge the value of the evidence. It's important to know if the causes and effects seem reliable and reasonable.

Considering the Purpose

Sometimes writers use cause-effect reasoning to convince you to take an action. In that case, ask yourself the following questions.

1. What does the author hope to gain by convincing me of this cause-effect relationship?
2. What is the author's background related to the subject?
3. What other explanations might there be?
4. What evidence might be missing?

INSIGHT

Never reject a point of view just because it doesn't match up to your own thinking. Remember, people used to quite reasonably believe that ice floats because it's thin. If they hadn't been prepared to entertain a better explanation, we might still be puzzled by ice *cubes*, which float despite being shaped like chunky rocks.

Review Reread the paragraph on page 258. Then discuss it with your classmates using the "purpose" questions above as a guide.

LO4 Reading and Reacting to a Student Paragraph

Read Read the following cause-effect paragraph about the history of family structure in the United States. Remember to use the steps in the reading process to help you gain a full understanding of the text. (See pages 14–15.)

The Reading Process

Prereading → Rereading

Reading → Reflecting

The Changing Family

Throughout U.S. history, the way that people make a living has   1
effected the family unit. Early on, much of the country consisted of
family farms clustered around small towns and villages. The families
on these farms were often multigenerational, with parents, children,
and grandparents all living under the same roof. With the rise of   5
industrialism, however, family farms gave way to large agribusinesses,
and much of the rural population moved to cities to work in factories
and offices. The "nuclear family" was born, consisting of father, mother,
and two or three children. When the children of these families reached
working age, they moved out to start their own nuclear families. Today,   10
with industrialism on the decline and the Information Age redefining
work, the United States is experiencing another shift in the family. Many
adult children are remaining at home. In some cases, parents, children,
and grandparents are again living together. In others, single parents or
same-sex couples are raising children, often with the help of siblings or   15
friends. Even single people find themselves rooming together in larger
groups. With all these changes, the "alternative family" concept is quickly
becoming a norm.

React Answer the following questions about the paragraph. Then discuss your answers with your classmates.

1. What is the main idea of this paragraph? Large-scale changes in the economy caused family units to change throughout U.S. history.

2. What causes and effects are included? Consider using a cause-effect organizer to help you answer this question. (See page 257.) _____

3. What are two things that you learned in this paragraph?

_____

4. How would you rate this paragraph and why?

   Weak ★ ★ ★ ★ ★ Strong

_____

A CLOSER LOOK at Considering the Evidence and Purpose

As you saw on page 259, cause-effect relationships are not always as simple as they might at first seem. It is important when reading to recognize the link between cause and effect and to make sure it is a reasonable one.

Identify Which of the following cause-effect patterns comes closest to the organization of the paragraph on the previous page? balanced

1. Cause-Focused

> Topic Sentence

Causes

Effects

> Closing Sentence

2. Effect-Focused

> Topic Sentence

Causes

Effects

> Closing Sentence

3. Balanced

> Topic Sentence

Causes

Effects

> Closing Sentence

Consider How does the topic sentence help you learn from this paragraph?

_____

_____

What purpose might the writer have had for explaining this cause-effect relationship?

_____

_____

What other reasons could there be for changes in the family unit?

_____

_____

What else would you like to know about the subject?

_____

_____

LO5 Practicing Reading Skills

Often in a cause-effect paragraph, you run into unfamiliar terms and you have to make sure that the causes described are really causes. This page will help.

Vocabulary: Word Parts and New Sentences

As you read cause-effect paragraphs, you may run into unfamiliar terms. Word parts can help you understand these terms, and using these terms in new sentences can cement the definitions in your mind. The example below shows how word parts and new sentences can help define the "autonomic" nervous system.

> **auto (self)   +   nomos (law)   +   ic (relating to)**
> *autonomic* is "related to ruling itself"
>
> The autonomic nervous system is the part of the brain that controls body functions such as breathing and heartbeat without requiring conscious effort.

Define Explore the word parts of the following examples by using the list of prefixes, suffixes, and roots on pages 549–557 (as well as your dictionary). Then write a definition for each word and use the word in a sentence.

1. redefine
   (page 260, line 11) _____
2. emitter
   (page 258, line 9) _____
3. multigenerational
   (page 260, line 4) _____
4. agribusiness
   (page 260, line 6) _____
5. concentration
   (page 258, line 2) _____
6. alternative
   (page 260, line 17) _____

Critical Thinking: Separating Causation and Correlation

You need to be able to tell the difference between correlation and causation. Correlation means that two things may occur together but have different causes. For example, you could say, "Every time my favorite show comes on, the tornado siren sounds." The favorite show doesn't set off the tornado siren. The favorite show airs Saturdays at noon, the same time when the city tests its tornado siren. The two are correlated, but there is no causation.

Check Indicate whether you think each situation represents correlation or causation. Explain your answers.

1. Whenever I brush my teeth, the meteorologist starts the weather report.
2. Whenever I forget to brush my teeth, my breath stinks.
3. I called my mother, and she started sneezing.
4. I showed my new cat to my mother, and she started sneezing.
5. Kennedy's secretary was Lincoln, and Lincoln's secretary was Kennedy.
6. Lee Harvey Oswald shot President Kennedy.
7. John Wilkes Booth shot President Lincoln.
8. John Wilkes Booth and Lee Harvey Oswald each had three names.

Writing

Beginning on this page, you will plan and write a cause-effect paragraph about a topic of your choice. Use the writing process to help you produce your best work. (See pages 68–73.)

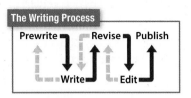

LO6 Planning a Cause-Effect Paragraph

To begin, you must choose a topic that both interests you and involves a cause-effect relationship.

Selecting a Topic

Think about the classes you are currently taking. What cause-effect ideas have you encountered in your studies? Also consider topics derived from the following categories.

- Family Life
- Politics
- Society

- Environment
- Entertainment
- Workplace

Select   List four cause-effect topics that interest you. Then circle the one you would like to write about.

1. Benefits of vegetarianism
2. Why people save things
3. Results of the 2009 jet landing on the Hudson River
4. How superhero movies affect our culture

Researching the Causes and Effects

Once you have selected a topic, research the causes and effects involved and list them for further use.

Identify   Use a cause-effect organizer to list possible causes and effects of your topic.

Subject	
Causes	Effects
-	-
-	-
-	-

Gathering and Evaluating Details

Effective cause-effect writing includes strong evidence. This means you must use trustworthy sources of information. Avoid sources that seems to approach your topic in a questionable way. Watch for sources that include the following types of information.

- **Broad generalization:** A statement that is based on too little evidence or allows no exceptions

> Video games are the reason that today's youth have a shorter attention span.
> *(This claim ignores the possibility of other reasons.)*

- **Straw man:** A claim that exaggerates or misinterprets an opponent's position

> If you cause deforestation, you hate the planet.

- **False cause:** A claim that confuses sequence with causation (If A comes before B, A must have caused B.)

> Since that new skate park opened, vandalism among young people has increased.
> *(The two factors may have no real connection.)*

Creating Your Topic Sentence

Your topic sentence should name your topic and identify what you plan on emphasizing about it. Use the following formula.

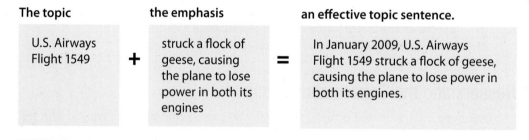

The topic		**the emphasis**		**an effective topic sentence.**
U.S. Airways Flight 1549	**+**	struck a flock of geese, causing the plane to lose power in both its engines	**=**	In January 2009, U.S. Airways Flight 1549 struck a flock of geese, causing the plane to lose power in both its engines.

Create Write your own topic sentence, following the example above.

The topic		**the emphasis**		**an effective topic sentence.**
	+		**=**	

LO7 Writing the First Draft

Your first draft is a first attempt to get your thoughts on paper in a reasonable order. It doesn't have to be perfect. You'll have time to polish it later.

Read Carefully read the following cause-effect paragraph about the emergency landing of Flight 1549.

Emergency Landing

Topic Sentence

In January 2009, U.S. Airways Flight 1549 struck a flock of geese, causing the plane to lose power in both its engines. The situation forced pilot Chesley "Sully" Sullenberger to perform an emergency landing on the Hudson River outside of New York City. Not only did he land safely, but all 150 passengers survived without a single serious injury. The event had many meaningful effects. Massive media coverage of the landing made "Sully" a household name. Many hailed him as

Body Sentences

an American hero. Meanwhile the passengers on the flight, though safe, suffered emotional trauma from the landing. Many refuse to step back onto a plane. Maybe the greatest effect, however, was the impact on the airline industry. The emergency landing led to a greater awareness of the dangers of bird populations near airways. Government agencies have gone so far as to wipe out geese populations in the proximity of airports. In the end, a tragic collision and remarkable

Closing Sentence

emergency landing may result in safer air travel for years to come.

1

5

10

15

Consider the Craft

1. What do you like best about this paragraph?

2. What are two of your favorite details?

3. Does the paragraph focus more on causes or effects?

4. What is the value of this paragraph?

The Working Parts of a Paragraph

As you can see from the previous page, a paragraph has three main parts, each with its own specific purpose.

Paragraph Outline

Topic Sentence: A topic sentence introduces your reader to your topic and identifies the main point about it that you want to stress.

Body Sentences: The body sentences support the topic sentence, adding specific details to make the causes and effects clear to the reader.

Closing Sentence: A closing sentence (or two) often summarizes the topic or may offer an interesting final idea.

Tip

Transition words that show cause-effect relationships: accordingly / as a result / because / consequently / for this purpose / for this reason / hence / just as / since / so / such as / therefore / thus / to illustrate / whereas

Drafting Tips

When you write a cause-effect paragraph, try to be both clear and interesting. To accomplish this, consider the following strategies.

In the topic sentence . . .
- Introduce the topic in a dramatic way that captures your reader's interest.
- State the main cause-effect connection clearly.

In the middle . . .
- Make sure that your cause-effect details follow logically and make sense.
- Use chronological order if the events follow a clear time sequence.
- Use order of importance (either most to least important or least to most important) if time sequence doesn't apply.
- Include enough details to explain each cause or effect.

In the closing sentence . . .
- End by reflecting on the main cause-effect connection.
- Leave the reader with an interesting idea to think about.
- Consider suggesting possibilities for further study or investigation.

INSIGHT

Journalism, the sciences, and even the arts often use the cause-effect approach when exploring a topic. Mastering this form will serve you well in all your college classes.

Write Prepare your first draft using the information on this page and your planning on pages 263–264 as a guide.

LO8 Revising the Writing

Start the revising process by reading your first draft two or three times to get a feel for your work so far. Then have one of your classmates read and react to your work using a response sheet as a guide. (See page 547.)

Using an Academic Style

Cause-effect paragraphs often require an academic style. Consider the quick tips below as you revise your paragraph.

Quick Tips for Academic Style

- **Avoid personal pronouns.** Avoid using personal pronouns such as *I, we,* and *you* in your cause-effect paragraph.
- **Define technical terms.** If your readers are not experts on your topic, define the specialized vocabulary or technical words you use.
- **Beware of unnecessary intensifiers.** Words such as *really, totally,* and *completely* are usually associated with a personal style.

Revising in Action:

Read aloud the unrevised and then the revised version of the following excerpt. Note how the changes improved the excerpt's academic style.

> Maybe the greatest effect, however, was the impact on the airline industry.
> ~~I think the greatest effect was the impact on aviation.~~ The emergency
> landing led to a ~~completely and totally~~ greater awareness of the dangers of bird
> airways.
> populations near ~~air hubs. You see~~ government agencies have . . .

Revise   Use the following checklist and your classmate's comments on the response sheet to improve your writing. Continue working until you can check off each item in the list.

Revising Checklist

Ideas

- [ ] 1. Does the topic sentence clearly introduce the topic and focus (causes, effects, or both) of the paragraph?
- [ ] 2. Do the causes and effects seem important and reliable?
- [ ] 3. Are all the links between the causes and effects clear and logical?

Organization

- [ ] 4. Do I include a topic sentence, body sentences, and a closing sentence?
- [ ] 5. Have I used transitions to show cause-effect relationships?

Voice

- [ ] 6. Have I used an appropriate voice—serious and academic or relaxed and personal?

LO9 Editing the Writing

Pronouns and their antecedents, the words that are replaced by the pronouns, must agree in three ways: in number, in person, and in gender. This page covers basic pronoun antecedent agreement

Basic Pronoun-Antecedent Agreement

Number

Somebody needs to bring his or her laptop to the meeting.

(The singular pronouns *his* or *her* agree with the singular antecedent *somebody*.)

Person

If students want to do better research, they should talk to a librarian.

(The third-person pronoun *they* agrees with the antecedent *students*.)

Gender

Chris picked up his lawn mower from his parents' garage.

(The masculine pronoun *his* agrees with the antecedent *Chris*.)

Practice   Read the sentences below. Correct the pronouns so that they agree with their antecedents in number, person, and gender.

1. The musicians strummed ~~his~~ their guitars.
2. After Shauna finished washing the dishes, ~~it~~ they sparkled.
3. If the waitress wants a better tip, ~~he~~ she should be more polite.
4. As the basketball players walked onto the court, ~~he~~ they waved to the crowd.
5. Mrs. Jackson started ~~their~~ her car.
6. Everyone can attend the extra study session if ~~they need~~ he or she needs help.
7. Eric poured root beer in ~~their~~ his favorite mug.

Additional Practice: For additional practice, see pages 446–447.

Apply   Read your cause-effect paragraph, watching for agreement issues with your pronouns and their antecedents. Correct any pronoun-antecedent agreement errors that you find.

Case of Pronouns

The case of a pronoun tells what role it can play in a sentence. There are three cases: *nominative, possessive,* and *objective.* Review the information below, which explains each case.

The nominative case is used for subjects and predicate nouns.
I, you, he, she, it, we, they

> She walked to the bank. It was she who needed more money.

The possessive case shows possession or ownership.
my, mine, our, ours, his, her, hers, their, theirs, its, your, yours

> The jacket is his. This jacket is mine. Your jacket is gone.

The objective case is used for direct or indirect objects and for objects of prepositions or infinitives.
me, us, you, him, her, it, them

> Reid told her that going to the movie was fine with him.

Practice   In each sentence below, select the correct pronoun in parentheses based on the case of the word.

1. Frank said that (he, him) needed someone to pick (his, him) up.
2. I looked over (their, them) expense report, and (they, them) went way over budget.
3. (She, her) worked on (she, her) new project.
4. The judge commended the competitor on (he, his) speed and agility.
5. (Their, them) lawn service is better than (our, ours) service.
6. It was (him, he) who spotted the bird.
7. The CEO increased (she, her) pay.
8. My brother and (I, me) attended the film festival.
9. (We, us) learned quickly how to recognize each other's voice.
10. On account of (I, me), my little brother does a lot of texting.

Additional Practice: For additional practice, see pages 444–445.

Apply   Read your cause-effect paragraph, checking the pronouns you've used. Make sure each pronoun is in the correct case.

Marking a Paragraph

The model that follows has a number of errors.

Editing Practice   Correct the following paragraph, using the marks below. One correction has been done for you.

Divided Along the 38th Parallel

Though the fighting ceased in 1953 the effects of the Korean War are   *1*

still felt today. The war began in 1950 when communist-occupied North

Korea, Waged war with south Korea. In a larger context, the war was

caused by the United States' desire to stop the spread of communism.

The effects of the conflict were considerable. Both sides suffered massive   *5*

casualties, and the Battle sparked the start of the cold war between the

United States and the Soviet Union. Today, Korea ~~remain~~ remains divided along

the 38th parallel. North Korea has a heavy military presence and has

suffered much poverty , while South Korea has thrived economically. Though the

countries have taken smalls steps toward political ~~piece~~ peace, the war has not   *10*

ended.

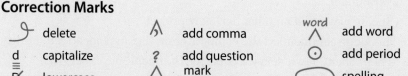

Correction Marks

℺ delete	⅄ add comma	*word* ∧ add word
d̲ capitalize	? ∧ add question mark	⊙ add period
∅ lowercase		⬭ spelling
∧ insert	v̆ insert an apostrophe	⏝ switch

INSIGHT

When checking for errors, it helps to use specific editing strategies. For example, to check for punctuation, you can circle all of the marks in your paper and check each one for correctness. To check for spelling, you should work from the bottom up in your writing. This strategy will help you focus on each word for spelling and usage. (See page 73 for more of these strategies.

Correcting Your Paragraph

Now it's time to correct your own paragraph.

Apply   Create a clean copy of your revised paragraph and use the following checklist to check for errors. Continue working until you can check off each item in the list.

Editing Checklist

Words

☐ 1. Have I used specific nouns and verbs? (See page 102.)

☐ 2. Have I used more action verbs than "be" verbs? (See page 458.)

Sentences

☐ 3. Have I varied the beginnings and lengths of sentences? (See pages 104–105.)

☐ 4. Have I combined short choppy sentences? (See page 105.)

☐ 5. Have I avoided sentence errors such as fragments and comma splices? (See pages 410–415.)

Conventions

☐ 6. Do I use correct verb forms (*he saw,* not *he seen*)? (See pages 464, 466.)

☐ 7. Do my subjects and verbs agree (*she speaks,* not *she speak*)? (See pages 394–403.)

☐ 8. Do my pronouns and antecedents agree?

☐ 9. Have I capitalized first words and proper nouns and adjectives? (See page 504.)

☐ 10. Have I carefully checked my spelling?

Adding a Title

Make sure to add an effective title. Here are two strategies for creating one.

- Grab the reader's attention:

  Emergency Landing

- Use an idea from the paragraph:

  The Changing Family

> "Our thoughts, deeds, and words return to us sooner or later, with astounding accuracy."
> —Florence Shinn

Review and Enrichment

In the first part of this chapter, you have read cause-effect paragraphs and written one of your own. In this part, you will read and react to a professional cause-effect essay. After that, you will find a number of writing ideas to choose from for a cause-effect paragraph or essay. The reading and writing that you do in these pages will reinforce and enrich the work you have already completed.

CONSIDER THE TRAITS

As you read the cause-effect essay in this part, consider first the **ideas** it contains—the topic, focus, and causes and effects. Then pay attention to the **organization**—the way the opening, middle, and closing parts are put together. Also think about the authors' **voice**—the overall tone or personality of the writing. Finally, ask yourself if these traits combine to produce a strong essay.

Prereading

The actions of people provide a common starting point for cause-effect writing. Or stated in another way, cause-effect writing often examines what we do and why we do it. The professional essay starting on the next page explains the causes and effects of a certain method of studying. As you should remember, the professional paragraph on page 258 explores the causes and effects of people burning tropical forests. And the student paragraph on page 265 explains the causes and effects of one pilot's heroic actions.

Identify List three or four actions you have observed, experienced, or read about that could provide topics for cause-effect essays or paragraphs. (One idea is provided for you.)

Seeing a young person helping an older person with a disability

_____

_____

_____

What do you think?

How would you explain the quotation above? And what does it have to do with causes and effects? Share your thoughts with your classmates.

Reading and Reacting

Read   Read the following cause-effect essay from *FOCUS on College and Career Success* by Constance Staley and Steve Staley. This essay explores a common but ineffective study strategy—cramming for tests. Use the reading process to help you gain a full understanding of the essay. (See pages 14–15.) And keep your class notebook handy for notes and personal thoughts at different points during your reading.

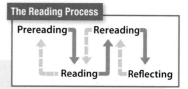

About the Authors

Constance Staley is a professor at the University of Colorado, Colorado Springs. During her time in the classroom, she has worked with thousands of students, helping them prepare for and succeed in college. *FOCUS on College and Career Success* puts in one place all of the valuable advice that she has shared with students over the years.

Steve Staley is dean of academics and professor of management and humanities at Colorado Technical University. He has also taught at the Air Force Academy, the Naval War College, and the University of Colorado, and has been an Air Force instructor pilot and served as director of corporate communications and educational development in a high-tech firm.

Cramming: Does "All or Nothing" Really Work?

Imagine yourself as the actor in the following scenarios. Compare these situations to cramming for tests.   *1*

- You haven't called your significant other since last year. Suddenly you appear at her door with candy, flowers, concert tickets, and dinner reservations at the most exclusive restaurant in town. You   *5* can't understand why she isn't happier to see you.

- You don't feed your dog for several months. When you finally bring him a plate loaded with ten T-bone steaks to make up for your neglect, you notice he's up and died on you. Oops!

Of course, these situations are ridiculous, aren't they? How could   *10* anyone ever neglect such basic necessities of life? There's an important point to be made here. Many things in life require continuous tending. If you ignore them for a time, catching up is next to impossible. Your college courses should be added to the list.

Believe it or not, some students give themselves permission to follow   *15*
this all-or-nothing principle of cramming in their academic work. They
sail along without investing much time or energy in their studies, and
then they try to make up for lost time right before an exam by cramming.
The word *cram* provokes a distinct visual image, and rightly so. Picture
yourself packing for a vacation in a warm, sunny place and hardly being   *20*
able to close your suitcase because it's crammed full. You can't decide what
to bring so you bring everything you can think of.

The same holds for cramming for a test. You try to stuff your brain full
of information, including things you won't need. Since you haven't taken
the time to keep up with learning as you go, you try to learn everything   *25*
at the last minute. Cramming is an attempt to overload information into
your unreliable working memory. It's only available for a very short time.
However, there are other reasons why cramming is a bad idea:

- Your anxiety level will rise quickly.

- Your sleep with suffer.   *30*

- Your immune system may go haywire.

- You may oversleep and miss the exam altogether.

Despite the warnings here, most student cram at some time or other
while taking college courses, and doing so may even give them a temporary
high and make them feel like they're suffering for a cause. But generally,   *35*
slow and steady wins the race.

"Cramming: Does 'All or Nothing' Really Work?" from STALEY/STALEY. *FOCUS on College and Career Success,* 1E. © 2012 Wadsworth, a part of Cengage Learning, Inc. Reproduced by permission. www.cengage.com/permissions

Vocabulary Practice

Explain or define the following words in the essay using your understanding of context clues and word parts as a guide. (See pages 24–25.) Also list the words and ideas in the text or any word parts that help you define each term.

- neglect
- tending
- investing
- overload

React   Answer the questions that follow about the essay on pages 273–274. Then discuss your responses with your classmates.

1. What is the main idea of the essay?

   Cramming for a test can cause many negative effects.

2. What causes and effects are covered? Consider filling in a cause-effect organizer to help you answer the question. (See page 257.)

Subject	
Causes	**Effects**
-	-
-	-
-	-

3. What are two things that you learned by reading this essay?

4. What questions, if any, do you still have about the topic?

5. How would you rate this essay and why?

   Weak ★ ★ ★ ★ ★ Strong

6. What was the authors' purpose for writing this essay?

Drawing Inferences

An *inference* is a logical conclusion you can make from context but that isn't specifically stated. However, a solid inference can result from a clear and careful understanding of a text. To practice drawing inferences, answer the following questions about the cause-effect selection on pages 273–274. Then share your answers with your classmates.

1. What conclusions can you draw from this essay about mindset of many students in terms of studying and school work?

2. How would the authors recommend that you study? What line or lines in the essay suggest this?

Writing

Use the guidelines on the next two pages to write your own cause-effect paragraph or cause-effect essay. Check with your instructor about any specific requirements he or she may have for this writing. And be sure to use the writing process to help you do your best work. (See pages 68–73.)

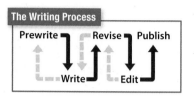

Prewriting

Choose one of the following or another appropriate idea for your cause-effect writing.

Writing Ideas

1. Write about one of the four cause-effect topics you identified in the planning activity on page 263.

2. Write about how a parent, teacher, or friend has affected your life.

3. Write about the causes and effects related to taking online classes.

4. Write about the effects of a movie or book on your life.

5. Write about the causes and effects of bottled water in our society.

6. Write about why people do or do not bother to vote.

7. Write about the widening gap between wealthy and poor Americans.

8. Write a cause-effect piece related to one of the photographs in *Fusion 1*.

When planning . . .

Refer to pages 263–264 to help with your prewriting and planning. Also use the tips below.

- Choose a topic you care about. Writing about something you find interesting is always the best choice. Make sure it will interest your readers as well.

- Make certain your listed causes and effects are clearly related and will make sense to your readers.

- Research any fuzzy areas so all the cause-effect connections are plain.

- If necessary, change your thesis or your topic sentence to match what you learn from your research.

Writing and Revising

Use the tips that follow and the information on pages 265–267 to help you with your drafting and revising.

When writing . . .

- Include an opening, a middle, and a closing part in your cause-effect piece. Each part has its own role to play. (See page 266.)
- Try to follow one of the general cause-effect organizations shown on page 261.
- Write your first draft freely, using your notes as a guide, but allowing yourself to explore new connections and explanations as they come to mind.
- If questions arise as you are writing the draft, make a note to return to these parts later.

When revising . . .

- Let your first draft sit unread for a while. Then read it critically, with fresh eyes. Also, reading a printed copy can help you see it differently.
- Ask a classmate or another writer to review and critique your writing. Use a peer-review sheet to guide the critique. (See page 547.)
- Make sure you have included enough details to explain the causes and effects.
- Consider the style of your writing. For most cause-effect writing, an academic style is appropriate. (See page 56.)

Editing

Refer to the checklist on page 271 when you are ready to edit your cause-effect writing for style and correctness.

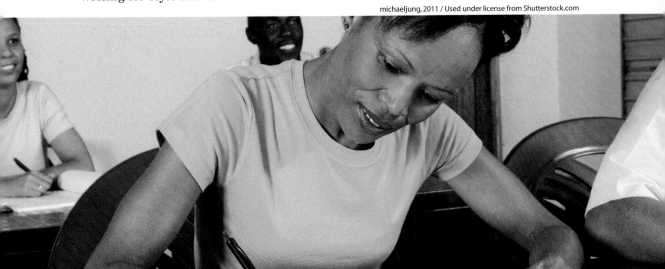

Reflecting on Classification Writing

Answer the following questions about your cause-effect reading and writing experiences in this chapter.

1. Why is cause-effect such a common structure in textbooks?

   _____

2. What is the most important thing you learned about reading a cause-effect paragraph or essay?

   _____

3. What reading strategy in this chapter do you find most helpful? Explain.

   _____

4. What is your favorite cause-effect piece in this chapter? Why?

   _____

5. What do you like most about the cause-effect paragraph you wrote for this chapter? Why?

   _____

6. What is one thing you would like to change in your paragraph?

   _____

7. What is the hardest part about cause-effect writing?

   _____

Key Terms to Remember

Whenever you read and write cause-effect paragraphs and essays, it's important to understand the following terms.

- **Causes**—the reasons for an action or a condition
- **Effects**—the results of a cause or an action
- **Cause-effect organizer**—a graphic organizer used to list causes in one column and effects in another
- **Evidence**—the facts and details that support or explain the main points in writing

13

"Another possible source of guidance for teenagers is television, but television's message has always been that the need for truth, wisdom, and world peace pales by comparison with the need for a toothpaste that offers whiter teeth and fresher breath."

—Dave Barry

Comparison

Take a close look at the photograph below. It is full of contrasts. A tree is contrasted with a man-made power station. The dark green and brown foreground is contrasted with the light blue background. And even the vertical stature of the tree and power station contrasts with the horizontal field and sky.

But the photo also contains some interesting comparisons. The water vapor from the power plant looks similar to the clouds overhead. The green leaves of the tree match the green grass. And the vegetation and the power station are both involved with energy use and production.

A paragraph that examines similarities and differences is called a comparison-contrast paragraph. In this chapter, you will read and react to comparison-contrast paragraphs and learn how to write one of your own.

Learning Outcomes

LO1 Understand comparison-contrast.
LO2 Learn about reading strategies.
LO3 Read and react to a professional paragraph.
LO4 Read and react to a student paragraph.
LO5 Practice reading strategies.
LO6 Plan a comparison-contrast paragraph.
LO7 Write the first draft.
LO8 Revise the writing.
LO9 Edit the writing.

What do you think?

What contrast is illustrated in the quotation above? Hint: The word *pales* means "to lack, or to be short of."

Hervé Hughes/Hemis/Corbis

LO1 Understanding Comparison-Contrast

Creating a ranking requires you to make comparisons. A food critic ranking the "5 Best Pizzerias in Town" would need to compare different pizza places to come up with an appropriate list. This same type of thinking is required to evaluate a ranking. If you disagreed with the food critic's list, you would need to make your own comparison: *The crust at La Familia's Pizza sets it apart from Ann's Pizza.*

The effectiveness of a ranking depends on the points of comparison that are made. In the example above, crust is used to compare two different pizzerias. The sauce, the toppings, or the staff's attentiveness could also serve as valuable points of comparison. As you study a ranking, always ask yourself if it is the result of a meaningful comparison. Ask the same question as you read and respond to a comparison-contrast paragraph.

> "There are dark shadows on the earth, but its lights are stronger in the contrast."
> —Charles Dickens

Comparing vs. Contrasting

When you compare, you look for similarities between subjects. When you contrast, you look for differences. Some comparison-contrast paragraphs focus on the similarities, while others focus on the differences. Still others may present a balanced analysis—equal numbers of similarities and differences. It all depends on the information the writer has discovered—and the points of comparison she or he makes.

INSIGHT

Related types of analysis include cause-effect and classification. These two forms require you to carefully examine the subjects, just as making comparisons requires. (See pages 231–254 and 255–278.)

Identify Write down a general field of study. Then write down jobs for people who graduate with that major. Finally, write two or three points of comparison for the jobs.

1. Field of study _____

2. Jobs in that field _____

_____

3. Points of comparison _____

_____

Reading

Comparison-contrast paragraphs involve two primary subjects, which must be evaluated equally. The strategies below will help you understand this type of paragraph.

LO2 Learning About Reading Strategies

Strategy 1: Recognizing Common Comparison-Contrast Patterns

Knowing the different patterns of organization used in comparison-contrast paragraphs will help you follow the main ideas in the text.

- **Point-by-point:** Some comparison-contrast writing is organized point by point. That is, each subject is addressed according to different points of comparison.
- **Subject-by-subject:** Other comparison-contrast writing discusses one subject in the first part and the other subject in the second part.
- **Similarities & differences:** Still other pieces address the similarities between the subjects in the first part and the differences in the second part.

> **INSIGHT**
>
> A writer may use a variation on one of the patterns, following it in general, but not exactly, from start to finish.

Point-by-Point

Topic Sentence

Point 1	
Subject 1	Subject 2

Point 2	
Subject 1	Subject 2

Point 3	
Subject 1	Subject 2

Closing Sentence

Subject-by-Subject

Topic Sentence

Subject 1

Subject 2

Closing Sentence

Similarities & Differences

Topic Sentence

Similarities

Differences

Closing Sentence

Strategy 2: Recognizing Comparison-Contrast Transitions

As you read comparison-contrast paragraphs, watch for transitions or linking words that alert you to specific comparisons and contrasts.

Transitions that show comparisons

also	both	in the same way	much as	likewise
much like	one way	similarly	another way	as

Transitions that show contrasts

although	even though	by contrast	but	however
on the one hand	on the other hand	otherwise	though	

LO3 Reading and Reacting to a Professional Paragraph

Read The following comparison-contrast paragraph comes from Gary Ferraro and Susan Andreatta's *Cultural Anthropology: An Applied Perspective,* a college textbook focusing on cultural anthropology. Remember to use the reading process to help you fully understand the text.

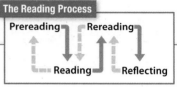

Cross-Cultural Miscues

Although both New Yorkers and Londoners speak English, there are   *1*
enough differences between American English and British English to
cause communication miscues. Speakers of English on opposite sides of the
Atlantic often use different words to refer to the same thing. To illustrate,
Londoners put their trash in a dustbin, not a garbage can; they take a   *5*
lift, not an elevator; and they live in flats, not apartments. To further
complicate matters, the same word used in England and the United States
can convey very different meanings. For example, in England the word
"homely" (as in the statement "I think your wife is very homely") means
warm and friendly, not plain . . . as in the United States; for the British,   *10*
the phrase "to table a motion" means to give an item a prominent place
on the agenda rather than to postpone taking action on an item, as in the
United States; and a rubber in British English is an eraser, not a condom.
These are just a few of the linguistic pitfalls that North Americans and
Brits may encounter when they attempt to communicate using their own   *15*
version of the "same" language.

"Cross-Cultural Miscues" from FERRARO/ANDREATTA. *Cultural Anthropology: An Applied Perspective,* 9E. © 2012 Wadsworth, a part of Cengage Learning, Inc.

React Answer the following questions about the paragraph. Then discuss your responses with your classmates.

1. What is the main point of this comparison-contrast paragraph? (See page 288.) There are major differences between American English and British English.

2. What pattern of organization do the authors use in the paragraph? (See page 281.) Point-by-Point

3. What transitions are used in the paragraph to help the reader follow the ideas? (See page 281.) although, for example, to illustrate

4. How would you rate this comparison-contrast paragraph and why? _____
   Weak ★ ★ ★ ★ ★ Strong

5. What did you learn about American English and British English? _____

A CLOSER LOOK   at Comparison

Using Comparison-Contrast Graphic Organizers

Comparison-contrast paragraphs focus on details that show similarities and differences. For help identifying and organizing such details, consider using one of the graphic organizers below.

Comparison T-Chart

A T-chart helps you gather details about the two topics of comparison. On one side of the chart, write details relating to the first subject, and on the second side, write details relating to the second subject.

> **CONSIDER THE READING-WRITING CONNECTION**
>
> Graphic organizers like the ones below help you analyze the details in a comparison-contrast paragraph. They will also help you gather details for your own comparison-contrast paragraphs.

Subject A	Subject B
Details	Details

Venn Diagram

A Venn diagram is a useful graphic organizer for any type of comparison writing. It is especially helpful for complex comparisons that examine both similarities and differences.

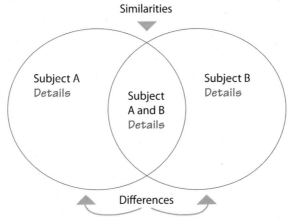

Graph Use one of the graphic organizers from above to identify the details of the next comparison-contrast paragraph that you read.

LO4 Reading and Reacting to a Student Paragraph

Read Read the following student paragraph, which compares the writer's father with the writer. Remember to use the steps in the reading process.

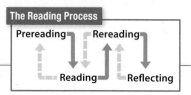

The Reading Process

Prereading   Rereading

Reading   Reflecting

Old Versus New

People often say I look like a younger version of my father, but in most   *1*
ways, we are very different. Our appearance is similar in that I have Dad's
brown eyes and black hair. We even have similar smiles, according to my
mom. But no one would say we look the same in the clothes we wear. Dad
dresses old school in work pants and button-down shirts, always tucked in.   *5*
For me, it's jeans and a Padres jersey, never tucked in. Our different dress
shows our different personalities. Dad is quiet, shy, and hardworking,
while I am very friendly and sometimes a little crazy. Neither of us,
however, is interested in causing trouble. Most of our differences come
from our different backgrounds. Dad was born in Mexico in a small town   *10*
south of Monterrey. He moved to San Diego as a young man and has
worked very long hours as a cook ever since. It has taken him a long time
to feel comfortable in this country, while the United States is all I have
ever known. Dad's tough life has made him more careful and serious than
I am, but if he had lived my life, he would be much more like me.   *15*

React Answer the following questions about the paragraph. Then discuss your answers with your classmates.

1. What is the main point of this comparison-contrast paragraph? (See page 288.) <u>The writer and his father look the same, but they are very different people.</u>

2. What pattern of organization does the author use in the paragraph? (See page 281.) <u>Similarities & Differences</u>

3. What key details (similarities and differences), does the author provide? Use a graphic organizer from page 283 to identify them.

   _____

   _____

4. How would you rate this comparison-contrast paragraph and why?

   Weak ★ ★ ★ ★ ★ Strong

   _____

   _____

A CLOSER LOOK at Analyzing the Details

Considering Points of Comparison

Points of comparison are the factors the author uses to compare two subjects. The paragraph on the previous page considers three factors in comparing and contrasting: appearance, personality, and background.

Identify Make a chart like the one below. Then fill it in with specific details about the writer and his father for each point of comparison

Point of comparison	Father	The Writer
Appearance (size, shape, hair color, clothing, etc.)		
Personality (attitude, outlook, feelings, actions, etc.)		
Background (place of birth, family, hometown, etc.)		

Identify As you read other comparison-contrast paragraphs in this chapter, identify the points of comparison. By doing so, you can better analyze the quality of the paragraph. An effective comparison-contrast paragraph …

- includes more than one point of comparison.
- provides details about both subjects for each point of comparison.

CONSIDER THE READING-WRITING CONNECTION

Points of comparison help readers analyze comparison-contrast paragraphs. They also help writers gather and organize their thoughts.

LO5 Practicing Reading Skills

When you read, you encounter new words and old words used in new ways. This page will help you understand these words.

Vocabulary: Using a Dictionary

A dictionary helps you understand the exact definition (denotation) of a word as well as how to pronounce it. A dictionary can also provide other information. Let's look at an example dictionary definition:

> pronunciation   part of speech   origin
> word ——**homely** \hom'-lē\ adj. [ME *hom,* fr. OE *haim* village, home + *ly* of, related to] 1. Plain or unattractive 2. Typical of a home 3. Comfortable and familiar 4. Natural and simple
> meanings (denotations)

Look Up   Each term below comes from the model paragraphs on pages 282 and 284. Use a dictionary to find and write down the pronunciation, part of speech, and at least one meaning of each term below.

1. miscues _____
2. prominent _____
3. agenda _____
4. postpone _____

5. linguistic _____
6. pitfall _____
7. jersey _____
8. hardworking _____

Vocabulary: Understanding Connotation

Often, in addition to having a literal definition, a word will have a connotation. A connotation is the implied meaning or feeling of a word. In the paragraph "Old Versus New," the writer uses words with differing connotations to describe his father and himself.

Father (Connotations)
old school (traditional)
work pants (practical)
tucked in (proper)
small town (rural)
long hours (hardworking)
tough life (determined)

Writer (Connotations)
jeans (youthful)
Padres shirt (sports fan)
untucked (relaxed)
San Diego (urban)
friendly (popular)
"a little crazy" (risk-taking)

Identify   For each word or phrase from "We Can Dance" on page 289, write a connotation.

1. basketball T-shirt _____
2. Obama country _____
3. sea of corn _____

4. hip-hop _____
5. techno _____
6. having a blast _____

Writing

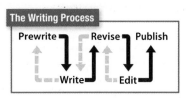

Starting on this page, you will plan and write a comparison-contrast paragraph about two people. Follow the writing process to help you do your best work. (See pages 68–73.)

LO6 Planning a Comparison-Contrast Paragraph

These two pages will help you gather your thoughts about your topic before you actually begin writing.

Selecting a Topic

Choose two people that interest you for your paragraph. They could be people you know well or complete strangers; people who are dead or alive; famous people or unknowns. You can even include yourself in the comparison.

Select For each heading below, identify two people you would like to compare and contrast. Then select the two people you would most like to write about in your paragraph.

Family   1. _____   2. _____

Friends   1. _____   2. _____

Role Models   1. _____   2. _____

Famous People   1. _____   2. _____

Experts in Your 1. _____   2. _____
Academic Major

Describing the People

Select Decide on three points of comparison to compare and contrast the two people. Consider the suggestions that follow.

- **Appearance:** Think of size, shape, hair color, eye color, skin color, gender, clothing, and so on.
- **Personality:** Think of attitude, outlook, feelings, actions, and so on.
- **Background:** Think of birthplace, schooling, hometown, family, and so on.
- **Interests:** Think of favorite activities, hobbies, friends, food, music, and so on.
- **Other**

Gathering Details

Below is an example of a Venn diagram that the author of the comparison-contrast paragraph on the next page used to note similarities and differences related to her three points of comparison.

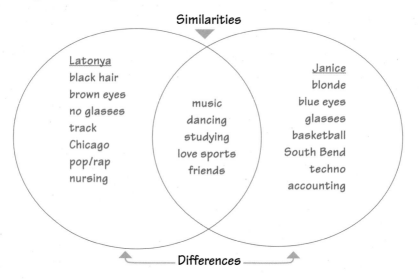

Similarities

Latonya
black hair
brown eyes
no glasses
track
Chicago
pop/rap
nursing

music
dancing
studying
love sports
friends

Janice
blonde
blue eyes
glasses
basketball
South Bend
techno
accounting

Differences

Gather Complete a Venn diagram with details that show the similarities and differences between your two subjects. At the top of your graphic organizer, name each subject. Then list your details in the appropriate spaces.

Tip

At this point, you may want to consider a pattern of organization for the main ideas of your paragraph. Consider the three common comparison-contrast patterns on page 281.

Writing a Topic Sentence

After collecting details for your paragraph, you are ready to write a topic sentence. This sentence should name your subjects and identify an important comparison between them.

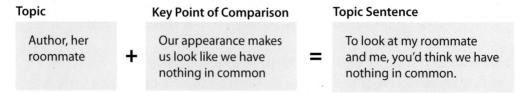

Topic		Key Point of Comparison		Topic Sentence
Author, her roommate	**+**	Our appearance makes us look like we have nothing in common	**=**	To look at my roommate and me, you'd think we have nothing in common.

Create Develop a topic sentence for your comparison-contrast paragraph, using the formula shown above as a guide. If necessary, write two or three versions until your statement says what you want it to say.

LO7 Writing the First Draft

Writing a first draft is your first attempt to connect all the thoughts you have gathered about your topic. Don't try to make everything perfect. Instead, simply get all your ideas on paper.

Read Carefully read through the paragraph. Note how the writer organizes the main ideas using the point-by-point pattern.

We Can Dance

Topic Sentence

To look at my roommate and me, you'd think we have   1
nothing in common. First of all, we look like complete
opposites. Janice is tall, with long blonde hair and blue eyes,
while I'm short, with black curly hair and brown eyes. Janice
loves wearing her basketball T-shirt from her Indiana State   5
Championship team. I prefer dressing in my cross-country
gear. We're also from completely different places. I'm a city

Body Sentences

girl, born and raised on the south side of Chicago, right in the
heart of Barack Obama country. Janice grew up on a farm
in a sea of corn, near South Bend, Indiana. So why do Janice   10
and I get along so well? Some might think it is our interest
in sports, but that's only part of it. When we first moved in
together, I turned on some hip-hop, and Janice started popping
and locking. She was good! So I showed her some of my moves,

Closing Sentence

and even tried the techno music she likes. Before you know it,   15
we came to be the best of friends, going to parties and dances
together and having a blast.

Consider the Craft

1. What do you like best about this paragraph?
2. What are your two favorite comparisons or contrasts?
3. Do you feel like the subjects make an interesting comparison?
4. How would you summarize the relationship between the two subjects?

Christos Georghiou, 2011 / Used under license from Shutterstock.com

The Working Parts of a Paragraph

A paragraph consists of three main parts, each of which has a special function. The information that follows explains each part.

Paragraph Outline

Topic Sentence: The topic sentence sets the stage for the paragraph. It should introduce both subjects and say something about the comparison. (See page 288 for the topic-sentence formula.)

Body Sentences: The body sentences share details about each subject for each point of comparison.

Closing Sentence: The closing sentence sums up the comparison by offering a final thought about the subjects.

Drafting Tips

When you write a comparison-contrast paragraph, you are showing how two subjects are alike or unalike. Consider the following techniques to give your reader a clear view of your subjects.

- **Use transitions that compare and contrast to connect ideas,** but be careful not to overuse them. Refer to page 281 for a full list of appropriate transitional words.

- **Address each subject with plenty of details,** making sure you use details that "show" rather than "tell." (See page 291.)

- **At the same time, don't overuse details that make your paragraph too long.** Use only those that offer a key similarity or difference between the two subjects.

- **Provide comparisons,** but always back them up with sound logic.

Write Develop your first draft using the information on this page and your planning on pages 287–288 as a guide.

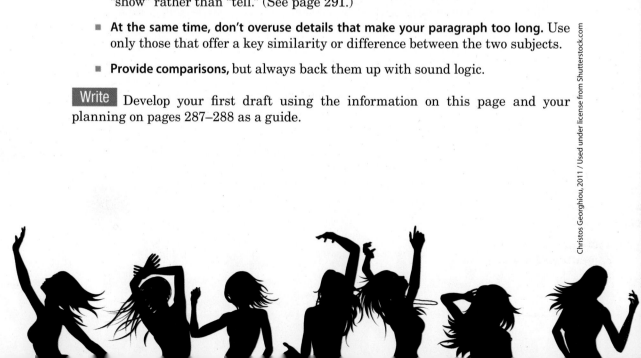

LO8 Revising the Writing

Start the revising process by reading your first draft two or three times to get a feel for your work so far. Then have one of your classmates read and react to your work using a response sheet as a guide. (See page 547.)

Show, Don't Tell

Your paragraph will be stronger if you show similarities and differences, not just tell about them. Consider the examples that follow.

Showing	vs.	Telling
She's popping and locking.		She likes to dance.
She lives on a farm in a sea of corn.		She is a country girl.
She lives in her championship jersey.		She is an athlete.

Revising in Action:

Read aloud the unrevised and then the revised version of the following excerpt. Note the improvements made by showing instead of telling.

> with long blonde hair and blue eyes,
>
> . . . First of all, we look like complete opposites. Janice is ~~white and~~ tall, ∧
>
> with black curly hair and brown eyes.
>
> while I'm ~~black and~~ short, ~~We like different sports.~~ Janice loves basketball,
>
> wearing her basketball T-shirt from her Indiana State Championship team.
>
> ~~and I like track.~~ We're also from completely different places. . . .
>
> I prefer dressing in my cross-country gear and taking off down the road.

Revise Improve your writing, using the following checklist and your classmate's comments on the response sheet. Continue working until you can check off each item in the list.

Revising Checklist

Ideas

☐ 1. Do I compare two interesting people?

☐ 2. Do I use three points of comparison?

☐ 3. Do I include details that show instead of tell?

Organization

☐ 4. Do I have a topic sentence, body sentences, and a closing sentence?

☐ 5. Have I used an appropriate organizational plan?

☐ 6. Have I used transitions to connect my sentences?

Voice

☐ 7. Do I sound knowledgeable and interested?

LO9 Editing the Writing

Commas tell the reader when to pause, making the writing easy to follow.

Commas After Introductory Words

Many sentences naturally start with the subject. Some sentences, however, start with an introductory phrase or clause. A comma is used to separate a long introductory word group from the rest of the sentence. When you read sentences like these out loud, you will naturally pause after the introductory words. That tells you that a comma is needed to separate these words from the rest of the sentence. See the examples that follow.

Introductory Word Groups:

After my third birthday, my brother was born. (prepositional phrase)

When he arrived on the scene, life changed for me. (dependent clause)

Punctuation Practice   Read the sentences below, out loud. Listen for the natural pause after an introductory phrase or clause. Place a comma to set off the introductory words.

1. When my younger brother was born, I was jealous.
2. Before he showed up, I had Mom all to myself.
3. At the beginning of our relationship, we didn't get along very well.
4. As the years passed, my brother stopped being a pest and became a friend.
5. As a matter of fact, we both came to love basketball.
6. Without my younger brother, I wouldn't have anyone to push my basketball skills.
7. Taking that into account, our long rivalry has helped us both.
8. Since our teenage years, we've become best friends.
9. Although we still tease each other, we're not being vicious.
10. When we bump fists, I sometimes remember when we bumped heads.

Apply   Read your comparison-contrast paragraph and look for sentences that begin with introductory phrases or clauses. If you do not find any, add an introductory phrase or clause to a few sentences to vary their beginnings. Does this help your writing read more smoothly? Remember to use a comma to separate a long introductory word group from the rest of the sentence. (For more information, see page 514 and 516.)

Commas with Extra Information

Some sentences include phrases or clauses that add information in the middle or at the end of sentences. This information should be set off with commas. You can recognize this extra information because it can be removed without changing the basic meaning of the sentence. When you read the sentence out loud, there's a natural pause before and after the phrase or clause. This indicates where you are to place the commas.

> **Extra Information:**
>
> I have a tough time waking up, not surprisingly.
>
> My mother, who works two jobs, makes me breakfast every morning.

Punctuation Practice   In each sentence, use a comma or commas to separate extra information. Listen for the natural pause. Some sentences may not have extra information.

1. My mother works as a waitress which is a tough job.
2. She also works as a licensed practical nurse which is an even tougher job.
3. The nursing home the one on Main and 7th is strict.
4. A time card punched one second late is docked fifteen minutes an unfair policy.
5. A time card punched ten minutes early does not earn overtime.
6. The restaurant job pays minimum wage which is not much.
7. Tips from a good lunch not the busiest time can double Mom's pay.
8. What I've learned about determination real grit I learned from Mom.
9. She wants to help me qualify for a better job a selfless goal.
10. I want exactly the same thing no surprise there.

Apply   Read your comparison paragraph and look for sentences that have extra information. If you haven't included any, add some extra information in a sentence or two. Do these additions make your writing more interesting? Remember to use commas to set off extra information in your sentences. (For more on comma use, see page 520.)

INSIGHT ————————————————————————————

Commas are very important in written English. For more practice with comma use, see pages 513–522.

Marking a Paragraph

The model that follows has a number of errors.

Editing Practice   Correct the following paragraph, using the correction marks below. One correction has been done for you.

Into the Spotlight

My wife and I love each other, but it's hard to imagine how we could be   *1*
more different. Lupe's a social butterfly. She been always meeting people
for coffee or talking to people on the phone. By contrast, I'm private. I
work at U.S. steel and come home. The only person I really want to be
with is Lupe, but she's always dragging me out to partys. Their is another   *5*
big difference. Lupe, who is a great singer and dancer, loves theater. She's
been in a dozen plays. When it come to me the idea of being on stage is
terrifying. She convinced me once to be in a play, I forgot my one line. so,
is there anything Lupe and I have in common? We love each other. Lupe
needs me to keep her grounded, and I need her to pry me out of the house.   *10*
We've even figured out a way to work around the theater thing. Next
play she is in, I'll work set crew. That's how we get along so well. I work
backstage, setting props for her, and getting what she needs. Then she
walks into the spotlight and performs.

Correction Marks

⌿	delete	⌃	add comma	⌃	add word
d͇	capitalize	?	add question mark	⊙	add period
ȼ	lowercase			⬭	spelling
⋀	insert	⌄	insert an apostrophe	⤸	switch

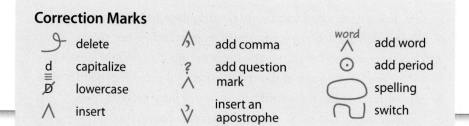

INSIGHT

As you've seen, commas are needed to set off extra information in a sentence. Sometimes the extra information comes between the subject and the verb:

Lupe, who is a great singer and dancer, loves theater.

But when there is no extra information to set off, do not separate the subject and verb with a comma.

Incorrect: Lupe, loves theater.   **Correct:** Lupe loves theater.

Correcting Your Paragraph

Now it's time to correct your own paragraph.

Edit Prepare a clean copy of your revised writing and use the following checklist to look for errors. Continue working until you can check off each item in the list.

Editing Checklist

Words
- [ ] 1. Have I used specific nouns and verbs? (See page 102.)
- [ ] 2. Have I used more action verbs than "be" verbs? (See page 458.)

Sentences
- [ ] 3. Have I varied the beginnings and lengths of sentences? (See pages 104–105.)
- [ ] 4. Have I combined short choppy sentences? (See page 105.)
- [ ] 5. Have I avoided shifts in sentences? (See page 422.)
- [ ] 6. Have I avoided fragments and run-ons? (See pages 410–413, 416–417.)

Conventions
- [ ] 7. Do I use correct verb forms (*he saw,* not *he seen*)? (See pages 464, 466.)
- [ ] 8. Do my subjects and verbs agree (*she speaks,* not *she speak*)? (See pages 394–403.)
- [ ] 9. Have I capitalized first words and proper nouns and adjectives?
- [ ] 10. Have I used commas after long introductory word groups? (See pages 574–577.)
- [ ] 11. Have I punctuated dialogue correctly? (See pages 148–149.)
- [ ] 12. Have I carefully checked my spelling?

Adding a Title

Make sure to add an attention-getting title. Here are three simple strategies for creating one.

- Use a phrase from the paragraph:

  Into the Spotlight

- Point to a similarity or difference:

  We Can Dance

- Use the word "versus":

  Old Versus New

Create Prepare a clean final copy of your paragraph and proofread it before sharing it.

"There is no teaching to compare with example."
—Sir Robert Baden-Powell

Review and Enrichment

You have been introduced to reading and writing comparison-contrast paragraphs. This section expands on that information by providing a comparison-contrast essay to read and respond to. You will also be given a number of writing ideas to choose from and develop. These activities will broaden your understanding of comparison.

Prereading

Many meaningful comparisons can be made about the places you have been, either in your hometown or on vacation. One neighborhood in your hometown may be very different from another. Or two places separated by an ocean may be more similar than you ever imagined.

CONSIDER THE TRAITS

As you read the essay that begins on the next page, focus first on the **ideas**. Then consider the **organization**—the comparison-contrast pattern used in the essay. Also note the author's **voice**—how he speaks to the reader. Finally, ask yourself if these traits combine to produce a satisfying reading experience.

Identify Think of two places you know a lot about. Then answer the following questions about both places. Share your thoughts with a classmate.

1. Write three adjectives to describe each place.

   Place 1: _____

   Place 2: _____

2. What is the main feature of each place?

   Place 1: _____

   Place 2: _____

3. What feeling do you get in each place?

   Place 1: _____

   Place 2: _____

What do you think?

Explain what you think Sir Robert Baden-Powell means in the quotation at the top of the page. Do you agree with him? Share your thoughts with your classmates.

Reading and Reacting

Read The following comparison-contrast essay takes a look at critical and creative thinking. The essay focuses on these subjects but also compares them to two types of breathing.

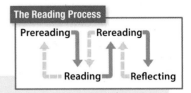

About the Author

Robert King is coauthor of *Inquire: A Guide to 21st Century Learning* as well as two dozen published novels.

Thinking Like Breathing

Which is more important for today's students, **critical thinking** or **creative thinking**? It's a trick question. I may as well ask which is more important, breathing out or breathing in? "Whichever one I need to do right now" is one good answer to this last question. Another is "Neither is *more* important since I need both to stay alive." It's the same with critical and creative thinking.   *5*

The Thought Exchange

Creative and critical thinking are two halves of a cycle: **inspiration** and **expiration**.

Creative thinking draws in possibilities. It is an expansive process,   *10* filling you with new ideas from the outside. Creativity reaches beyond what is known and into the unknown . . . to discover something new. Creativity is not necessarily discerning. You don't separate **nitrogen** from **oxygen** before you breathe it in. Your chest simply expands, and in it comes. Creative thinking floods you with new possibilities.   *15*

Critical thinking, on the other hand, sorts through the possibilities to do something practical. Critical thinking analyzes, applies, and evaluates. It categorizes, compares, contrasts, and traces causes and effects. It's like separating oxygen from the air to enrich your cells, or extracting the **carbon dioxide** from your blood to get rid of the waste. Critical thinking   *20*

1

takes what creative thinking has amassed and sorts it, keeping the best and discarding the worst.

Thinking as Respiration

All sorts of activities require this exchange between critical and creative thinking. For example, think of the process of solving a problem. *25* You start by analyzing the problem (critical), and then you brainstorm solutions (creative). Next you evaluate the solutions and choose the best one (critical). At that point, you have to create your solution (creative). Once it is done, you need to test it and evaluate it (critical). Finally, you can make improvements to your solution and put it into practice (creative). *30*

You'll find you use a similar process when you write an essay, create a college schedule, and even plan a party. Most activities require an interchange between critical and creative thinking, and you switch back and forth as easily as breathing.

Vocabulary

critical thinking
close, careful thinking that analyzes a topic, seeking realities

creative thinking
open-minded exploration of a topic, seeking possibilities

inspiration
breathing in; also, something that provides an idea

expiration
breathing out

nitrogen
gas that makes up most of our environment

oxygen
gas needed to support animal life

carbon dioxide
gas waste product of animal respiration

respiration
the act of breathing

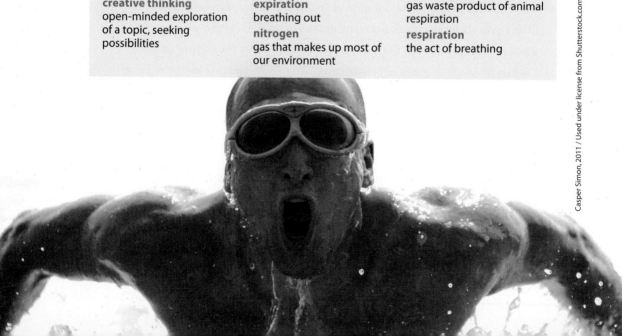

Casper Simon, 2011 / Used under license from Shutterstock.com

React Answer the following questions about "Thinking Like Breathing." Then share your responses with your classmates.

1. What are the two main subjects of this essay?

   critical thinking and creative thinking
   _____

2. Does this essay focus on the similarities or differences of the two subjects? Explain.

   differences
   _____

3. What details are provided about the two subjects? Use a T-chart or a Venn diagram to identify them.

   _____

   _____

4. How does the use of headings help you understand the essay's organization?

   _____

   _____

5. How would you rate this essay and why?

   Weak ★ ★ ★ ★ ★ Strong

   _____

   _____

6. What did you learn about the two subjects?

   _____

   _____

Vocabulary Practice

Explain or define the following words in the essay by using context clues and your understanding of word parts. (See pages 24–25.) Also list the clues or word parts that help you define the terms.

- expansive (line 10)
- discerning (line 13)
- extracting (line 19)
- amassed (line 21)

Writing

Write a comparison-contrast paragraph or essay following the guidelines on the next two pages. Check with your instructor about any specific requirements that he or she may have.

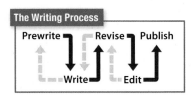

Prewriting

Choose one of the following writing ideas for your comparison-contrast writing or find an appropriate topic of your own.

Writing Ideas

1. Write about the pair of places you chose to compare in the activity on page 296.

2. Write a review comparing two of your favorite restaurants.

3. Write about the music of two bands or artists from a similar genre.

4. Write a comparison of two historical figures.

5. Write a comparison of two of your professors' teaching styles.

Leah-Anne Thompson, 2011 / Used under license from Shutterstock.com

When planning . . .

Refer to pages 287–288 to help you with your prewriting and planning. Also use the tips that follow.

- Choose subjects that are specific enough for a paragraph or an essay and that you know a lot about or can research effectively.
- Choose appropriate points of comparison and a pattern of organization. (See pages 285 and 281.)
- Collect plenty of details relating to those points of comparison. Use a graphic organizer to collect and organize the details. (See page 283.)
- Review the examples of comparison-contrast writing in this chapter to see how they are developed.

Writing and Revising

Refer to pages 289–291 to help you write and revise your first draft. Also use the tips that follow.

When writing . . .

- Include opening, middle, and closing parts in your writing. Each part has a specific role. (See page 290.)
- Follow the pattern of organization and points of comparison you chose during your planning, but be open to making changes in organization or content if the writing is not logically coming together.
- Use transitional words to help the reader follow your ideas. (See page 281.)

When revising . . .

- Ask yourself if your paragraph or essay contains any dead spots that either need more details or should be cut back.
- Decide if any parts are confusing or cause you to stumble. Rewrite these parts as needed.
- Determine if you have organized your details in the best way.
- Have at least one trusted peer react to your writing.

Editing

Refer to the checklist on page 295 when you are ready to edit your comparison-contrast writing for style and correctness.

ene, 2011 / Used under license from Shutterstock.com

Reflecting on Comparison-Contrast Writing

Answer the following questions about your reading and writing experiences in this chapter.

1. What makes a comparison-contrast paragraph enjoyable to read?

   _____

2. What is your favorite paragraph in this chapter?

   _____

3. Which reading strategy in this chapter seems the most helpful? Explain.

   _____

4. What is the most important thing you have learned about reading comparison-contrast paragraphs?

   _____

5. What do you like most about the first comparison-contrast paragraph that you wrote in this chapter? Explain.

   _____

6. What is one thing that you would like to change in your paragraph?

   _____

7. What is the most important thing that you have learned about comparison-contrast writing?

   _____

8. What is the hardest thing about this type of writing? The easiest?

   _____

Key Terms to Remember

When you read and write comparison-contrast paragraphs and essays, it's important to understand the following terms.

- **Comparing**—showing how two or more subjects are similar
- **Contrasting**—showing how two or more subjects are different
- **Points of comparison**—the special elements or features used to make a comparison (size, strength, appearance, and so on)
- **Patterns of organization for comparison-contrast writing**—point-by-point, subject-by-subject, or similarities and differences. (See page 281.)

14

Argumentation

"Use soft words and hard arguments."
—English Proverb

Have you ever wondered why political candidates participate in debates? It's no accident. Argumentation plays a central role in any civilization. Given our variety of personalities, backgrounds, values, and assumptions, the only way of coming to a consensus is to discuss our opinions. That discussion requires the ability to argue in its original sense: to clearly state a position, to back it up with reasonable support, and to address any arguments against it.

Of course, argumentation plays its daily role outside of politics, as well. Every day in school, at work, and at home, we present our opinions and the reasons to support them. In this chapter, you will learn to refine your own ability to present arguments.

Learning Outcomes

LO1 Understand argumentation.

LO2 Learn about reading strategies.

LO3 Read and react to a professional paragraph.

LO4 Read and react to a student paragraph.

LO5 Practice reading skills.

LO6 Plan an argumentation paragraph.

LO7 Write the first draft.

LO8 Revise the writing.

LO9 Edit the writing.

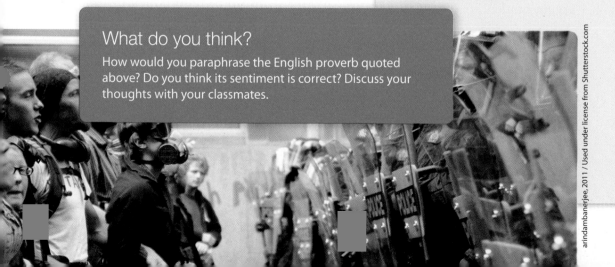

What do you think?

How would you paraphrase the English proverb quoted above? Do you think its sentiment is correct? Discuss your thoughts with your classmates.

arindambanerjee, 2011 / Used under license from Shutterstock.com

LO1 Understanding Argumentation

As the quotation below shows, the word "argument" is commonly misused. It doesn't mean to bicker, squabble, or fight. Those things happen when people don't engage in honest debate.

To argue means to present and support a disputable position. It assumes first considering all sides of a situation and then coming to an opinion. This is why Andre Maurois says, "The difficult part in an argument is not to defend one's opinion, but rather to know it."

Once you've done your research, you will be prepared to argue a position convincingly. It's simply a matter of organizing and presenting the support that led you to your conclusion. As Dale Carnegie puts it, "The best argument is that which seems merely an explanation."

> "People generally quarrel because they cannot argue."
> —Gilbert K. Chesterton

Argumentation Versus Persuasion

The main purpose of persuasion is to be convincing. A campaigning politician trying to gain votes through persuasion will very likely appeal more to the voters' personal interests—"Follow me. I can fix the economy!"—than to logic and reason. A thorough, logical argument may be persuasive, but that is not its main purpose. Its real intent is to prove the strength of a certain line of thinking.

Identify Brainstorm a list of debatable topics you would like to know more about. (Avoid topics on which you already have a firm opinion, unless you are honestly prepared to have that opinion challenged.) Compare your list with those of your classmates, and chose an interesting topic to explore in a paragraph of argumentation.

INSIGHT
In order to be convincing, you must be aware of opposing viewpoints on your topic and either counter them directly or present a weight of evidence that overshadows them. Notice how the examples in this chapter address counterarguments.

_____

_____

_____

_____

_____

Reading

Reading argument paragraphs requires a close examination of the main claim and supporting details. This section provides valuable reading practice.

LO2 Learning About Reading Strategies

In an argument, the author takes a position, supports it with evidence, and addresses counterclaims. The reader considers the evidence presented and decides whether to accept the author's position.

Strategy 1: Considering the Author's Background

Before you read, consider the author's background with the topic. This can help you understand the writer's authority or possible bias. (Often, you can find details about the author in the writing or a short biography that accompanies it. Sometimes you may have to do a Web search or other research to learn more.) Fill in a chart like the following one.

Topic	
Author:	
Author's Position	
Author's Background	

Strategy 2: Considering the Reader's Background

Also review your own background and assumptions about a topic before reading. That way, you'll be best prepared to reflect sincerely on the author's argument. To the chart above, add the following:

My Position:	
My Background:	

LO3 Reading and Reacting to a Professional Essay

Read In this argumentation paragraph, the author discusses benefits of "wind farming." Use the reading process to get the most from the paragraph, along with the reading strategies on page 305.

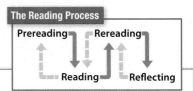

The Reading Process

Prereading → Rereading

Reading → Reflecting

Support Wind Farm Energy

To counteract its dependence on fossil fuels, the United States must invest in wind farms for its energy needs. A wind farm is made up of a group of large wind turbines, which convert wind into electric energy. The benefits of wind farms are numerous. First, wind is a free and renewable source of energy. In comparison, fossil fuels like oil and coal are limited in supply and cost money to extract from the earth. Secondly, wind farms are a clean energy source. Unlike power plants, which emit dangerous pollutants, wind farms release no pollution into the air or water, meaning less smog, less acid rain, and fewer green house emissions. And then there's this: the National Wind Resource Center reports that running a single wind turbine has the potential to displace 2,000 tons of carbon dioxide, or the equivalent of one square mile of forest trees ("The Opportunity"). But despite being the fastest growing energy source in the U.S., wind energy accounts for only one percent of power supplied in the country ("Renewable"). If the United States wants to limit carbon emissions and lessen its dependence on fossil fuels, it must act now and invest more money in wind farms. The answer is in the air.

1

5

10

15

Works Cited

"The Opportunity." *Windcenter.com*. NWRC, n.d. Web. 31 Jan. 2012.
"Renewable Energy Sources in the United States." *nationalatlas.gov*. National Atlas of the United States, 26 Jan. 2011. Web. 31 Jan. 2012.

React Answer the following questions. Then discuss your responses with your classmates.

1. What is the paragraph's main idea? The United States must invest more in wind energy, as a means of using less fossil fuels.

2. What main claims does the author offer to support this idea? _____

3. How are alternatives (counterclaims) addressed? _____

4. How would you rate this paragraph? **Weak** ★ ★ ★ ★ ★ **Strong** Why?

_____

A CLOSER LOOK at Argumentation

When reading argumentation, it is important to keep an open mind but watch for bias. To do so, consider the writer's treatment of claims and counter claims.

Identifying Claims

You can use a graphic like the one below to help identify the claims in an argument. List each claim separately, and then write any supporting details below it.

Position: _____

Claim 1: _____

Supporting Evidence: _____

_____

Claim 2: _____

Supporting Evidence: _____

_____

Considering Counterclaims

Also consider any counterclaims addressed in the writing. List each separately, with reasons given to dismiss them.

Counterclaim 1: _____

Dismissing Arguments: _____

_____

Counterclaim 2: _____

Dismissing Arguments: _____

_____

Identify Use graphics like the ones above to list claims, evidence, counterclaims, and dismissing arguments for the paragraph on page 306.

LO4 Reading and Reacting to a Student Paragraph

Read Read the following argument paragraph about text messaging while driving. Remember to use the steps in the reading process. (See pages 14–15.)

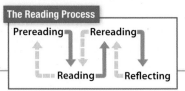

The Reading Process

Prereading → Rereading
Reading → Reflecting

Text Messaging and Driving Don't Mix

Text messaging while driving should be banned in all states because the   1
practice is making U.S. roadways dangerous. Car crashes rank among the
leading causes of death in the United States, but many blame the frequency
of drinking and driving and ignore the dangers of texting and driving.
Studies by the National Highway Traffic Safety Administration show that   5
text messaging while driving is about six times more likely to result in an
accident than drunk driving (Pennsylvania Truck Accident Lawyers). And
according to the Human Factors and Ergonomics Society, mobile devices
contribute to 2,600 deaths and 330,000 injuries per year ("The Use of Cell
Phones"). The major danger associated with texting is the distraction   10
it causes to the driver. A driver whose eyes are concentrating on a phone
instead of the road is more likely to get in an accident. Some critics say
teenage drivers are the problem, but 20 percent of adults in a recent AAA
study admitted to regularly sending text messages while driving ("Text
Messaging"). At least 34 states and the District of Columbia understand   15
the aforementioned dangers and have passed bans on texting while driving
("Cell Phone"). Let's make all of our roads a safer place; the time has come
to make text messaging while driving illegal in every state.

Works Cited

"Cell Phone and Texting Laws." *GHSA.org*. Governors Highway Safety Association,
Sept. 2011. Web. 31 Jan. 2012.
"Text Messaging and Cell Phone Use While Driving." *AAAFoundation.org*. AAA, 12
Oct. 2009. PDF file.
"The Use of Cell Phones While Driving." *USLegal.com*. US Legal, Inc., 2010. Web.
31 Jan. 2012.
Pennsylvania Truck Accident Lawyers. "Teens, Texting and Driving." *Findlaw.com*.
Findlaw, 1 Oct. 2009. Web. 31 Jan. 2012.

React Answer the following questions. Then discuss your responses with your classmates.

1. What is the main idea in this paragraph? What claims does the writer make to support this idea? _Text messaging while driving should be banned in all_ _states because it is dangerous._

2. What counterclaims does he address? _____

3. How effective is this paragraph? **Weak** ★ ★ ★ ★ ★ **Strong** Why? _____

A CLOSER LOOK at Considering Counterclaims

A good argument does not ignore opposing viewpoints. Instead, it acknowledges them and explains why they don't destroy the argument. When reading, notice how well the author does or does not address your ideas to the contrary. When writing, the better you predict your own reader's possible objections to your argument, the better you can address them, thereby making your argument stronger.

Identify On your own paper, make a chart like the one below. List two counterclaims addressed in the paragraph on page 308. Then explain how the writer responds to those counterclaims. Finally, list any other objections readers might have, and provide an idea of how you might address them.

Position:

Counterclaim 1:	Response:
Counterclaim 2:	Response:
Reader Objection:	Your Response:

INSIGHT

Not all possible objections need be addressed in argument writing. By countering the most important ones and providing plenty of support for your own position, you may outweigh minor objections without actually stating them. For example, the writer of the paragraph on the previous page doesn't address the possible objection, "Sometimes a text message is important," because his statistics ("six times more likely to result in an accident than drunk driving" and "2,600 deaths per year") already overshadow that counterclaim.

LO5 Practicing Reading Skills

As you read an argument, watch for the difference between facts and opinions. This page will help you understand the difference.

Critical Thinking: Separating Facts and Opinions

A fact is a statement that can be directly proven to be true. An opinion is a personal belief that is disputable because it cannot be directly proven. Opinions often present the meaning of facts, give suggestions for policies, or predict what might happen in the future. Note how a fact (shown below in the center) can spawn opposite opinions.

Opinions ◄———	Facts ———►	Opinions
We need to build many more wind farms.	Wind energy currently accounts for only 1 percent of power supplied in the country.	Wind energy will never be able to replace fossil fuels.
Wind farms should be built in forests to double the carbon savings.	A single wind turbine can displace 2,000 tons of carbon dioxide, the same amount as 1 square mile of forest.	Trees should never be felled to make room for wind farms.

Identify   Tell whether each piece of text below is an opinion or a fact.

1. Text messaging while driving should be banned. _opinion_____

2. Mobile devices contribute to 2,600 deaths per year. _fact_____

3. Thirty-four states have banned texting while driving. _fact_____

4. Teenagers are the problem. _opinion_____

5. Twenty percent of adults admit to texting while driving. _fact_____

6. The time has come to outlaw texting while driving. _opinion_____

Write   For each fact listed below, write two opposite opinions.

Opinions ◄———	Facts ———►	Opinions
	Wind turbines can produce electrical energy only when the wind is blowing.	
	The four most productive wind turbines operate in Denmark, while the tallest wind turbine at 205 meters is in Germany.	

Writing

In your own argument paragraph, you will develop a claim about a debatable topic. Be sure to write about a topic that you truly care about. Use the writing process to help you do your best work. (See pages 68–73.)

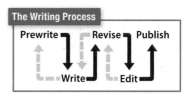

LO6 Prewriting: Planning

Your prewriting begins by selecting a topic that interests you, developing a position about it, and refining that position.

Selecting a Topic

Will began his topic search by browsing newspapers, magazines, and the Internet for current issues that people have strong feelings about. When a friend of his almost ran off the road because of texting, Will had found his topic.

Select List three or four debatable issues you could write about in an argument paragraph. Choose your favorite topic.

_____   _____

_____   _____

Stating a Position

Once you decide on a topic, you need to state a preliminary position about it. In one sentence, write a defensible position statement using the formula below.

Topic		Position	Position Statement
Text messaging while driving	**+** *would, should, must, ought to, needs* **+**	be banned in all states **=**	Text messaging while driving should be banned in all states.

Create Write a position statement by providing the topic, selecting a verb, and indicating your position.

would, should, must, ought to, needs

Topic: _____ **+** **+**

Position: _____ **=**

Position Statement: _____

Refining Your Position

With your initial position written, use the following strategies to develop and refine your opinion on the issue:

- **Research** all possible positions on the issue. Who supports each position and why? Who opposes your position and why?
- **Gather** solid evidence regarding your issue. Does the most compelling evidence support or oppose your position?
- **Refine** your position. At this point, you may have new convictions about your position, or you may have changed your mind about it. Before you are ready to write, clarify your position statement.

Gathering Details

When you take a stand on an issue, you must gather convincing support to defend your position. The writer of the paragraph on page 308 gathered four different types of details to support his position: **facts**, **statistics**, **testimonials**, and **predictions**.

Support Chart

Fact	At least 34 states and the District of Columbia have passed laws against text messaging while driving.
Statistic	According to the U.S. Department of Transportation, mobile devices contribute to 2,600 deaths per year.
Testimony	In the words of U.S. Secretary of Transportation Ray LaHood, "This is an important safety step, and we will be taking more to eliminate the threat of distracted driving."
Prediction	Roads will be safer if texting while driving is banned in all states.

Gather Create a support chart below with the research you have gathered about your issue. Try to include at least one fact, statistic, piece of testimony, and prediction. If you have not found supporting details for each category, consider doing additional research.

Vocabulary

facts
details that offer statements or claims of verified information

statistics
details that offer concrete numbers about a topic

testimonials
details that offer insight from an authority on the topic

predictions
details that offer insights into possible outcomes or consequences by forecasting what might happen under certain conditions

LO7 Writing the First Draft

Let your first draft be an experiment to get your thoughts and research down on paper. Don't worry about trying to get everything perfect.

Read Read and consider the following argument for a mandatory public service program.

Citizen Service

Topic Sentence

Our country and our youth would benefit from a one- or two-year period of national service after high school. Democracy has a long history of service by private citizens. Think of the citizen soldiers of Ancient Greece or the Minutemen of colonial America. Consider today's National Guard members, Reservists, and Peace Corps volunteers. Ask most people who have served, and they will tell you the experience helped them grow up and discover their potential. It also made them more conscious of their responsibility to their nation. Of course, some may object that mandatory service would violate our liberties. However, we already require public education from kindergarten through high school. Adding another year or two shouldn't matter, especially since people would have a choice of how they wished to serve. The military's various branches would offer possibilities, as would the Peace Corps, Americorps, and other civilian volunteer organizations. In these various services, people would learn life and career skills, and under a bill currently going through Congress, they could also earn grants for college ("Mandatory"). A nation is only as good as its people. Adding a year or two of public service to our educational track would benefit us all.

Body Sentences

Closing Sentence

Works Cited

"Mandatory Public Service." *FactCheck.org*. U. of Penn., 21 Apr. 2009. Web. 31 Jan. 2012.

Consider the Craft

1. How effectively does the paragraph make its claim?
2. How effectively does it address counterclaims?
3. What do you like most about this paragraph?
4. What improvements might you suggest?

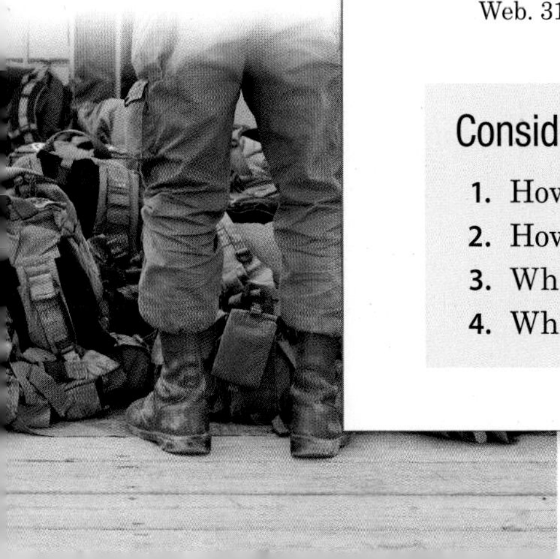

dominique landau, 2011 / Used under license from Shutterstock.com

The Working Parts of a Paragraph

As the previous page shows, a paragraph has three main parts, each with its own purpose.

Paragraph Outline

Topic Sentence: The topic sentence states your position.

Body Sentences: The body sentences support the position using logical reasoning and reliable details. These sentences also address counterclaims.

Closing Sentence: A closing sentence (or two) reinforces your argument and (if appropriate) encourages your reader to adopt it.

Drafting Tips

When writing an argument paragraph, appeal to the reader with logical reasoning and compelling evidence.

In the opening…

- Lead up to your claim, if necessary, by providing reasonable background.
- Make your claim firmly but respectfully.

In the middle…

- Give the reader plenty of solid reasons to adopt your point of view.
- Use valid research to back up your position.
- Address any counterclaims politely, providing a convincing argument against them.

In the closing…

- Restate your position in light of the reasons you have provided.
- If appropriate, give your reader a call to action.

TRAITS

Transition words that show importance:
first of all / to begin / secondly / another reason / the best reason / also / in addition / more importantly / most importantly / finally

Write Prepare the first draft of your argument paragraph using the information on this page and the planning on pages 311–312 as a guide.

LO8 Revising the Writing

Start the revising process by reading your first draft two or three times to get a feel for your work so far. Then have one of your classmates read and react to your work using a response sheet as a guide. (See page 547.)

Five Common Logical Fallacies

A logical fallacy is a false assertion that weakens an argument. Below are five common logical fallacies that should be removed from your writing.

- A **bare assertion** denies that an issue is debatable, claiming, "That's just how it is."

  Withdrawal of troops is our only option for peace.

  (The claim discourages discussion of other ways to promote peace.)

- A **threat** is a simple way to sabotage an argument, claiming, "If you don't agree with me, you'll regret it."

  If you don't accept alternative fuel sources, get ready to move back to the Stone Age.

- A **slippery slope** fallacy argues that a single step will start an unstoppable chain of events.

  If we build a skate park, vandalism is going to run rampant in our city.

- An **unreliable testimonial** is a statement made by a biased or unqualified source. A testimonial only has force if it is made by an authority.

  As TV's Dr. Daniels, I recommend Xanax for all my patients.

- A **half-truth** contains part of but not the whole truth.

  Three out of five doctors recommend ibuprofen, according to a recent study.

  (This may be true in this one study but not universally.)

Revise Improve your writing using the following checklist and your partner's comments on the response sheet. Continue until you can check off each item.

Revising Checklist

Ideas
- [ ] 1. Does my topic sentence identify an issue and my position?
- [ ] 2. Do I include a variety of supporting details?
- [ ] 3. Do I avoid errors in logic?

Organization
- [ ] 4. Do I have a topic sentence, body sentences, and a closing sentence?
- [ ] 5. Have I used transitions to connect my ideas?

Voice
- [ ] 6. Do I sound knowledgeable and passionate about the issue?

LO9 Editing: Mechanics

"Mechanics" refers to the standards of presenting written language; capitalization and number use are two of the mechanics issues writers encounter.

Capitalization Errors

Capitalizing proper nouns and proper adjectives (adjectives derived from proper nouns) is a basic rule of capitalization. There are times, however, when certain words are capitalized in one instance but not in another. The quick guide below refers to a number of these special cases. (Also see pages 504–512.).

Capitalize	Do Not Capitalize
American	un-American
January, May	winter, spring
The South is quite conservative	Turn south at the stop sign.
Duluth City College	a Duluth college
Chancellor John Bohm	John Bohm, our chancellor
President Obama	the president of the United States
Earth (planet name)	the earth
Internet	electronic communications network

Proofreading Practice In each sentence below, indicate which words should be capitalized, using the correction mark (≡).

1. with november around the corner, it's only so long until winter engulfs minnesota.

2. Flag burning is the definition of an un-american activity.

3. I caught up with chancellor Greg Williams of the university of pittsburgh.

4. I used the internet to find out that Missouri is nicknamed the show-me state.

5. My favorite french restaurant rests in a quiet neighborhood off college avenue.

6. The west coast is known for its laid-back lifestyle.

7. Does the winter sports season begin before or after december?

8. The president of the united states lives in the white house.

INSIGHT

Different languages use capitalization differently. Even different Englishes (U.S. and British, for example) treat capitals differently. For more practice see pages 504–512.

Apply As you edit your paragraph, be careful to discern common nouns from proper nouns. Remember: Do not capitalize common nouns and titles that appear near, but are not part of, a proper noun.

Using Numbers

When a paragraph includes numbers or statistics, you will have to know whether to write them as words or as numerals. Below are three basic rules to follow.

Numerals or Words

Numbers from one to one hundred are usually written as words; numbers 101 and greater are usually written as numerals.

two	seven	twenty-five	103	1,489

Numerals Only

Use numerals for the following forms: decimals, percentages, pages, chapters, addresses, dates, telephone numbers, identification numbers, and statistics.

13.1	**20** percent	Highway **41**	chapter **6**
February **12, 2010**	**(273) 289-2288**	**2.4** feet	

Words Only

Use words to express numbers that begin a sentence.

Thirteen players suffered from food poisoning.

Proofreading Practice In each sentence below, cross out any incorrect numbers and write the correct form above.

1. My ~~2~~ ^{two} cousins, Braden and Candace, live ~~4~~ ^{four} miles apart on Highway ~~Eleven~~ ¹¹.

2. ~~300~~ ^{Three hundred} raffle tickets were bought at the gates.

3. The results showed ~~twenty-five~~ ²⁵ percent of participants were born before January ~~first~~, 1985.

4. Please review chapter ~~seventeen~~ ¹⁷ for the test on Monday.

5. The coastal reef is ~~two point eight~~ ^{2.8} knots away.

6. ~~15~~ ^{Fifteen} of us are hoping to complete the ~~three point one~~ ^{3.1}-mile race.

Apply Read your argument paragraph, paying special attention to sentences that include numbers and statistics. Present numbers in the correct way: either as numerals or as words.

Marking a Paragraph

Before you finish editing your revised paragraph, you can practice by editing the following model.

Editing Practice   Correct the following paragraph, using the marks below. One correction has been done for you.

A Super Blow to Roscoe

For the good of the local economy, the Roscoe City Council must vote   *1*
down a proposal to build a SuperMart store on Highway Thirty-One.
The discount chain may slash prices, but it will slash local businesses in the
process. a University of Iowa study showed a group of small towns lost up
to 47 percent of they're retail trade after ten years of a SuperMart moving   *5*
in nearby. Grocery stores and retail businesses were hit the hardest. If a
SuperMart comes to Roscoe local grocers like Troyer's will have to lower
wages or risk closing. A 2007 study showed how a SuperMart caused
a one point five percent reduction in earnings for local grocery stores.
Proponents of a SuperMart expansion says the store will bring new jobs,   *10*
more sales taxes, and great bargains. But all SuperMart will accomplish
is reallocating where existing income is spent. The Roscoe City Council
should look for alternatives to jump-start the community's economy vote no
for SuperMart.

Correction Marks

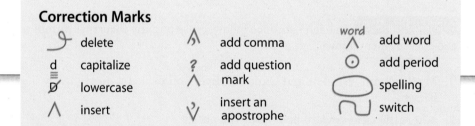

⌿ delete	⋀ add comma	word ⋀ add word
d̲ capitalize	? ⋀ add question mark	⊙ add period
⌿ lowercase		⬭ spelling
⋀ insert	⋁ insert an apostrophe	∿ switch

INSIGHT

On the previous page, you learned some basic rules for using numbers in your writing. Here is another useful guideline:

■ Use numerals when the time of day is expressed with an abbreviation; spell out the number when time is expressed in words.

6:00 p.m. or **six o'clock** (not *6 o'clock*)

the **2:15** p.m. train (not *two-fifteen p.m. train*)

an **eleven o'clock** wake-up call (not *an 11 o'clock wake-up call*)

Correcting Your Paragraph

Now it's time to correct your own paragraph.

Apply Create a clean copy of your paragraph and use the following checklist to check for errors. When you can answer *yes* to a question, check it off. Continue working until all items are checked.

Editing Checklist

Words

☐ 1. Have I used specific nouns and verbs? (See page 102.)

☐ 2. Have I used more action verbs than "be" verbs? (See page 458.)

Sentences

☐ 3. Have I varied the beginnings and lengths of sentences? (See pages 104–105.)

☐ 4. Have I combined short choppy sentences? (See page 105.)

☐ 5. Have I avoided shifts in sentences? (See page 422.)

☐ 6. Have I avoided fragments and run-ons? (See pages 410–413, 416–417.)

Conventions

☐ 7. Do I use correct verb forms (*he saw,* not *he seen*)? (See pages 464, 466.)

☐ 8. Do my subjects and verbs agree (*she speaks,* not *she speak*)? (See pages 394–403.)

☐ 9. Have I used the right words (*their, there, they're*)?

☐ 10. Have I capitalized first words and proper nouns and adjectives? (See page 504.)

☐ 11. Have I used commas after long introductory word groups? (See pages 514–517.)

☐ 12. Have I carefully checked my spelling?

Adding a Title

Make sure to add an attention-getting title. Here are three simple strategies for creating one.

- Create a slogan:

  Support Wind Farm Energy

- Sum up your argument:

  Texting and Driving Don't Mix

- Use a play on words:

  A Super Blow to Roscoe

Create Prepare a clean final copy of your paragraph and proofread it.

> "When I'm getting ready to reason with a man, I spend one-third of my time thinking about myself and what I am going to say—and two-thirds thinking about him and what he is going to say."
>
> — Abraham Lincoln

Review and Enrichment

On the next seven pages you will be asked to read and respond to a professional argument essay about how personal lawsuits are brought against corporations. You will also encounter several ideas for writing your own argument.

Prereading

Social issues can be complicated. Each of us comes to a social topic with our own assumptions based on our backgrounds, our needs, and our desires. Somehow we all have to come to a consensus about what is best, meshing the rights of the individual with the workings of a civilization.

Argumentation plays a central role in that process. It allows us each to present and support our positions, so that they can all be weighed against one another to come up with the best solutions for our common challenges.

Identify Think of a local issue that matters a lot to you: a shortage of student parking space; a need for more bike paths; class scheduling conflicts; gender, age, or ethnicity issues in employment; and so on. Freewrite for 5 to 10 minutes about why that issue is important to you.

_____

_____

_____

CONSIDER THE TRAITS

As you read the argumentation essay that follows, pay attention to the **ideas** first—the claims and counterclaims, and how they are either supported or answered. Then note the essay's **organization**—the way in which the opening introduces the topic, the body expands upon it, and the closing revisits it.

What do you think?

What does the Abraham Lincoln quotation above tell you about presenting an effective argument? With your classmates, discuss your reaction to this quotation.

Reading and Reacting

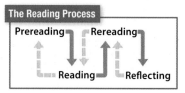

Read Read the following argumentative essay about "frivolous lawsuits." Notice the variety of details used to illustrate the topic's impact upon and importance to our society. Use the reading process (see pages 14–15) for the most effective reading.

About the Author

Laraine Flemming is a textbook writer with 20 years' experience teaching, from elementary to college level, but her first teaching position was in a psychiatric hospital in Vinita, Oklahoma. It was there that she became utterly convinced of the transformative power of reading, which led her eventually to publish reading texts of her own. Flemming has a Ph.D. from State University of New York in Buffalo.

What Exactly Is a Frivolous Lawsuit?

The lawsuit of seventy-nine-year-old Stella Liebeck, launched against McDonald's in 1994 after spilling hot coffee on herself as she went through the drive-through lane, immediately became the stuff of comedy. A *Seinfeld* episode even used it, making one of the characters sue for damages after he spilled coffee on himself. But the general attitude toward the suit, on television and off, was summed up in the response of another *Seinfeld* character, Elaine, who expressed puzzlement at the very idea of a lawsuit involving hot coffee being spilled and McDonald's being somehow liable, "Who ever heard of this anyway? Suing a company because their coffee is too hot? Coffee is supposed to be hot." In other words, the suit was a ridiculous joke.   10

What got left out of all the jokes, though, were the actual details of the case. Liebeck suffered third-degree burns. Third-degree burns are the most serious kind, especially for a woman of her age. Plus, there had been at least 700 previous cases of people being scalded by McDonald's coffee before Liebeck went to court. McDonald's had settled other claims but did not want to give   15
Liebeck the $20,000 compensation she had requested. So she sued and the case went to court.

What Liebeck's lawyers proved was that McDonald's was making its coffee 30 to 50 degrees hotter than other restaurants. In fact, the Shriner Burn Institute had already warned McDonald's not to serve coffee above 130   20
degrees. Yet the liquid that burned Liebeck was the usual temperature for McDonald's brew—about 190 degrees. As a result of Liebeck's suit, McDonald's coffee is now sold at the same temperature as most other restaurants.

Yes, there probably are trivial lawsuits filed on a regular basis. But Liebeck's wasn't one of them. It's actually ironic that the "hot coffee" lawsuit,   25
as it's come to be called, is often cited as an illustration of why the country desperately needs tort reform. Yet a closer examination of this issue suggests that citizens might want to think twice before joining in the chorus of calls to enact tort reform.

Tort reform legislation, in place or pending, differs from state to state.   30
Thus one of the questions involved in the debate is how tort reform should go forward. Should it be on a state or federal level?

In general, though, the tort reform movement focuses on three goals: (1) the need to limit the circumstances under which injured people may file a lawsuit after being injured by a product or procedure, (2) the goal of making it more difficult for people injured by a product or procedure to obtain a trial by jury, and (3) the desire to place limits on the amount of money injured parties may be awarded. 35

In the eyes of some, like political activist and organizer Jon Greenbaum, the idea that the country is desperately in need of tort reform is a myth. From his perspective, the right to sue corporations or companies if their products were defective or their procedures badly managed or fraudulent was a consumer victory won in the 1950s. In his eyes, now is not the time to abandon that right. He thinks implementing tort reform would be a step backward for consumers, not a step forward: "It will limit our ability to hold corporations accountable for their misdeeds. Corporate America has succeeded to a great extent by buying up our legislators and capturing regulatory bodies. We must not let them wrest control of the judicial system as well." 40, 45

That, however, would not be the position of Court Koenning, the president of Citizens Against Lawsuit Abuse of Houston. For him, lawsuits demanding compensation for injury due to defective products or procedures reveal a growing canker on American society—the abdication of personal responsibility. As he writes, "The somebody's gotta pay attitude is pervasive and that does not bode well for future generations. We need to reacquaint ourselves with personal responsibility and stop playing the blame game. We need to realize that every dilemma or personal disappointment is not fodder for a lawsuit and does not warrant a treasure trove of cash." 50, 55

These are all stirring sentiments. But they need to be viewed in the light of what consumers "playing the blame game" in court have actually tried to accomplish. In Los Angeles, California, consumers have gone to court to stop health insurers from canceling policies of people newly diagnosed with a serious illness. The insurance cancellations, usually based on technicalities, seem to target people who will require long-term and expensive care, for which the insurance companies would have to pay if the policies weren't cancelled. 60

In Harrisburg, Pennsylvania, consumers turned to the courts to take action against "mortgage rescue" companies who, for a fee, claimed they could help those falling behind on their payments. But after the fee was paid, no help was forthcoming. In Hartford, Connecticut, consumers also went to court against a pharmaceutical company that was blocking generic alternatives to the high-priced drugs on which the company's profits were based. 65, 70

This is not to say that all personal injury complaints taken to court are worthy of respect. Did anyone really want to see the woman who sued a cosmetics company for changing the shade of her hair become a millionaire? But many of the personal injury lawsuits brought by consumers do real good, helping not just the litigant but the public in general. We might want to consider that fact next time we hear or read another argument in favor of tort reform because what we might be reforming is our own right to seek justice by legal means. 75

Sources: Court Koenning, "Starbucks 'Hot Tea' Lawsuit Highlights a Void in Personal Responsibility," www.setexasrecord.com; Jon Greenbaum, "McDonald's Hot Coffee Lawsuit and Beyond: The Tort Reform Myth Machine," CommonDreams.org 80

React   Answer the following questions about the argumentative essay. Share your responses with your classmates.

1. What is Flemming's position (main claim) in the essay?

   The American public should rethink tort reform, as lawsuits deemed "frivolous" by the public
   are not always as frivolous as they seem.

2. How might her personal or professional background have influenced this position?

   _____

3. What was your own opinion about the topic before reading the essay?

   _____

4. How might your own background have influenced your opinion?

   _____

5. What claims and counterclaims does the author include in the essay? (List at least three.)

   _____

   _____

   _____

6. How are her claims supported? How are counterclaims answered?

   _____

7. How would you rate this argument and why?

   Weak ★ ★ ★ ★ ★ Strong

   _____

8. What did you learn from the argument that you hadn't known before?

   _____

Writing

Follow the guidelines on the next two pages to write your own paragraph or essay of argumentation. Check with your instructor about any specific requirements that he or she may have.

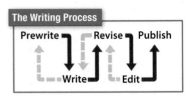

Prewriting

Choose one of the following ideas for your argumentative writing. Or decide upon another idea of your own.

Writing Ideas

1. Choose one of the debatable topics you brainstormed on page 304, or one of the local issues you identified on page 311.

2. Think about a problem you would like to see fixed. Use an argumentation essay to suggest a solution.

3. Choose a cause that you believe needs to be championed. Use an argumentation essay to explain what is threatening it and why it must succeed.

4. Challenge yourself by arguing the other side. Select a current topic of debate and argue against your own opinion on it, in favor of an opposing viewpoint. (This mental exercise is an extension of Abraham Lincoln's on page 320.)

5. Think about an important person in your life. What one opinion does that person hold strongest? Write an argumentation essay either supporting or challenging that opinion. (Consider sharing your essay with the person after it is finished.)

When planning . . .

Refer to pages 311–312 to help with your prewriting and planning. Also use the tips below.

- State your main idea clearly, so that you can remain focused during writing.

- Consider your reader. What opinion will that person likely have about the subject? What questions or objections might your reader have?

- Consider your purpose. If your reader's opinion matches your own, your purpose will be to further the reader's understanding of the topic and any counterarguments. If your reader's opinion is contrary to yours, your purpose will be to soothe any objections and provide convincing support for yours.

- Consider your voice. For a paragraph or an essay of argument, your voice should usually be respectful but confident.

Writing and Revising

Refer to pages 313–315 to help you write and review your first draft. Also use the tips below to help with your drafting and revising.

When writing . . .

- Include an opening, a middle, and a closing in your argument. Each part has a specific role to play. (See page 314.)
- Follow your planning notes, but remain free to expand upon new ideas.
- If you encounter a claim or counterclaim that you have not researched, note it in your text and keep on writing. Research that claim or counterclaim after finishing your first draft rather than getting sidetracked during writing.
- Try to keep your intended audience in mind. Picture someone in particular and keep your voice appropriately confident and respectful.

When revising . . .

- Be prepared to reorganize your ideas for better impact. Often a new arrangement will suggest itself as you reread your first draft.
- Make sure your writing doesn't antagonize the reader by taking on a negative or condescending tone.
- Also make sure your writing sounds confident, not apologetic.
- Watch for spots where your argument seems "thin." If a point needs more support, find it. If an important counterclaim has not been mentioned, address it.
- Ask a classmate or another writer to review and critique your writing. Use a peer-review sheet to guide the critique. (See page 547.)

Editing

Refer to the checklist on page 319 when you are ready to edit your argument for style and correctness.

Reflecting on Argument Writing

Answer the following questions about your argumentation reading and writing experience in this chapter.

1. Why is argumentation so important?

   _____

2. What is your favorite sample argument in this chapter? Why?

   _____

3. What reading strategy in this chapter do you find most helpful? Explain.

   _____

4. What is the most important thing you learned about reading a paragraph or an essay of argumentation?

   _____

5. What do you like most about the paragraph of argumentation you wrote for this chapter? Why?

   _____

6. What is one thing you would like to change in your paragraph?

   _____

7. What is the most important thing you have learned about writing paragraphs and essays of argumentation?

   _____

Key Terms to Remember

Whenever you read and write argumentation, it's important to understand the following terms.

- **Claims**—reasons in support of the main topic. Without claims to support it, an argument is merely an unfounded opinion.
- **Counterclaims**—reasons against the main topic. When addressed respectfully and confidently, counterclaims can actually strengthen an argument by showing that you have carefully thought over the entire subject.
- **Logical fallacies**—false assertions. These actually weaken an argument by making it seem less than carefully considered.

15

Summarizing

> "If you can't explain it simply, you don't understand it well enough."
> —Albert Einstein

Longer forms of academic reading and writing, like essays, are often packed with important information. For a reader, memorizing all the key details in longer texts can be a tall order. Summarizing the writing is a more effective way to learn the information. Summarization is the process of identifying and explaining the key ideas of a reading in your own words.

Writing a summary is one of the best ways of becoming actively involved in your reading. Summarizing a text also helps you to evaluate how much you know about the material and to remember what you read. If you have trouble explaining any ideas, then you know you need to reread the passage.

In this chapter, you will read and summarize a number of academic passages. You will also learn strategies for identifying key ideas and explaining them in your own words.

Learning Outcomes

LO1 Understand summarizing.

LO2 Learn about reading strategies.

LO3 Read and react to a summary.

LO4 Write a summary.

LO5 Practice additional summary writing.

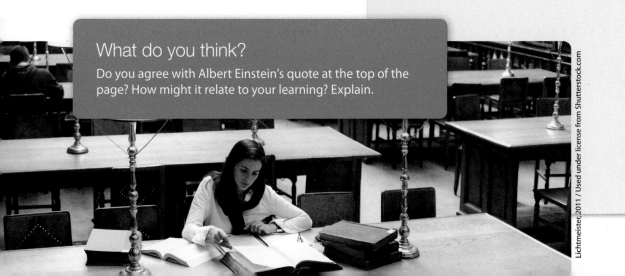

What do you think?

Do you agree with Albert Einstein's quote at the top of the page? How might it relate to your learning? Explain.

LO1 Understanding Summarizing

In some ways you practice summarizing every day in conversations with your friends, family members, and co-workers. For example, when someone asks you what you did over the weekend, you wouldn't tell every detail about it. Instead you would summarize or highlight the most important points in your own words.

When you write a summary, you should use your own words, except for any specific, essential words for ideas from the text. The key is to share only the main ideas of the text, rather than every last detail. Your goal is to provide a glimpse of the whole text, not a detailed look at the parts.

> "The simpler you say it, the more eloquent it is."
> —August Wilson

Summary Versus Paraphrase

A paraphrase, also written in your own words, does not reduce a text to its basic meaning. Rather, it explains the full meaning of a challenging reading. Because a paraphrase often includes explanations or interpretations, it can actually be longer than the original. A summary, by contrast, provides a brief explanation of the main ideas in the text and should be about one-third the length of the original.

Identify Telling friends about a movie is one example of informal summarizing. List three or four other examples of summaries that commonly occur in your conversations.

INSIGHT

A typical one- or two-page essay can be summarized in one well-formed paragraph. The first sentence in a summary is the topic sentence. The sentences that follow must support the topic sentence.

1. <u>Recapping a television episode for a friend is one example of informal summarizing</u>

2. _____

3. _____

4. _____

Reading

Summarizing is an important learning tool in all of your class work, especially for report and research assignments. But to summarize a text, you need to understand it in its original form. The strategies below will help.

LO2 Learning About Reading Strategies

Strategy 1: Using a Table Diagram

Part of the challenge when reading a text is keeping track of the main idea and key supporting points. A graphic organizer called a table diagram works well for this purpose. Identify the thesis, or main idea, of the reading on the table top and list the key supporting points underneath. Then refer to this information as you write a summary of the text.

Table Diagram

Thesis or main idea

supporting points	supporting points	supporting points	supporting points

ajt, 2011 / Used under license from Shutterstock.com

Strategy 2: Understanding the Structure of Writing

Most informational texts are shaped in the following way: The first part introduces the topic and states the thesis or main idea. The middle paragraphs support and develop the thesis. The closing part usually reviews what has been said and may offer an additional idea or two. Keeping this structure in mind should help you find the key information in a text.

Beginning

Middle

Ending

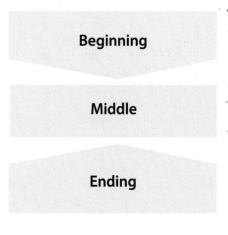

LO3 Reading and Reacting to a Summary

In order to read and react to a summary, you must first read and react to the text that is being summarized. What follows is an academic text followed by a model summary of the text.

Read Read the following passage from the article entitled, "How Our Skins Got Their Color," by Marvin Harris. Use the reading process to help you fully understand the text. (See pages 14–15.)

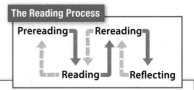

The Reading Process

Prereading Rereading

Reading Reflecting

How Our Skins Got Their Color

Human skin owes its color to the presence of particles known as   1
melanin. The primary function of melanin is to protect the upper levels of
the skin from being damaged by the sun's ultraviolet rays. This radiation
poses a critical problem for our kind because we lack the **dense** coat of hair
that acts as a sunscreen for most mammals. . . . Hairlessness exposes us to   5
two kinds of radiation hazards: ordinary sunburn, with its blisters, rashes,
and risk of infection; and skin cancers, including malignant melanoma,
one of the deadliest diseases known. Melanin is the body's first line of
defense against these afflictions. The more melanin particles, the darker
the skin, and the lower the risk of sunburn and all forms of skin cancer.   10
This explains why the highest rates for skin cancer are found in sun-
drenched lands such as Australia, where light-skinned people of European
descent spend a good part of their lives outdoors wearing scanty attire.
Very dark-skinned people such as heavily **pigmented** Africans of Zaire
seldom get skin cancer, but when they do, they get it on depigmented parts 15
of their bodies—palms and lips.

If exposure to solar radiation had nothing but harmful effects,
natural selection would have favored inky black as the color for all human
populations. But the sun's rays do not present an **unmitigated** threat. As it
falls on the skin, sunshine converts a fatty substance in the **epidermis** into 20
vitamin D. The blood carries vitamin D from the skin to the intestines,
where it plays a vital role in the absorption of calcium. In turn, calcium
is vital for strong bones. Without it, people fall victim to the crippling
diseases **rickets** and **osteomalacia**. In women, calcium deficiencies can
result in a deformed birth canal, which makes childbirth lethal for both   25
mother and fetus.

Vitamin D can be obtained from a few foods, primarily the oils and
livers of marine fish. But inland populations must rely on the sun's rays
and their own skins for this crucial substance. The particular color of a

maxstockphoto, 2011 / Used under license from Shutterstock.com

human population's skin, therefore, represents in large degree a trade-off   *30*
between the hazards of too much versus too little solar radiation: acute
sunburn and skin cancer on the one hand, and rickets and osteomalacia on
the other. It is this trade-off that largely accounts for the **preponderance**
of brown people in the world and for the general tendency for skin color to
be darkest among **equatorial populations** and lightest among populations   *35*
dwelling at higher latitudes.

Marvin Harris, "How Our Skins Got Their Color," Our Kind: Who We Are, Where We Came From,
and Where We Are Going, Harper Collins, 1989.

Vocabulary

dense
thick

pigmented
colored by pigment

unmitigated
not made less severe

epidermis
uppermost layer of skin

rickets
softening of bones in the
young

osteomalacia
softening of bones in adults

preponderance
majority

equatorial populations
people who live close to the
earth's equator

React   Answer the questions below about the essay on the previous page. Then
discuss your responses with your classmates.

1. What is the thesis or main idea of the text? _____

2. What key points are explained in the middle paragraph? _____

3. What example does the author use in the third paragraph to explain the
   relationship between the benefits and hazards of sunlight to the skin? _____

4. How would you rate this passage and why?

   Weak ★ ★ ★ ★ ★ Strong _____

Drawing Inferences

An *inference* is a logical conclusion that you can make about something that is
not actually said or stated in a text. A worthy inference does, however, result from
a clear and careful understanding of what *is* said. To practice drawing inferences,
answer the following questions about the text on pages 330–331. Afterward,
share your responses with your classmates.

1. Reread the first two sentences of the last paragraph. What inference
   related to vitamin D and diet can you make about populations who live
   near marine life?

2. Using the information from the passage, what can you infer about your
   own skin color?

Read   Carefully read the following summary of the text about skin and sunlight. Notice that it is not more than one-third the length of the original text.

Summary of the Text

> In the passage from "How Our Skins Got Their Color," Marvin Harris explores the impact of sunlight on skin health and skin color. There are two main dangers caused by overexposure to the sun. They are sunburn and skin cancer. The presence of melanin particles protects skin from these dangers. Melanin also influences skin color—the more melanin particles present, the darker the skin. But while too much sunlight can cause health problems, so too can lack of sunlight, since sunlight provides the body with vitamin D. Lack of vitamin D can cause a person's bones to soften. The author concludes that this balancing act between too much and too little sun exposure is why a large percentage of the world's population has brown skin.

React   Answer the following questions about the summary. Then share your responses with your classmates.

1. What information is provided in the topic sentence of the summary?

   The title, author, and brief description of the reading
   _____

2. What information is provided in the body or middle sentences? Name three ideas.

   _____

3. What information is provided in the closing sentence?

   _____

4. Does the writer of the summary use his own words for the most part? Why do you think this is important?

   _____

5. Does the summary help you understand the original passage? Explain.

   _____

INSIGHT

When you are writing a summary for a report or research paper, note the source of the text (title of the text, author, page number, and so on). This will make it easier for you to acknowledge or cite the source in your actual report.

LO4 Writing a Summary

In this part of the chapter, you will write a summary of your own following the guidelines presented in this section.

Read To get started, read and react to the article below by Constance Staley and Steve Staley. Use the reading process to help you gain a complete understanding of the text. (See pages 68–73.)

About the Authors

Constance Staley is an author and educator. She is an expert in helping students prepare for and succeed in college. *FOCUS on College and Career Success* puts in one place all of the valuable advice she has shared with students over the years.

Steve Staley is dean of academics and professor of management and humanities at Colorado Technical University. He has also taught at the Air Force Academy, the Naval War College, and the University of Colorado.

Get Physically Energized

To make sure you're physically energized, try these suggestions.   *1*

1. **Snap to your body's rhythm.** Have you noticed times of the day when it's easier to concentrate than others? Perhaps you regularly crash in the middle of the afternoon, for example, so you go for a chocolate fix, or a coffee pick-me-up. Everyone has a biological clock. Paying attention   *5* to your body's natural rhythms is important. Plan to do activities that require you to be alert during your natural productivity peaks. That's better than plodding although a tough assignment when the energy just isn't there. Use low energy times to take care of mindless chores that require little to no brainpower.   *10*

2. **Up and at 'em.** What about 8:00 a.m. classes? Don't use your body's natural rhythms as an excuse to sleep through class! ("I'm just not a morning person . . .") If you're truly not a morning person, don't sign up for early morning classes. If you are coming off working a night shift, you may need some rest first. Sleeping through your obligations won't   *15* do much for your success—and you'll be playing a continual game of catch-up, which takes even more time. Some experts advise that you start your day as early as possible. Marking six items off your to-do list before lunch can give you a real high.

3. **Sleep at night, study during the day.** Burning the midnight oil and   *20* pulling all-nighters aren't the best ideas, either. It only takes one all-nighter to help you realize that a lack of sleep translates into a drop in performance. Without proper sleep, your ability to understand and remember course material is impaired. Research shows that the

Artur Synenko, 2011 / Used under license from Shutterstock.com

`8:00`

average adult requires seven to eight hours of sleep each night. If 25
you can't get that much for whatever reason, take a short afternoon
nap. Did you know that the Three Mile Island nuclear meltdown in
Pennsylvania in 1979 and the Chernobyl disaster in the Ukraine in
1986 took place at 4 a.m. and 1:23 a.m., respectively? Experts believe
it's no coincidence that both these events took place when workers 30
would normally be sleeping.

4. **"Burn the premium fuel."** You've heard it before: Food is the fuel that
makes us run. The better the fuel, the smoother we run. It's that
simple. . . . When the demands on your energy are high, such as exam
week, use premium fuel. If you don't believe it, think about how many 35
people you know get sick during times of high stress. Watch how
many of your classmates are hacking and coughing their way through
exams—or in bed missing them altogether.

"Get Physically Energized" from STALEY/STALEY. *FOCUS on College and Career Success*, 1E. ©
2012 Wadsworth, a part of Cengage Learning, Inc.

React Answer the following questions about the reading. Your responses to these questions will help you write your summary.

1. What is the thesis or main idea of the text? (See pages 30–31.) _____

2. What key points in the middle paragraphs explain or develop the thesis? Consider listing them on a table diagram. (See page 329.) _____

Thesis or main idea			
supporting points	supporting points	supporting points	supporting points

3. How does the structure of the text help you identify the key points? _____

4. How would you rate this essay and why?

   Weak ★ ★ ★ ★ ★ Strong _____

Vocabulary Practice

Explain or define the following words in the text by using context clues and your understanding of word parts. (See pages 24–25.) List the word or word parts that help you define each term.

- plodding (line 8)
- obligations (line 15)
- impaired (line 24)
- premium (line 32)

Writing Guidelines

The following guidelines will help you write a paragraph summary of an essay or extended passage.

Planning Your Summary

Most of your prewriting and planning will occur when you read and react to the text. During your planning . . .

- Name the thesis or main idea of the text.
- Identify the key points that support the thesis.

> **INSIGHT**
>
> In academic texts, each middle paragraph often addresses one key supporting point. This point is usually stated in the topic sentence.

Writing the First Draft

Remember that you are writing a paragraph, starting with a topic sentence and following with supporting ideas. As you write your first draft . . .

- Use your own words as much as possible.
- Start with a topic sentence, naming the title, author, and topic of the text.
- Continue with the key points that explain the thesis. (Avoid specific details.)
- Arrange your ideas in the most logical order.
- Add a closing sentence, if one seems necessary.

Revising the Writing

Remember that your summary should address just the essential information from the original text. As you review your first draft . . .

- Determine if it identifies the main idea of the text.
- Decide if you've limited yourself to key supporting information.
- See if your summary reads smoothly and logically.
- Determine if you've used your own words, except for key ideas. (See the next page.)

Editing the Writing

Be sure that your summary is clear and accurate if you are turning it in for evaluation. As you edit your revised summary . . .

- Check that you've used complete sentences.
- Check for spelling, capitalization, and punctuation errors. Pay special attention to titles and quoted material. (See the next page.)
- Check for proper usage and grammar.

Write Write a paragraph summary of the text on pages 333–334 using the information above as a guide. Be prepared to refer to the original text many times as you develop your writing.

A CLOSER LOOK at Revising and Editing

Revising

The information that follows will help you check your summary for (1) recognizing the source and (2) identifying exact ideas from the text.

Recognizing the Source Follow your instructor's guidelines for identifying the source of your summary (if you are turning it in for evaluation). The following example shows you how to identify the title and author in the topic sentence of your summary.

- In this passage from "Religious Faith Versus Spirituality," author Neil Bissoondath explores spirituality. . . .

Identifying Exact Ideas from the Text In your summary, you may find it necessary to include a few exact ideas or specialized words from the original text. When this type of information is taken directly from the text, enclose it within quotation marks.

- **Exact idea:** The author describes himself as "soaring with a lightness I'd never known before" after the ceremony.
- **Specialized word:** One teacher recognized as a master teacher serves as a "standard-bearer" for all great teachers.

Editing

This information will help you correctly capitalize and punctuate titles and quoted materials.

Capitalizing Titles Capitalize the first and last words in a title and all important words in between. Do not capitalize words such as *a, for, by, in, and,* and *the* if they occur within the title. (See pages 508–509 for more.)

- **Title:** Chinese Space, American Space *(All the words are important so they are all capitalized.)*
- **Title:** Catcher in the Rye *("In" and "the" occur within the title so they are lowercased.)*

Punctuating Titles Use quotation marks to set off the titles of chapters, essays, articles, and so on. Italicize or underline the titles of books, magazines, newspapers, Web sites, and so on.

- **Title of an Essay:** "Chinese Space, American Space"
- **Title of a Book:** *Catcher in the Rye*

Placement of Other Punctuation Place commas and periods inside quotation marks. Place question marks or exclamation marks inside the quotation marks when they punctuate the quotation and outside when they punctuate the sentence.

- **Placement of a Comma:** In this passage from "Religious Faith Versus Spirituality," author Neil Bissoondath explores spirituality. *(Commas and periods are always placed inside the quotation marks.)*

- **Placement of a Question Mark:** The essay "Yes, Accidents Happen. But Why?" analyzes the causes of accidents. *(The question mark punctuates the quotation, so it is placed inside the quotation marks.)*

- Have you read "Spanglish Spoken Here"? *(The question mark punctuates the entire sentence, so it is placed outside the quotation marks.)*

Check Be sure to use the information on these two pages to help you revise and edit your summary, correctly capitalizing and punctuating titles and quoted material.

Supri Suharjoto, 2011 / Used under license from Shutterstock.com

LO5 Practicing Additional Summary Writing

This section includes two texts that you can use for additional summary-writing practice. Always read and react to the text before writing your summary

First Text

Read   Read the following passage from *Living in the Environment* by G. Tyler Miller and Scott Spoolman. The writing discusses a common misconception about sharks and explains why they are important to the environment.

About the Authors

G. Tyler Miller and Scott Spoolman are textbook writers, specializing in environmental science.

Why Should We Protect Sharks?

More than 400 known **species** of sharks inhabit the world's oceans. They vary widely in size and behavior, from the goldfish-sized dwarf dog shark to the whale shark, which can grow to a length of 18 meters (60 feet) and weigh as much as two full-grown African elephants. . . .   *1*

Sharks have been around for more than 400 million years. As keystone species, some shark species play **crucial** roles in helping to keep their **ecosystems** functioning. Feeding at or near the tops of food webs, they remove injured and sick animals from the ocean. Without this service provided by sharks, the oceans would be teeming with dead and dying fish and marine mammals.   *5*   *10*

In addition to playing their important ecological roles, sharks could help to save human lives. If we learn why they almost never get cancer, we could possibly use this information to fight cancer in our own species. Scientists are also studying their highly effective immune systems, which allow wounds in sharks to heal without becoming infected.   *15*

Many people argue that we should protect sharks simply because they, like any other species, have a right to exist. But another reason for the importance of sustaining this threatened portion of the earth's **biodiversity** is that some sharks are keystone species, which means that we and other species need them.

"Why Should We Protect Sharks?" from MILLER. *Living in the Environment,* 17E. © 2012 Brooks/ Cole, a part of Cengage Learning, Inc.

Vocabulary

species
kinds

ecosystems
a community of organisms
and the environment they
life in

crucial
very important

biodiversity
the number of plants and
animals living in the same
place

React   Answer the questions below about the text on page 338. Then discuss your responses with your classmates.

1. What is the thesis or main idea of the text? (See pages 30–31.) _____

2. What key points in the middle paragraphs explain or develop the thesis? Consider listing them on a table diagram. (See page 329.) _____

Thesis or main idea			
supporting points	supporting points	supporting points	supporting points

3. How would you rate this text and why?

   Weak ★ ★ ★ ★ ★ Strong _____

4. What did you learn abut the topic? Name at least two things. _____

Drawing Inferences

   An *inference* is a logical conclusion that you can make about something that is not actually said or stated in a text. A worthy inference does, however, result from a clear and careful understanding of what *is* said. To practice drawing inferences, answer the following questions about the text on page 338. Afterward, share your responses with your classmates.

1. What conclusions can you draw about the authors' personal feelings toward sharks?

2. What conclusions can you draw about sharks from the title of the article?

Write   Write a summary of this text using your responses above and the information on page 335 as a basic guide.

Second Text

Read   Read the following passage from *Sociology: Your Compass for a New World,* a sociology text by Robert J. Brym and John Lie. In the passage, the authors discuss the idea that all people are connected by six degrees of separation, using actor Kevin Bacon as the prime example.

About the Authors

Robert J. Brym is a professor of sociology at the University of Toronto. He has won numerous awards for his teaching and scholarly work.

John Lie is a professor of social theory and political economy at the University of California, Berkley.

Six Degrees of Kevin Bacon

The *Internet Movie Database* (2003) contains information on the half   1
million actors who have ever performed in a commercially released movie.
While this number is large, you might be surprised to learn that, socially,
they form a small world. We can demonstrate this fact by first selecting an
actor who is not an especially big star—someone like Kevin Bacon. We can   5
then use the *Internet Movie Database* to find out which other actors have
ever been in a movie with him (University of Virginia, 2003). Acting in a
movie with *another* actor **constitutes** a link. Actors two links away from
Bacon have never been in a movie with him but have been in a movie with
another actor who has been in a movie with him. **Remarkably** more than   10
85 percent of the half million actors in the database have one, two, or three
links to Bacon. We conclude that although film acting stretches back more
than a century and has involved people in many countries, the half million
people who have ever acted in films form a pretty small world.

What is true for the world of film actors turns out to be true for the   15
rest of us, too. Jeffrey Travers and Stanley Milgram (1969) conducted a
famous study in which they asked 300 randomly selected people to mail a
document to a complete stranger. However, the people could not mail the
document directly to them. They had to mail it to a person they knew on
a first-name basis, who, in turn, could send it only to a person he or she   20
knew on a first name basis, and so forth. Travers and Milgram defined
this passing of a letter from one person to another as a link, or a "degree of
separation." Remarkably, it took only six links on average for the document
to reach the stranger. The idea soon became **widespread** that there are no
more than six degrees of separation between any two people in the United   25
States.

"Six Degrees of Kevin Bacon" from BRYM/LIE. *Sociology: Your Compass for a New World,* 2E. ©
2006 Thompson, a part of Cengage Learning, Inc.

Vocabulary

constitutes	**remarkably**	**widespread**
forms	worthy of attention	found by a large spread of people

React   Answer the questions below about the text on page 340. Then discuss your responses with your classmates.

1. What is the thesis or main idea of the text? (See pages 30–31.)
   Although the United States is heavily populated, any two people are socially connected by no more than six degrees of separation.

2. What key points explain or develop the thesis? Consider using a table diagram to list these points. (See page 329.)

Thesis or main idea

supporting points	supporting points	supporting points	supporting points

3. How would you rate this text and why?

   Weak ★ ★ ★ ★ ★ Strong _____

4. What did you learn about the topic? Name at least two things.

   _____

Drawing Inferences

An *inference* is a logical conclusion that you can make about something that is not actually said or stated in a text. A worthy inference does, however, result from a clear and careful understanding of what *is* said. To practice drawing inferences, answer the following questions about the text on page 340. Afterward, share your responses with your classmates.

1. What conclusion do the writers make about people in the film industry? How does it relate to the United States as a whole?

2. Why might it be difficult to complete the study in the second paragraph?

Write   Write a summary of this text using your responses above and the information on page 335 as a basic guide.

Reflecting on Summary Writing

Answer the following questions about your summary-writing experiences in this chapter.

1. Why is summary writing valuable?

   _____

2. How is careful reading connected to effective summary writing?

   _____

3. What are three important things to remember when writing a summary?

   _____

4. Which of the reading strategies is most helpful when it comes to aiding your summary writing? Explain.

   _____

5. What do you like most about the summary you wrote in this chapter? Explain.

   _____

6. What one thing would you like to change in your summary?

   _____

7. When will you use summary writing in the future?

   _____

Key Terms to Remember

When you write summaries, it's important to understand the following terms.

- **Summary**—the core of a text presented in a condensed form
- **Paraphrase**—a form of summary writing with explanations and interpretations; may be as long or longer than the source text
- **Table diagram**—a graphic organizer for identifying the thesis and key supporting points in a text

16

> "I won't say ours was a tough school, but we had our own coroner. We used to write essays like: What I'm going to be if I grow up."
> —Lenny Bruce

Reading and Writing Essays

As you have seen in previous chapters, a paragraph can be a self-contained unit with an opening, a middle, and a closing. The opening introduces your topic; the middle provides support; the closing gives a last thought about the topic.

Often a topic is simply too big to cover in a single paragraph. That is when an essay becomes necessary.

Like a standalone paragraph, an essay has an opening, a middle, and a closing. However, the opening of an essay is a full paragraph itself. The middle of an essay consists of one or more paragraphs of support. And the closing is also a separate paragraph. Sometimes, in a longer essay, the opening or closing may use more than one paragraph.

In this chapter, you will be introduced to the workings of an essay of definition. You will read and react to a professional essay and then write an essay of your own. Along the way, you will learn how paragraphs in an essay are similar to and different from the paragraphs you have previously read and written.

Learning Outcomes

LO1 Understand essays of definition.

LO2 Learn about reading strategies.

LO3 Read and react to a professional essay.

LO4 Plan an essay.

LO5 Write the first draft.

LO6 Revise the writing.

LO7 Edit the writing.

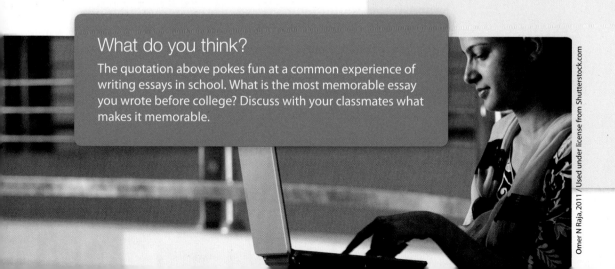

What do you think?

The quotation above pokes fun at a common experience of writing essays in school. What is the most memorable essay you wrote before college? Discuss with your classmates what makes it memorable.

LO1 Understanding Essays of Definition

As the earlier chapter on definition explains, definition writing is often done to convey information. Much of the writing in your various textbooks is intended to define terms, for instance. A definition essay may instead explore an idea. Much of the writing in academic journals is this sort of exploration. Lastly, an essay of definition can simply be an explanation of what something means to the writer: kindness, art, the power of music, and so on.

> "In high school, I won a prize for an essay on tuberculosis. When I got through writing the essay, I was sure I had the disease."
> —Constance Baker Motley

Often, writing an essay of definition requires research. The writer must understand the term well enough to write an effective opening paragraph and thesis statement. Then the writer must supply effective support in the body paragraphs, each with its own topic sentence and supporting details. Finally, the closing paragraph should present a new insight into the term defined, based upon the details in the body.

INSIGHT

Sometimes a definition can open our eyes to a topic we had not noticed before. In *The Non-Designer's Design Book,* graphic designer Robin Williams describes reading about Joshua trees while visiting her parents. After that reading, she finally noticed the Joshua tree standing in their front yard, and in every yard in the neighborhood. Have you had an experience similar to Williams' or Motley's? Discuss it with your classmates.

Marie Lumiere, 2011 / Used under license from Shutterstock.com

Identify Identify at least one possible topic for definition in each of the following categories. (One example is provided.) Then discuss your responses with your classmates.

Arts and Crafts: _____

History: _____

Journalism: _____

Nutrition: _____

Reading

An essay of definition can broaden your knowledge of the world by introducing you to an unfamiliar topic.

LO2 Learning About Reading Strategies

The following strategies will help you to quickly grasp the information in an essay of definition.

Strategy 1: Outlining the Essay

To understand the overall structure of an essay, make an outline like the one below.

- **Start with the essay's thesis statement.** This is often the final sentence of the opening paragraph.
- **Then find the topic sentence in each body paragraph.** This is often (but not always) the first sentence of the paragraph.
- **Find the closing thought.** This restatement of the thesis may be located near the beginning of the closing paragraph or at its end.

Thesis Statement: _____
    Topic Sentence A. _____
    Topic Sentence B. _____
    Topic Sentence C. _____
    Topic Sentence D. _____
    Topic Sentence E. _____
Closing Thought: _____

Strategy 2: Summarizing the Essay

Once you have outlined the specifics of the essay, write a one-paragraph summary of it in your own words. Rewrite the idea of thesis statement as your topic sentence. Then rewrite the idea of each topic sentence from the essay, making them the supporting points of your paragraph. Finally, conclude by rewriting the closing thought. (See chapter 15 for more about writing summaries.)

Topic Sentence: _____
Support: _____
_____
_____
_____
Conclusion: _____

LO3 Reading and Reacting to a Professional Essay

Read   Use the reading process as you go through this definition of life stages, from the book *Diversified Health Occupations*.

The Reading Process

Prereading   Rereading

Reading   Reflecting

About the Authors

Louise Simmers is a retired medical educator with a BS in nursing from the University of Maryland and a M.Ed from Kent State University. She has worked as a medical-surgical, coronary-intensive care, and public health nurse and has won two Ohio state awards for outstanding health-occupational teaching.

Karen Simmers-Nartker has a BS in nursing from Kent State and special certifications from the Emergency Nurses Association and the American Heart Association. She is the charge nurse for an intensive-care unit. Sharon Simmers-Kobelak has a Bachelor of Business Administration degree from Miami University, Ohio. She works in the educational publishing industry.

Life Stages

Even though individuals differ greatly, each person passes through   *1*
certain stages of growth and development from birth to death. These
stages are frequently called life stages. A common method of classifying
life stages is as follows:
- Infancy: birth to 1 year   *5*
- Early childhood: 1-6 years
- Late childhood: 6-12 years
- **Adolescence**: 12-18 years
- Early adulthood: 40-65 years
- Late adulthood: 65 years and older   *10*

As individuals pass through these life stages, four main types of
growth and development occur: physical, mental or **cognitive**, emotional,
and social. Physical refers to body growth and includes height and weight
changes, muscle and nerve development, and changes in body organs.
Mental or cognitive refers to **intellectual** development and includes   *15*
learning how to solve problems, make judgments, and deal with situations.
Emotional refers to feelings and includes dealings with love, hate, joy, fear,
excitement, and other similar feelings. Social refers to interactions and
relationships with other people.

Each stage of growth and development has its own characteristics   *20*
and has specific developmental tasks that an individual must master.
These tasks progress from the simple to the more complex. For example,

an individual first learns to sit, then crawl, then stand, then walk, and then, finally, run. Each stage establishes the foundation for the next stage. In this way, growth and development proceeds in an orderly pattern. It is important to remember, however, that the rate of progress varies among individuals. Some children master speech early, others master it later. Similarly, an individual may experience a sudden growth spurt and then maintain the same height for a period of time.   25

Erik Erikson, a **psychoanalyst**, has identified eight states of **psychosocial** development. His eight stages of development, the basic conflict or need that must be resolved at each stage, and ways to resolve the conflict are shown in [the] table [below]. Erikson believes that if an individual is not able to resolve a conflict at the appropriate stage, the individual will struggle with the same conflict later in life. For example, if a toddler is not allowed to learn and become independent by mastering basic tasks, the toddler may develop a sense of doubt in his or her abilities. This sense of doubt will interfere with later attempts at mastering independence.   30   35

Health care providers must understand that each life stage creates certain needs in individuals. Likewise, other factors can affect life stages and needs. An individual's sex, race, heredity (factors inherited from parents, such as hair color and body structure), culture, life experiences, and health status can influence needs. Injury or illness usually has a negative effect and can change needs or **impair** development.   40   45

Erikson's Eight Stages of Psychosocial Development*		
Stage of Development	*Basic Conflict*	*Major Life Event*
Infancy: Birth to 1 Year; Oral-Sensory	Trust vs. Mistrust	Feeding
Toddler: 1-3 Years; Muscular-Anal	Autonomy vs. Shame/Doubt	Toilet Training
Preschool: 3-6 Years; Locomotor	Initiative vs. Guilt	Independence
School-Age: 6-12 Years; Latency	Industry vs. Inferiority	School
Adolescence: 12-18 Years	Identity vs. Role Confusion	Peer
Young Adulthood: 19-40 Years	Intimacy vs. Isolation	Love Relationships
Middle Adulthood: 40-65 Years	Generativity vs. Stagnation	Parenting
Older Adulthood: 66 Years to Death	Ego Identity vs. Despair	Reflection on and Acceptance of Life

*Table adapted from *Diversified Health Occupations,* minus the "Ways to Resolve Conflict" column.

"Life Stages" from SIMMERS. *Diversified Health Occupations,* 7E. © 2009 Delmar Learning, a part of Cengage Learning, Inc. Reproduced by permission. www.cengage.com/permissions

Vocabulary

adolescence
a period of development between childhood and adulthood

cognitive
having to do with thought

intellectual
involving thinking

psychoanalyst
a therapist who deals with the mind

psychosocial
relating to both mental and social topics

impair
weaken or harm

React   Answer the following questions to help your understanding of the essay, "Life Stages." Then discuss your answers with your classmates.

Outlining to Understand

1. What is the thesis statement of this essay?

   Each person passes through similar life stages, from birth until death.

   _____

2. What is the topic sentence of each body paragraph?

   a. As individuals pass through these life stages, four main types of growth and development

   occur: physical, mental or cognitive, emotional, and social.

   b. Each stage of growth and development has its own characteristics and has specific

   developmental tasks that an individual must master.

   c. Erik Erikson, a psychoanalyst, has identified eight states of psychosocial development.

   _____

3. What is the topic sentence of the closing paragraph?

   Health care providers must understand that each life stage creates certain needs in individuals.

   _____

Summarizing to Understand

In your own words, write a one-paragraph summary of the essay, using the outline above as a guide. Compare your summary with those of your classmates. (See chapter 15 for more about writing summaries.)

Topic Sentence: _____

Support: _____

_____

_____

_____

_____

Conclusion: _____

Writing

Starting on this page, you will plan and write an essay of definition about a topic you are studying. Be sure to use the writing process to do your best work. (See pages 68–73.)

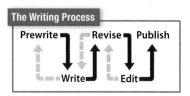

The Writing Process

Prewrite → Revise → Publish
Write → Edit

LO4 Planning an Essay of Definition

While an essay of definition can change its readers, it can also change its writer. Writing an essay of definition is a chance to explore a topic more fully than you have before. As a result, your understanding of the topic will deepen. At the same time, your writing skills will improve.

Selecting a Topic

Below are listed four topics Azzie listed as possible topics for definition, using the categories from page 344. She decided to write about marriage.

- Arts: _Self-expression_
- Journalism: _Slanted language_
- History: (_Marriage_)
- Nutrition: _Vegetarianism_

Select   On page 344 you listed a topic for each of the categories, Arts, Journalism, History, and Nutrition. Choose one of the topics you listed and use it for your own essay of definition.

"The point of the essay is to change things."
—Edward Tufte

hektor2, 2011 / Used under license from Shutterstock.com

Using Resources to Gather Details

There are many resources you can use to begin developing your essay of definition. Here are a few of the most helpful.

- **Dictionary:** Often, your term will have a specific definition in a dictionary. This can be a good starting place for understanding the term. Just make sure to use the correct definition—many words have several possible meanings.
- **Thesaurus:** A thesaurus lists synonyms—words with similar meanings. It also lists antonyms—words with opposite meanings. A synonym or an antonym may be useful in your opening statement.
- **Negative definition:** Sometimes explaining what a term is not can help to reveal what it is.
- **Examples:** Specific examples or instances can help your reader to understand your definition.
- **Function or purpose:** Explaining what something does can help to define that thing.
- **Description:** If what you are defining can be divided into parts, a description of those parts can help make it clear.

The writer of the essay on the next page started a sheet to gather details about marriage from various resources.

Dictionary:	"1 a (1) : the state of being united to a person of the opposite sex as husband or wife in a consensual and contractual relationship recognized by law" *Merriam-Webster's Dictionary*
Thesaurus:	"wedding, matrimony, nuptials." Microsoft Word
Negative definition:	In my opinion, marriage is not just a contract between people. Nor is it always feelings of love.
Examples:	My parents have been married for 35 years. I still see them talking and laughing a lot. Sometimes they also argue.
Function/purpose:	A way of protecting children while they grow. (But what about after children are grown and gone?)
Description:	Joy and passion come and go. So do pain and disappointment. A good marriage seems to be about care and respect beneath it all.

Collect Use a table like the one above to gather your own details about your topic.

LO6 Writing the First Draft

When writing your first draft, don't worry about making everything perfect. Just get your thoughts down on paper.

Read Carefully read and consider the following definition essay about marriage.

Let's Talk Marriage

The thesis statement introduces the topic.

Weddings are great, but marriages can be tough. Many marriages end early, and divorces can be ugly. We might wonder why anyone bothers to get married in the first place. Still, something about marriage keeps people coming back for more. | 1

The author builds upon a dictionary definition.

Historically, marriage has been a public contract between two people, promising to support each other until death. In many cultures, it has also been a contract between two families, each giving something to help launch the new couple. Biologically, marriage has also provided a safe haven for children to grow to adulthood. | 5 ... 10

Negative definitions put the topic in a new perspective.

However, nowadays that contract and safe haven seem to matter less. Our society has less of a stigma about divorce than in previous decades. Many people argue that it is better for children to grow up with separated parents than with parents who argue all the time. The topic of "being in love" seems to be most important. People say, "I love you. Let's get married," then, "I don't love you anymore. Let's get divorced." That seems a pretty narrow definition of love. | 15

Examples are used to round out the definition.

My parents have been married for 35 years, and I think they know true love. Sometimes they argue. I've seen my mom cry over some of their fights. I've seen my dad cry, too. Often their fights have been over how to raise their children. I've also seen my parents support each other through tough times, like when my dad had to have back surgery, or when my mom lost her favorite job. The most important thing is, I see how much they like to spend time together, even just sitting and talking. I see how they still make each other laugh. | 20 ... 25

The author uses further examples to discuss one aspect of the definition.

As for raising children, I'm starting to think that never ends. My brothers and I are all out of the house, but our mom and dad still help out when we need something. Also, when I think about it, I can remember hearing my mom or dad on the phone asking their own parents for advice. | 30

The closing paragraph gives a final thought about the topic.

All things considered, successful marriages seem to be about respect and care. Joys come and goes. Passion comes and goes. Pain comes and goes. Disappointments come and go. Good marriages show a type of love that outlasts them all. | 35

The Working Parts of an Essay

As you saw from the outline and paragraph format on page 345, a paragraph and an essay have certain things in common. Both have an opening, a middle, and an ending, and each of those parts plays its own role. Compare the two graphics below.

Parts of a Paragraph

Thesis Statement

Detail Sentence

Detail Sentence

Detail Sentence

Detail Sentence

Closing Statement

Parts of an Essay

Opening paragraph
(leads to thesis statement)

Supporting paragraph

Supporting paragraph

Supporting paragraph

Supporting paragraph

Ending paragraph
(leads to closing sentence)

Noting Differences

While the two structures bear similarities, note these important differences.

Paragraph	Essay
The parts of a paragraph are sentences.	Each part of an essay is a full paragraph
A standalone paragraph opens with a thesis statement and ends with a closing statement.	The first paragraph usually builds toward the thesis statement.
	Middle paragraphs usually open with a topic sentence.
	The final paragraph builds toward a strong closing sentence.
Sentences are arranged in a spatial, chronological (time), or logical order.	Paragraphs use transitions to lead from one to the next. (See page 354.)

Write Develop your first draft using the information on this page, plus your planning on pages 349–350 as a guide.

LO7 Revising: Improving the Writing

Ernest Hemingway said, "I rewrote the ending of *Farewell to Arms,* the last page of it, 39 times before I was satisfied." Most of us don't make that many revisions, but the fact is, professional writers revise. They know that adding, cutting, rearranging, and rewording are what make writing come to life.

To do your best revision, let your first draft sit for a few days if possible, so that you can view it with fresh eyes. Then read it a number of times looking for strong and weak parts. Be sure to read it aloud at least once. Then have at least one classmate or other peer read and react to your work. Use the response sheet below to guide that conversation.

INSIGHT

Write clear comments and notes in the margins and between the lines of your writing to guide your revision. Make these marks as soon as they occur to you, so that you won't forget.

Peer Review Sheet

Essay title: _____

Writer: _____

Reviewer: _____

1. Which part seems best: Introductory paragraph, a middle paragraph, or closing paragraph? Why?

   _____

   _____

2. Which part needs some work? Why?

   _____

   _____

3. Does the essay adequately define the term? Explain why or why not.

   _____

   _____

4. Does the essay make you think? Explain your thoughts after reading it.

   _____

   _____

Using Transitions Between Paragraphs

Sometimes a thought is enough to lead a reader from one paragraph to the next. Consider the relationship between the final sentence of this paragraph and the first sentence of the next one:

> . . . That seems a pretty narrow definition of love.
>
> My parents have been married for 35 years, and I think they know true love.

Often, however, a transition word or phrase is needed to signal the relationship of one paragraph to the next. In this sentence, "However, nowadays that contract and safe haven seem to matter less," the writer uses the word *however* to contrast the thoughts of two paragraphs.

INSIGHT

Transition words can also lead from sentence to sentence within a paragraph.

Transition Words

- **Words used to show location:**

above	away from	beyond	into	over
across	behind	by	near	throughout
against	below	down	off	to the right
along	beneath	in back of	on top of	under
among	beside	in front of	onto	
around	between	inside	outside	

- **Words used to show time:**

about	before	later	soon	until
after	during	meanwhile	then	when
afterward	finally	next	third	yesterday
as soon as	first	next week	today	
at	immediately	second	tomorrow	

- **Words used to compare things (show similarities):**

also	in the same way	likewise
as	like	similarly

- **Words used to contrast things (show differences):**

although	even though	on the other hand	still
but	however	otherwise	yet

- **Words used to emphasize a point:**

again	for this reason	particularly	to repeat
even	in fact	to emphasize	truly

- **Words used to conclude or summarize:**

all in all	finally	in summary	therefore
as a result	in conclusion	last	to sum up

- **Words used to add information:**

additionally	and	equally important	in addition
again	another	finally	likewise
along with	as well	for example	next
also	besides	for instance	second

- **Words used to clarify:**

for instance	in other words	put another way	that is

Revise   Review your first draft and have someone else read it as well. (See the peer review sheet on page 353.) Then use the following checklist to guide your revision. Keep revising until you can check off each item in the list.

Ideas

☐ 1. Does my essay define an interesting topic?

☐ 2. Do I use various types of sources to make my definition?

☐ 3. Do I thoroughly explore the idea?

Organization

☐ 4. Does my opening paragraph clearly identify the topic?

☐ 5. Do my middle paragraphs all reveal something interesting about the topic?

☐ 6. Does my closing paragraph lead to a strong closing statement?

Voice

☐ 7. Does my writing voice show my interest in the topic?

☐ 8. Does my voice engage the reader?

LO8 Editing: Checking for Correctness

Edit   Create a clean copy of your paragraph and use the following checklist to check it for words, sentences, and conventions.

Words

☐ 1. Have I used specific nouns and verbs? (See page 102.)

☐ 2. Have I used more action verbs than "be" verbs? (See page 458.)

Sentences

☐ 3. Have I varied the beginnings and lengths of sentences? (See pages 104–105.)

☐ 4. Have I combined short choppy sentences? (See page 105.)

☐ 5. Have I avoided shifts in sentences? (See page 422.)

☐ 6. Have I avoided fragments and run-ons? (See pages 410–413, 416–417.)

Conventions

☐ 7. Do I use correct verb forms (*he saw,* not *he seen*)? (See pages 464, 466.)

☐ 8. Do my subjects and verbs agree (*she speaks,* not *she speak*)? (See pages 394–403.)

☐ 9. Have I used the right words (*their, there, they're*)?

☐ 10. Have I capitalized first words and proper nouns and adjectives? (See page 504.)

☐ 11. Have I used commas after long introductory word groups? (See pages 514–517.)

☐ 12. Have I carefully checked my spelling?

> "People are pretty much alike. It's only that our differences are more susceptible to definition than our similarities."
> —Linda Ellerbee

Review and Writing Enrichment

On the next six pages, you will find a professional essay of definition to read and respond to, followed by several ideas for writing your own definitions. Completing these activities will deepen your understanding of writing essays, particularly essays of definition.

Reading

It is human nature to classify things. We lump one group of creatures together as "fish," another group as "birds." Then we offer definitions to make our classifications clear. Often, we have to further those definitions to account for special cases—like penguins and ostriches.

Much of your education is spent learning definitions, evaluating them, and offering definitions of your own. Defining helps us to understand.

Identify Consider two courses you are currently taking in school. List one topic in each that you would like to understand more fully. Share your thoughts with your classmates.

Course: _____

      Topic: _____

Course: _____

      Topic: _____

What do you think?

Do you agree with Linda Ellerbee that "people are pretty much alike"? What do you think she means by the sentence after that? Do you agree with her conclusion? Share your thoughts with your classmates.

Reading and Reacting

Read   This section from *An Invitation to Health: Choosing to Change, Brief Edition,* defines the word "forgive" and explains the health benefits of practicing forgiveness. Use the reading process to get the most out of this brief essay.

The Reading Process

Prereading — Rereading

Reading — Reflecting

About the Author

Dianne Hales is a nationally known freelance journalist, author of more than a dozen books, and recipient of more than a dozen writing awards.

"Forgiving"

While "I forgive you" may be three of the most difficult words to say, they are also three of the most powerful—and the most beneficial for the body as well as the soul. Being angry, harboring resentments, or reliving hurts over and over again is bad for your health in general and your heart in particular. The word forgive comes from the Greek word for "letting go," and that's what happens when you forgive: You let go of all the anger and pain that have been demanding your time and wasting your energy.   *1*   *5*

To some people, forgiveness seems a sign of weakness or submission. People may feel more in control, more powerful, when they're filled with anger, but forgiving instills a much greater sense of power. Forgiving a friend or family member may be more difficult than forgiving a stranger because the hurt occurs in a context in which people deliberately make themselves vulnerable (Fincham).   *10*

When you forgive, you reclaim your power to choose. It doesn't matter whether someone deserves to be forgiven; you deserve to be free. However, forgiveness isn't easy. It's not a one-time thing but a process that takes a lot of time and work involving both the conscious and unconscious mind (Karremans). Most people pass through several stages in their journey to forgiveness. The initial response may involve anger, sadness, shame, or other negative feelings. Later there's a reevaluation of what happened, then reframing to try to make sense of it or to take mitigating circumstances into account. This may lead to a reduction in negative feelings, especially if the initial hurt turns out to be accidental rather than intentional.   *15*   *20*

Works Cited

Fincham, Frank. "Forgiveness: Integral to a Science of Close Relationships?" *Prosocial Motives, Emotions, and Behavior: The Better Angels of our Nature.* Mario Mikulincer and Phillip R. Shaver (Eds.), Washington, DC: American Psychological Association, 2010, pp. 347-365.

Karremans, J. C., et al. "The Malleability of Forgiveness." *Prosocial Motives, Emotions, and Behavior: The Better Angels of our Nature.* Mario Mikulincer and Phillip R. Shaver (Eds.), Washington, DC: American Psychological Association, 2010, pp. 285-301.

React Answer the following questions about Dianne Hales' essay of definition. Share your responses with your classmates.

1. What term is defined by the essay?

   Forgiving

2. What is the thesis of the essay? Write it in your own words.

   _____

3. What origin of "forgive" does the author give?

   The essay mentions that "forgive" comes from the Greek word for letting go.

4. What negative definition or definitions does the author give?

   The author mentions that some people think of forgiveness as a sign of weakness or submission.

5. According to the author, what is the function, or purpose of forgiving?
   The function of forgiving is to let go of all the anger and pain that have been demanding your time and wasting your energy.

6. How would you rate this essay and why?

   Weak ★ ★ ★ ★ ★ Strong

   _____

7. What did you learn from this essay?

   _____

Drawing Inferences

An *inference* is a logical conclusion you can make about something not actually stated in a text, but which is based upon clues in the text. To practice drawing inferences, respond to the following questions about the essay on page 357. Then share your answers with your classmates.

1. What is meant in line 10: "but forgiving instills a much greater sense of power"?

2. How do "anger, sadness, shame, or other negative feelings" relate to forgiveness? Provide an example of each.

Writing

Write an essay of definition following the guidelines on the next two pages. Check with your instructor for any specific requirements she or he may have.

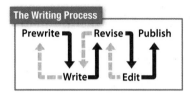

Prewriting

Choose one of the following writing ideas for your essay of definition. Or come up with one of your own.

Writing Ideas

1. Write about one of the topics you identified in the prereading activity on page 344.

2. Write to define an emotion.

3. Write to define an abstract noun such as friendship, enemy, charity, nature, or the like.

4. Write to define a topic you wish everyone found exciting. Use your definition to explain what makes that topic so fascinating to you.

5. Expand your definition paragraph from pages 191–199 to turn it into a more complete and detailed definition, gathering details from the resources described on page 350.

6. Choose a word from a dictionary and write a definition essay about it, expanding it with synonyms and antonyms, negative definitions, real-life examples, explanations of function or purpose, and descriptions of parts.

When planning . . .

Refer to pages 349–350 to help guide your prewriting and planning. Also use the tips below.

- Choose a term to define that will support an essay. Your topic should be broad enough to allow for some exploration and discussion.

- Choose a topic that you feel a strong interest in. Writing about a subject you care about is always easiest and leads to best results.

- Gather plenty of details about your topic so that you will have enough material to draw from when writing.

- Arrange those details in an order that seems sensible to you. (You can always adjust that order when writing or revising.)

Writing and Revising

Refer to pages 351–355 to help as you write your first draft and revise it. Also use the following tips to help with the process.

When writing . . .

- Include an opening paragraph that draws the reader in and leads to your thesis statement.
- Include several middle paragraphs, each exploring one main idea about your topic.
- Include a closing paragraph that rewords your thesis and leads to a strong closing sentence.
- Use transitions to lead from one paragraph to the next.
- Follow your planning notes, but also feel free to explore new ideas that come to mind as you write.
- Use many types of details to help define your chosen subject.

When revising . . .

- Let your essay sit for a few days if possible, then reread it aloud.
- Ask if your definition will interest and engage a reader. If it doesn't, determine what changes need to be made.
- Ask if your middle paragraphs are in the best order. If they aren't, rearrange them to make the best sense and to lead the reader from one idea to the next.
- Ask if any areas need transitions to help carry the reader along. Insert any needed transitions. (See page 354.)
- Have at least one trusted peer read your essay. Ask for an honest reaction. (See page 353.)

Supri Suharjoto, 2011 / Used under license from Shutterstock.com

Editing

Refer to the checklist on page 355 when editing your essay of definition for style and correctness.

Reflecting on Argument Writing

Answer the following questions about your reading and writing experiences in this chapter.

1. What do you find enjoyable about reading essays of definition?

   _____

2. What is your favorite essay in this chapter? Explain.

   _____

3. Which reading strategy in this chapter do you find most helpful? Explain.

   _____

4. What is the most important thing you have learned about reading an essay of definition?

   _____

5. What do you like most about the essay of definition you wrote in this chapter? Explain.

   _____

6. What is one thing you would like to change about that essay?

   _____

7. What is the most important thing you have learned about writing an essay of definition?

   _____

Key Terms to Remember

When you read and write definition essays, it's important to understand the following terms.

- **Transition**—a connecting word, phrase, or thought that leads from one paragraph to another, or from one sentence to another within a paragraph
- **Synonyms**—words that are similar in meaning
- **Antonyms**—words that are opposite in meaning
- **Negative definition**—an explanation of what something is not, which by contrast helps to reveal what it is

Part III: Sentence Workshops

17

"Grasp the subject; the words will follow."
—Cato the Elder

Sentence Basics

All right, soldiers, fall in for basic training. Of course, you've studied all of this before, so the following pages will be a review. And the basics of sentences really are basic. A sentence is the connection between a noun and a verb (or a subject and a predicate), with all of the other words modifying those two parts. These are the building blocks of thought.

In the pages that follow, you will explore the ins and outs of subjects and predicates, as well as the words, phrases, and clauses that describe them. Fear not. These are sentence basics, and we'll make sure they are easy to understand.

Learning Outcomes

LO1 Understand subjects and predicates.

LO2 Work with special subjects.

LO3 Work with special predicates.

LO4 Understand adjectives.

LO5 Understand adverbs.

LO6 Use prepositional phrases.

LO7 Use clauses.

LO8 Apply sentence basics in a real-world context.

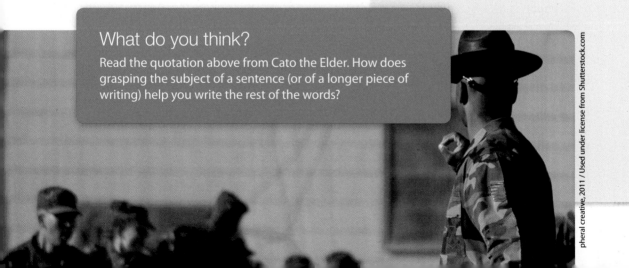

What do you think?

Read the quotation above from Cato the Elder. How does grasping the subject of a sentence (or of a longer piece of writing) help you write the rest of the words?

pheral creative, 2011 / Used under license from Shutterstock.com

LO1 Subjects and Verbs (Predicates)

The subject of a sentence tells what the sentence is about. The verb (predicate) of a sentence tells what the subject does or is.

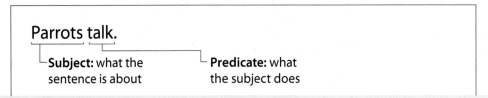

Simple Subject and Simple Predicate

The **simple subject** is the subject without any modifiers, and the **simple predicate** is the verb and any helping verbs without modifiers or objects.

The red and black parrot sang the song all day.
                    simple subject   simple predicate

Complete Subject and Complete Predicate

The **complete subject** is the subject with modifiers, and the **complete predicate** is the predicate with modifiers and objects.

The red and black parrot sang the song all day.
        complete subject   complete predicate

Implied Subject

In commands, the subject *you* is implied. Commands are the only type of sentence in English that can have an **implied subject**.

(You)   Stop singing!
implied subject   complete predicate

Inverted Order

Most often in English, the subject comes before the predicate. However, in questions and sentences that begin with *here* or *there*, the subject comes after the predicate.

    subject   subject
Why are you so loud?   Here is a cracker.
    predicate   predicate

Creating Subjects and Verbs (Predicates)

Identify/Write For each sentence below, identify the simple subject (SS) and simple predicate (SP). Then write a similar sentence of your own and identify the simple subject and simple predicate in the same way.

1. In the wild, parrots gather in large groups.
   SS   SP
   Answers will vary.

2. In a person's home, a parrot needs constant companionship.
   SS   SP

3. Without enough attention, some parrots pluck their feathers.
   SS   SP

4. A caring pet owner understands the parrot's need for attention.
   SS   SP

Identify/Write For each sentence below, identify the complete subject (CS) and complete predicate (CP). Then write a similar sentence of your own and identify the complete subject and complete predicate in the same way.

1. A typical pet parrot can live to be eighty years old.
   CS   CP

2. A baby parrot could outlive the person.
   CS   CP

3. Parrot owners often place their parrots in their wills.
   CS   CP

4. Why do parrots live so long?
   CP   CS   CP

5. There must be an explanation.
   CP   CS

Vocabulary

simple subject
the subject without any modifiers

simple predicate
the verb and any helping verbs without modifiers or objects

complete subject
the subject with modifiers

complete predicate
the predicate with modifiers and objects

implied subject
the word *you* implied in command sentences

LO2 Special Types of Subjects

As you work with subjects, watch for these special types.

Compound Subjects

A **compound subject** is two or more subjects connected by *and* or *or*.

My brother and sister swim well. Dajohn, Larinda, and I love to dive.
   compound subject   compound subject

"To" Words (Infinitives) as Subjects

An **infinitive** can function as a subject. An infinitive is a verbal form that begins with *to* and may be followed by objects or modifiers.

To complete a one-and-a-half flip is my goal.
          infinitive subject

"Ing" Words (Gerunds) as Subjects

A **gerund** can function as a subject. A gerund is a verb form that ends in *ing* and may be followed by objects or modifiers.

Swimming is his favorite sport.   Handing him the goggles would be nice.
gerund subject   gerund subject

Noun Clause as Subject

A **noun clause** can function as a subject. The clause itself has a subject and a verb but cannot stand alone as a sentence. Noun clauses are introduced by words like *what, that, when, why, how, whatever,* or *whichever.*

Whoever wants to go swimming must remember to bring a swimsuit.
        noun clause subject

Whatever remains of the afternoon will be spent at the pool.
        noun clause subject

CONSIDER THE TRAITS

Note that each of these special subjects still functions as a noun or a group of nouns. A sentence is still, at root, the connection between a noun and a verb.

Say It

Pair up with a partner and read each sentence aloud. Take turns identifying the type of subject—compound subject, infinitive subject, gerund subject, or noun-clause subject. Discuss your answers.

1. Swimming across the pool underwater is challenging.
2. To get a lifesaving certificate is hard work.
3. Whoever gets a certificate can be a lifeguard.
4. You and I should go swimming sometime.

Creating Special Subjects

Identify/Write   For each sentence below, identify the complete subject as a compound subject (CS), infinitive (I), gerund (G), or noun clause (NC). Then write a similar sentence of your own and identify the complete subject in the same way.

1. <u>To clean the car thoroughly</u> requires a vacuum. Answers will vary.
   I

2. <u>Wishing for better weather</u> won't stop the rain.
   G

3. <u>The river and the lake</u> are flooding into the streets.
   CS

4. <u>Whoever needs to set the table</u> should get started now.
   NC

5. <u>Shoes, shirts, and pants</u> are required in this restaurant.
   CS

6. <u>Reading us the riot act</u> is not the best way to win us over.
   G

7. <u>To reassure your boss about the expenditures</u> is your first priority.
   I

8. <u>Whatever you plan</u> needs to be simple and affordable.
   NC

9. Are <u>Jason, Micah, and Eli</u> in the play?
   CS

10. <u>Helping us change the tire</u> will speed everything along.
    G

Vocabulary

compound subject
two or more subjects connected by *and* or *or*

infinitive
a verb form that begins with *to* and can be used as a noun (or as an adjective or adverb)

gerund
a verb form that ends in *ing* and is used as a noun

noun clause
a group of words beginning with words like *that, what, whoever,* and so on; containing a subject and a verb but unable to function as a sentence

LO3 Special Verbs (Predicates)

As you work with predicates, watch for these special types.

Compound Predicates

A **compound predicate** consists of two or more predicates joined by *and* or *or*.

I sang and danced. The audience laughed, clapped, and sang along.
    compound predicate   compound predicate

Predicates with Direct Objects

A **direct object** follows a transitive verb and tells what or who receives the action of the verb.

I sang a song. I danced a few dances. I told a joke or two.
    direct object   direct object   direct objects

Predicates with Indirect Objects

An **indirect object** comes between a transitive verb and a direct object and tells to whom or for whom an action was done.

I sang Jim his favorite song. I told Ellen her favorite joke.
    indirect object   indirect object

Passive Predicates

When a predicate is **passive**, the subject of the sentence is being acted upon rather than acting. Often, the actor is the object of the preposition in a phrase that starts with *by*. To make the sentence **active**, rewrite it, turning the object of the preposition into the subject.

Passive

Teri was serenaded by Josh.
subject   passive verb   object of the preposition

Active

Josh serenaded Teri.
subject └ active verb └─ direct object

Say It

Pair up with a partner and read each sentence aloud. Take turns identifying the sentence as active or passive. If the sentence is passive, speak the active version out loud.

1. I threw out my back.
2. My friends were warned by the bouncer.
3. A camera crew was escorted to the exit by the guard.
4. I plan to go.

Creating Special Predicates

Identify/Write For each sentence below, identify any compound predicate (CP), direct object (DO), and indirect object (IO). Then write a similar sentence of your own and identify the compound predicate and direct or indirect object.

1. Everyone at the party danced and sang. _Answers will vary._
   CP
2. The DJ played dance music. _____
   DO
3. I gave him a request. _____
   IO   DO
4. The crowd twisted and shouted. _____
   CP
5. I gave my date a kiss. _____
   IO   DO
6. The music rattled and boomed. _____
   CP
7. The DJ provided everyone some awesome entertainment. ____
   IO   DO

Identify/Write For each passive sentence below, identify the simple subject (SS), the simple predicate (SP), and the object of the preposition *by* (O). Then rewrite each sentence, making it active.

1. Many songs were played by the DJ. _The DJ played many songs._
   SS   SP   O
2. A good time was had by the partygoers. _The partygoers had a good time._
      SS   SP   O
3. My friend was asked by Sarah to the next party. _Sarah asked my friend to the_
      SS   SP   O   _next party._

Vocabulary

compound predicate
two or more predicates joined by *and* or *or*

direct object
a word that follows a transitive verb and tells what or who receives the action of the verb

indirect object
a word that comes between a transitive verb and a direct object and tells to whom or for whom an action was done

passive
the voice created when a subject is being acted upon

active
the voice created when a subject is acting

LO4 Adjectives

To modify a noun, use an adjective or a phrase or clause acting as an adjective.

Adjectives

Adjectives answer these basic questions: *which, what kind of, how many, how much.*

To modify the noun **books,** ask . . .

Which books? ⟶ hardbound books

What kind of books? ⟶ old books

How many books? ⟶ five books

five old hardbound books

Adjective Phrases and Clauses

Phrases and clauses can also act as adjectives to modify nouns.

To modify the noun **books,** ask . . .

What kind of books? ⟶ books about women's issues

⟶ books showing their age

Which books? ⟶ books that my mother gave me

Showing their age, the books that my mother gave me about women's issues rest on the top shelf.

INSIGHT

It's less important to know the name of a phrase or clause than to know how it functions. If a group of words answers one of the adjective questions, the words are probably functioning as an adjective.

| Say It |

Pair up with a classmate to find adjectives—words, phrases, or clauses—that modify the nouns below. Take turns asking the questions while the other person answers.

1. **Cars**
   Which cars?
   What kind of cars?
   How many cars?

2. **Trees**
   Which trees?
   What kind of trees?
   How many trees?

Use Adjectives

Answer/Write For each noun, answer the questions using adjectives—words, phrases, or clauses. Then write a sentence using two or more of your answers.

1. **Dogs** Answers will vary.

   Which dogs? Labrador dogs

   What kind of dogs? black dogs

   How many dogs? two dogs

   Sentence: Two black Labrador dogs played in the yard.

2. **Classes** Answers will vary.

   Which classes? business classes

   What kind of classes? core classes

   How many classes? three classes

   Sentence: I took three core business classes during my freshman year.

3. **Ideas** Answers will vary.

   Which ideas? Jason's idea

   What kind of ideas? practical ideas

   How many ideas? one idea

   Sentence: Jason's one practical idea helped us get out of a jam.

LO5 Adverbs

To modify a verb, use an adverb or a phrase or clause acting as an adverb.

Adverbs

Adverbs answer these basic questions: *how, when, where, why, how long, and how often.*

To modify the verb **jumped,** ask . . .

How did they jump?	⟶	jumped exuberantly
When did they jump?	⟶	jumped today
Where did they jump?	⟶	jumped there
How often did they jump?	⟶	jumped often

> The children jumped exuberantly and often today, there on the pile of old mattresses.

Adverb Phrases and Clauses

Phrases and clauses can also act as adverbs to modify verbs.

To modify the verb **jumped,** ask . . .

How did they jump?	⟶	jumped with great enthusiasm
When did they jump?	⟶	jumped before lunchtime
Where did they jump?	⟶	jumped on the trampoline
Why did they jump?	⟶	jumped to get some exercise
	⟶	jumped because it's fun
How long did they jump?	⟶	jumped for an hour

> To get some exercise before lunchtime, the children jumped on the trampoline with great enthusiasm. I think, though, that they jumped for an hour just because it's fun!

CONSIDER SPEAKING AND LISTENING

Read the last two sentences aloud. Though they may look imposing on the page, they sound natural, probably because adverbs and adjectives are a common part of our speech. Experiment with these modifiers in your writing as well.

Using Adverbs

Answer/Write   For each verb, answer the questions using adverbs—words, phrases, or clauses. Then write a sentence using three or more of your answers.

1. Sang Answers will vary.

How did they sing? _sang beautifully_

When did they sing? _sang last night_

Where did they sing? _sang here_

Why did they sing? _sang to provide entertainment_

How long did they sing? _sang for 15 minutes_

How often did they sing? _sang often_

Sentence: _Kristie sang beautifully here last night._

2. **Ate** Answers will vary.

How did they eat? _ate sloppily_

When did they eat? _ate two hours ago_

Where did they eat? _ate at Rick's BBQ_

Why did they eat? _ate to fulfill a craving_

How long did they eat? _ate for hours_

How often did they eat? _ate every Friday_

Sentence: _Every Friday JT and Alex ate at Rick's BBQ to fulfill a craving._

LO6 Prepositional Phrases

One of the simplest and most versatile types of phrases in English is the **prepositional phrase**. A prepositional phrase can function as an adjective or an adverb.

Building Prepositional Phrases

A prepositional phrase is a preposition followed by an object (a noun or pronoun) and any modifiers.

Preposition	+	Object	=	Prepositional Phrase
at		noon		at noon
in		an hour		in an hour
beside		the green clock		beside the green clock
in front of		my aunt's vinyl purse		in front of my aunt's vinyl purse

As you can see, a propositional phrase can be just two words long, or many words long. As you can also see, some prepositions are themselves made up of more than one word. Here is a list of common prepositions.

Prepositions

aboard	back of	except for	near to	round
about	because of	excepting	notwithstanding	save
above	before	for	of	since
according to	behind	from	off	subsequent to
across	below	from among	on	through
across from	beneath	from between	on account of	throughout
after	beside	from under	on behalf of	'til
against	besides	in	onto	to
along	between	in addition to	on top of	together with
alongside	beyond	in behalf of	opposite	toward
alongside of	but	in front of	out	under
along with	by	in place of	out of	underneath
amid	by means of	in regard to	outside	until
among	concerning	inside	outside of	unto
apart from	considering	inside of	over	up
around	despite	in spite of	over to	upon
as far as	down	instead of	owing to	up to
aside from	down from	into	past	with
at	during	like	prior to	within
away from	except	near	regarding	without

INSIGHT

A preposition is pre-positioned before the other words it introduces to form a phrase. Other languages have post-positional words that follow their objects.

Using Phrases

Create For each item below, create a prepositional phrase by writing a preposition in the first box and an object (and any modifiers) in the second box. Then write a sentence using the prepositional phrase.

1.
Preposition	$+$	Object (and any modifiers)
Answers will vary.		Answers will vary.

Sentence: Answers will vary.

2.
Preposition	$+$	Object (and any modifiers)

Sentence: _____

3.
Preposition	$+$	Object (and any modifiers)

Sentence: _____

4.
Preposition	$+$	Object (and any modifiers)

Sentence: _____

5.
Preposition	$+$	Object (and any modifiers)

Sentence: _____

Vocabulary

prepositional phrase
a group of words beginning with a preposition and including an object (noun or pronoun) and any modifiers

LO7 Clauses

A clause is a group of words with a subject and a predicate. If a clause can stand on its own as a sentence, it is an **independent clause**, but if it cannot, it is a **dependent clause**.

Independent Clause

An independent clause has a subject and a predicate and expresses a complete thought. It is the same as a simple sentence.

> I have nineteen pets.

Dependent Clause

A dependent clause has a subject and a predicate but does not express a complete thought. Instead, it is used as an **adverb clause**, an **adjective clause**, or a **noun clause**.

An adverb clause begins with a subordinating conjunction (see below) and functions as an adverb, so it must be connected to an independent clause to be complete.

CONSIDER SPEAKING AND LISTENING

In each example below, read the dependent clause out loud. (The dependent clause is in red.) Can you hear how each dependent clause sounds incomplete? Read it to another person, and the listener will probably say, "What about it?" These clauses depend on a complete thought to make sense.

after	as long as	given that	since	unless	where
although	because	if	so that	until	whereas
as	before	in order that	that	when	while
as if	even though	provided that	though	whenever	

> Because I have nineteen pets, I have a big pet-food bill.

An adjective clause begins with a relative pronoun *(which, that, who)* and functions as an adjective, so it must be connected to an independent clause to be complete.

> My oldest pet is a cat that thinks he is a person.

A noun clause begins with words like those below and functions as a noun. It is used as a subject or an object in a sentence.

| how | what | whoever | whomever |
| that | whatever | whom | why |

> My cat doesn't care about what I think.

Using Clauses

Identify/Write For each sentence below, identify any adverb clauses (ADVC), adjective clauses (ADJC), or noun clauses (NC). Then write a similar sentence of your own and identify the clauses.

1. I know a woman <u>who has fifteen cats</u>.
   Answers will vary.   ADJC

2. The number is so high <u>because she takes care of shelter kittens</u>.
                                              ADVC

3. <u>When a pregnant cat is dropped at the shelter</u>, this woman takes her home.
                     ADVC

4. She provides <u>what the mother and the kittens need</u>.
                              NC

5. <u>Whatever cat comes to her</u> receives good care.
              NC

6. People <u>who are cruel to animals</u> should not have pets.
                    ADJC

7. <u>When I visit my friend</u>, I see plenty of kittens.
              ADVC

8. All are safe <u>provided that they don't escape</u>.
                           ADVC

9. My friend has a shirt <u>that has the words "Cat Lady" printed on it</u>.
                                      ADJC

10. <u>Though others might scoff</u>, my friend is proud of what she does.
                 ADVC

Vocabulary

independent clause
a group of words with a subject and predicate that expresses a complete thought

dependent clause
a group of words with a subject and predicate that does not express a complete thought

adverb clause
a dependent clause beginning with a subordinating conjunction and functioning as an adverb

adjective clause
a dependent clause beginning with a relative pronoun and functioning as an adjective

noun clause
a dependent clause beginning with a subordinating word and functioning as a noun

LO8 Real-World Application

Identify Write down the simple subject and simple predicate of each sentence in the e-mail below. Identify dependent clauses.

| Send | Attach | Fonts | Colors | Save As Draft |

To: Robert Pastorelli

Subject: Meeting to Discuss Benefits and Policies

Dear Robert:

I am pleased that you have accepted the Production Manager position at Rankin Technologies. I believe that you'll find many opportunities for professional growth with us.

Our Human Resources Department is here to help you grow. To that end, I would like to discuss Rankin's benefit package, policies, and procedures. Specifically, I'd like to share the following information:
- Profit-sharing plan
- Medical-plan benefits for you and your family
- Procedures for submitting dental and optometry receipts
- Counseling services
- Continuing-education programs
- Advancement policies and procedures
- Workplace policies

On Friday, I will arrange a convenient time for your orientation meeting. In the meantime, if you have questions, please contact me at extension 3925 or simply reply to this message.

Sincerely,
Julia

1

5

10

15

Expand Answer the adjective and adverb questions below. Then expand the sentence using some of the words, phrases, and clauses you have created.

The manager spoke.

Which manager? _____

What kind of manager? _____

Spoke *how?* _____

Spoke *when?* _____

Sentence: _____

18

"A complex system that works is invariably found to have evolved from a simple system that works."

—John Gaule

Simple, Compound, and Complex Sentences

A two-by-four is a simple thing—a board with standard dimensions. But two-by-fours can be used to create everything from a shed to a mansion. It's the way that the boards are connected and combined that determines the proportions of the final structure.

A sentence can be a simple thing as well, just a subject and a verb. But sentences can also be connected to become compound or complex sentences. The way in which writers use simple, compound, and complex sentences determines the maturity of their writing.

Learning Outcomes

LO1 Create simple sentences.

LO2 Create simple sentences with compound subjects.

LO3 Create simple sentences with compound verbs (predicates).

LO4 Create compound sentences.

LO5 Create complex sentences.

LO6 Create complex sentences with relative clauses.

LO7 Apply simple, compound, and complex sentences in a real-world context.

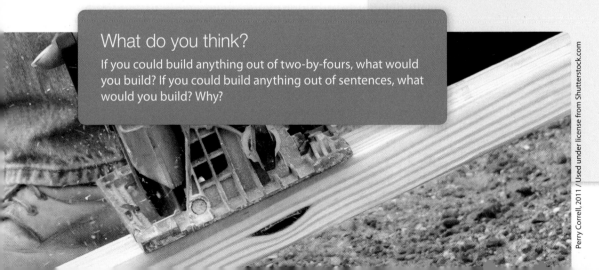

What do you think?

If you could build anything out of two-by-fours, what would you build? If you could build anything out of sentences, what would you build? Why?

Perry Correll, 2011 / Used under license from Shutterstock.com

LO1 Simple Sentences

A **simple sentence** consists of a subject and a verb. The subject is a noun or pronoun that names what the sentence is about. The verb tells what the subject does or is.

> Terrance played.
> subject verb

Modifiers

Other words can modify the subject. Words and phrases that modify the subject answer the adjective questions: *which, what kind of, how many, how much.*

> My longtime friend Terrance played.
> (The phrase tells *which Terrance.*)

Other words can also modify the verb. These words and phrases answer the adverb questions: *how, when, where, why, how long,* and *how often.*

> Terrance played all afternoon and into the evening.
> (The phrases tell *when Terrance played.*)

Direct and Indirect Objects

The verb may also be followed by a **direct object**, a noun or pronoun that receives the action of the verb. The direct object answers the question *what* or *whom.*

> Terrance played basketball.
> (*Basketball* tells *what Terrance played.*)

A noun or pronoun that comes between the verb and its direct object is called an **indirect object**. The indirect object answers the question *to whom* or *for whom* an action is done.

> Terrance passed me the basketball.
> (*Me* tells *to whom Terrance passed the basketball.*)

Creating Simple Sentences

Create Provide a noun for a subject and a verb for a predicate. Then write a sentence with the noun and verb, adding details that answer the questions asked. The first question has been done for you.

1.

Subject The Raiders	Verb won

Which? _____

Simple Sentence: _The Raiders won._____

2.

Subject	Verb

What kind of? _____

Simple Sentence: _____

3.

Subject	Verb

When? _____

Simple Sentence: _____

4.

Subject	Verb

Where? _____

Simple Sentence: _____

5.

Subject	Verb

How? _____

Simple Sentence: _____

Vocabulary

simple sentence
a subject and a verb that together form a complete thought

direct object
a noun or pronoun that follows a verb and receives its action

indirect object
a noun or pronoun that comes between a verb and a direct object, telling *to whom* or *for whom* an action is done

LO2 Simple Sentences with Compound Subjects

A simple sentence can have a **compound subject** (two or more subjects).

A Simple Sentence with Two Subjects

To write a simple sentence with two subjects, join them using *and* or *or*.

One Subject: Chan collected donations for the animal shelter.

Two Subjects: Chan and Lynn collected donations for the animal shelter.
Chan or Lynn collected the most donations.

One Subject: The president of the shelter gave Lynn an award.

Two Subjects: The president and vice president of the shelter gave Lynn an award.
The president or the vice president of the shelter thanked her for her hard work.

A Simple Sentence with Three or More Subjects

To write a simple sentence with three or more subjects, create a series, using *and* or *or* before the last one.

Three Subjects: Chan, Lynn, and I went out to celebrate.

Five Subjects: Chan, Lynn, the president, the vice president, and I were interviewed by a reporter.

NOTE: When a compound subject is joined by *and,* the subject is plural and requires a plural verb. When a compound subject is joined by *or,* the verb should match the last subject.

Chan and Lynn plan to help out again next year.

Chan or Lynn plans to help out again next year.

CONSIDER THE TRAITS

Using a compound subject in a simple sentence does not make the sentence compound. As long as the subjects connect to the same verb, the sentence is still considered simple.

Say It

Speak each of the following sentences out loud.
1. Chan *volunteers* regularly.
2. Chan *and* Lynn *volunteer* regularly.
3. Chan *or* Lynn *volunteers* once a month.
4. Chan, Lynn, *and* Dave *help* at the shelter each week.
5. Chan, Lynn, *or* Dave *helps* at the shelter each week.

Using Compound Subjects

Create For each item below, write subjects in the boxes provided. Then connect the subjects using *and* or *or* and use the compound subject in a simple sentence.

1. | Subject Answers will vary. | Verb Answers will vary. |

   Simple Sentence: Answers will vary. _____

2. | Subject | Verb |

   Simple Sentence: _____

3. | Subject | Verb |

   Simple Sentence: _____

4. | Subject | Verb |

   Simple Sentence: _____

5. | Subject | Verb |

   Simple Sentence: _____

Vocabulary

compound subject
two or more subjects joined
by the conjunction *or* or *and*

LO3 Simple Sentences with Compound Verbs

A simple sentence can have a **compound verb** (two or more verbs).

A Simple Sentence with Two Verbs

To write a simple sentence with two verbs, join them using *and* or *or*.

One Verb: The tornado roared.

Two Verbs: The tornado roared and twisted.

Remember that the predicate often includes words that modify or complete the verbs.

One Verb: A tornado tore through our town.

Two Verbs: A tornado tore through our town and damaged buildings.

A Simple Sentence with Three or More Verbs

To write a simple sentence with three or more verbs, create a series, using *and* or *or* before the last one.

Three Verbs: The tornado roared, twisted, and shuddered.

Five Verbs: People shouted, ran, gathered, hid, and waited.

Each verb in a series can also include modifiers or completing words (direct and indirect objects).

The tornado tore apart a warehouse, ripped the roofs from homes, and flattened trailers in a local park.

CONSIDER THE TRAITS

Using a compound verb in a simple sentence does not make the sentence compound. As long as the verbs connect to the same subject, the sentence is still considered simple.

Using Compound Verbs

Create For each subject below, write verbs, along with modifiers or completing words, in the boxes provided. (See page 384.) Then create a compound verb using *and* or *or* and write the complete simple sentence on the lines.

1. The hailstorm

> Verb Answers will vary.

> Verb Answers will vary.

Simple Sentence: _Answers will vary._

2. Driving rain

> Verb

> Verb

Simple Sentence: _____

3. A news crew

> Verb

> Verb

Simple Sentence: _____

4. Many homes

> Verb

> Verb

Simple Sentence: _____

Vocabulary

compound verb
two or more subjects joined
by the conjunction *or* or *and*

LO4 Compound Sentences

A **compound sentence** is made out of simple sentences joined by a coordinating conjunction: *and, but, or, nor, for, so,* or *yet.*

Compound of Two Sentences

Most compound sentences connect two simple sentences, or independent clauses. Connect the sentences by placing a comma and a coordinating conjunction between them.

Two Sentences: We drove all night. The sun rose behind us.

Compound Sentence: We drove all night, and the sun rose behind us.

You can also join two sentences with a semicolon.

Compound Sentence: We drove all night; the sun rose behind us.

Compound of Three or More Sentences

Sometimes, you may want to join three or more short sentences to form a compound sentence.

Three Sentences: I drove. Janice navigated. Paulo slept.

Compound Sentence: I drove, Janice navigated, and Paulo slept.

You can also join the sentences with semicolons. This approach works well for sharing a long, involved process or a flurry of activity.

I took the shift from Williamsburg to Monticello; Janice drove from Monticello to Louisville; Paulo brought us from Louisville to Indianapolis.

NOTE: Remember that a compound sentence is made of two or more simple sentences, each containing its own subject and verb.

CONSIDER THE TRAITS

Using a compound verb in a simple sentence does not make the sentence compound. As long as the verbs connect to the same subject, the sentence is still considered simple.

Create Compound Sentences

Write   Write a simple sentence for each prompt; then combine them into a compound sentence.

1. What did you do on a road trip? Answers will vary. _____

   What did a different person do? Answers will vary. _____

   Compound sentence: Answers will vary. _____

   _____

2. What do you like to eat? _____

   What does a friend like to eat? _____

   Compound sentence: _____

   _____

3. What did you do last weekend? _____

   What did a friend do? _____

   What did a relative do? _____

   Compound sentence: _____

   _____

4. Where do you want to go? _____

   Where does a friend want to go? _____

   Where does a relative want to go? _____

   Compound sentence: _____

   _____

5. What is your favorite place? _____

   What is a friend's favorite place? _____

   What is a relative's favorite place? _____

   Compound sentence: _____

   _____

Vocabulary

compound sentence
two or more simple sentences joined with a coordinating conjunction

LO5 Complex Sentences

A **complex sentence** shows a special relationship between two ideas. Instead of connecting two sentences as equal ideas (as in a compound sentence), a complex sentence shows that one idea depends on the other.

Using a Subordinating Conjunction

You can create a complex sentence by placing a subordinating conjunction before the sentence that is less important. Here are common subordinating conjunctions:

after	before	so that	when
although	even though	that	where
as	if	though	whereas
as if	in order that	till	while
as long as	provided that	'til	
because	since	until	

The subordinating conjunction shows that the one sentence depends on the other and cannot stand on its own.

Two Sentences:	We searched the package. We found no instructions.
Complex Sentence:	Though we searched the package, we found no instructions.
	We found no instructions though we searched the package.

NOTE: The subordinating conjunction begins the dependent clause, but the two clauses can be in either order. When the dependent clause comes second, it is usually not separated by a comma.

Compound-Complex

You can also create a **compound-complex sentence** by placing a subordinating conjunction before a simple sentence and connecting it to a compound sentence.

Simple Sentence:	I wouldn't give up.
Compound Sentence:	Jan went to watch TV, and Bill joined her.
Compound-Complex:	Although I wouldn't give up, Jan went to watch TV, and Bill joined her.

Create Complex Sentences

Write Write a simple sentence for each prompt. Then select a subordinating conjunction from the facing page, place it at the beginning of one sentence, and combine the two sentences into a single complex sentence.

1. What did you look for? _Answers will vary._

   What did you find? _Answers will vary._

   Complex sentence: _Answers will vary._

2. Who helped you? _____

   Who did not help? _____

   Complex sentence: _____

3. What do you need? _____

   What did you get? _____

   Complex sentence: _____

4. What did you see? _____

   What did a friend see? _____

   Complex sentence: _____

5. Whom did you meet? _____

   Whom did you avoid? _____

   Complex sentence: _____

6. What did you win? _____

   What did you lose? _____

   Complex sentence: _____

CONSIDER SPEAKING AND LISTENING

Read the example complex and compound-complex sentences aloud. Despite their daunting names, these sentences aren't that complicated and are used often in speech. Experiment with them in your writing.

WilleeCole, 2011 / Used under license from Shutterstock.com

LO6 Complex Sentences with Relative Clauses

In a complex sentence, one idea depends on the other. You've seen how a dependent clause can start with a subordinating conjunction. Another type of dependent clause starts with a relative pronoun.

Relative Clauses

A **relative clause** is a group of words that begins with a **relative pronoun** (*that, which, who, whom*) and includes a verb and any words that modify or complete it.

Relative Clauses: that celebrates my promotion
which is very generous
who comes to the party

Each relative clause above has a subject and a verb, but none of the clauses is a complete sentence. All need to be connected to independent clauses to complete their meaning.

Complex Sentences: I hope you come to the party that celebrates my promotion.
My boss gave me an office, which is very generous.
I'll have a gift for everyone who comes to the party.

That and *Which*

The pronoun *that* signals information that is necessary to the meaning of the sentence. The pronoun *which* signals information that is not necessary, so the clause is set off with a comma.

That: Please reserve the room that we will use. (The clause beginning with *that* defines the room.)

Which: We'll have cheesecake, which I love. (The clause beginning with *which* just adds information about the cake.)

Who and *Whom*

The pronoun *who* is the subject of the relative clause that it introduces. The pronoun *whom* is a direct object in the clause it introduces.

Who: I spoke to the woman who baked the cake. (*Who* is the subject.)

Whom: I greeted the Joneses, whom I invited. (*Whom* is the direct object.)

Create Complex Sentences with Relative Clauses

Write For each item, write a relative clause beginning with the pronoun provided. Then write a complex sentence that includes the relative clause. (If you need a topic idea, consider writing about a party, concert, or family gathering you attended.)

1. Relative clause: that _____

   Complex sentence: Answers will vary. _____

   _____

2. Relative clause: who _____

   Complex sentence: _____

   _____

3. Relative clause: which _____

   Complex sentence: _____

   _____

4. Relative clause: whom _____

   Complex sentence: _____

   _____

5. Relative clause: that _____

   Complex sentence: _____

   _____

6. Relative clause: which _____

   Complex sentence: _____

   _____

INSIGHT

In some languages, if the relative pronoun is the object of the clause it introduces, another pronoun is inserted in the clause:

> *I liked the gift that my boss gave it to me.*

In English, no additional pronoun is inserted:

> *I liked the gift that my boss gave to me.*

Vocabulary

relative clause
a group of words that begins with a relative pronoun and includes a verb but cannot stand alone as a sentence

relative pronoun
a word (*that, which, who, whom*) that relates a dependent clause to another word in the sentence

LO7 Real-World Application

Rewrite Read the following invitation to a party. Note how every sentence is a simple sentence. Rewrite the invitation, combining some sentences into compound or complex sentences to improve the flow.

Dear Ms. Jamison:

You are invited to a party. The party celebrates my promotion to store manager. I've been working toward this promotion all year. The store owner notified me yesterday. This is a big step for me. I want to share my day with you.

The party takes place Tuesday, July 13, at 8:00 p.m. at the Lucky Star restaurant. I've invited my colleagues and friends. Don't bring a gift. Just bring an appetite and a party spirit. I will provide beverages and cake. You've been a great support. I hope to see you there.

Dear Ms. Jamison:

Answers will vary.

Dear Ms. Jamison:

You are invited to a party that celebrates my promotion to store manager. I've been working toward this promotion all year, and the store owner notified me yesterday. This is a big step for me, and I want to share my day with you.

The party takes place Tuesday, July 13, at 8:00 p.m. at the Lucky Star restaurant. I've invited my colleagues and friends. Don't bring a gift; just bring an appetite and a party spirit, because I will provide beverages and cake. You've been a great support, and I hope to see you there.

INSIGHT ——————————————————————————————————

Using a variety of sentences in workplace writing will improve the flow of ideas and give the organization a polished, capable image.

19

Agreement

"Men keep agreements when it is to the advantage of neither to break them."
—Solon

When people come to an agreement, they can begin to work together. Until an agreement is reached, the people most often work against each other, or perhaps have no working relationship at all.

The same goes for subjects and verbs. If the verb does not agree with the subject in number, both being either singular or plural, these two crucial sentence parts cannot work together. They fight each other, or even disconnect. And the same happens when pronouns and antecedents don't agree. Sentences break down.

This chapter helps you recognize and correct agreement errors. It also focuses on a few other pronoun problems. After you review the information and complete the exercises, you will be prepared to write well-connected sentences that work.

Learning Outcomes

LO1 Make subjects and verbs agree.

LO2 Make two subjects agree with verbs.

LO3 Practice agreement with *I* and *you*.

LO4 Practice agreement with indefinite pronouns.

LO5 Practice pronoun-antecedent agreement.

LO6 Correct other pronoun problems.

LO7 Check agreement in a real-world context.

What do you think?

What would happen if all agreements that have been made were suddenly broken?

LO1 Subject-Verb Agreement

A verb must **agree in number** with the subject of the sentence. If the subject is singular, the verb must be singular. If the subject is plural, the verb must be plural.

| singular subject | **+** | singular verb | **=** | agreement | | plural subject | **+** | plural verb | **=** | agreement |

The truck needs a tune-up. | The trucks need tune-ups.

NOTE: Plural subjects often end in *s*, but plural verbs usually do not. Also note that only present tense verbs and certain *be* verbs have separate singular and plural forms.

Present:	singular	plural		Past:	singular	plural
	walks	walk			walked	walked
	sees	see			saw	saw
	eats	eat			ate	ate
	is/am	are			was	were

To make most verbs singular, add just an *s*.

run—runs   write—writes   stay—stays

The verbs *do* and *go* are made singular by adding an *es*.

do—does   go—goes

When a verb ends in *ch, sh, x,* or *z,* make it singular by adding *es*.

latch—latches   wish—wishes   fix—fixes   buzz—buzzes

When a verb ends in a consonant followed by a *y,* change the *y* to *i* and add *es*.

try—tries   fly—flies   cry—cries   quantify—quantifies

INSIGHT

The "Say It" activity on the next page will help you become familiar with the subject-verb agreement patterns in English. Practice it aloud, and for added practice, write the sentences as well.

Say It

Read the following sentences aloud, emphasizing the words in italics.
1. The alarm *rings*. The alarms *ring*. The dog *barks*. The dogs *bark*.
2. The man *is*. The men *are*. The woman *is*. The women *are*.
3. She *sits*. They *sit*. He *walks*. They *walk*.
4. The woman *tries*. The women *try*. The man *does*. The men *do*.
5. The door *latches*. The doors *latch*. The bee *buzzes*. The bees *buzz*.

Correcting Basic Subject-Verb Agreement

Write For each sentence below, write the correct form of the verb in parentheses.
1. The people at the help desk _____are_____ knowledgeable. (is)
2. They _____know_____ more about computers than most. (know)
3. Any question _____receives_____ a quick, helpful answer. (receive)
4. One student _____asks_____ about the "any" key. (ask)
5. The instructions _____say_____ to press the "any" key. (say)
6. One tech helper _____tapes_____ the word "any" to space bars. (tape)
7. That sign _____does_____ prevent many questions. (do)
8. The tech also _____fixes_____ any computer that breaks down. (fix)
9. Or at least the tech _____tries_____ to fix any problems. (try)
10. Most users _____are_____ glad they don't have to fix the computers. (is)

Correct Correct any agreement errors you find by writing the line number and the verb you would change. Cross it out and write the correct present tense verb.

> Those who study computer science ~~has~~ have a challenging career. Since   1
> computer technology ~~change~~ changes so quickly, the things students ~~learns~~ learn when
> they ~~is~~ are starting out will probably be outdated by the time they ~~graduates~~ graduate.
> Memory capacity ~~double~~ doubles every few years, and high-speed connections
> ~~creates~~ create new possibilities. Innovations on the Web and in handheld devices   5
> ~~drives~~ drive change in all areas. One computer-science major ~~confess~~ confesses, "Students
> ~~doesn't~~ don't have the luxury of being amazed by new technology. As soon as
> they ~~hears~~ hear about a new software or hardware development, they ~~has~~ have to
> check it out and get on board—or they ~~gets~~ get left behind."

Write For each plural verb below, write one sentence using the verb in its singular form. Answers will vary.
1. do ___(does)___
2. go ___(goes)___
3. wash ___(washes)___
4. scratch ___(scratches)___

Vocabulary

agree in number
match, as when a subject and verb are both singular, or when they are both plural

LO2 Agreement with Two Subjects

Sentences with **compound subjects** have special rules to make sure that they agree.

When a sentence has two or more subjects joined by *and*, the verb should be plural.

plural subject **+** plural verb **=** agreement

Bill and Sue try new hairstyles.

Rubberball/Corbis

When a sentence has two or more subjects joined by *or, nor,* or *but also,* the verb should agree with the last subject.

singular subject **+** singular verb **=** agreement

Either Bill or Sue tries a new hairstyle.

Not only Bill but also Sue looks cool.

Say It

Read the following sentences aloud, emphasizing the words in *italics*.

1. The woman *and* man *talk.* The woman *or* man *talks.*
2. A mouse *and* gerbil *run.* A mouse *or* a gerbil *runs.*
3. Either Sarah *or* Steve *phones.* Neither Sarah *nor* Steve *phones.*
4. Not only Jim *but also* Patty *responds.*
5. A man, woman, *and* child *arrive.* A man, a woman, *or* a child *arrives.*

CONSIDER TEST TAKING

For more practice with compound subjects, see pages 382–383.

Fixing Agreement with Two Subjects

Write For each sentence below, write the correct form of the verb in parentheses.

1. The office manager and secretary _____have_____ to multitask. (has)

2. The secretary or manager _____acts_____ as receptionist. (act)

3. Calls and faxes _____arrive_____ every few minutes. (arrive)

4. Customer service and satisfaction _____are_____ the keys to their jobs. (is)

5. Neither the secretary nor the manager _____minds_____ the rush. (mind)

6. Not only excitement but also challenge _____comes_____ with each call. (come)

7. Either the manager or the secretary _____greets_____ visitors as well. (greet)

8. A friendly smile and a polite word _____smooth_____ the conversations. (smooth)

9. Praise or complaints _____receive_____ the same professional reply. (receive)

10. Not only the manager but also the secretary _____was_____ voted employee of the month. (was)

Correct Correct any agreement errors you find by writing the line number and incorrect verb, crossing it out, and writing the correct present tense verb.

Multitasking is the ability to do more than two things at a time.   *1*
Talking on the phone and cooking dinner ~~makes~~ *make* a person focus on both
tasks at once. Multitaskers and nonmultitaskers ~~disagrees~~ *disagree* about the
value of doing more than one thing. Cooking, cleaning, and taking care
of children ~~is~~ *are* daily tasks for stay-at-home parents. Office workers and   *5*
blue collar workers often ~~focuses~~ *focus* on one task at a time. Who gets more
done? Multitaskers and nonmultitaskers ~~sees~~ *see* it differently. Dinner, a
clean house, and happy kids ~~is~~ *are* the results of a multitasker's labor at
home. A job done right and another job underway ~~is~~ *are* the product of a
nonmultitasker's attention at work. Both approaches ~~succeeds~~ *succeed*. Not only   *10*
the multitasker but also the nonmultitasker ~~work~~ *works* efficiently and ~~complete~~ *completes*
the task. The difference is perhaps not in the person but in the work.

Write Write a sentence with a compound subject joined by *and*. Write a sentence with a compound subject joined by *or*. Check subject-verb agreement.

Answers will vary.

_____

_____

Vocabulary

compound subject
two or more subjects that share the same verb or verbs

LO3 Agreement with *I* and *You*

The pronouns *I* and *you* usually take plural verbs, even though they are singular.

plural verb

Correct: I sit here and think. You talk to me.

singular verb

Incorrect: I sits here and thinks. You talks to me.

NOTE: The pronoun *I* takes the singular verbs *am* and *was*. **Do not** use *I* with *be* or *is*.

Correct: I am glad. I was hoping to go. I am excited to see the show.

Incorrect: I are glad. I were hoping to go. I is excited to see the show.

Quick Guide

Using *am, is, are, was,* and *were*

	Singular	Plural
Present Tense	I *am* you *are* he *is* she *is* it *is*	we *are* you *are* they *are*
Past Tense	I *was* you *were* he *was* she *was* it *was*	we *were* you *were* they *were*

INSIGHT

The word *am* exists for one reason only, to go along with the word *I*. There is no other subject for the verb *am.* In academic or formal writing, *I* should never be used with *be* or *is.* Think of René Descartes saying, "I think, therefore I am."

Say It

Read the following word groups aloud, emphasizing the words in *italics*.
1. I *walk* / You *walk* / She *walks* / They *walk*
2. I *drive* / You *drive* / He *drives* / They *drive*
3. I *do* / You *do* / He *does* / They *do*
4. I *am* / You *are* / She *is* / They *are*
5. I *was* / You *were* / He *was* / They *were*

Correcting Agreement with *I* and *You*

Write For each blank below, write the correct forms of the verb in parentheses. (Do not change the tense.)

1. I _____work_____ as hard as he _____works_____ . (work)

2. You _____sing_____ as beautifully as she _____sings_____ . (sing)

3. The group _____decides_____ together, or you _____decide_____ alone. (decide)

4. My brother _____plays_____ guitar while I _____play_____ piano. (play)

5. I _____forgive_____ you if you _____forgive_____ me. (forgive)

6. I _____applaud_____ just as loudly as she _____applauds_____ . (applaud)

7. I _____am_____ tired, but he _____is_____ tired, too. (is)

8. You _____are_____ full of energy, and she _____is_____ also. (is)

9. Yesterday, I _____was_____ late, but you _____were_____ late, too. (was)

10. You _____are_____ my friend; I hope I _____am_____ yours. (is)

Correct Correct any agreement errors you find by writing the line number and incorrect verb. Cross it out and write the correct verb.

>   want   am
>   I ~~wants~~ to thank you for such a wonderful day yesterday. I ~~is~~ still   *1*
> smiling to think about the art exhibit. You ~~knows~~ so much about the
> history of art, and you ~~shares~~ what you ~~knows~~ so willingly. You ~~am~~ my
> new favorite tour guide. I ~~be~~ happy to go back to the art institute any
> time you ~~wants~~.   *5*
>   What were my favorite paintings? I ~~were~~ thrilled by the   wasn't
> Impressionist paintings, especially the Monets and Manets. I ~~weren't~~
> even sure there was a difference before yesterday. You ~~was~~ very gentle to
> point out they ~~was~~ two different people. I ~~be~~ glad to know that now.
>   Thank you again for the guided tour. You ~~is~~ generous with your time,   *10*
> and I ~~is~~ always interested to hear what you ~~says~~ about each artwork.
> Next time you ~~is~~ going, give me a call!

Write Write two sentences using "I" as the subject. Then write two more using "you" as the subject. Check your subject-verb agreement.

Answers will vary.

LO4 Agreement with Singular Indefinite Pronouns

An **indefinite pronoun** is intentionally vague. Instead of referring to a specific person, place, or thing, it refers to something general or unknown.

Singular Indefinite Pronouns

Singular indefinite pronouns take singular verbs:

Singular
someone
somebody
something
anyone
anybody
anything
no one
nobody
nothing
everyone
everybody
everything
one
each
either
neither

Someone donates $10 a week.

No one knows who it is.

Everyone appreciates the generosity.

Note that indefinite pronouns that end in *one, body,* or *thing* are singular, just as these words themselves are singular. Just as you would write, "That thing is missing," so you would write "Something is missing." The words *one, each, either,* and *neither* can be tricky because they are often followed by a prepositional phrase that contains a plural noun. The verb should still be singular.

One of our roommates is generous.

Each of us wants to cook as well as he does.

Remember that a compound subject joined with *and* needs a plural verb, and a compound subject joined with *or* needs a verb that matches the last subject.

Everybody and everything need to stay out of my way.

Something or someone prevents us from succeeding.

Say It

Read the following word groups aloud, emphasizing the words in *italics*.

1. Someone *is* / Somebody *has* / Something *does*

2. Anyone *is* / Anybody *has* / Anything *does*

3. One of the books *is* / Each of the books *has* /
   Either of the books *does*

Correcting Indefinite Pronoun Agreement I

Write For each sentence below, write the correct form of the verb in parentheses. (Do not change the tense.)

1. Someone _____ needs _____ a new muffler. (need)
2. Each of the cars _____ needs _____ repair. (need)
3. Something _____ rattles _____ when I turn the ignition. (rattle)
4. Either of the garages _____ does _____ good work. (do)
5. Neither of the options _____ is _____ very affordable. (is)
6. Somebody _____ has _____ to fix the tailgate. (have)
7. Nobody _____ wants _____ to drive a broken-down car. (want)
8. Nobody and nothing _____ deter _____ me from fixing the car. (deters)
9. Either of the repair jobs _____ costs _____ a fortune. (cost)
10. One of my paychecks _____ vanishes _____ each time I get repairs. (vanish)

Write Write sentences using each indefinite pronoun as a subject. Choose present tense verbs and check subject-verb agreement.

1. Everyone Answers will vary. _____

_____

2. Each _____

_____

3. No one _____

_____

4. Anything _____

_____

5. One _____

_____

6. Either _____

_____

Vocabulary

indefinite pronoun
a special type of pronoun that does not refer to a specific person or thing

Agreement with Other Indefinite Pronouns

Other indefinite pronouns are always plural, or have a singular or plural form, depending on how they are used.

Plural Indefinite Pronouns

Plural indefinite pronouns take plural verbs:

Plural
both
few
many
several

Both of us match the donation.

Many are wishing they did.

Singular or Plural Indefinite Pronouns

Some indefinite pronouns or quantity words are singular or plural. If the object of the preposition in the phrase following the pronoun is singular, the pronoun takes a singular verb; if the object is plural, the pronoun takes a plural verb.

Singular or Plural
all
any
half
part
most
none
some

All of the pizza is gone.

All of the pizzas are gone.

Notice the shift in meaning, depending on the prepositional phrase. "All of the pizza" means that one pizza is gone. "All of the pizzas" means that all of many pizzas are gone. Here's another startling difference.

Half of the mortgage is paid off.

Half of the mortgages are paid off.

In the first example, half of one mortgage is paid off. In the second, half of a number of mortgages are paid off. What a difference one *s* can make!

Say It

Read the following word groups aloud, emphasizing the words in *italics*.

1. Both *are* / Few *have* / Many *do* / Several *were*
2. All of the budget *is* / Any of the budgets *are* / Half of the budget *does*
3. Part of the pie *is* / Most of the pies *are* / None of the foods *are* / Some of the food *is*

Correcting Indefinite Pronoun Agreement II

Write For each blank below, write the correct form of the verb in parentheses. (Do not change the tense.)

1. Someone _____provides_____ for others, but both of us _____provide_____ for ourselves. (provide)

2. All of the book _____was_____ scary, but all of the scares _____were_____ fun. (was)

3. Some of my friends _____have_____ Facebook pages, and part of my Facebook page _____has_____ photos of friends. (have)

4. Everyone _____wants_____ to be famous, but few _____want_____ to be followed day and night. (want)

5. One of my friends _____broadcasts_____ a Webcast show; several episodes _____broadcast_____ in a row. (broadcast)

6. Either _____is_____ a valuable idea, and neither _____is_____ expensive. (is)

7. Few _____have_____ thought about the final exam, though all of the students _____have_____ reason to study. (has)

8. Of the competing bids, several _____are_____ desirable, but none of them _____are_____ affordable. (is)

9. Most of us _____watch_____ the lions pace, though some of the lions _____watch_____ us. (watch)

10. Half of the car _____was_____ submerged, and half of the spectators _____were_____ gasping. (was)

CONSIDER SPEAKING AND LISTENING

After completing the sentences in the first exercise, say them aloud, emphasizing the underlined verbs.

Write Write sentences using each indefinite pronoun as a subject. Choose present tense verbs and check subject-verb agreement.

1. Several ____Answers will vary._____

2. Few _____

3. All _____

4. Most _____

5. Part _____

6. Both _____

LO5 Pronoun-Antecedent Agreement

A pronoun must agree in **person**, **number**, and **gender** with its **antecedent**. (The antecedent is the word the pronoun replaces.)

The man went to lunch but forgot his lunch box.

antecedent + **pronoun** = **agreement**
(third person   (third person
singular   singular
masculine)   masculine)

Quick Guide

	Singular	Plural
First Person:	I, me (my, mine)	we, us (our, ours)
Second Person:	you (your, yours)	you (your, yours)
Third Person: masculine feminine neuter	 he, him (his) she, her (her, hers) it (its)	 they, them (their, theirs) they, them (their, theirs) they, them (their, theirs)

Two or More Antecedents

When two or more antecedents are joined by *and,* the pronoun should be plural.

Juan and Maria will do their dance.

When two or more singular antecedents are joined by *or, nor,* or *but also,* the pronoun or pronouns should be singular.

Juan or Maria will do his or her dance.

Not only Juan but also Maria presses his or her own costume.

NOTE: Avoid sexism when choosing pronouns that agree in number.

Ocean/Corbis

Sexist: Each student should bring his basket.
Correct: Each student should bring her or his basket.
Correct: Students should bring their baskets.

Correcting Pronoun-Antecedent Agreement

Write   For each blank below, write the pronoun that agrees with the underlined word or words.

1. The <u>cha-cha-cha</u> began in Cuba, and _____it_____ got its name from the shuffling sound of the dancers' feet.

2. In the 1950s, <u>Monsieur Pierre</u> traveled to Cuba, where _____he_____ studied dance styles and from them created the ballroom rumba.

3. <u>Pepe Sanchez</u> is the father of the Cuban bolero, even though _____he_____ was untrained as a musician and dancer.

4. The <u>paso doble</u> came from bullfight music, so _____it_____ depicts the lead dancer as the bullfighter and the follower as the cape.

5. In the early twentieth century, <u>Brazilians</u> created the samba, and _____they_____ danced three steps for each two-count measure.

6. The <u>tango</u> had _____its_____ start in Argentina and Uruguay.

7. Stiff and stylized, the tango is performed with the <u>man</u> holding _____his_____ arms in a rigid frame and the <u>woman</u> matching _____her_____ steps to her partner's.

8. Salsa dancing combines other <u>styles</u> and blends _____them_____ together like the ingredients in hot sauce.

9. Most of these styles require hip <u>movements</u> from side to side; _____they_____ reflect a sensuous nature.

10. Northern European dancing, however, calls for straight hips and leaping, hopping <u>movements</u>; _____they_____ may help the dancers stay warm.

Revise   Rewrite each of the following sentences to avoid sexism.

1. Every dancer should put on his shoes.

   Every dancer should put on her or his shoes.

2. Each dancer must keep track of her equipment.

   Each dancer must keep track of his or her equipment.

3. One of the applicants will have his application accepted.

   One of the applicants will have her or his application accepted.

Vocabulary

person
the person speaking (first person—*I, we*), the person being spoken to (second person—*you*), or the person being spoken about (third person—*he, she, it, they*)

number
singular or plural

gender
masculine, feminine, neuter, or indefinite

antecedent
the noun (or pronoun) that a pronoun refers to or replaces

LO6 Other Pronoun Problems

Missing Antecedent

If no clear antecedent is provided, the reader doesn't know what or whom the pronoun refers to.

Confusing: In Wisconsin, they produce many types of cheese.
(Who does "they" refer to?)

Clear: In Wisconsin, cheese makers produce many types of cheese.

Vague Pronoun

If the pronoun could refer to two or more words, the passage is **ambiguous**.

Indefinite: Ben told his son to use his new surfboard.
(To whom does the pronoun "his" refer, Ben or Ben's son?)

Clumsy: Ben told his son to use Ben's new surfboard.

Clear: Ben lent his new surfboard to his son.

Double Subject

If a pronoun is used right after the subject, an error called a double subject occurs.

Incorrect: My grandmother, she is a good baker.

Correct: My grandmother is a great baker.

INSIGHT

Use *my* before the thing possessed and use *mine* afterward: *my cat,* but *that cat is mine.* Do the same with *our/ours, your/yours, her/hers,* and *their/theirs.*

Incorrect Case

Personal pronouns can function as subjects, objects, or possessives. If the wrong case is used, an error occurs.

Incorrect: Them are the wrong size.

Correct: They are the wrong size.

Subject	Object	Possessive
I	me	my, mine
we	us	our, ours
you	you	your, yours
he	him	his
she	her	her, hers
it	it	its
they	them	their, theirs

The list on the right tells you which pronouns to use in each case.

Correcting Other Pronoun Problems

Write For each blank below, write the correct pronoun from the choices in parentheses.

1. _____I_____ want to give _____you_____ some advice.

   (I, me, my, mine)   (you, your, yours)

2. _____You_____ should watch _____him_____ and learn what _____he_____ does.

   (you, your, yours)   (he, him, his)   (he, him, his)

3. _____She_____ agreed to lend _____me_____ that book of _____hers_____ .

   (she, her, hers)   (I, me, my, mine)   (she, her, hers)

4. _____I_____ grant _____my_____ permission for _____her_____ to go.

   (I, me, my, mine)   (I, me, my, mine)   (she, her, hers)

5. _____We_____ watched _____our_____ dog do tricks for _____us_____ .

   (we, us, our, ours)   (we, us, our, ours)   (we, us, our, ours)

Revise Rewrite each sentence below, correcting the pronoun problems.

Answers will vary.

1. David and Jerry took his car to the shop.

   David and Jerry took their car to the shop.

2. Clare needed to work with Linda, but she had no time.

   Clare needed to work with Linda, but Linda had no time.

3. After driving all the way, it gave out.

   After driving all the way, the engine gave out.

4. When are they going to make an effective vaccine?

   When is the World Health Organization going to make an effective vaccine?

5. Bill and Sarah, they went to the movies.

   Bill and Sarah went to the movies.

6. Steve told Dave to bring his book.

   Steve told Dave to bring Dave's book.

Vocabulary

ambiguous
unclear, confusing

LO7 Real-World Application

Correct In the letter below, correct the agreement errors. Write the line number and any word you would change. Then show the change. Use the correction marks at the bottom of the page.

Hope Services Child Development Center

2141 South Fifth Place, Seattle, WA 90761
414-555-1400 www.hopeserv.org

---

1 May 17, 2010
    Mr. Donald Keebler
    Keebler Electronics
    466 Hanover Boulevard
5 Penticton, BC V2A 5S1

    Dear Mr. Keebler:

    Everyone at Hope Services ~~want~~ *wants* to thank you for helping us choose a
    sound system that fits both our needs and our budget. I ~~is~~ *am* especially
    thankful for the way you worked around our schedule during installation.

10 We found that the system meets all ~~their~~ *our* needs. Being able to adjust
    sound input and output for different uses in different rooms has been
    wonderful. The system ~~help~~ *helps* staff in the family room with play-based
    assessment, and team members are tuning in to different conversations
    as if they were in the room ~~himself~~ *themselves.* As a result, children who might feel
15 overwhelmed with too many people in the room ~~relaxes~~ *relax*
    and ~~plays~~ *play* naturally. In addition, parents use the sound
    system to listen in on sessions in the therapy room as
    therapists model constructive one-on-one communication
    methods with children.

20 You ~~does~~ *do* excellent work, Donald. I ~~are~~ *am* happy to
    recommend your services to anyone needing sound
    equipment.

    ~~Yours~~ *Your* friend,

    Barbara Talbot

25 Barbara Talbot
    Executive Director

Correction Marks

℔	delete
d̲	capitalize
ⱷ	lowercase
∧	insert
⌃	add comma
? ∧	add question mark
word ∧	add word
⊙	add period
◠	spelling
◡	switch

20

"Another way to look at sentences is to see them as carriers of 'news.'"
—Scott Rice

Sentence Problems

Mathematics is full of problems. The whole point of math is to puzzle out a solution. And for each problem, there should be only one or, occasionally, a small set of right answers.

Writing is different. Sentences should not be full of problems. If a reader has to puzzle out the meaning of a sentence, the sentence *is* a problem. Sometimes a shift has occurred in person, tense, or voice. At other times, a modifier is misplaced or dangling. The result can be a sentence that confuses instead of communicates.

This chapter focuses on correcting these additional sentence problems. You'll find exercises for each type of problem as well as a real-world application.

Learning Outcomes

LO1 Correct common fragments.

LO2 Correct tricky fragments.

LO3 Correct comma splices.

LO4 Correct run-on sentences.

LO5 Correct rambling sentences.

LO6 Correct misplaced and dangling modifiers.

LO7 Correct shifts in sentence construction.

LO8 Check for fragments in a real-world context.

LO9 Correct comma splices and run-ons in a real-world context.

LO10 Correct sentence problems in a real-world context.

What do you think?

How do sentence problems impact the sentence's ability to be a carrier of news?

LO1 Common Fragments

In spoken communication and informal writing, sentence fragments are occasionally used and understood. In formal writing, fragments should be avoided.

Missing Parts

A sentence requires a subject and a predicate. If one or the other or both are missing, the sentence is a **fragment**. Such fragments can be fixed by supplying the missing part.

Fragment:	Went to the concert.
Fragment + Subject:	We went to the concert.
Fragment:	Everyone from Westville Community College.
Fragment + Predicate:	Everyone from Westville Community College may participate.
Fragment:	For the sake of student safety.
Fragment + Subject and Predicate:	The president set up a curfew for the sake of student safety.

Incomplete Thoughts

A sentence also must express a complete thought. Some fragments have a subject and a verb but do not express a complete thought. These fragments can be corrected by providing words that complete the thought.

Fragment:	The concert will include.
Completing Thought:	The concert will include an amazing light show.
Fragment:	If we arrive in time.
Completing Thought:	If we arrive in time, we'll get front-row seats.
Fragment:	That opened the concert.
Completing Thought:	I liked the band that opened the concert.

Say It

Read these fragments aloud. Then read each one again, but this time supply the necessary words to form a complete thought.

1. The student union building.
2. Where you can buy used books.
3. Walked to class every morning.
4. When the instructor is sick.
5. The cop was.

Correct   Add words to correct each fragment below. Write the complete sentence on the lines provided.

1. Groceries for our special meal.

Answers will vary.

_____

2. While I made the pasta, Maya prepared.

_____

_____

3. Finished everything within forty-five minutes.

_____

_____

4. Easily, the best meal ever.

_____

_____

5. Not everyone likes.

_____

_____

Correct   The following paragraph contains numerous fragments. Either add what is missing or combine fragments with other sentences to make them complete. Use the correction marks shown below.

Answers will vary.

The kitchen truly needs a new coat of paint. Everyone who uses the   1
kitchen. Should help out. Need lots of help. If you have next Saturday
afternoon to spare, plan to paint. Ben and I will provide. We'll try to pick a
color that goes with the cabinets. When we are finished. The kitchen will
be more pleasant for everyone to use. However, we won't guarantee that   5
the food will taste any better.

Correction Marks

✄	delete	⌃	add comma	⌃ word	add word
d̲	capitalize	?	add question mark	⊙	add period
ø̸	lowercase			⬭	spelling
⌃	insert	⌄	insert an apostrophe	∿	switch

Correct   On your own paper or orally, correct the following fragments by supplying the missing parts. Use your imagination. Answers will vary.

1. The front hall of the dorm.
2. When I arrived.
3. Was filled with new students.
4. Worked hard all morning.
5. Which was more than most people had done.

Vocabulary

fragment
a group of words that is missing a subject or a predicate (or both) or that does not express a complete thought

LO2 Tricky Fragments

Some fragments are more difficult to find and correct. They creep into our writing because they are often part of the way we communicate in our speaking.

Absolute Phrases

An **absolute phrase** looks like a sentence that is missing its helping verb. An absolute phrase can be made into a sentence by adding the helping verb or by connecting the phrase to a complete sentence.

Absolute Phrase (Fragment):	Our legs trembling from the hike.
Absolute Phrase + Helping Verb:	Our legs were trembling from the hike.
Absolute Phrase + Complete Sentence:	We collapsed on the couch, our legs trembling from the hike.

Informal Fragments

Fragments that are commonly used in speech should be eliminated from formal writing. Avoid the following types of fragments unless you are writing dialogue.

Interjections:	Hey! Yeah!	**Questions:**	How come? Why not? What?
Exclamations:	What a nuisance! How fun!		
Greetings:	Hi, everybody. Good afternoon.	**Answers:**	About three or four. As soon as possible.

NOTE: Sentences that begin with *here* or *there* have a **delayed subject**, which appears after the verb. Other sentences (commands) have an **implied subject** (*you*). Such sentences are not fragments.

Delayed Subject:	Here are some crazy fans wearing wild hats.
Implied Subject:	Tackle him! Bring him down!

Say It

Read these fragments aloud. Then add words to form a complete thought.
1. Are three types of laptop computers.
2. Our instructor explaining the assignment.
3. About three in the morning.
4. Is my favorite Web site.
5. My friend working at a half-priced disk shop.

Fixing Tricky Fragments

Practice A Rewrite each tricky fragment below, making it a sentence.

1. Their hearts melting at the sight of the orphaned pets.

> Their hearts melted at the sight of the orphaned pets.

2. The dogs yelping hellos and wagging their tails.

> The dogs were yelping hellos and wagging their tails.

3. Our cats and dogs chasing each other and playing together.

> Our cats and dogs are chasing each other and playing together.

4. Are many benefits to pet ownership.

> There are many benefits to pet ownership.

5. The vet's office teeming with a variety of pets.

> The vet's office is teaming with a variety of pets.

Practice B The following paragraph contains a number of informal fragments. Identify and delete each one. Reread the paragraph and listen for the difference.

> Both dogs and cats have long been companions to humans. ~~Awesome!~~ *1*
> Dogs started off as wolves at the end of the last Ice Age. ~~What then?~~
> Human hunters killed off wolves that tried to take their food, but a wolf
> that was neither afraid of humans nor aggressive toward them might
> be spared. Living alongside people meant wolves were beginning to be   *5*
> domesticated, or comfortable in a human environment.
>   Cats, however, came a bit later, when humans had become farmers.
> ~~Yeah.~~ Ancient "barn cats" were probably the first kind. They loved to eat
> the mice and rats that fed on stored grains, and farmers let them. ~~Perfect!~~
> If kittens are handled by humans, they become tame. If they are not, they   *10*
> stay wild.
>   That's why dogs like walks and cats like to stay home. Dogs joined us
> when we were walking everywhere, and cats arrived when we were staying
> put. ~~Yessir!~~

Vocabulary

absolute phrase
a group of words with a noun and a participle (a word ending in *ing* or *ed*) and the words that modify them

delayed subject
a subject that appears after the verb, as in a sentence that begins with *here* or *there* or a sentence that asks a question

implied subject
the word *you*, assumed to begin command sentences

LO3 Comma Splices

Comma splices occur when two sentences are connected with only a comma. A comma splice can be fixed by adding a coordinating conjunction (*and, but, or, nor, for, so,* or *yet*) or a subordinating conjunction (*while, after, when,* and so on). The two sentences could also be joined by a semicolon (;) or separated by a period.

Comma Splice: The winners were announced, we were not mentioned.

Corrected by adding a coordinating conjunction:	The winners were announced, but we were not mentioned.
Corrected by adding a subordinating conjunction:	When the winners were announced, we were not mentioned.
Corrected by replacing the comma with a semicolon:	The winners were announced; we were not mentioned.

INSIGHT

A comma is not strong enough to join sentences without a conjunction. A semicolon can join two closely related sentences. A period or question mark can separate two sentences.

Comma Splice: An engineer named George Washington Gale Ferris planned the first Ferris wheel, many people thought he was crazy.

Corrected by adding a coordinating conjunction:	Our instructor praised our efforts, and he thought we deserved an award.
Corrected by adding a subordinating conjunction:	Our instructor praised our efforts because he thought we deserved an award.
Corrected by replacing the comma with a period:	Our instructor praised our efforts. He thought we deserved an award.

Correcting Comma Splices

Practice A Correct the following comma splices by adding a coordinating conjunction (*and, but, yet, or, nor, for, so*), adding a subordinating conjunction (*when, while, because,* and so on), or replacing the comma with a semicolon or period. Use the approach that makes the sentence read most smoothly.

1. Contests are set up to have many participants, very few actually win.
2. Businesses run contests to stir up buzz, they are trying to advertise.
3. The business gives away a few prizes, it brings in many names and addresses.
4. Most people enter a contest for one reason, they want the prize, of course.
5. A business should follow up with entrants, they provide a marketing opportunity.
6. Both Bill and I entered the contest, we both were disappointed.
7. Then we received discount coupons, we were happy to get them.
8. Winning is a long shot, there are other benefits to entering.
9. We each used our coupons, the discount was significant.
10. We're on the lookout for another contest, maybe we'll have better luck in the future.

Practice B Rewrite the following paragraph, correcting any comma splices that you find.

> Braille is a system of communication used by the blind. It was developed by Louis Braille in 1824. The system uses combinations of small raised dots to create an alphabet, the dots are imprinted on paper and can be felt. A blind person reads the page by running his or her fingers across the dots. The basic unit is called a cell, a cell is two dots wide and three dots high. Numbers, punctuation marks, and written music can be expressed with this system. Braille has allowed the blind to read, it is truly a great invention.
>
> Braille is a system of communication used by the blind. It was developed by Louis Braille in 1824. The system uses combinations of small raised dots to create an alphabet, and the dots are imprinted on paper and can be felt. A blind person reads the page by running his or her fingers across the dots. The basic unit is called a cell, which is two dots wide and three dots high. Numbers, punctuation marks, and written music can be expressed with this system. Braille has allowed the blind to read, and it is truly a great invention.

Vocabulary

comma splice
a sentence error that occurs when two sentences are connected with only a comma

LO4 Run-On Sentences

A **run-on sentence** occurs when two sentences are joined without punctuation or a connecting word. A run-on can be corrected by adding a comma and a conjunction or by inserting a semicolon or period between the two sentences.

Run-On: I was feeling lucky I was totally wrong.

Corrected by adding a comma and coordinating conjunction:	I was feeling lucky, but I was totally wrong.
Corrected by adding a subordinating conjunction and a comma:	Although I was feeling lucky, I was totally wrong.
Corrected by inserting a semicolon:	I was feeling lucky; I was totally wrong.

INSIGHT

As you can see, run-ons and comma splices are very similar. As such, they can be corrected in the same basic ways.

Run-On: I signed up for the contest I had to write a story about robotic life.

Corrected by adding a comma and a coordinating conjunction:	I signed up for the contest, so I had to write a story about robotic life.
Corrected by adding a subordinating conjunction and a comma:	When I signed up for the contest, I had to write a story about robotic life.
Corrected by inserting a period:	I signed up for the contest. I had to write a story about robotic life.

Correcting Run-On Sentences

Correct Correct the following run-on sentences. Use the approach that makes the sentence read most smoothly. Answers will vary.

1. John McCarthy coined the term artificial intelligence ⊙̲ this field deals with the intelligence of machines.

2. Thinking machines first appeared in Greek myths ∧ᵃⁿᵈ they have been a common feature in fiction since the 1800s.

3. True artificial intelligence could become a reality ∧ⁱᶠ an electronic brain could be produced.

4. ∧ᵂʰᵉⁿ Scientists had computers solving algebra word problems ∧, people knew these machines could do incredible things.

5. Reports criticized the artificial intelligence movement ∧ˢᵒ∧ funding for research stopped.

6. Funding is again very strong today ∙∧ᵃⁿᵈ artificial intelligence plays an important role in the technology industry.

7. Computers solve problems in one way ∧; human beings solve them in other ways.

8. ∧ᴬˡᵗʰᵒᵘᵍʰ People acquire a great deal of basic knowledge ∧, it would not be so easy to build this knowledge into machines.

Rewrite Rewrite the following paragraph, correcting any run-on sentences that you find. Answers will vary.

> Smart Cars look like little water bugs on the road. They are only ₁ about eight feet long they are less than five feet wide. You can fit two or three smart cars in a typical parking space. Smart Cars have been quite popular in Europe it remains to be seen how they will be received in the United States. By the way, the two co-stars in *Da Vinci Code* raced ₅ around Rome in one of these cars. Some versions of the Smart Car run on a three-cylinder engine they still can go from zero to 60 in about 15 seconds. They can get about 33 miles per gallon in the city and 41 miles per gallon on the highway.

Vocabulary

run-on sentence
a sentence error that occurs when two sentences are joined without punctuation *or* a connecting word

LO5 Rambling Sentences

A rambling sentence occurs when a long series of separate ideas are connected by one *and, but,* or *so* after another. The result is an unfocused sentence that goes on and on. To correct a rambling sentence, break it into smaller units, adding and cutting words as needed.

> **Rambling:** When we first signed up for the contest, I had no thought that we would win, but then my brother started talking about how he would spend the money and he asked me if he could have my share of it, so we were counting on winning even though we really had no chance and as it turned out we of course didn't win.
>
> **Corrected:** When we first signed up for the contest, I had no thought that we would win. Then my brother started talking about how he would spend the money. He even asked for my share. Soon, we were counting on winning even though we had no chance. As it turned out, we didn't win.

Say It

Read the following rambling sentences aloud. Afterward, circle all of the connecting words (*and, but, so*), and be prepared to suggest different ways to break each rambling idea into more manageable units.

1. I enjoyed touring the hospital and I would enjoy joining the nursing staff and I believe that my prior work experience will be an asset but I also know that I have a lot more to learn.

2. The electronics store claims to offer "one-stop shopping" and they can take care of all of a customer's computer needs and they have a fully trained staff to answer questions and solve problems so there is really no need to go anywhere else.

webphotographer / istockphoto.com

Correct Correct the following rambling sentences by dividing some of the ideas into separate sentences.

1. The cat entered silently through the window and next he jumped onto a chair and darted behind the curtain so he could hide from everyone and then he curled up and relaxed for a while.

   The cat entered silently through the window. Next he jumped onto a chair, darted behind the

   curtain, and hid from everyone. Then he curled up and relaxed for a while.

2. I went to the dentist yesterday and when I got there, I had to wait forever to see him and when he finally examined my teeth, he found two cavities and now I have to go back next week to get fillings and I don't want to go.

   I went to the dentist yesterday. When I got there, I had to wait forever to see him. When he

   finally examined my teeth, he found two cavities. Now I have to go back next week to get

   fillings, and I don't want to go.

3. We use trampolines for entertainment but they were used for other purposes a long time ago and Eskimos once used a form of a trampoline made from skins to watch for whales and seals and I think that is a much better use of a trampoline than to just jump up and down on it so I wonder what practical way we can use them today.

   We use trampolines for entertainment, but they were used for other purposes a long time

   ago. Eskimos once used a form of a trampoline made from skins to watch for whales and

   seals. I think that is a much better use of a trampoline than to just jump up and down on it. I

   wonder what practical way we can use them today.

Correct In the space provided below, write a rambling sentence or idea about a topic of your own choosing. Afterward, exchange your work with a classmate, and correct each other's rambling idea.

Answers will vary.

LO6 Misplaced / Dangling Modifiers

Dangling Modifiers

A modifier is a word, phrase, or clause that functions as an adjective or adverb. When the modifier does not clearly modify another word in the sentence, it is called a **dangling modifier**. This error can be corrected by inserting the missing word and/or rewriting the sentence.

Dangling Modifier: After buckling the fancy red collar around his neck, my dog pranced proudly down the street. *(The dog could buckle his own collar?)*

Corrected: After I buckled the fancy red collar around his neck, my dog pranced proudly down the street.

Dangling Modifier: Trying desperately to chase a rabbit, I was pulled toward the bushes. *(The person was chasing the rabbit?)*

Corrected: Trying desperately to chase a rabbit, my dog pulled me toward the bushes.

Misplaced Modifiers

When a modifier is placed beside a word that it does not modify, the modifier is misplaced and often results in an amusing or **illogical** statement. A **misplaced modifier** can be corrected by moving it next to the word that it modifies.

Misplaced Modifier: The dog was diagnosed by the vet with mange. *(The vet has mange?)*

Corrected: The vet diagnosed the dog with mange.

Misplaced Modifier: The vet's assistant gave a chewable pill to the dog tasting like liver. *(The dog tastes like liver?)*

Corrected: The vet gave my cat a pill tasting like fish.

INSIGHT

Avoid placing any adverb modifiers between a verb and its direct object.
  Misplaced: I will throw quickly the ball.
  Corrected: I will quickly throw the ball.
Also, do not separate two-word verbs with an adverb modifier.
  Misplaced: Please take immediately out the trash.
  Corrected: Please immediately take out the trash.

Say It

Read the following sentences aloud, noting the dangling or misplaced modifier in each one. Then tell a classmate how you would correct each error.

1. The new dog park makes good use of vacant property called Dog Heaven.
2. You will usually find an old basset hound running around the park with extremely stubby legs.

Correcting Dangling and Misplaced Modifiers

Rewrite Rewrite each of the sentences below, correcting the misplaced and dangling modifiers.

1. We saw a buck and a doe on the way to marriage counseling.

   We saw a buck and a doe on the way to marriage counseling.

2. The car was reported stolen by the police.

   The car was reported stolen by the police.

3. We have new phones for hard-of-hearing people with loud ring tones.

   We have new phones for hard-of-hearing people with loud ring tones.

4. Please present the proposal that is attached to Mr. Brumbly.

   Please present the proposal that is attached to Mr. Brumbly.

5. I drove with Jennie to the place where we live in a Buick.

   I drove with Jennie to the place where we live in a Buick.

6. I found some moldy cheese in the fridge that doesn't belong to me.

   I found some moldy cheese in the fridge that doesn't belong to me.

7. I bought a parrot for my brother named Squawky.

   I bought a parrot for my brother named Squawky.

Correct For each sentence, correct the placement of the adverb.

1. Provide promptly the form to Human Resources.

   Provide promptly the form to Human Resources.

2. We will initiate immediately your new insurance.

   We will initiate immediately your new insurance.

3. Please fill carefully out the form.

   Please fill carefully out the form.

Vocabulary

dangling modifier
a modifying word, phrase, or clause that appears to modify the wrong word or a word that isn't in the sentence

illogical
without logic; senseless, false, or untrue

misplaced modifier
a modifying word, phrase, or clause that has been placed incorrectly in a sentence, often creating an amusing or illogical idea

LO7 Shifts in Sentences

Shift in Person

A **shift in person** is an error that occurs when first, second, and/or third person are improperly mixed in a sentence.

Shift in person:	Once you feel better, you can do everything an individual loves to do. (The sentence improperly shifts from second person—*you*—to third person—*individual*.)
Corrected:	Once you feel better, you can do everything you love to do.

Shift in Tense

A **shift in tense** is an error that occurs when more than one verb tense is improperly used in a sentence. (See pages 464–471 for more about tense.)

Shift in tense:	I searched everywhere before I find my essay. (The sentence improperly shifts from past tense—*searched*—to present tense—*find*.)
Corrected:	I searched everywhere before I found my essay.

Shift in Voice

A **shift in voice** is an error that occurs when active voice and passive voice are mixed in a sentence.

Shift in voice:	As you search for your essay, your keys may also be found. (The sentence improperly shifts from active voice—*search*—to passive voice—*may be found*.)
Corrected:	As you search for your essay, you may also find your keys.

Say It

Read the following sentences aloud, paying careful attention to the improper shift each contains. Then tell a classmate how you would correct each error.

1. Margo drinks plenty of fluids and got plenty of rest.
2. Landon is running again and many new routes are being discovered by him.
3. When you are ready to work, a person can search for jobs online.
4. Charley served as a tutor in the writing lab and helps English language learners with their writing.

Correcting Improper Shifts in Sentences

Rewrite Rewrite each sentence below, correcting any improper shifts in construction.

1. I jogged along the wooded path until I feel exhausted.

  I jogged along the wooded path until I felt exhausted.

2. As we drove to the movie theater, favorite comedies had been discussed by us.

  As we drove to the movie theater, we discussed our favorite comedies.

3. When you drop off my toolbox, can he or she also return my grill?

  When you drop off my toolbox, can you also return my grill?

Correct Correct the improper shifts in person, tense, or voice in the following paragraph. Use the correction marks below when you make your changes.

> When you think about today's technology, the first word that comes to   1
> mind was convenience. For instance, if you traveled before the creation of
> the Internet, printed maps were used by you. And if you were traveling out
> of state, a person needed to purchase other state maps from a gas station
> or convenience store. You would unfold each map and the best possible   5
> route was planned by you. Now you have access to digital maps, personal
> navigation systems, and Web sites to find your way. You probably enjoy
> the ease and speed of the new technology and thought the old methods are
> tiresome.

Correction Marks

℘ delete	⑃ add comma	word ∧ add word
d̲ capitalize	? add question	⊙ add period
D̶ lowercase	∧ mark	⌒ spelling
∧ insert	⌄ insert an apostrophe	⌐⌐ switch

Vocabulary

person
first person (*I* or *we*—the person speaking), second person (*you*—the person spoken to), or third person (*he, she, it,* or *they*—the person or thing spoken about)

voice of verb
whether the subject is doing the action of the verb (active voice) or is being acted upon (passive voice) (See page 462.)

shift in person
an error that occurs when first, second, and third person are improperly mixed in a sentence

shift in tense
an error that occurs when more than one verb tense is improperly used in a sentence

shift in voice
an error that occurs when active voice and passive voice are mixed in a sentence

LO8 Real-World Application

Correct Correct any sentence fragments in the following business memo. Use the correction marks below.

3041 45th Avenue   *1*
Lake City, WI 53000
November 14, 2010

Ms. Colleen Turner
Human Resource Director   *5*
Western Printing Company
100 Mound Avenue
Racine, WI 53001

Dear Ms. Turner:

In response to your advertisement in the *Racine Standard Press* on   *10*
November 12, I am writing to apply for the position of Graphic Designer.
I Have worked as a designer for Alpha Publications in Brookfield, Wisconsin,
for the past three years.

I worked with a team of talented designers to create business handbooks
and workbooks, including the award-winning handbook *Write for Business*.   *15*
Our team creates each product from early design ideas to preparation of the final
disk. My special skills include coloring illustrations and incorporating
graphics in page design.

My experience with design software packages includes, Adobe InDesign,
Photoshop, and Illustrator.   *20*

Enclosed is my résumé. It Gives more information about my qualifications
and training. I look forward to hearing from you and can be reached at
(200) 555-6655 or at aposada@atz.com. Thank you for your consideration.

Sincerely,

Anna Posada   *25*

Anna Posada
Encl. résumé

Correction Marks

✄ delete	⌃ add comma	word ⌃ add word
d̲ capitalize	? add question mark	⊙ add period
⌀ lowercase		⬭ spelling
⌃ insert	⌄ insert an apostrophe	⤮ switch

LO9 Real-World Application

Correct Correct any comma splices or run-on sentences in the following sales letter.

Dale's Garden Center
405 Cherry Lane
Flower City, IL 53185

NOTE: An *ing* or *ed* phrase is called a participial phrase and serves as an adjective in a sentence. (See page 472 for more information.)

February 1, 2011

Dear Gateway College Student:

Did one of your science instructors ever tell you that plants can talk? Well,   *1*
they can Dale's flowers speak the language of romance.

With Valentine's Day just two weeks away, let Dale's flowers give you the
words to share with your sweetheart. Red roses share your love in the
traditional way, while a Southern Charm Bouquet says the same thing with a   *5*
little more class. Or send "poetry" by choosing our Valentine Special in a
porcelain vase!

Check out the enclosed selection guide then place your order by phoning
1-800-555-LEAF. If you call by February 13, we promise delivery of fresh
flowers on Valentine's Day.   *10*

Let Dale's flowers help you start a conversation that could last a lifetime!

Sincerely,

Dale Brown

P.S. Long-distance romances are not a problem, for we deliver flowers
anywhere in the world.   *15*

Extend Correct each of the following comma splices or run-on sentences by changing one of the sentences into an *ing* or *ed* phrase and connecting it to the other sentence. The first one has been done for you.

1. Carnations are a very popular flower they show love and wonder.

   Carnations are a very popular flower, showing love and wonder.

2. The iris is an elegant flower, it is distinguished by its special blue color.

   Distinguished by its special blue color, the iris is an elegant flower.

LO10 Real-World Application

Correct Correct any dangling modifiers, misplaced modifiers, or shifts in construction in the following message. (Only one sentence is free of errors.) Use the correction marks below.

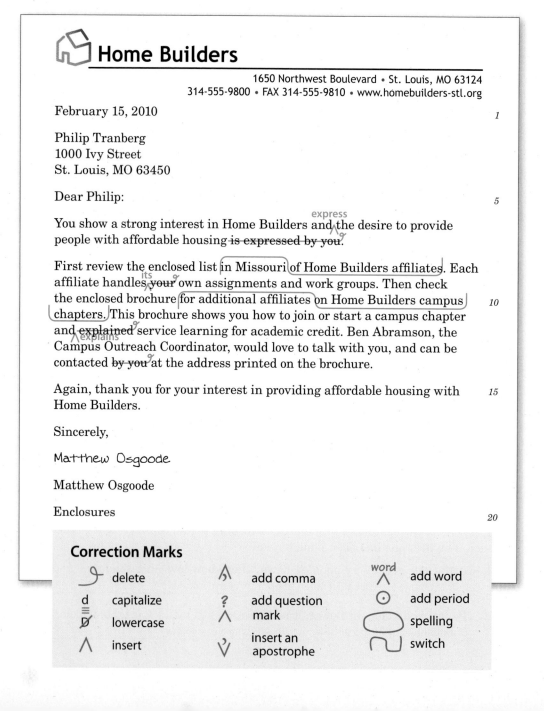

Home Builders

1650 Northwest Boulevard • St. Louis, MO 63124
314-555-9800 • FAX 314-555-9810 • www.homebuilders-stl.org

February 15, 2010   *1*

Philip Tranberg
1000 Ivy Street
St. Louis, MO 63450

Dear Philip: *5*

You show a strong interest in Home Builders and ⟨express⟩ the desire to provide people with affordable housing ~~is expressed by you~~.

First review the enclosed list |in Missouri| of Home Builders affiliates. Each affiliate handles ⟨its⟩ ~~your~~ own assignments and work groups. Then check the enclosed brochure |for additional affiliates on Home Builders campus| *10* ⌊chapters.⌋ This brochure shows you how to join or start a campus chapter and ~~explained~~ ⟨explains⟩ service learning for academic credit. Ben Abramson, the Campus Outreach Coordinator, would love to talk with you, and can be contacted ~~by you~~ at the address printed on the brochure.

Again, thank you for your interest in providing affordable housing with   *15* Home Builders.

Sincerely,

Matthew Osgoode

Matthew Osgoode

Enclosures   *20*

Correction Marks

⟿ delete	⌅ add comma	⟨word⟩ ∧ add word
d̲ capitalize	? ∧ add question mark	⊙ add period
Ø̶ lowercase		⬭ spelling
∧ insert	V̇ insert an apostrophe	⎇ switch

Rewrite   The sentences that follow come from *The Suspended Sentence* by Roscoe C. Born. Born found these sentences in newspaper and magazine articles, and each one contains a misplaced modifier. (Yes, even the professionals sometime make mistakes.) Working with a partner, rewrite each sentence to correct the error.

1. The Pistons' general manager wants a big guy who can bang in Tuesday's National Basketball Association draft.

   In Tuesday's National Basketball Association draft, the Pistons' general manager wants a big
   guy who can bang.

2. Fiekens is to make a final decision on how the contractors, Vista and Michigan Disposal, Inc., can continue to haul Detroit sludge in a meeting next Monday with their lawyers.

   In a meeting next Monday with the contractors' lawyers, Fiekens is to make a final decision on
   how the contractors, Vista and Michigan Disposal, Inc., can continue to haul Detroit sludge.

3. Jessica W., 28, and Abernathy A., 26, both of Detroit, were charged with delivery of cocaine after the raid.

   After the raid, Jessica W., 28, and Abernathy A., 26, both of Detroit, were charged with delivery
   of cocaine.

4. In 1935 he joined the embryonic [Count] Basie group and remained with what many consider the greatest jazz organization of all time until 1948.

   In 1935 he joined the embryonic [Count] Basie group, what many consider the greatest jazz
   organization of all time, and remained in the group until 1948.

Write   Write the first draft of a personal narrative (true story) in which you share a time when you misplaced or lost something important to you or to someone else. Here are some tips for adding interest to your story:

- Start right in the middle of the action.
- Build suspense to keep the reader's interest.
- Use dialogue.
- Use sensory details (what you heard, saw, felt, and so on).

Afterward, exchange your writing with a classmate. Read each other's narrative first for enjoyment and a second time to check it for the sentence errors discussed in this chapter.

CONSIDER THE WORKPLACE

Journalists and publishers need to be especially careful to avoid mistakes in their writing. But errors in writing reflect badly on all professionals.

Part IV: Word Workshops

21

> "Mathematics, rightly viewed, possesses not only truth, but supreme beauty—a beauty cold and austere, like that of sculpture."
>
> —Bertrand Russell

Noun

You have probably heard that a noun names a person, place, or thing. For example, the words *man* and *woman* are nouns. The words *Millennium Park* and *lakefront* also are nouns. And the words *sculpture* and *bean* are nouns as well.

But you may not know that nouns can also name ideas. The word *beauty* is a noun, for example, as are *artistry, mathematics,* and *awe.* You can't see these things, but they are real, and they change the world. At one point, this sculpture was only an idea in the mind of Anish Kapoor, who wanted to create a polished drop of mercury hovering above the ground. Years and $26 million dollars later, the "Cloud Gate" has become a real thing—one of the most popular attractions along the Chicago lakefront.

This chapter helps you find the right nouns to name people, places, things, and ideas. You'll learn about the different classes of nouns, singular and plural nouns, count and noncount nouns, and noun markers. Last, you'll get to apply what you have learned in a real-world document.

Learning Outcomes

LO1 Understand classes of nouns.

LO2 Use singular and plural nouns.

LO3 Form tricky plurals.

LO4 Use count and noncount nouns.

LO5 Use articles.

LO6 Use other noun markers.

LO7 Use nouns correctly in a real-world context.

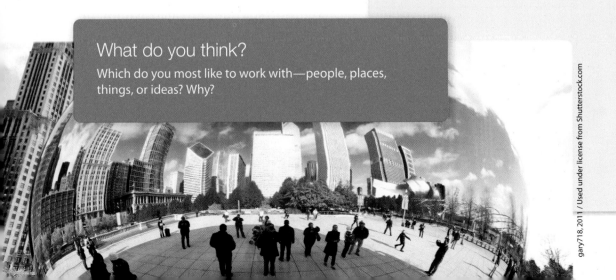

What do you think?
Which do you most like to work with—people, places, things, or ideas? Why?

gary718, 2011 / Used under license from Shutterstock.com

LO1 Classes of Nouns

All nouns are either *common* or *proper*. They can also be *individual* or *collective, concrete* or *abstract*.

Common or Proper Nouns

Common nouns name a general person, place, thing, or idea. They are not capitalized as names. **Proper nouns** name a specific person, place, thing, or idea, and they are capitalized as names.

	Common Nouns	**Proper Nouns**
Person:	rapper	P. Diddy
Place:	memorial	Vietnam Veterans Memorial
Thing:	car	Ford
Idea:	religion	Islam

Individual or Collective Nouns

Most nouns are **individual**: They refer to one person or thing. Other nouns are **collective**, referring most commonly to a group of people or animals.

	Individual Nouns	**Collective Nouns**
Person:	chairperson	committee
	quarterback	team
	tourist	crowd
	son	family
Animal:	bird	flock
	gnat	swarm
	lion	pride
	whale	pod
	fish	school

Concrete or Abstract

If a noun refers to something that can be seen, heard, smelled, tasted, or touched, it is a **concrete noun**. If a noun refers to something that can't be sensed, it is an **abstract noun**. Abstract nouns name ideas, conditions, or feelings.

Concrete Nouns	**Abstract Nouns**
cathedral	Catholicism
heart	love
skin	health

Using Different Classes of Nouns

Identify In each sentence below, identify the underlined nouns as common (C) or proper (P).

1. Waterfalls capture the imagination.
   C   C
2. Niagara Falls is the most powerful set of falls in North America.
   P   C   C   P
3. Niagara Falls is nearly 4,400 feet wide, but Victoria Falls is well over 5,500 feet wide.
   P   P
4. Every second, 85,000 gallons of water rush over Niagara Falls.
                        C   C   P

Identify In each sentence below, identify the underlined nouns as individual (I) or collective (CL).

1. The tallest cascade is Angel Falls in Venezuela at 3,212 feet.
                I   I   CL
2. A team of explorers led by Ruth Robertson measured the height of Angel Falls in 1949.
     CL   I   I   I
          CL
3. In 1937, Jimmie Angel crash-landed on the falls; a crew had to bring the plane down.
       I   CL
            I
4. The company that made Up drew inspiration for Paradise Falls from Angel Falls.
       CL   I   I
5.

Identify In each sentence below, identify the underlined nouns as concrete (CT) or abstract (A).

1. Iguazu Falls is at the border of Argentina and Brazil.
   CT   CT   CT   CT
2. Tourists gaze with wonder and amazement at 275 falls spread over 1.9 miles.
   CT   A   A   CT
   CT
3. The largest fall, Devil's Throat, roars like a devil full of rage.
                CT   CT   A   A
4. When Eleanor Roosevelt saw them, she said in awe, "Poor Niagara!"
        CT   A   CT

Vocabulary

common noun
noun referring to a general person, place, thing, or idea; not capitalized as a name

proper noun
noun referring to a specific person, place, thing, or idea; capitalized as a name

individual noun
noun referring to one person or thing

collective noun
noun referring to a group of people or animals

concrete noun
noun referring to something that can be sensed

abstract noun
noun referring to an idea, a condition, or a feeling—something that cannot be sensed

LO2 Singular or Plural

The **number** of a noun indicates whether it is singular or plural. A **singular** noun refers to one person, place, thing, or idea. A **plural** noun refers to more than one person, place, thing, or idea. For most words, the plural is formed by adding *s*. For nouns ending in *ch, s, sh, x,* or *z,* add an *es*.

	Most Nouns Add *s*		Nouns Ending in *ch, s, sh, x, or z* Add *es*	
	Singular	Plural	Singular	Plural
Person:	sister	sisters	coach	coaches
Place:	park	parks	church	churches
Thing:	spoon	spoons	kiss	kisses
Idea:	solution	solutions	wish	wishes

Same in Both Forms or Usually Plural

Some nouns are the same in both forms, and others are usually plural:

Same in Both Forms		Usually Plural	
Singular	Plural	Plural	
deer	deer	clothes	series
fish	fish	glasses	shears
moose	moose	pants	shorts
salmon	salmon	proceeds	species
sheep	sheep	savings	tongs
swine	swine	scissors	trousers

Irregular Plurals

Irregular plurals are formed by changing the words themselves. That is because the plural form comes from Old English or Latin.

From Old English		From Latin	
Singular	Plural	Singular	Plural
child	children	alumnus	alumni
foot	feet	axis	axes
goose	geese	crisis	crises
man	men	datum	data
mouse	mice	millennium	millennia
person	people	medium	media
tooth	teeth	nucleus	nuclei
woman	women	phenomenon	phenomena

Using Singular and Plural Nouns

Identify For each word, fill in the blank with either the singular or plural form, whichever is missing. If the word usually uses the plural form or is the same in both forms, write an X on the line.

1. boy — boys
2. girl — girls
3. child — children
4. man — men
5. woman — women
6. deer — X
7. X — clothes
8. X — species
9. swine — X
10. axis — axes
11. tooth — teeth
12. millennium — millennia
13. automobile — automobiles
14. tree — trees
15. X — pants
16. X — moose
17. phenomenon — phenomena
18. crisis — crises
19. mouse — mice
20. X — savings
21. datum — data
22. alumnus — alumni
23. goose — geese
24. fish — X
25. X — shears

Vocabulary

number
whether a word is singular or plural

singular
referring to one thing

plural
referring to more than one thing

irregular plural
a plural noun formed by changing the word rather than by adding *s*

LO3 Tricky Plurals

Some plural nouns are more challenging to form. Words ending in *y, f,* or *fe* and certain compound nouns require special consideration.

Nouns Ending in *y*

If a common noun ends in *y* after a consonant, change the y to *i* and add *es*. If the noun ends in *y* after a vowel, leave the *y* and add *s*.

y After a Consonant		*y* After a Vowel	
Singular	**Plural**	**Singular**	**Plural**
fly	flies	bay	bays
lady	ladies	key	keys
penny	pennies	toy	toys
story	stories	tray	trays

Nouns Ending in *f* or *fe*

If a common noun ends in *f* or *fe,* change the *f* or *fe* to a *v* and add *es*—unless the *f* sound remains in the plural form. Then just add an *s*.

v Sound in Plural		*f* Sound in Plural	
Singular	**Plural**	**Singular**	**Plural**
calf	calves	belief	beliefs
life	lives	chef	chefs
self	selves	proof	proofs
shelf	shelves	safe	safes

Compound Nouns

A **compound noun** is made up of two or more words that function together as a single noun. Whether the compound is hyphenated or not, make it plural by placing the *s* or *es* on the most important word in the compound.

Important Word First		Important Word Last	
Singular	**Plural**	**Singular**	**Plural**
editor in chief	editors in chief	bird-watcher	bird-watchers
mother-in-law	mothers-in-law	human being	human beings
professor emeritus	professors emeritus	test tube	test tubes
secretary of state	secretaries of state	well-wisher	well-wishers

Forming Tricky Plurals

Form Plurals For each word below, create the correct plural form.

1. ray ___rays___
2. elf ___elves___
3. high school ___high schools___
4. bunny ___bunnies___
5. boy ___boys___
6. leaf ___leaves___
7. reef ___reefs___
8. calf ___calves___
9. guy ___guys___
10. credit card ___credit cards___

11. brother-in-law ___brothers-in-law___
12. day ___days___
13. patty ___patties___
14. café ___cafés___
15. sister-in-law ___sisters-in-law___
16. fife ___fifes___
17. rear guard ___rear guards___
18. jury ___juries___
19. power of attorney ___powers of attorney___
20. poppy ___poppies___

Form Plurals In the sentences below, correct the plural errors by writing the correct forms.

1. I read two different (storys) about (ladys) that swallowed (flys).
   stories   ladies   flies
2. The (toies) on the (shelfs) belong to my (stepchilds).
   toys   shelves   stepchildren
3. The (cheves) served salmon (pattys) with the (soup) of the (days).
   chefs   patties   soups   day
4. After a few (daies), the (daisys) sprouted in the (flowers box).
   days   daisies   flower boxes
5. The (secretary of states) from both (countrys) discussed the (treatys).
   secretaries of state   countries   treaties
6. I saw mud (puppys) and (rivers) otter on my hike.
   puppies   river   otters
7. He gave me four (pennys), which I divided between
   the two take-a-penny (traies).
   pennies   trays
8. The (keis) for my (carries-on) are missing.
   keys   carry-ons
9. Why is ("elfs") spelled one way and ("dwarves") is
   spelled the other?
   elves   dwarfs
10. The (crys) of (babys) usually alert parents.
    cries   babies

Steve Collender/ Used under license from Shutterstock.com

Vocabulary

compound noun
noun made up of two or
more words

LO4 Count and Noncount Nouns

Some nouns name things that can be counted, and other nouns name things that cannot. Different rules apply to each type.

Count Nouns

Count nouns name things that can be counted—*pens, people, votes, cats,* and so forth. They can be singular or plural, and they can be preceded by numbers or articles (*a, an,* or *the*).

Singular	Plural
grape	grapes
dog	dogs
car	cars
idea	ideas

INSIGHT

Many native English speakers aren't even aware of count and noncount nouns, though they use them correctly out of habit. Listen for their use of count and noncount nouns.

Noncount Nouns

Noncount nouns name things that cannot be counted. They are used in singular form, and they can be preceded by *the,* but not by *a* or *an.*

This semester, I'm taking **mathematics** and **biology** as well as **Spanish**.

Substances	Foods	Activities	Science	Languages	Abstractions
wood	water	reading	oxygen	Spanish	experience
cloth	milk	boating	weather	English	harm
ice	wine	smoking	heat	Mandarin	publicity
plastic	sugar	dancing	sunshine	Farsi	advice
wool	rice	swimming	electricity	Greek	happiness
steel	meat	soccer	lightning	Latin	health
aluminum	cheese	hockey	biology	French	joy
metal	flour	photography	history	Japanese	love
leather	pasta	writing	mathematics	Afrikaans	anger
porcelain	gravy	homework	economics	German	fame

Two-Way Nouns

Two-way nouns can function as count or noncount nouns, depending on their context.

Please set a **glass** in front of each place mat. (count noun)

The display case was made of tempered **glass**. (noncount noun)

Using Count and Noncount Nouns

Sort Read the list of nouns below and sort the words into columns of count and noncount nouns.

door	wool	vacation	happiness	sunshine
heat	tablecloth	wagon	photography	flour
swimming	cherry	French	ruler	tablespoon

door	heat
tablecloth	swimming
cherry	wool
vacation	French
wagon	happiness
ruler	photography
tablespoon	sunshine
	flour

Using Count and Noncount Nouns

Correct Read the following paragraph and correct the noun errors. Write down the line number and any words you would change. Then show what changes you would make. The first one has been done for you.

There are different activities for four different weathers. For days   1

with sunshines, outdoor activities are best. Some people enjoy swimmings,

others like boatings, and even more play soccers. For days in the

spring or fall, quieter activities work well. Writing poetries and enjoying

photographies are good pastimes, as well as dancings. During the winter,   5

there are readings and homeworks to do. The key to happinesses is to enjoy

whatever you are doing.

Correction Marks

ℒ delete	⋀ add comma	⋀ word add word	
d ≡ capitalize	? add question mark	⊙ add period	
⋀ insert	⋁ insert an apostrophe	spelling switch	

Vocabulary

count noun
noun naming something that can be counted

noncount noun
noun naming something that cannot be counted

two-way noun
noun that can function as either a count or a noncount noun

LO5 Articles

Articles help you to know if a noun refers to a specific thing or to a general thing. There are two basic types of articles—definite and indefinite.

Definite Article

The **definite article** is the word *the*. It signals that the noun refers to one specific person, place, thing, or idea.

> Fluffy slept on the laptop.
> (Fluffy slept on a specific laptop.)
>
> > NOTE: *The* can be used with most nouns, but usually not with proper nouns.
>
> **Incorrect:** The Fluffy got off the laptop.
> **Correct:** Fluffy got off the laptop.

INSIGHT ————————————————————————————————

If your heritage language does not use articles, pay close attention to the way native English speakers use *the* when referring to a specific thing. Note, however, that *the* is not usually used with proper nouns naming people or animals.

Indefinite Articles

The **indefinite articles** are the words *a* and *an*. They signal that the noun refers to a general person, place, thing, or idea. The word *a* is used before nouns that begin with consonant sounds, and the word *an* is used before nouns that begin with vowel sounds.

> Chan needs a laptop.
> (He'll take any laptop.)
>
> > NOTE: Don't use *a* or *an* with noncount nouns or plural count nouns.
>
> **Incorrect:** Pass me a cheese.
> **Correct:** Pass me the cheese.
>
> > NOTE: If a word begins with an *h* that is pronounced, use *a*. If the *h* is silent, use *an*.
>
> **Incorrect:** It is a honor.
> **Correct:** It is an honor.

Using Articles

Identify Add the appropriate indefinite article (*a* or *an*) to each of the words below. The first one has been done for you.

1. __an__ anthill
2. _____ pear
3. _____ hog
4. _____ hour
5. _____ apple

6. _____ ad
7. _____ heap
8. _____ honor
9. _____ dolphin
10. _____ egg

11. _____ euro
12. _____ honest man
13. _____ idea
14. _____ exaggeration
15. _____ handshake

Correct In the following paragraph, delete or replace any articles that are incorrectly used. Write down the line number and any words you would change. Then show what changes you would make. The first sentence has been done for you.

Scientists wonder whether a planet Neptune collided with the "super-   1
Earth" when a solar system was forming. The Neptune emits much more
radiation than the Uranus, though they are otherwise twins in a solar
system. An extra radiation may be left over from this collision with the planet
twice the size of an Earth. The Neptune's large moon, the Triton, rotates   5
in an opposite direction to a planet's spin. That fact shows that a Triton
was probably a moon of the super-Earth and was captured. If scientists are
right, the Neptune holds another planet inside its gassy belly.

Correction Marks

⌿	delete	⋏	add comma	⋏ *word*	add word
d	capitalize	?	add question mark	⊙	add period
Ø	lowercase				spelling
⋏	insert	⋁	insert an apostrophe	∿	switch

Vocabulary

article
the most common type of noun marker (*a, an,* or *the*)

definite article
the word *the,* used to mark a noun that refers to a specific person, place, or thing

indefinite article
the words *a* or *an,* used to mark a noun that refers to a general person, place, or thing

LO6 Other Noun Markers

Other words help provide information about nouns.

Possessive Adjective

A **possessive adjective** is the possessive form of a noun or pronoun. Possessive adjectives can be formed by adding *'s* to singular nouns and *'* to plural nouns.

Dave's e-mail came back, but **Ellen's** didn't.

Milwaukee's harbor is usually calm.

The **Smiths'** house needs painting.

That is **my** car. That car is **mine**.

It's **your** book. The book is **yours**.

Possessive Pronouns

	Singular		Plural	
	Before	After	Before	After
First Person	my	mine	our	ours
Second Person	your	yours	your	yours
Third Person	his	his	their	theirs
	her	hers	their	theirs
	its	its	their	theirs

Indefinite Adjectives

An **indefinite adjective** signals that the noun it marks refers to a general person, place, thing, or idea. Some indefinite adjectives mark count nouns and others mark noncount nouns.

All people are welcome to join. **Much** celebrating will be done.

With Count Nouns			With Noncount Nouns	With Count or Noncount		
each	either	every	much	all	any	more
few	many	neither		most	some	
several						

Demonstrative Adjectives

A **demonstrative adjective** marks a specific noun. The words *this* and *that* (singular) or *these* and *those* (plural) demonstrate exactly which one is meant.

These songs are by **that** artist.   **This** song includes **those** lyrics.

Quantifiers

A **quantifier** tells *how many* or *how much* there is of something.

With Count Nouns		With Noncount Nouns		With Count or Noncount		
each	a couple of	a bag of	a little	no	a lot of	most
several	every	a bowl of	much	not any	lots of	all
a number of	many	a piece of	a great deal of	some	plenty of	
both	a few					
nine						

Using Noun Markers

Identify   Indicate the appropriate noun marker in parentheses for each sentence.

1. Please leave (*your*, *yours*) phone number after the beep.
2. Is this phone number (*your*, *yours*)?
3. How (*many*, *much*) students are allowed in the class?
4. The professor did not give us (*any*, *each*) homework.
5. I want to buy (*this*, *these*) shirts.
6. The resident assistant didn't like (*that*, *those*) idea.
7. After making the dough, we had (*several*, *a little*) flour left.
8. I liked (*a number of*, *much*) the suggestions.
9. The proposal was originally (*her*, *hers*).
10. Let's make sure to return (*their*, *theirs*) pillows.

Correct   In the following paragraph, delete or replace any noun markers that are incorrectly used. Write down the line number and any words you would change. Then show what changes you would make. The first line has been done for you.

> What is ~~yours~~ *your* major? You probably have heard that ~~much~~ *many* times. But   *1*
> taking a ~~little~~ *few* courses in one area does not mean it is ~~yours~~ *your* major. ~~Much~~ *Many*
> students don't choose a major until ~~theirs~~ *their* junior year. ~~This~~ *These* students have
> to explore ~~theirs~~ *their* options before making up ~~theirs~~ *their* minds. ~~Those~~ *That* delay isn't
> a problem. ~~Those~~ *This* exploration is the point of undergraduate study. Until you   *5*
> know for sure a major is ~~your~~ *yours*, you should taste-test ~~much~~ *many* fields. In ~~mine~~ *my*
> junior year, I was told I would not graduate unless I picked ~~mine~~ *my* major. I
> added up ~~mine~~ *my* hours, and that total showed I was
> closest to English. Two weeks later, the head of the
> English Department called and said, "I thought we   *10*
> should meet since you are one of ~~mine~~ *my* majors."

Correction Marks

ℒ	delete
d̲̲	capitalize
D̸	lowercase
∧	insert
⌃	add comma
?	add question mark
∧ word	add word
⊙	add period
◯	spelling
∿	switch

Vocabulary

possessive adjective
the possessive form of a noun or pronoun, showing ownership of another noun

indefinite adjective
an indefinite pronoun (*many, much, some*) used as an adjective to mark a nonspecific noun

demonstrative adjective
a demonstrative pronoun (*this, that, those*) used as an adjective to mark a specific noun

quantifier
a modifier that tells *how many* or *how much*

LO7 Real-World Application

Correct In the following letter, correct any errors with nouns, articles, or other noun markers. Write down the line number and any words you would change. Then show what changes you would make.

Dale's Garden Center
405 Cherry Lane Flower City, IL 53185

February 1, 2010   *1*

Dear Student:

Did one of yours [your] science professors ever tell you that plants can talk?
Well, they can. Dale [Dale's] flowers speak a language of love to the womans [women] or
mans [men] in your life.   *5*

If you're at an [a] loss for words with valentine's day just two weeks away,
let Dale's flowers give you the words. Red roses share yours [your] love in the
language of Romance. A Southern charm bouquet says it with class and
a [an] added touch of Magnolias. Or send poetries [poetry] by choosing our Valentine's
Day special in a porcelain vase!   *10*

Come browse our shelfs [shelves]. Or check out the enclosed catalog and place
yours [your] order by phoning 1-800-555-LEAF. If you call by february 13,
we guarantee delivery of fresh flowers on Valentine's Day. Order by
Februaries [February] 10, and you'll receive an [a] 20-percent discount.

Let Dales [Dale's] flowers help you start a conversation that could last a lifetime!   *15*

Sincerely,

Jerilynn Bostwick

Jerilynn Bostwick
Sales Manager

P.S. Is your [yours] a long-distance romance? Remember, we deliver flowers   *20*
anywhere in the world through the telefloral network.

22

Pronoun

"The personal pronoun in English has three cases, the dominative, the objectionable, and the oppressive."
—Ambrose Bierce

Mannequins are everywhere—trying to sell this dress or that shirt, trying to show you a suit or a pair of shorts. The reason mannequins are everywhere is that it would be too expensive and boring for real people to stand around all day showing off clothing.

Pronouns are like mannequins—they are stand-ins for nouns. They aren't nouns, but they refer back to them. Writing that has no pronouns quickly becomes overloaded with nouns, repetitive and hard to read. So a pronoun can take the noun's place.

This chapter will show you how to make sure your pronoun stand-ins work well.

Learning Outcomes

LO1 Understand personal pronouns.

LO2 Create pronoun-antecedent agreement.

LO3 Correct other pronoun problems.

LO4 Create agreement with indefinite pronouns.

LO5 Use relative pronouns.

LO6 Use other pronouns.

LO7 Use pronouns correctly in a real-world context.

What do you think?

How do sentence problems impact the sentence's ability to be a carrier of news?

LO1 Personal Pronouns

A **pronoun** is a word that takes the place of a noun or another pronoun. The most common type of pronoun is the **personal pronoun**. Personal pronouns indicate whether the person is speaking, is being spoken to, or is being spoken about.

Person	Singular			Plural		
	Nom.	Obj.	Poss.	Nom.	Obj.	Poss.
First (speaking)	I	me	my/mine	we	us	our/ours
Second (spoken to)	you	you	your/yours	you	you	your/yours
Third (spoken about) masculine	he	him	his	they	them	their/theirs
feminine	she	her	her/hers	they	them	their/theirs
neuter	it	it	its	they	them	their/theirs

Nom. = nominative case / **Obj.** = objective case / **Poss.** = possessive case

Case of Pronouns

The **case** of a personal pronoun indicates how it can be used.

■ **Nominative** pronouns are used as the subjects of sentences or as subject complements (following the linking verbs *am, is, are, was, were, be, being,* or *been*).

> I was nominated, but the person selected was she.

■ **Objective** pronouns are used as direct objects, indirect objects, or objects of prepositions.

> The professor lectured them about it.

■ **Possessive** pronouns show ownership and function as adjectives.

> My notebook has fewer notes than hers.

Gender

Pronouns can be **masculine**, **feminine**, or **neuter**.

> She helped him with it.

Say It

Read the following aloud.
1. *I* am / *You* are / *He* is / *She* is / *It* is / *We* are / *They* are
2. Help *me* / Help *you* / Help *him* / Help *her* / Help *it* / Help *us* / Help *them*

Using Personal Pronouns

Select For each sentence below, select the correct personal pronoun in parentheses.

1. The dorm cafeteria is where (*I, me, my*) friends gather.
2. (*We, Us, Our*) talk about classes and also about each other.
3. I told Emily that I would help (*she, her, hers*) with her homework.
4. I have a heavy schedule, but not as heavy as (*she, her, hers*) is.
5. (*I, Me, My, Mine*) 18 credits require less work than (*she, her, hers*) 20.

Correct In the following paragraph, correct the pronouns. Write the line number and any incorrect pronoun. Cross it out and write a correction beside it.

> I asked ~~me~~ ^{my} sons if ~~them~~ ^{they} would like to take a walk around Lake   1
> Geneva. ~~Them~~ ^{They} asked how ~~us~~ ^{we} could walk around the lake. I told ~~they~~ ^{them} that
> a path goes all the way around the lake, and ~~its~~ ^{it} is open to the public. My
> sons said that ~~them~~ ^{they} wanted to go, but ~~them~~ ^{they} wondered how far the walk
> was. ~~Me~~ ^I told ~~they~~ ^{them} that it was about 30 miles. ~~They~~ ^{Their} mouths dropped open.   5
> ~~Them~~ ^{They} couldn't figure out what to say to ~~I~~ ^{me}. My sons and ~~me~~ ^I looked at each
> other. Then I said ~~them~~ ^{they} needed to get ~~theirs~~ ^{their} backpacks and shoes. They
> told me that I should get a life. But I convinced ~~they~~ ^{them}, and ~~us~~ ^{we} hiked all the
> way around Lake Geneva. When it was over, I wished I had listened to
> ~~they~~ ^{them}. My legs hurt so much!   10

Vocabulary

pronoun
a word that takes the place of a noun or other pronoun

personal pronoun
a pronoun that indicates whether the person is speaking, is spoken to, or is spoken about

case
whether a pronoun is used as a subject, an object, or a possessive

nominative
used as a subject or subject complement

objective
used as a direct object, an indirect object, or an object of

a preposition

possessive
used to show ownership

masculine
male

feminine
female

neuter
neither male nor female

LO2 Pronoun-Antecedent Agreement

The **antecedent** is the word that a pronoun refers to or replaces. A pronoun must have the same person, number, and gender as the antecedent, which is called **pronoun-antecedent agreement**.

> **third-person**   **singular feminine**
> Linda asked to borrow a pen but then found hers.

Agreement in Person

A pronoun needs to match its antecedent in **person** (first, second, or third).

> **third person**   **second person**
> **Incorrect:** If people look hard, you might find some good deals.
> **Correct:** If you look hard, you might find some good deals.
> **Correct:** If people look hard, they might find some good deals.

Agreement in Number

A pronoun needs to match its antecedent in **number** (singular or plural).

> **singular**   **plural**
> **Incorrect:** Each student should bring their assignment.
> **Correct:** Students should bring their assignments.
> **Correct:** Each student should bring her or his assignment.

Agreement in Gender

A pronoun needs to match its antecedent in **gender** (masculine, feminine, or neuter).

> **feminine**   **masculine**
> **Incorrect:** Janae will share his project.
> **Correct:** Janae will share her project.

Correcting Agreement Errors

Correct Person   Rewrite each sentence to correct the person error.

1. If both of you go to the job fair, they will probably find job opportunities.

   If both of you go to the job fair, **you** will probably find job opportunities.

2. We went to the fair last year, and they landed some good jobs.

   We went to the fair last year, and **we** landed some good jobs.

3. If the graduates fill out applications, you may find jobs.

   If the graduates fill out applications, **they** may find jobs.

4. One considers the future when you attend the fair.

   One considers the future when **one** attends the fair.

Correct Number   Rewrite each sentence to correct the number error.

5. Each applicant should put down their name.

   Applicants should put down their **names**.

6. An employee will greet you, and they will interview you.

   An employee will greet you, and **she or he** will interview you.

7. Applicants should supply his contact information.

   Applicants should supply **their** contact information.

Correct Gender   Rewrite each sentence to correct the gender error.

8. If Lionel goes, she can drive others.

   If Lionel goes, **he** can drive others

9. Tawny said he was going.

   Tawny said **she** was going.

10. Ask David if she is planning to attend.

    Ask David if **he** is planning to attend.

11. The hall is big, and she sits at a major intersection.

    The hall is big, and **it** sits at a major intersection.

Vocabulary

antecedent
the word that a pronoun refers to or replaces

pronoun-antecedent agreement
matching a pronoun to its antecedent in terms of person, number, and gender

person
whether the pronoun is speaking, being spoken to, or being spoken about

number
whether the pronoun is singular or plural

gender
whether the pronoun is masculine, feminine, or neuter

LO3 Other Pronoun Problems

Pronouns are very useful parts of speech, but if they are mishandled, they can cause problems.

Vague Pronoun

Do not use a pronoun that could refer to more than one antecedent.

> **Unclear:** Lupe spoke to her roommate and her sister.
> **Clear:** Lupe spoke to her roommate and her roommate's sister.

Missing Antecedent

Avoid using *it* or *they* without clear antecedents.

> **Unclear:** It says in the tabloid that a donkey-boy was born.
> **Clear:** The tabloid says that a donkey-boy was born.
> **Unclear:** They have found one of the causes of arthritis.
> **Clear:** Scientists have found one of the causes of arthritis.

Double Subjects

Do not place a pronoun right after the subject. Doing so creates an error called a **double subject**, which is not a standard construction.

> **Incorrect:** Kyle and Jules, they went to the movies.
> **Correct:** Kyle and Jules went to the movies.

Usage Errors *(They're, You're, It's)*

Do not confuse possessive pronouns (*your, their, its*) with contractions (*you're, they're, it's*). Remember that contractions use apostrophes in place of missing letters.

> **Incorrect:** Please place you're plastic bottles in they're recycling bin.
> **Correct:** Please place your plastic bottles in their recycling bin.

CONSIDER SPEAKING AND LISTENING

The pronoun problems on this page may not cause confusion in spoken English. In written English, these problems can derail meaning. Correct them in your writing.

Correcting Other Pronoun Problems

Rewrite Rewrite each sentence to correct the pronoun-reference problems.

1. Raul asked his father and his friend to help him move.

   Raul asked his father and his father's friend to help him move.

2. It says in the article that three people are trapped.

   The article says that three people are trapped.

3. They are proposing an amendment to the Constitution.

   Congress is proposing an amendment to the Constitution.

4. Shakira wants her sister and her friend to help.

   Shakira wants her sister and her sister's friend to help.

5. It says in the news report that stocks are down.

   The news report says that stocks are down.

6. They have a new cure for baldness.

   Scientists have a new cure for baldness.

Correct In the following paragraph, correct the pronoun errors. Write the line number and any words you would change. Then show how you would change them.

>   ~~It says on~~ the Internet that many major companies have pulled April   *1*
> Fool's Day pranks. ~~They~~ replaced the name "Google" with the name
> "Topeka," for one. ~~It~~ says also that a rare baby skeksis was born in a
> zoo, but ~~it~~ exists only in the film *The Dark Crystal*. One classical music
> station, ~~it~~ claimed that a British billionaire was sending a violinist to   *5*
> the moon in a special spaceship. ~~It's~~ console had a button to make the
> ship's cockpit sound like the Royal Albert Hall. ~~They~~ had a lot of fun
> with ~~they're~~ gags, but gullible people kept getting tripped up all day. ~~It~~
> also claims that in the UK, Australia, and South Africa, the gags stop at
> noon, but ~~they're~~ citizens, ~~they~~ still get pranked by Americans all day.   *10*
>
> Annotations (handwritten corrections): *An article on* (line 1), *says* (line 1), *Google* (line 2), *The article* (line 3), *a skeksis* (line 4), *The spaceship's* (line 6), *The station* (line 7), *The article* (line 8), *their* (line 8), *their* (line 10)

Vocabulary

vague pronoun
using a pronoun that could refer to more than one antecedent

missing antecedent
using a pronoun that has no clear antecedent

double subject
error created by following a subject with a pronoun

usage error
using the wrong word (e.g., *they're* instead of *their*)

LO4 Indefinite Pronouns

An **indefinite pronoun** does not have an antecedent, and it does not refer to a specific person, place, thing, or idea. These pronouns pose unique issues with subject-verb and pronoun-antecedent agreement.

Singular Indefinite Pronouns

Some indefinite pronouns are singular. When they are used as subjects, they require a singular verb. As antecedents, they must be matched to singular pronouns.

each	anyone	anybody	anything
either	someone	somebody	something
neither	everyone	everybody	everything
another	no one	nobody	nothing
one			

> Someone is supposed to empty the dishwasher.
>
> No one has said he will do it.

Plural Indefinite Pronouns

Some indefinite pronouns are plural. As subjects, they require a plural verb, and as antecedents, they require a plural pronoun.

both	few	several	many

> A few of the housemates leave dirty dishes everywhere.
>
> Several of their friends said they are fed up.

Singular or Plural Indefinite Pronouns

Some indefinite pronouns can be singular or plural, depending on the object of the preposition in the phrase that follows them.

all	any	most	none	some

> All of the pies were eaten.
>
> All of the pie was eaten.

INSIGHT

For more practice with indefinite pronouns, see pages 400–403.

Correcting Agreement

Correct Rewrite each sentence to correct the agreement errors. (Hint: The sentences are about a group of male campers.)

1. Everyone needs to wash their own dishes.

   Everyone needs to wash his own dishes.

2. No one are exempt.

   No one is exempt.

3. Anyone not washing their dishes must wash everyone else's.

   Anyone not washing his dishes must wash everyone else's.

4. Nothing short of illness are an excuse.

   Nothing short of illness is an excuse.

5. Few is arguing with the new policy.

   Few are arguing with the new policy.

6. Several says it is about time.

   Several say it is about time.

7. Many expresses their appreciation.

   Many express their appreciation.

8. For a week, all of the dishes has been washed.

   For a week, all of the dishes have been washed.

9. Ted made sure all of his plates was washed and put away.

   Ted made sure all of his plates were washed and put away.

10. Most of the roommates agrees that this works.

    Most of the roommates agree that this works.

11. Most of the morning are spent cleaning up.

    Most of the morning is spent cleaning up.

12. None of the dishes is left lying about.

    None of the dishes are left lying about.

13. None of the food are left to eat either, since everybody have forgotten to go shopping.

    None of the food is left to eat either, since everybody

    has forgotten to go shopping.

Vocabulary

indefinite pronoun
a pronoun that does not refer to a specific person, place, thing, or idea

LO5 Relative Pronouns

A **relative pronoun** introduces a dependent clause and relates it to the rest of the sentence.

who	whom	which	whose
whoever	whomever	that	

relative clause

I would like to meet the man who invented the World Wide Web.

Who/Whoever and Whom/Whomever

Who, whoever, whom, and *whomever* refer to people. *Who* or *whoever* functions as the subject of the relative clause, while *whom* or *whomever* functions as the object of the clause.

I would like to thank whoever chose the playlist for this party.

The person whom I thanked had terrific taste in music.

relative clause   **relative clause**

NOTE: In the second **relative clause**, *whom* introduces the clause even though it is the direct object, not the subject *(I thanked whom).*

That and Which

That and *which* usually refer to things. When *that* introduces the clause, the clause **is not** set off with commas. When *which* introduces the clause, the clause **is** set off with commas.

I read the book that told of Teddy Roosevelt's journey down the Amazon.

I enjoyed *The River of Doubt,* which was a $29 hardback.

relative clause   **relative clause**

Whose

Whose shows ownership or connection.

relative clause

The mechanic whose hand got cut was fixing our car.

NOTE: Do not confuse *whose* with the contraction *who's* (who is).

Using Relative Pronouns

Select   For each sentence, select the correct relative pronoun.

1. Theo Jansen is an engineer and artist *(who, whom)* is creating new life.

2. He builds sculptures *(that, which)* harness the wind to walk.

3. Theo refers to his sculptures as animals, *(that, which)* is unusual for an engineer.

4. These animals are built of plastic pipe, *(that, which)* is inexpensive and strong.

5. Another engineer and artist *(who, whom)* Jansen admires is Leonardo da Vinci.

6. Theo's creations are on display for *(whoever, whomever)* is on the beach.

7. His most famous creation is the Strandbeest, *(that, which)* has wings on top.

8. The wings pump air into plastic bottles, *(that, which)* store it up.

9. The air powers "muscles" *(that, which)* are made of sliding tubes.

10. Muscles open taps that activate other muscles, *(that, which)* makes the beast walk.

11. Theo Jansen, *(who, whose)* creations are spellbinding, hopes these "animals" will roam on their own one day.

12. Theo feels that the boundary between art and engineering is only in our minds, *(that, which)* allows him to create such creatures.

Write   Write a relative clause for each of these relative pronouns:

1. who   3. whom   5. which

2. whoever   4. whomever   6. that

Write a sentence including one of your clauses.
Answers will vary.

Vocabulary

relative pronoun
a pronoun that begins a relative clause, connecting it to a sentence

relative clause
a type of dependent clause that begins with a relative pronoun that is either the subject or the direct object of the clause

INSIGHT

For more practice with relative pronouns, see pages 390–391.

LO6 Other Pronoun Types

Other types of pronouns have specific uses in your writing: asking questions, pointing to specific things, reflecting back on a noun (or pronoun), or intensifying a noun (or pronoun).

Interrogative Pronoun

An **interrogative pronoun** asks a question—*who, whose, whom, which, what.*

> Who will help me make the salads? What is your favorite dressing?

Demonstrative Pronoun

A **demonstrative pronoun** points to a specific thing—*this, that, these, those.*

> This is the best of times! These are wonderful days!

Reflexive Pronoun

A **reflexive pronoun** reflects back to the subject of a sentence or clause—*myself, ourselves, yourself, yourselves, himself, herself, itself, themselves.*

> I e-mailed myself the file. You can send yourself the vacation photos.

Intensive Pronoun

An **intensive pronoun** emphasizes the noun or pronoun it refers to—*myself, ourselves, yourself, yourselves, himself, herself, itself, themselves.*

> I myself will be there. You yourself will see me.

Reciprocal Pronoun

A **reciprocal pronoun** refers to two things in an equal way—*each other, one another.*

> We should apologize to each other. We should love one another.

> **Say It**
>
> Speak the following words aloud.
> 1. Interrogative: *Who* is? / *Whose* is? / *Which* is? / *What* is? / *Whom* do you see?
> 2. Demonstrative: *This* is / *That* is / *These* are / *Those* are
> 3. Reflexive: I helped *myself.* / You helped *yourself.* / They helped *themselves*
> 4. Intensive: I *myself* / You *yourself* / She *herself* / He *himself* / They *themselves*
> 5. Reciprocal: We helped *each other.* / We helped *one another.*

Using Other Types of Pronouns

Identify   Indicate the type of each underlined pronoun: *interrogative, demonstrative, reflexive, intensive,* or *reciprocal.*

1. <u>That</u> is the reason we should fill the tank.   demonstrative

2. <u>What</u> should we use to pay for gas?   interrogative

3. I <u>myself</u> expected you to bring money.   intensive

4. You should pat <u>yourself</u> on the back.   reflexive

5. <u>That</u> is all the money you have?   demonstrative

6. The change <u>itself</u> won't be enough.   intensive

7. <u>Who</u> gets $1.73 worth of gas?   interrogative

8. <u>That</u> won't get us far.   demonstrative

9. <u>This</u> is ridiculous.   demonstrative

10. <u>What</u> should we do?   interrogative

11. I <u>myself</u> am prepared to push.   intensive

12. We should be ashamed of <u>ourselves</u>.   reflexive

13. We shouldn't blame <u>each other</u>.   reciprocal

14. Let's help <u>one another</u> move this car.   reciprocal

15. Then let's get <u>ourselves</u> a soda.   reflexive

Write   Create a sentence using *myself* as a reflexive pronoun, and a second using *myself* as an intensive pronoun.

1. Answers will vary.

2. _____

LO7 Real-World Application

Correct Correct any pronoun errors in the letter that follows. Write the line number and any words you would change. Cross out the word and show the change you would make.

Rankin Technologies
401 South Manheim Road, Albany, NY 12236 ▪ Ph: 708.555.1980 ▪ Fax: 708.555.0056

1   April 28, 2010

Mr. Henry Danburn
Construction Manager
Titan Industrial Construction, Inc.
5   P.O. Box 2112
Phoenix, AZ 85009-3887

Dear Mr. Danburn:

Thank you for meeting with ~~I~~ [me] last week at the National Convention
in Las Vegas. I want to follow up on ~~ours~~ [our] discussion of ways ~~which~~ [that]
10   Rankin Technologies could work with Titan Industrial Construction.

Enclosed is the information that ~~your~~ [you] requested. I believe this
material demonstrates ~~what~~ [why] Rankin Technologies would be a solid
match for ~~yours~~ [your] projects in western Illinois.
You ~~yourselves~~ [yourself] are the construction manager for the Arrow Mills
15   renovation project in California. Rankin did the electrical installation
on that project initially, and ~~us~~ [we] would be very interested in working
with you on the renovation. Someone ~~whom~~ [who] is familiar
with our work at Arrow Mills is Mike Knowlan. ~~She~~ [He] is
the plant manager and can be reached at 606-555-6328.
20   ~~Us~~ [We] are excited about working with ~~yous~~ [you] on any future
projects, and on the Arrow Mills project in particular.
Please call ~~I~~ [me] with any questions (708-555-1980).

Sincerely,

James Gabriel

25   James Gabriel
Vice President
Enclosures 5

INSIGHT ─────────────────────────────
In workplace documents, correct grammar is critical
to creating a strong impression.

Correction Marks

ℐ	delete
d	capitalize
D	lowercase
∧	insert
∧	add comma
? ∧	add question mark
word ∧	add word
⊙	add period
⌒	spelling
∾	switch

23

Verb

> "I think I am a verb."
> —R. Buckminster Fuller

Of course, we call ourselves human beings, but a few people have suggested we should think of ourselves as human doings. They would argue that our actions define us more than who we are.

Whether you are a human being or a human doing, you are thinking of yourself as a verb. Verbs express states of being and actions (doing). They give a sentence energy, movement, and meaning. This chapter provides practice working with these amazing words.

Learning Outcomes

LO1 Understand and use verb classes.
LO2 Work with number and person.
LO3 Work with voice.
LO4 Form present and future tenses.
LO5 Form past tense.
LO6 Form progressive tense.
LO7 Form perfect tense.
LO8 Understand verbals.
LO9 Use verbals as objects.
LO10 Apply learning to real-world examples.

What do you think?

Are you a human being or a human doing? Why?

LO1 Verb Classes

Verbs show action or states of being. Different classes of verbs do these jobs.

Action Verbs

Verbs that show action are called **action verbs**. Some action verbs are **transitive**, which means that they transfer action to a direct object.

Bill clutches the pillow.
(The verb *clutches* transfers action to the direct object *pillow*.)

Others are **intransitive**: They don't transfer action to a direct object.

Bill sleeps.
(The verb *sleeps* does not transfer action to a direct object.)

Linking Verbs

Verbs that link the subject to a noun, a pronoun, or an adjective are **linking verbs**. Predicates with linking verbs express a state of being.

Bill is a heavy sleeper.
(The linking verb *is* connects *Bill* to the noun *sleeper*.)

He seems weary.
(The linking verb *seems* connects *He* to the adjective *weary*.)

Linking Verbs

is	am	are	was	were	be	being	been	become
grow	feel	seem	look	smell	taste	sound	appear	remain

NOTE: The bottom-row words are linking verbs if they don't show action.

INSIGHT

If you are mathematically minded, think of a linking verb as an equal sign. It indicates that the subject equals (or is similar to) what is in the predicate.

Helping Verbs

A verb that works with an action or linking verb is a **helping** (or auxiliary) verb. A helping verb helps the main verb form tense, mood, and voice.

Bill has slept till noon before, and today he will be sleeping even longer.
(The helping verb *has* works with the main verb *slept;* the helping verbs *will be* work with *sleeping.* Both form special tenses.)

NOTE: Helping verbs work with verbs ending in *ing* or in past tense form.

Helping Verbs

am	been	could	does	have	might	should	will
are	being	did	had	is	must	was	would
be	can	do	has	may	shall	were	

Using Verb Classes

Identify/Write For each sentence below, identify the underlined verbs as transitive action verbs (T), intransitive action verbs (I), linking verbs (L), or helping verbs (H). Then write your own sentence using the same class of verb.

1. I <u>need</u> eight hours of sleep per night, but I often <u>get</u> only six. <u>Answers will vary.</u>

2. This weekend, I <u>will be</u> getting even less sleep. _____

3. One of my favorite bands is <u>playing</u> in town. _____

4. They <u>rock</u>, and whenever I <u>see</u> a concert of theirs, I hardly <u>sleep</u>. _____

5. I <u>am</u> eager, but after the weekend, I <u>will</u> be worn out. _____

6. The problem with having too much fun on the weekend <u>is</u> the week after. ___

7. Maybe I <u>should</u> go to bed earlier so that I <u>can</u> store up sleep. _____

8. I <u>feel</u> awake now, but next week I will <u>look</u> weary. _____

Vocabulary

action verb
word that expresses action

transitive verb
action verb that transfers action to a direct object

intransitive verb
action verb that does not transfer action to a direct object

linking verb
verb that connects the subject with a noun, a pronoun, or an adjective in the predicate

helping (auxiliary) verb
verb that works with a main verb to form some tenses, mood, and voice

LO2 Number and Person of Verb

Verbs reflect number (singular or plural) and person (first person, second person, or third person).

Number

The **number** of the verb indicates whether the subject is singular or plural. Note that most present tense singular verbs end in *s*, while most present tense plural verbs do not.

Singular: The Gettysburg Address speaks of those who "gave the last full measure of devotion."

Plural: Many historians speak of it as the greatest American speech.

Person

The **person** of the verb indicates whether the subject is speaking, being spoken to, or being spoken about.

	Singular	**Plural**
First Person:	(I) am	(we) are
Second Person:	(you) are	(you) are
Third Person:	(she) is	(they) are

Note that the pronoun *I* takes a special form of the *be* verb—*am.*

Correct: I am excited about going to Gettysburg.
Incorrect: I is excited about going to Gettysburg.

The pronoun *I* also is paired with plural present tense verbs.

Correct: I want to go with you.
Incorrect: I wants to go with you.

In a similar way, the singular pronoun *you* takes the plural form of the *be* verb—*are, were.*

Correct: You are going to the Gettysburg National Military Park.
Incorrect: You is going to the Gettysburg National Military Park.

Correct: You were my first choice.
Incorrect: You was my first choice.

Using Number and Person

Provide   For each sentence below, provide the correct person and number of the present tense *be* verb *(is, am, are)*.

1. We _____are_____ interested in going to Gettysburg.

2. It _____is_____ a town in Pennsylvania where a great battle took place.

3. You _____are_____ welcome to come on the trip with us.

4. Little Round Top _____is_____ a hill where the fighting focused.

5. The Union troops _____are_____ memorialized in statues on the hill.

6. You _____are_____ standing on a piece of American history.

7. Pickett's Charge _____is_____ considered General Lee's greatest mistake.

8. Troops from both sides _____are_____ buried in the cemetery.

9. I _____am_____ eager to see where Lincoln gave the Gettysburg Address.

10. We _____are_____ hoping to spend two days in Gettysburg.

Rewrite   Rewrite each sentence below to fix the errors in the number and person of the verb.

1. I listens as the tour guide describe the last day of battle.

   I listen as the tour guide describes the last day of battle.

2. Rifle shots hails down on the Confederate soldiers.

   Rifle shots hail down on the Confederate soldiers.

3. General Pickett order them to charge Little Round Top.

   General Pickett orders them to charge Little Round Top.

4. Flying lead kill many Southern soldiers.

   Flying lead kills many Southern soldiers.

5. The Union troops repels the charge and wins the day.

   The Union troops repel the charge and win the day.

6. President Lincoln deliver the Gettysburg Address.

   President Lincoln delivers the Gettysburg Address.

Vocabulary

number
singular or plural

person
whether the subject is speaking *(I, we)*, is being spoken to *(you)*, or is being spoken about *(he, she, it, they)*

LO3 Voice of the Verb

The **voice** of the verb indicates whether the subject is acting or being acted upon.

Voice

An **active voice** means that the subject is acting. A **passive voice** means that the subject is acted on.

Active: The usher led us to our seats.
Passive: We were led by the usher to our seats.

	Active Voice		Passive Voice	
	Singular	Plural	Singular	Plural
Present Tense	I see you see he/she/it sees	we see you see they see	I am seen you are seen he/she/it is seen	we are seen you are seen they are seen
Past Tense	I saw you saw he saw	we saw you saw they saw	I was seen you were seen it was seen	we were seen you were seen they were seen
Future Tense	I will see you will see he will see	we will see you will see they will see	I will be seen you will be seen it will be seen	we will be seen you will be seen they will be seen
Present Perfect Tense	I have seen you have seen he has seen	we have seen you have seen they have seen	I have been seen you have been seen it has been seen	we have been seen you have been seen they have been seen
Past Perfect Tense	I had seen you had seen he had seen	we had seen you had seen they had seen	I had been seen you had been seen it had been seen	we had been seen you had been seen they had been seen
Future Perfect Tense	I will have seen you will have seen he will have seen	we will have seen you will have seen they will have seen	I will have been seen you will have been seen it will have been seen	we will have been seen you will have been seen they will have been seen

Active voice is preferred for most writing because it is direct and energetic.

Active: We gave the band a standing ovation.
Passive: The band was given a standing ovation by us.

Passive voice is preferred when the focus is on the receiver of the action or when the subject is unknown.

Passive: A rose was thrown on stage.
Active: Someone threw a rose on stage.

Using Voice of a Verb

Rewrite Read each passive sentence below and rewrite it to be active. Think about what is performing the action and make that the subject.

1. The concert was attended by 3,000 fans.

   Three thousand fans attended the concert.

2. A good time was had by everyone.

   Everyone had a good time.

3. The ten greatest hits of the band were played by them.

   The band played their ten greatest hits.

4. Three concert T-shirts were bought by my friends and me.

   My friends and I bought three concert T-shirts.

5. The opening acts were tolerated by the crowd.

   The crowd tolerated the opening acts.

6. The air was electrified by the appearance of the main act.

   The appearance of the main act electrified the air.

7. I was not disappointed by their performance.

   Their performance did not disappoint me.

8. My short friend's view was blocked by a tall guy.

   A tall guy blocked my short friend's view.

9. The guy was asked by my friend to switch seats.

   My friend asked the guy to switch seats.

10. Every new song was cheered by the crowd.

    The crowd cheered for every new song.

Write Using the chart on the facing page, write a sentence for each situation below.

1. (A present tense singular active sentence) Answers will vary.

2. (A past tense plural passive sentence) _____

CONSIDER THE WORKPLACE

In workplace writing, use active voice for most messages. Use passive voice to deliver bad news.

Vocabulary

voice
active or passive

active voice
voice created when the subject is performing the action of the verb

passive voice
voice created when the subject is receiving the action of the verb

LO4 Present and Future Tense Verbs

Basic verb tenses tell whether action happens in the past, in the present, or in the future.

Present Tense

Present tense verbs indicate that action is happening right now.

A cruise ship arrives in Cabo San Lucas, Mexico.

Present tense verbs also can indicate that action happens routinely or continually.

Every day, ships drop anchor outside of the harbor.

Present Tense in Academic Writing

Use present tense verbs to describe current conditions.

Cabo San Lucas makes most of its income through tourism.

Use present tense verbs also to discuss the ideas in literature or to use historical quotations in a modern context. This use is called the "historical present," which allows writers to continue speaking.

Some say that those who see Cabo do not truly see Mexico, or as G. K. Chesterton writes, "The traveler sees what he sees; the tourist sees what he has come to see."

NOTE: It is important to write a paragraph or an essay in one tense. Avoid shifting needlessly from tense to tense as you write.

Future Tense

Future tense verbs indicate that action will happen later on.

Cruise ships will visit Cabo San Lucas for many years to come.

Using Present and Future Verb Tenses

Write   For each sentence below, supply the present tense form of the verb indicated in parentheses.

1. Many visitors _____snorkel_____ in Cabo's warm waters. (snorkeled)

2. White, sandy beaches _____attract_____ many swimmers. (attracted)

3. Parasailors _____fly_____ overhead from parachutes. (flew)

4. Waves _____pick up_____ if winds are strong. (picked up)

5. Boats _____run_____ people from cruise ships to shore. (ran)

Change   Replace the verbs in the following paragraph, making them all present tense. Write the line number and the present tense verb.

>   go   is
> We ~~went~~ to Lover's Beach in Cabo San Lucas. The beach ~~was~~ very   *1*
>   sunbathe   scuba dive
> busy. About a third of the people ~~sunbathed~~, a third ~~scuba dived~~, and a
>   splash   are
> third just ~~splashed~~ in the waves. The waves ~~were~~ large because the wind
> is   swim   returns
> ~~was~~ strong. We ~~swam~~ all afternoon until the water taxi ~~returned~~ for us.
>   spend   is
> The day we ~~spent~~ in Cabo San Lucas ~~was~~ one of our favorite days of the   *5*
> trip.

Write   Write a sentence of your own, using each word below in the form indicated in parentheses.

1. enjoy (present) _Answers will vary._____

2. swim (future) _____

3. realize (present) _____

4. complete (future) _____

Vocabulary

present tense
verb tense indicating that action is happening now

future tense
verb tense indicating that action will happen later

LO5 Past Tense Verbs

Past tense verbs indicate that action happened in the past.

When referring to his campaign in England, Julius Caesar reported, "I came. I saw. I conquered."

Forming Past Tense

Most verbs form their past tense by adding *ed*. If the word ends in a silent *e*, drop the *e* before adding *ed*.

help ⟶ helped
look ⟶ looked

love ⟶ loved
hope ⟶ hoped

If the word ends in a consonant before a single vowel and the last syllable is stressed, double the final consonant before adding *ed*.

stop ⟶ stopped
plan ⟶ planned

occur ⟶ occur**red**
refer ⟶ refer**red**

If the word ends in a *y* preceded by a consonant, change the *y* to *i* before adding *ed*.

study ⟶ studied
worry ⟶ worried

hurry ⟶ hurried
carry ⟶ carried

Irregular Verbs

Some of the most commonly used verbs form past tense by changing the verb itself. See the chart below:

Pres.	Past	Pres.	Past	Pres.	Past	Pres.	Past	Pres.	Past	Pres.	Past
am	was, were	dig	dug	fly	flew	hide	hid	see	saw	stand	stood
become	became	do	did	forget	forgot	keep	kept	shake	shook	steal	stole
begin	began	draw	drew	freeze	froze	know	knew	shine	shone	swim	swam
blow	blew	drink	drank	get	got	lead	led	show	showed	swing	swung
break	broke	drive	drove	give	gave	pay	paid	shrink	shrank	take	took
bring	brought	eat	ate	go	went	prove	proved	sing	sang	teach	taught
buy	bought	fall	fell	grow	grew	ride	rode	sink	sank	tear	tore
catch	caught	feel	felt	hang	hung	ring	rang	sit	sat	throw	threw
choose	chose	fight	fought	have	had	rise	rose	sleep	slept	wear	wore
come	came	find	found	hear	heard	run	ran	speak	spoke	write	wrote

Using Past Tense Verbs

Write For each verb, write the correct past tense form.

1. give _gave_
2. shop _shopped_
3. trick _tricked_
4. type _typed_
5. teach _taught_
6. cry _cried_
7. sing _sang_
8. soap _soaped_

9. cap _capped_
10. cope _coped_
11. try _tried_
12. fly _flew_
13. think _thought_
14. grip _gripped_
15. gripe _griped_
16. pour _poured_

Edit Make changes to the following paragraph, converting it from present tense to past tense. Write the line number and any word you would change. Cross it out and write the change.

>   During my junior year of high school, I ~~become~~ *became* a lifeguard at a   *1*
> campground pool. I ~~think~~ *thought* it ~~is~~ *was* a cushy job, sitting poolside all summer.
> However, this pool ~~hosts~~ *hosted* many day camps, meaning hundreds of little
> kids with little supervision. I quickly ~~discover~~ *discovered* that the other guards and
> I ~~are~~ *were* the supervision. It ~~is~~ *was* hard to yell at kids all day, but it is more   *5*
> dangerous to stay silent. They ~~run~~ *ran* on the deck or ~~dive~~ *dove* into shallow water
> or ~~jump~~ *jumped* into deep water when they ~~don't~~ *didn't* know how to swim. Worse yet,
> families ~~come~~ *came*, and when their kids ~~do~~ *did* the same things and I ~~yell~~ *yelled*, parents
> ~~tell~~ *told* me their kids ~~can~~ *could* run on deck if they ~~want~~ *wanted*. Facing down adults at
> sixteen ~~isn't~~ *wasn't* easy. Still, my brother's summer job ~~is~~ *was* mowing lawns at the   *10*
> same campground. When he ~~walks~~ *walked* by, drenched in sweat, my job sitting
> in my lifeguard chair suddenly ~~seems~~ *seemed* cushy.

Correction Marks

℘ delete	⅄ add comma	word ∧ add word
d capitalize	? add question mark	⊙ add period
Ð lowercase		spelling
∧ insert	⌄ insert an apostrophe	switch

Vocabulary

past tense
verb tense indicating that action happened previously

LO6 Progressive Tense Verbs

The basic tenses of past, present, and future tell when action takes place. The progressive tense or aspect tells that action is ongoing.

Progressive Tense

Progressive tense indicates that action is ongoing. Progressive tense is formed by using a helping verb along with the *ing* form of the main verb.

Scientists are studying the growth of human populations.

There are past, present, and future progressive tenses. Each uses a helping verb in the appropriate tense.

In 1804, one billion people were sharing the globe.

Currently, about seven billion people are living on Earth.

In 2040, about nine billion people will be calling this planet home.

Forming Progressive Tense

Past:	was/were	+	main verb	+	ing
Present:	am/is/are	+	main verb	+	ing
Future:	will be	+	main verb	+	ing

INSIGHT

Avoid using progressive tense with the following:

- Verbs that express thoughts, attitudes, and desires: *know, understand, want, prefer*
- Verbs that describe appearances: *seem, resemble*
- Verbs that indicate possession: *belong, have, own, possess*
- Verbs that signify inclusion: *contain, hold*

       Correct: I **know** your name.
     Incorrect: I **am knowing** your name.

Using Progressive Tense

Form Rewrite each sentence three times, changing the tenses as requested in parentheses.

Epidemics drop populations, but vaccination leads to upswings.

1. (present progressive) Epidemics are dropping populations, but vaccination is leading to upswings.

2. (past progressive) Epidemics were dropping populations, but vaccination was leading to upswings.

3. (future progressive) Epidemics will be dropping populations, but vaccination will be leading to upswings.

Though food production grows by addition, population grows by multiplication.

4. (present progressive) Though food production is growing by addition, population is growing by multiplication.

5. (past progressive) Though food production was growing by addition, population was growing by multiplication.

6. (future progressive) Though food production will be growing by addition, population will be growing by multiplication.

Improved public-health programs led to lower mortality rates.

7. (present progressive) Improved public-health programs are leading to lower mortality rates.

8. (past progressive) Improved public-health programs were leading to lower mortality rates.

9. (future progressive) Improved public-health programs will be leading to lower mortality rates.

Vocabulary

progressive tense
verb tense that expresses ongoing action

LO7 Perfect Tense Verbs

The perfect tense tells that action is not ongoing, but is finished, whether in the past, present, or future.

Perfect Tense

Perfect tense indicates that action is completed. Perfect tense is formed by using a helping verb along with the past tense form of the main verb.

> An estimated 110 billion people have lived on earth.

There are past, present, and future perfect tenses. These tenses are formed by using helping verbs in past, present, and future tenses.

> By 1804, the world population had reached one billion.
>
> We have added another billion people in the last 13 years.
>
> In 13 more years, we will have welcomed another billion.

Forming Perfect Tense

Past:	had	+	past tense main verb
Present:	has/have	+	past tense main verb
Future:	will have	+	past tense main verb

Perfect Tense with Irregular Verbs

To form perfect tense with irregular verbs, use the past participle form instead of the past tense form. Here are the past participles of common irregular verbs.

Pres.	Past Part.	Pres.	Past Part.	Pres.	Past Part.	Pres.	Past Part.	Pres.	Past Part.	Pres.	Past Part.
am, be	been	dig	dug	fly	flown	hide	hidden	see	seen	stand	stood
become	become	do	done	forget	forgotten	keep	kept	shake	shaken	steal	stolen
begin	begun	draw	drawn	freeze	frozen	know	known	shine	shone	swim	swum
blow	blown	drink	drunk	get	gotten	lead	led	show	shown	swing	swung
break	broken	drive	driven	give	given	pay	paid	shrink	shrunk	take	taken
bring	brought	eat	eaten	go	gone	prove	proven	sing	sung	teach	taught
buy	bought	fall	fallen	grow	grown	ride	ridden	sink	sunk	tear	torn
catch	caught	feel	felt	hang	hung	ring	rung	sit	sat	throw	thrown
choose	chosen	fight	fought	have	had	rise	risen	sleep	slept	wear	worn
come	come	find	found	hear	heard	run	run	speak	spoken	write	written

Using Perfect Tense

Form Rewrite each sentence three times, changing the tenses as requested in parentheses.

According to scientists, the earth circles the sun over 4.5 billion times.

1. (past perfect) According to scientists, the earth had circled the sun over 4.5 billion times.

2. (present perfect) According to scientists, the earth has circled the sun over 4.5 billion times.

3. (future perfect) According to scientists, the earth will have circled the sun over 4.5 billion times.

The sun lives half of its lifetime.

4. (past perfect) The sun had lived half of its lifetime.

5. (present perfect) The sun has lived half of its lifetime.

6. (future perfect) The sun will have lived half of its lifetime.

Two stars within our galaxy go supernova.

7. (past perfect) Two stars within our galaxy had gone supernova.

8. (present perfect) Two stars within our galaxy have gone supernova.

9. (future perfect) Two stars within our galaxy will have gone supernova.

Vocabulary

perfect tense
verb tense that expresses completed action

LO8 Verbals

A **verbal** is formed from a verb but functions as a noun, an adjective, or an adverb. Each type of verbal—gerund, participle, and infinitive—can appear alone or can begin a **verbal phrase**.

Gerund

A **gerund** is formed from a verb ending in *ing,* and it functions as a noun.

Swimming is my favorite pastime. (subject)
I love swimming. (direct object)

A **gerund phrase** begins with a gerund and includes any objects and modifiers.

Swimming laps at the pool builds endurance. (subject)
I prefer swimming laps in pools rather than in lakes. (direct object)

Participle

A **participle** is formed from a verb ending in *ing* or *ed,* and it functions as an adjective.

Excited, I received my lifesaving certification! (*excited* modifies *I*)
What an exciting day! (*exciting* modifies *day*)

A **participial phrase** begins with a participle and includes any objects and modifiers.

Exciting the crowd of young swimmers, I said we were diving today.

Infinitive

An **infinitive** is formed from *to* and a present tense verb, and it functions as a noun, an adjective, or an adverb.

To teach is a noble profession. (noun)
This is an important point to remember. (adjective)
Students must pay attention to understand. (adverb)

An **infinitive phrase** begins with an infinitive and includes any objects or modifiers.

I plan lessons to teach an easy progression of swimming skills.

Using Verbals

Identify Identify each underlined verbal by selecting the correct choice in parentheses (gerund, participle, infinitive).

1. <u>Jogging</u> is another excellent exercise. (**gerund**, participle, infinitive)
2. You should plan <u>to jog</u> three times a week. (gerund, participle, **infinitive**)
3. <u>Jogging</u> with friends, you can also be social. (gerund, **participle**, infinitive)
4. Try <u>to wear</u> good shoes. (gerund, participle, **infinitive**)
5. <u>Avoiding</u> joint injury is important. (**gerund**, participle, infinitive)
6. <u>Toned</u> through exercise, your body will look better. (gerund, **participle**, infinitive)

Form Complete each sentence below by supplying the type of verbal requested in parentheses. *Answers will vary.*

1. The exercise I would choose is _____ . (gerund)
2. _____ , I would lose weight. (participle)
3. _____ is a good toning exercise. (infinitive)
4. I would also like to try _____ . (gerund)
5. When exercising, remember _____ . (infinitive)
6. _____ , I'll be in great shape. (participle)

Write For each verbal phrase below, write a sentence that correctly uses it.

1. to lift weights *Answers will vary.* _____
2. preparing myself for a marathon _____
3. filled with anticipation _____

Vocabulary

verbal
gerund, participle, or infinitive; a construction formed from a verb but functioning as a noun, an adjective, or an adverb

verbal phrase
phrase beginning with a gerund, a participle, or an infinitive

gerund
verbal ending in *ing* and functioning as a noun

gerund phrase
phrase beginning with a gerund and including objects and modifiers

participle
verbal ending in *ing* or *ed* and functioning as an adjective

participial phrase
phrase beginning with a participle and including objects and modifiers

infinitive
verbal beginning with *to* and functioning as a noun, an adjective, or an adverb

infinitive phrase
phrase beginning with an infinitive and including objects and modifiers

LO9 Verbals as Objects

Though both infinitives and gerunds can function as nouns, they can't be used interchangeably as direct objects. Some verbs take infinitives and not gerunds. Other verbs take only gerunds and not infinitives.

Gerunds as Objects

Verbs that express facts are followed by **gerunds**.

admit	deny	enjoy	miss	recommend
avoid	discuss	finish	quit	regret
consider	dislike	imagine	recall	

> I enjoy playing cards.
> **not** I enjoy to play cards.
>
> I imagine winning a poker tournament.
> **not** I imagine to win a poker tournament.

Infinitives as Objects

Verbs that express intentions, hopes, and desires are followed by **infinitives**.

agree	demand	hope	prepare	volunteer
appear	deserve	intend	promise	want
attempt	endeavor	need	refuse	wish
consent	fail	offer	seem	
decide	hesitate	plan	tend	

> I attempt to win every hand.
> **not** I attempt winning every hand.
>
> I need to get a better poker face.
> **not** I need getting a better poker face.

Gerunds or Infinitives as Objects

Some verbs can be followed by either a gerund or an infinitive.

begin	hate	love	remember	stop
continue	like	prefer	start	try

> I love to play poker.
> **or** I love playing poker.

Using Verbals as Objects

Select   For each sentence below, select the appropriate verbal in parentheses.

1. I enjoy (to play, playing) canasta.
2. We should promise (to play, playing) canasta this weekend.
3. In canasta, you need (to get, getting) seven-card melds.
4. You and a partner endeavor (to meld, melding) suits.
5. You and your partner can discuss (to go, going) out.
6. The rules recommend (to keep, keeping) other table talk down.
7. I recall (to win, winning) three hands in a row.
8. If you lose a hand, you'll regret (to have, having) wild cards.
9. If you fail (to use, using) a wild card, it costs.
10. You'll dislike (to get, getting) penalized 50 points.

Write   For each verb below, write your own sentence using the verb and following it with a gerund or an infinitive, as appropriate.

1. deny

   Answers will vary.

2. promise

3. refuse

4. consider

5. recommend

6. avoid

Vocabulary

gerund
verbal ending in *ing* and functioning as a noun

infinitive
verbal beginning with *to* and functioning as a noun, an adjective, or an adverb

LO10 Real-World Application

Revise   Rewrite the following paragraph, changing passive verbs to active verbs.

> Your request to send all the sales reps to the Adobe training seminar in Cincinnati was reviewed by me. Your idea that this training would help your staff is agreed to by me. Our training budget was reviewed by me to see if the seminar could be afforded by us.
>
> _I reviewed your request to send all the sales reps to the Adobe training seminar in_
>
> _Cincinnati. I agree with your idea that this training would help your staff. I reviewed our_
>
> _training budget to see if we could afford the seminar._

Revise   In the following paragraph, change future perfect verbs into past perfect verbs. Write the line number and the words you would change. Then show the change.

>   _had_
> We ~~will have~~ used a large portion of our budget to upgrade design   1
>   _had_
> software for the engineering staff. In addition, we ~~will have~~ made prior   2
>   _had not_
> commitments to train office staff in August. As a result, we ~~will not have~~   3
> reserved enough money to send all sales reps to Cincinnati.   4

Revise   In the following paragraph, correct misused verbals. Write the line number and the words you would change. Then show the change.

>   _to explore_   _sending_
> I want ~~exploring~~ other solutions with you. Do you recommend ~~to send~~   1
>   _doing_
> two reps who then could train others? I recall ~~to do~~ that in previous   2
>   _agreeing_
> situations. I admit ~~to agree~~ that this isn't the optimal course, but I hope   3
> _to do_
> ~~doing~~ something.   4

24

Adjective and Adverb

All right, so you have a car. Lots of people have cars. It's a vintage Volkswagen beetle? Nice. And it's decked out with custom paint, toys, barrettes, and words like "smile," "laugh," and "let flow"? You call it your "crazy, lovey, hippy, dippy, vintage buggy"? Wow, do you have a car!

The owner of the car above has totally modified it and then has used strings of modifying words and phrases to describe it. That's what adjectives and adverbs do. They add color, texture, shape, size, and many more vivid details to each picture. Remember, though, that too many modifiers can overload a sentence—much as bric-a-brac can overwhelm a car.

Learning Outcomes

LO1 Understand adjective basics.

LO2 Put adjectives in order.

LO3 Use adjectivals.

LO4 Understand adverb basics.

LO5 Place adverbs well.

LO6 Use adverbials.

LO7 Apply adjectives and adverbs in real-world contexts.

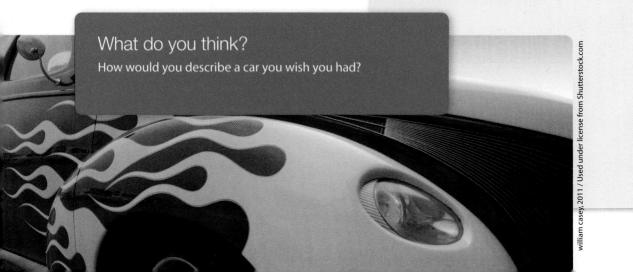

What do you think?

How would you describe a car you wish you had?

LO1 Adjective Basics

An **adjective** is a word that modifies a noun or pronoun. Even **articles** such as *a, an,* and *the* are adjectives, because they indicate whether you mean a general or specific thing. Adjectives answer these basic questions: *which, what kind of, how many/how much.*

Adjectives often appear before the word they modify.

You have a cute, fluffy dog.

A **predicate adjective** appears after the noun it modifies and is linked to the word by a linking verb.

Your dog is cute and fluffy.

Proper adjectives come from proper nouns and are capitalized.

He is a Yorkshire terrier.

Forms of Adjectives

Adjectives come in three forms: positive, comparative, and superlative.

- **Positive adjectives** describe one thing without making any comparisons.

Keats is a friendly dog.

- **Comparative adjectives** compare the thing to something else.

Keats is friendlier than our cat, Yeats.

- **Superlative adjectives** compare the thing to two or more other things.

He is the friendliest dog you will ever meet.

NOTE: For one- and two-syllable words, create the comparative form by adding *er,* and create the superlative form by added *est.* For words of three syllables or more, use *more* (or *less*) for comparatives and *most* (or *least*) for superlatives. Also note that *good* and *bad* have special superlative forms:

Positive		Comparative		Superlative	
good	happy	better	happier	best	happiest
bad	wonderful	worse	more wonderful	worst	most wonderful
big		bigger		biggest	

Using the Forms of Adjectives

Identify/Write For each sentence below, identify the underlined adjectives as positive (P), comparative (C), or superlative (S). Then write a new sentence about a different topic, but use the same adjectives. Answers will vary.

1. We once had a <u>beautiful</u> collie with a <u>long</u>, <u>shiny</u> coat.
   P   P   P

2. She was <u>smarter</u> than our last dog, perhaps the <u>smartest</u> pet we've owned.
   C   S

3. She thought she was the <u>alpha</u> female and my wife was the <u>beta</u> female.
   P   P

4. My wife became even <u>more unhappy</u> when the dog tore up her <u>best</u> couch.
   C   S

5. My wife was <u>happiest</u> on the day we gave the dog to a farmer.
   S

Correct Read the paragraph below and correct adjective errors, using the correction marks below. The first one has been done for you.

> Did you know there is an ~~I~~ntelligence test for dogs? It includes   *1*
> ~~v~~arious tasks to check the dog's ~~A~~daptive intelligence or problem-solving
> ability. The ~~most~~ smartest dogs can quickly find a treat under one of
> three buckets, get a treat from under a piece of furniture, find its ~~f~~avorite
> spot after a room is rearranged, and ~~gets~~ get a towel off its head. In tests,   *5*
> border collies, poodles, and german shepherds have tested as the ~~most~~
> smartest, and afghan hounds, british bulldogs, and chow chows tested at
> the ~~most low~~ lowest end. Even if they aren't the ~~intelligentest~~ most intelligent, these dogs might
> still be the ~~most~~ cuddliest.

Correction Marks

℘ delete	⅄ add comma	^word add word
d̳ capitalize	? add question mark	⊙ add period
∅̳ lowercase	∧	⌒ spelling
∧ insert	ⱽ insert an apostrophe	⌓ switch

Vocabulary

adjective
word that modifies a noun or pronoun

articles
the adjectives *a, an,* and *the*

predicate adjective
adjective that appears after a linking verb and describes the subject

positive adjective
word that modifies a noun or pronoun without comparing it

comparative adjective
word that modifies a noun or pronoun by comparing it to something else

superlative adjective
word that modifies a noun or pronoun by comparing it to two or more things

LO2 Adjective Order

Adjectives aren't all created equally. Native English speakers use a specific order when putting multiple adjectives before a noun, and all speakers of English can benefit from understanding this order.

Begin with . . .

1.	articles	a, an, the
	demonstrative adjectives	that, this, these, those
	possessives	my, our, her, their, Kayla's

Then position adjectives that tell . . .

2.	time	first, second, next, last
3.	how many	three, few, some, many
4.	value	important, prized, fine
5.	size	giant, puny, hulking
6.	shape	spiky, blocky, square
7.	condition	clean, tattered, repaired
8.	age	old, new, classic
9.	color	blue, scarlet, salmon
10.	nationality	French, Chinese, Cuban
11.	religion	Baptist, Buddhist, Hindu
12.	material	cloth, stone, wood, bronze

Finally place . . .

13.	nouns used as adjectives	baby [seat], shoe [lace]

Example:

that gorgeous old French shrimp boat
(**1** + **7** + **8** + **10** + **13** **noun**)

NOTE: Avoid using too many adjectives before a noun. An article and one or two adjectives are usually enough. More adjectives may overload the noun.

Too many:	my last three spiky old blue Cuban coral souvenirs
Effective:	my last three coral souvenirs

Placing Adjectives in Order

Order   Rearrange each set of adjectives and articles so that they are in the correct order. The first one has been done for you.

1. purple   rectangular   this

_____this rectangular purple_____ carton

2. your   Mexican   beautiful

_____your beautiful Mexican_____ guitar

3. wooden   worn-out   many

_____many worn-out wooden_____ blocks

4. precious   the   Islamic

_____the precious Islamic_____ mosaic

5. traditional   several   Russian

_____several traditional Russian_____ dolls

6. stone   chess   Doug's

_____Doug's stone chess_____ pieces

7. pen   French   my

_____my French pen_____ pal

8. broken-down   that   old

_____that broken-down old_____ sedan

9. felt   his   pin-striped

_____his pin-striped felt_____ fedora

10. old   the   mossy

_____the mossy old_____ temple

11. original   three   piano

_____three original piano_____ pieces

12. first   real   our

_____our first real_____ vacation

LO3 Adjective Questions and Adjectivals

Adjectives answer four basic questions: *which, what kind of, how many/how much.*

Children	
Which?	those children
What kind of?	smiling Indian children
How many/how much?	many children

those many smiling Indian children

> **INSIGHT**
>
> Instead of trying to memorize the names of different types of phrases and clauses, just remember the adjective questions. Turn them into a cheer—*which, what kind of, how many/how much.*

Adjectivals

A single word that answers one of these questions is called an adjective. If a phrase or clause answers one of these questions, it is an **adjectival** phrase or clause.

Children	
Which?	children who were waiting to vote
What kind of?	children wanting to get photographed

Wanting to get photographed, the children who were waiting to vote crowded my camera.

The following types of phrases and clauses can be adjectivals:

Prepositional phrase:	from the school
Participial phrase:	standing in a line
Adjective clause:	who greeted me warmly

Say It

Partner with a classmate. One of you should say the noun, and the other should ask the adjective questions. Then the first person should answer each question with adjectives or adjectivals.

1. **mini-vans**
   Which mini-vans?
   What kind of mini-vans?
   How many mini-vans?

2. **shampoo**
   Which shampoo?
   What kind of shampoo?
   How much shampoo?

Using Adjectives and Adjectivals

Answer/Write For each word, answer the adjective questions using adjectives and adjectivals. Then write a sentence using two or more of your answers.

1. **Cats**

   Which cats? _Answers will vary._____

   What kind of cats? _____

   How many cats? _____

   Sentence: _____

   _____

2. **Hobbies**

   Which hobbies? _____

   What kind of hobbies? _____

   How many hobbies? _____

   Sentence: _____

   _____

3. **Plans**

   Which plans? _____

   What kind of plans? _____

   How many plans? _____

   Sentence: _____

   _____

Vocabulary

adjectival
phrase or clause that answers one of the adjective questions and modifies a noun or pronoun

prepositional phrase
phrase that starts with a preposition and includes an object and modifiers

participial phrase
phrase beginning with a participle (*ing* or *ed* form of verb) plus objects and modifiers; used as an adjective

adjective clause
clause beginning with a relative pronoun and including a verb, but not able to stand alone; functioning as an adjective

LO4 Adverb Basics

An **adverb** modifies a verb, a **verbal**, an adjective, an adverb, or a whole sentence. An adverb answers five basic questions: *how, when, where, why, to what degree, how often.*

He danced boldly.
(*Boldly* modifies the verb *danced.*)

He leaped very high.
(*Very* modifies the adverb *high,* which modifies *leaped.*)

Apparently, he has had dance training.
(*Apparently* modifies the whole sentence.)

NOTE: Most adverbs end in *ly.* Some can be written with or without the *ly,* but when in doubt, use the *ly* form.

loud ⟶ loudly   tight ⟶ tightly   deep ⟶ deeply

Forms of Adverbs

Adverbs have three forms: positive, comparative, and superlative.

- **Positive adverbs** describe without comparing.

He danced skillfully.

- **Comparative adverbs** (*er, more,* or *less*) describe by comparing with one other action.

He danced more skillfully than his brother.

- **Superlative adverbs** (*est, most,* or *least*) describe by comparing with more than one action.

He danced most skillfully of any of those trying out.

NOTE: Some adjectives change form to create comparative or superlative forms.

well ⟶ better ⟶ best   badly ⟶ worse ⟶ worst

Using the Forms of Adverbs

Provide For each sentence below, provide the correct form of the adverb in parentheses—positive, comparative, or superlative.

1. I like to dance _____ fast _____ (fast).

2. I dance _____ faster _____ (fast) than any of my friends.

3. My moves are the _____ fastest _____ (fast) of anyone on the floor.

4. My brother moves _____ well _____ (well) for an older guy.

5. He eats _____ better _____ (well) than a spoiled child.

6. But I dance _____ best _____ (well) in my family.

7. I ask the band to play the song _____ quickly _____ (quickly).

8. They sometimes play it _____ more quickly _____ (quickly) than I intended.

9. A thrash band played _____ most quickly _____ (quickly) of any band I've heard.

10. That's when I danced _____ worst _____ (badly) in my whole life.

Choose In each sentence, write the correct word in parentheses. If the word modifies a noun or pronoun, choose the adjective form (*good, bad*). If the word modifies a verb, a verbal, an adjective, or an adverb, choose the adverb form (*well, badly.*)

1. I hope this turns out to be a (good, well) movie.

2. Even if the actors do (good, well), the plot might not be (good, well).

3. I don't want to spend (good, well) money on a (bad, badly) movie.

4. I wanted to see this movie (bad, badly).

5. Every time Richard comes along, he behaves (bad, badly).

6. If I tell him to straighten up, he takes it (bad, badly).

7. That guy has a (bad, badly) attitude.

8. I have done (good, well) not to invite him.

Vocabulary

adverb
word that modifies a verb, a verbal, an adjective, an adverb, or a whole sentence

verbal
word formed from a verb but functioning as a noun, an adjective, or an adverb

positive adverb
adverb that modifies without comparing

comparative adverb
adverb that modifies by comparing with one other thing

superlative adverb
adverb that modifies by comparing to two or more things

LO5 Placement of Adverbs

Adverbs should be placed in different places in sentences, depending on their use.

How Adverbs

Adverbs that tell *how* can appear anywhere except between a verb and a direct object.

Furiously we paddled the raft.	We paddled the raft furiously.
We furiously paddled the raft.	**not** We paddled furiously the raft.

When Adverbs

Adverbs that tell *when* should go at the beginning or end of the sentence.

We ran the white water yesterday. Today we'll tackle the course again.

Where Adverbs

Adverbs that tell *where* should follow the verb they modify, but should not come between the verb and the direct object. (NOTE: Prepositional phrases often function as *where* adverbs.)

Our guide shouted instructions from the back of the boat.
not Our guide shouted from the back of the boat instructions.

To What Degree Adverbs

Adverbs that tell *to what degree* go right before the adverb they modify.

I learned very quickly to hang on tight.

How Often Adverbs

Adverbs that tell *how often* should go right before an action verb, even if the verb has a helping verb.

I often dreamed about going white-water rafting.
Before that trip, I had never gotten to go.

Placing Adverbs Well

Place For each sentence below, insert the adverb (in parentheses) in the most appropriate position. The first one has been done for you.

1. The instructor *often* reminded us to stay alert. (often)
2. He began our training by *thoroughly* explaining the equipment. (thoroughly)
3. *Next* We got our paddles and helmets. (next)
4. The instructor was *very* careful about safety. (very)
5. We took our positions *in the raft*. (in the raft)
6. *Soon* The rapids chattered all around us. (soon)
7. We *often* went over challenging rapids. (often)
8. *Fortunately* No one fell out. (fortunately)
9. I would *highly* recommend that guide. (highly)
10. I hope to go rafting again *someday*. (someday)

Revise Rewrite the paragraph below, moving adverbs that incorrectly come between a verb and a direct object to the correct position.

Adrenaline junkies seek often thrills by putting themselves in danger. Dangerous situations trigger usually the release of adrenaline. Adrenaline is a hormone that causes typically the heart rate to increase. It triggers also the fight-or-flight response. Adrenaline junkies enjoy very much this feeling and seek often it out through high-risk activities. They try frequently skydiving or bungee jumping. Some use repeatedly white-water rafting to get their thrills.

LO5 Adverb Questions and Adverbials

Adverbs answer six basic questions: *how, when, where, why, to what degree,* and *how often.*

Yesterday, they repeatedly, spontaneously, and extremely joyously bounced around.

NOTE: Avoid this sort of adverb overload in your sentences.

They bounced.

How?	bounced joyously
When?	bounced yesterday
Where?	bounced around
Why?	bounced spontaneously
To what degree?	extremely joyously
How often?	bounced repeatedly

Piotr Wawrzyniuk, 2011 / Used under license from Shutterstock.com

Adverbials

Often, the adverb questions are answered by **adverbial** phrases and clauses, which answer the same six questions.

They bounced.

How?	bounced doing the splits
When?	bounced during the Fun Day Festival
Where?	bounced in the inflatable castle
Why?	bounced because they had been studying too much
To what degree?	bounced until they got sick
How often?	bounced throughout the afternoon

Because they had been studying too much, they bounced in the inflatable castle throughout the afternoon until they got sick.

NOTE: Again, avoid this sort of adverbial overload in your sentences.

The following types of phrases and clauses can be adverbials:

Prepositional phrase:	in the inflatable castle
Participial phrase:	doing the splits
Dependent clause:	because they had been studying too much

Using Adverbials

Answer/Write For each sentence, answer the adverb questions using adverbs and adverbials. Then write a sentence using three or more of your answers.

1. **They ran.** _Answers will vary._ _____

   How did they run? _____

   When did they run? _____

   Where did they run? _____

   Why did they run? _____

   To what degree did they run? _____

   How often did they run? _____

   Sentence: _____

   _____

2. **They laughed.**

   How did they laugh? _Answers will vary._ _____

   When did they laugh? _____

   Where did they laugh? _____

   Why did they laugh? _____

   To what degree did they laugh? _____

   How often did they laugh? _____

   Sentence: _____

   _____

INSIGHT

The adverb questions can be memorized by turning them into a cheer: *how, when, where, why, to what degree, how often!*

Vocabulary

adverbial
phrase or clause that answers one of the
adverb questions

LO7 Real-World Application

Correct   In the following document, correct the use of adjectives and adverbs. Use the correction marks below.

Verdant Landscaping

1500 West Ridge Avenue
Tacoma, WA 98466

1   January 6, 2012

Ms. Karen Bledsoe
Blixen Furniture
1430 North Bel Air Drive
5   Tacoma, WA 98466-6970

Dear Ms. Bledsoe:

We miss you! Verdant Landscaping has not been scheduled ~~not~~ to care for your grounds since fall 2008. You were a valued customer. Did our service fall short in some way? Whatever prompted you to make a change, we would like to dis-
10   cuss ways we could serve you ~~gooder.~~ better

During the past year, Verdant has added these three important new services ~~important these new three services~~: A full-time landscape architect helps happily you improve your grounds with flower beds, hardy shrubs, and blooming trees. A tree surgeon can give at a moment's notice you help with diseased or damaged trees. And our lawn crews
15   offer now mulching services. We provide the ~~most good~~ best service and value at the ~~most good~~ best price!

I'd like to call next week you to discuss whatever concerns you may have, and to offer you a 10-percent discount on a lawn-service new agreement. I can answer at that time any
20   questions you may have about our new services as they are described in the enclosed brochure.

Sincerely,
~~Sincere,~~

Stephen Bates

Stephen Bates
25   Customer Service

Enclosure

Correction Marks

ℐ	delete
d̲	capitalize
D̸	lowercase
∧	insert
↶	add comma
? ∧	add question mark
word ∧	add word
⊙	add period
◯	spelling
∏	switch

25

Conjunction and Preposition

Every relationship is different. A boyfriend and girlfriend will probably be equals, but a mother and daughter probably won't be. In fact, the daughter may be legally classified as a dependent.

Ideas have relationships, too. Sometimes ideas are equal—you can tell by the conjunction that connects them. At other times, one idea depends on another. There are conjunctions for that situation, too. And when words form a special relationship, prepositions are there to connect them.

Conjunctions and prepositions make connections in your writing and help your ideas relate to each other. This chapter shows how.

Learning Outcomes

LO1 Use coordinating and correlative conjunctions.

LO2 Use subordinating conjunctions.

LO3 Understand common prepositions.

LO4 Use *by, at, on,* and *in.*

LO5 Use conjunctions and prepositions in real-world documents.

What do you think?
What kind of relationship does the photo suggest?

LO1 Coordinating and Correlative Conjunctions

A **conjunction** is a word or word group that joins parts of a sentence—words, phrases, or clauses.

Coordinating Conjunctions

A **coordinating conjunction** joins grammatically equal parts—a word to a word, a phrase to a phrase, or a clause to a clause. (A clause is basically a sentence.)

Coordinating Conjunctions						
and	but	or	nor	for	so	yet

Equal importance: A coordinating conjunction shows that the two things joined are of equal importance.

Ted and Jana like rhythm and blues.
(*And* joins words in an equal way.)

I have R&B songs on my iPod and on CDs.
(*And* joins the phrases *on my iPod* and *on CDs*.)

I want to download more, but I lost my USB cord.
(*But* joins the two clauses, with a comma after the first.)

Items in a series: A coordinating conjunction can also join more than two equal things in a series.

Ted, Jana, and I are planning to attend an R&B festival.
(*And* joins *Ted, Jana,* and *I*. A comma follows each word except the last.)

We will drive to the fest, check out the acts, and buy our tickets.
(*And* joins three parts of a compound verb.)

Correlative Conjunctions

Correlative conjunctions consist of a coordinating conjunction paired with another word. They also join equal grammatical parts: word to word, phrase to phrase, or clause to clause.

Correlative Conjunctions				
either/or	neither/nor	whether/or	both/and	not only/but also

Stressing equality: Correlative conjunctions stress the equality of parts.

I like not only rock but also classical.
(*Not only/but also* stresses the equality of *rock* and *classical*.)

Using Coordinating and Correlative Conjunctions

Correct For each sentence below, write the best coordinating conjunction in parentheses.

1. I should buy an MP3 player (but, (for), or) an iPod.

2. Kelly, Eli, ((and), nor, yet) I sometimes share music.

3. We have different tastes, (or, (so), yet) we get to hear a variety.

4. Kelly likes hip-hop, (nor, (but), for) I like Latin music.

5. Eli likes classic rock, (but, yet, (so)) he shares '70s bands.

6. Each week, Kelly, Eli, ((and), but, or) I meet to talk about music.

7. We want to broaden our tastes, (and, or, (yet)) we don't like everything we hear.

8. I like rhythm, Kelly likes words, ((and), nor, so) Eli likes melodies.

9. Ask us for recommendations, (and, (for), so) we are committed fans.

10. We'll tell you what we like, ((but), nor, for) you have to choose for yourself.

Write Create sentences of your own, using a coordinating conjunction (*and, but, or, nor, for, so, yet*) as requested.

1. joining two words: _Answers will vary._ _____

2. joining two phrases: _____

3. creating a series: _____

4. joining two clauses (place a comma after the first clause, before the conjunction): _____

Write Create a sentence using a pair of correlative conjunctions:

Answers will vary. _____

CONSIDER THE TRAITS

When two ideas correlate, they work together. They co-relate. Thinking in this way can help you remember the term *correlative conjunctions*.

Vocabulary

conjunction
word or word group that joins parts of a sentence

coordinating conjunction
conjunction that joins grammatically equal components

correlative conjunction
pair of conjunctions that stress the equality of the parts that are joined

LO2 Subordinating Conjunctions

A **subordinating conjunction** is a word or word group that connects two clauses of different importance. (A clause is basically a sentence.)

Subordinating Conjunctions

after	as long as	if	so that	till	whenever
although	because	in order that	than	unless	where
as	before	provided that	that	until	whereas
as if	even though	since	though	when	while

Subordinate clause: The subordinating conjunction comes at the beginning of the less-important clause, making it subordinate (it can't stand on its own). The **subordinate clause** can come before or after the more important clause (the **independent clause**).

I go out to eat. I like to order Mexican food.
(two clauses)

Whenever I go out to eat, I like to order Mexican food.
(*Whenever* introduces the subordinate clause, which is followed by a comma.)

I like to order Mexican food whenever I go out to eat.
(If the subordinate clause comes second, a comma usually isn't needed.)

Special relationship: A subordinating conjunction shows a special relationship between ideas. Here are the relationships that subordinating conjunctions show:

Time	after, as, before, since, till, until, when, whenever, while
Cause	as, as long as, because, before, if, in order that, provided that, since, so that, that, till, until, when, whenever
Contrast	although, as if, even though, though, unless, whereas

Whenever Mexican food is on the menu, I will order it.
(time)

I order it extra spicy because I love to feel the burn.
(cause)

Even though I ask for extra heat, I often still have to add hot sauce.
(contrast)

Using Subordinating Conjunctions

Write For the blank in each sentence, provide an appropriate subordinating conjunction. Then write what type of relationship it shows.

1. _____ Answers will vary. _____ we washed the car, I got sprayed many times.
   (time, cause, contrast)

2. Car washing is work _____ it feels like play.
   (time, cause, contrast)

3. _____ the hoses go on, a splash fight is inevitable.
   (time, cause, contrast)

4. I usually don't start the fight _____ I'm willing to join in.
   (time, cause, contrast)

5. _____ people can't resist sudsy buckets, the fight begins.
   (time, cause, contrast)

6. The car may not get clean _____ the people do.
   (time, cause, contrast)

7. _____ I first get sprayed, I yell in shock.
   (time, cause, contrast)

8. _____ I get used to it, all bets are off.
   (time, cause, contrast)

9. I can be pretty ruthless _____ I have a hose in hand.
   (time, cause, contrast)

10. _____ people have such fun, not much washing gets done.
    (time, cause, contrast)

Write Create three of your own sentences, one for each type of relationship.

1. time: Answers will vary. _____

2. cause: _____

3. contrast: _____

Vocabulary

subordinating conjunction
word or word group that connects clauses of different importance

subordinate clause
word group that begins with a subordinating conjunction and has a subject and verb but can't stand alone as a sentence

independent clause
group of words with a subject and verb and that expresses a complete thought; it can stand alone as a sentence

LO3 Common Prepositions

A **preposition** is a word or word group that shows a relationship between a noun or pronoun and another word. Here are common prepositions:

Prepositions

aboard	back of	except for	near to	round
about	because of	excepting	notwithstanding	save
above	before	for	of	since
according to	behind	from	off	subsequent to
across	below	from among	on	through
across from	beneath	from between	on account of	throughout
after	beside	from under	on behalf of	'til
against	besides	in	onto	to
along	between	in addition to	on top of	together with
alongside	beyond	in behalf of	opposite	toward
alongside of	but	in front of	out	under
along with	by	in place of	out of	underneath
amid	by means of	in regard to	outside	until
among	concerning	inside	outside of	unto
apart from	considering	inside of	over	up
around	despite	in spite of	over to	upon
as far as	down	instead of	owing to	up to
aside from	down from	into	past	with
at	during	like	prior to	within
away from	except	near	regarding	without

Prepositional Phrases

A **prepositional phrase** starts with a preposition and includes an object of the preposition (a noun or pronoun) and any modifiers. A prepositional phrase functions as an adjective or adverb.

The store at the corner advertises in the newspaper.
(*At the corner* modifies *store,* and *in the newspaper* modifies *advertises.*)

Hand me the keys on the rack by the side of the door.
(*On the rack* modifies *keys; by the side* modifies *rack; of the door* modifies *side.*)

Margoe Edwards, 2011 / Used under license from Shutterstock.com

Using Common Prepositions

Create   For each sentence, fill in the blanks with prepositional phrases. Create them from the prepositions on the facing page and nouns or pronouns of your own choosing. Be creative!

1. This morning, I drove ___Answers will vary._____ .

2. Another driver _____ honked loudly.

3. I was so startled, I swerved _____ .

4. The other driver swerved _____ .

5. We both had looks of shock _____ .

6. I accelerated _____ .

7. Next thing I knew, I was _____ .

8. The incident _____ was a lesson.

9. The lesson was never to drive _____ .

Model   Read each sentence below and write another sentence modeled on it. Note how the writer uses prepositional phrases to create specific effects.

1. The boat went through the rapids, down a bowl, into the air, and over the falls.
   ___Answers will vary._____

2. I don't want to talk at you, but to you—but with you.
   _____

3. After days of arguing and hours of negotiation, the Senate compromised.
   _____

4. Go through the back door, up the stairs, past the security guard, and into the party.
   _____

Vocabulary

preposition
word or word group that creates a relationship between a noun or pronoun and another word

prepositional phrase
phrase that starts with a preposition; includes an object of the preposition (noun or pronoun) and any modifiers; and functions as an adjective or adverb

VR Photos, 2011 / Used under license from Shutterstock.com

LO4 *By, At, On,* and *In*

Prepositions often show the physical position of things—above, below, beside, around, and so on. Four specific prepositions show position but also get a lot of other use in English.

Uses for *By, At, On,* and *In*

By means "beside" or "up to a certain place or time."

> by the shed, by the road, by midnight, by April 15

At refers to a specific place or time.

> at the corner, at the station, at 4:35 p.m., at noon

On refers to a surface, a day or date, or an electronic medium.

> on the desk, on the cover
>
> on June 9, on Tuesday
>
> on the disk, on TV, on the computer

In refers to an enclosed space; a geographical location; an hour, a month, or a year; or a print medium.

> in the drawer, in the room, in Seattle, in Britain
>
> in an hour, in May, in 2012, in the book, in the newspaper

Say It

Team up with a partner. Have the first person read one of the words below, and have the second person use it in a prepositional phrase beginning with *by, at, on,* or *in.* The first person should check if the form is correct. (Some have more than one correct answer.) Then you should switch roles.

1. the living room
2. October 9
3. 11:15 a.m.
4. the cell phone
5. the edge
6. Chicago
7. the table
8. the restaurant
9. sunrise
10. the magazine

INSIGHT ——————————————————————————————————————

Native English speakers follow these rules without thinking about them. Listen to the way native English speakers use *by, at, on,* and *in,* and practice their use until it seems second-nature.

Using *By, At, On,* and *In*

Provide   For each sentence, circle the correct preposition in parentheses.

1. Please arrive (by, on, in) 11:55 p.m. because we will leave promptly (at, on, in) noon.

2. Make sure your carry-on fits (by, at, on, in) the overhead compartment or (by, at, on, in) the foot well in front of you.

3. I looked for a science article (by, at, on, in) the journal but could find only one (by, at, on, in) the Internet.

4. Though we sat (by, at, on, in) the waiting room, we weren't called (by, on, in) 3:15 p.m. for our appointment.

5. Four people standing (by, at, in) the corner reported a fire (at, on, in) a nearby garbage can.

6. (By, At, On, In) July 20, 1969, Neil Armstrong stepped (by, at, on, in) the surface of the moon.

7. I will meet you (by, at, on) the restaurant for our dinner reservation (by, at, on, in) 8:00 p.m.

8. Please place your check (by, at, on, in) the envelope, seal it, and write the following address (by, at, on, in) the envelope.

9. A parrot sat (by, at, on, in) the pirate's shoulder and looked me (by, at, on, in) the eye.

10. The song goes, "Under the boardwalk, down (by, at, on, in) the sea, (by, at, on, in) a blanket with my baby is where I'll be."

Write   Write a sentence that uses all four of these prepositions in phrases: *by, at, on, in.*

Answers will vary.

_____

_____

_____

LO5 Real-World Application

Revise Read the following e-mail, noting how choppy it sounds because all of the sentences are short. Rewrite the e-mail. Connect some of the sentences using a coordinating conjunction and a comma, and connect others using a subordinating conjunction. You can also change other words as needed. Reread the e-mail to make sure it sounds smooth.

Subordinating Conjunctions

after	as long as	if	so that	till	whenever
although	because	in order that	than	unless	where
as	before	provided that	that	until	whereas
as if	even though	since	though	when	while

Coordinating Conjunctions

and	but	or	nor
for	so	yet	

Send	Attach	Fonts	Colors	Save As Draft

To:	mwilliams@bramfeldpub.com
Subject:	ESleightner@bramfeldpub.com
Attach:	Update on Book Revision

Dear Ed: Answers will vary.   1

Thank you for writing about the revision. It is going well. It should be complete in two weeks. I have finished most chapters. I have addressed the main points. It is easy to forget to apply a change throughout. I will read the whole book to watch for changes.   5

Some of the graphics are still rough. I will need to finalize them. The maps for the inside covers are drawn. They need to be professionally inked.

The permissions requests are still pending. I have gotten permissions for three of the five excerpts. The fee for using the material was reasonable. If the fees for the other two are not, I will replace them.   10

I will wrap up the revision in two weeks. You can plan to start editing then.

Thanks,

Maurice Williams
Author

Correct Read the following party invitation, noting the incorrect use of the prepositions *by, at, on,* and *in.* (See page 498.) Correct the errors by deleting the prepositions and replacing them.

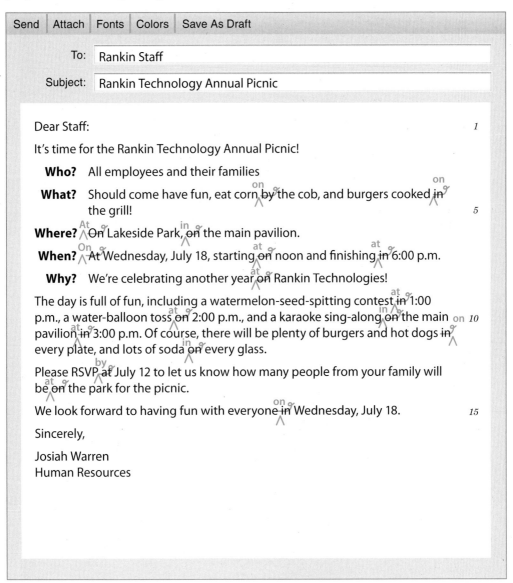

Send	Attach	Fonts	Colors	Save As Draft

To: Rankin Staff

Subject: Rankin Technology Annual Picnic

Dear Staff: *1*

It's time for the Rankin Technology Annual Picnic!

Who?   All employees and their families

What?   Should come have fun, eat corn ~~by~~ on the cob, and burgers cooked ~~in~~ on

       the grill!   *5*

Where?   ~~On~~ At Lakeside Park, ~~on~~ in the main pavilion.

When?   ~~At~~ On Wednesday, July 18, starting ~~on~~ at noon and finishing ~~in~~ at 6:00 p.m.

Why?   We're celebrating another year ~~on~~ at Rankin Technologies!

The day is full of fun, including a watermelon-seed-spitting contest ~~in~~ at 1:00
p.m., a water-balloon toss ~~on~~ at 2:00 p.m., and a karaoke sing-along ~~on~~ in the main on *10*
pavilion ~~in~~ at 3:00 p.m. Of course, there will be plenty of burgers and hot dogs ~~in~~ on
every plate, and lots of soda ~~on~~ in every glass.

Please RSVP ~~at~~ by July 12 to let us know how many people from your family will
be ~~on~~ at the park for the picnic.

We look forward to having fun with everyone ~~in~~ on Wednesday, July 18.   *15*

Sincerely,

Josiah Warren
Human Resources

CONSIDER THE WORKPLACE

Correct use of *by, at, on,* and *in* will mark you as a writer comfortable with English.

Part V: Punctuation and Mechanics Workshops

26

> "Words, once they are printed,
> have a life of their own."
> —Carol Burnett

Capitalization

By now you know writing requires correct capitalization. You know that every first word in a sentence should be capitalized and so should all proper nouns and proper adjectives. But what are the special uses of capitalization? And why are some nouns capitalized in one instance but not another?

This chapter will guide you in the conventional use of capital letters in writing. Throughout the section, examples demonstrate correct capitalization and serve as a handy reference during editing and proofreading.

Learning Outcomes

LO1 Understand basic capitalization rules.

LO2 Understand advanced capitalization rules.

LO3 Understand capitalization of titles, organizations, abbreviations, and letters.

LO4 Understand capitalization of names, courses, and Web terms.

LO5 Apply capitalization in real-world documents.

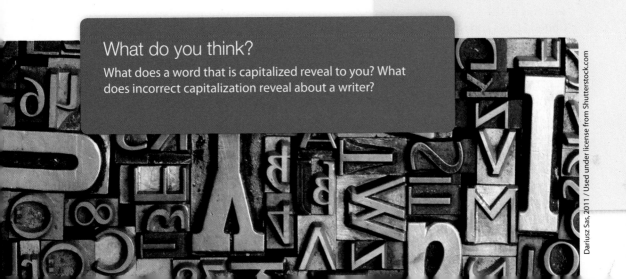

What do you think?

What does a word that is capitalized reveal to you? What does incorrect capitalization reveal about a writer?

Dariusz Sas, 2011 / Used under license from Shutterstock.com

LO1 Basic Capitalization

All first words, proper nouns, and proper adjectives must be capitalized. The following guidelines and examples will help explain these rules.

Proper Nouns and Adjectives

Capitalize all proper nouns and all proper adjectives (adjectives derived from proper nouns). The chart below provides a quick overview of capitalization.

Quick Guide: Capitalization at a Glance

Days of the week	Saturday, Sunday, Tuesday
Months	March, August, December
Holidays, holy days	Christmas, Hanukah, Presidents' Day
Periods, events in history	the Renaissance, Middle Ages
Special events	Tate Memorial Dedication Ceremony
Political parties	Republican Party, Green Party
Official documents	Bill of Rights
Trade names	Frisbee disc, Heinz ketchup
Formal epithets	Alexander the Great
Official titles	Vice-President Al Gore, Senator Davis
Official state nicknames	the Garden State, the Beaver State
Planets, heavenly bodies	Earth, Mars, the Milky Way
Continents	Asia, Australia, Europe
Countries	France, Brazil, Japan, Pakistan
States, provinces	Montana, Nebraska, Alberta, Ontario
Cities, towns, villages	Portland, Brookfield, Broad Ripple
Streets, roads, highways	Rodeo Drive, Route 66, Interstate 55
Sections of the United States and the world	the West Coast, the Middle East
Landforms	Appalachian Mountains, Kalahari Desert
Bodies of water	Lake Erie, Tiber River, Atlantic Ocean
Public areas	Central Park, Rocky Mountain National Park

First Words

Capitalize the first word in every sentence and the first word in a direct quotation that is a full sentence.

Preparing for the final exam will help you get a good grade.

Shawna asked, "**Does** anyone want to study with me at the coffee house?"

Correcting Capitalization

Practice A   In each sentence below, capitalize the appropriate words.

1. Singer jack johnson finds musical inspiration in his hometown of oahu, hawaii.

2. Hawaii is the only state made up entirely of islands and is located in the pacific ocean.

3. Known as the aloha state, it's home to the hawaii volcanoes national park.

4. Another national park, the U.S.S. *arizona* memorial, is dedicated to the navy members who were lost during the attack on pearl harbor.

5. On december, 7, 1941, the United States naval base at pearl harbor, Hawaii, was attacked by japan.

6. The attack triggered the united states' entry in world war II.

7. President franklin d. roosevelt declared December 7 as "a day that will live in infamy."

8. Hawaii's beautiful beaches and tropical temperatures attract tourists from the midwest to the far east.

Practice B   Decide what words should be capitalized. Write them down.

My favorite holiday is thanksgiving. every november family members   *1*
from illinois, indiana, and Michigan travel to my parents' house to
celebrate the best thursday of the year. While Mom and my aunts work
on the dressing and mashed potatoes, my cousins and I watch football on
the fox network. it has long been a tradition for the Detroit lions to play a   *5*
home game every thanksgiving. By the time the game is finished, the food
is ready and the feast is on. Turkey, gravy, and green-bean casserole—you
can't beat thanksgiving.

INSIGHT

Different languages use capitalization differently. For example, German capitalizes not just proper nouns but all important nouns. Compare and contrast capitalization styles between your heritage language and English.

LO2 Advanced Capitalization

Sentences in Parentheses

Capitalize the first word in a sentence that is enclosed in parentheses if that sentence is not combined within another complete sentence.

My favorite designer is hosting a fashion show for her new collection.
(**Now** I just need a ticket.)

NOTE: Do *not* capitalize a sentence that is enclosed in parentheses and is located in the middle of another sentence.

Rachel's cousin (his name is Carl) can't make it tonight.

Sentences Following Colons

Capitalize a complete sentence that follows a colon when that sentence is a formal statement, a quotation, or a sentence that you want to emphasize.

I would like to paraphrase Patrick Henry: Give me chocolate or give me death.

Salutation and Complimentary Closing

In a letter, capitalize the first and all major words of the salutation. Capitalize only the first word of the complimentary closing.

Dear Dr. Howard: **Sincerely** yours,

Sections of the Country

Words that indicate sections of the country are proper nouns and should be capitalized; words that simply indicate directions are not proper nouns.

I'm thinking about moving to the **West Coast.** *(section of country)*
I'm thinking about driving **west** to California. *(direction)*

Languages, Ethnic Groups, Nationalities, and Religions

Capitalize languages, ethnic groups, nationalities, religions, Supreme Beings, and holy books.

African	**Navajo**	**Islam**	**God**	**Allah**
Jehovah	the **Koran**	**Exodus**		the **Bible**

Correcting Capitalization

Practice A In each sentence below, capitalize the appropriate words.

1. The midwest region of the United States is made up of 12 states.

2. The bible and the koran are considered holy books.

3. The navajo indians of the southwest have significant populations in an area known as the Four Corners (arizona, new mexico, utah, and Colorado).

4. Mark Twain once said this about adversity: "it's not the size of the dog in the fight; it's the size of the fight in the dog."

5. My brother Phil is starting college today. (my mom finally has the house to herself.)

6. I'm a proud member of the latino community in Miami.

7. In Quebec, Canada, many citizens speak both english and french.

Practice B Read the following paragraph. Then capitalize the appropriate words.

> I ate the best seafood of my life at a new england restaurant. The small, coastal restaurant in Massachusetts features fresh seafood from the atlantic ocean. I ordered the maine lobster, and I have one impression: it was awesome. If you have never tried fresh lobster before, I highly recommend it. You won't be disappointed. (now I need to figure out when I can go back.)   *1*   *5*

Practice C Decide what words should be capitalized. Write them down.

tomorrow   hanukah   wednesday   bank   frisbee

u.s. bank   flying disc   russia   tree

INSIGHT ————————————————————————————————

Do not capitalize words used to indicate direction or position.

Turn **south** at the stop sign. *(South refers to direction.)*
The **South** is known for its great Cajun food. *(South refers to a region of the country.)*

LO3 Other Capitalization Rules I

Titles

Capitalize the first word of a title, the last word, and every word in between except articles *(a, an, the)*, short prepositions, *to* in an infinitive, and coordinating conjunctions. Follow this rule for titles of books, newspapers, magazines, poems, plays, songs, articles, films, works of art, and stories.

The Curious Case of Benjamin Button	*New York Times*
"**Cry Me** a **River**"	"**Cashing** in on **Kids**"
A Midsummer Night's Dream	*The Da Vinci Code*

Organizations

Capitalize the name of an organization or a team and its members.

American Indian Movement	**Democratic Party**
Lance Armstrong Foundation	**Indiana Pacers**
Susan G. Komen for the **Cure**	**Boston Red Sox**

Abbreviations

Capitalize abbreviations of titles and organizations.

M.D.	**Ph.D.**	**NAACP**	**C.E.**	**B.C.E.**	**GPA**

Letters

Capitalize letters used to indicate a form or shape.

U-turn	**I**-beam	**V**-shaped	**T**-shirt

INSIGHT

Note that the American Psychological Association has a different style for capitalizing the titles of smaller works. Be sure you know the style required for a specific class.

Correcting Capitalization

Practice A   In the sentences below, capitalize the appropriate words.

1. I'm stopping by the gas station to pick up the sunday *Chicago tribune*.
2. The Los Angeles lakers play in the staples center.
3. At the next stoplight, you will need to take a u-turn.
4. My favorite author is Malcolm Gladwell, who wrote the best-sellers *blink* and *The tipping point*.
5. How many times have you heard the song "I got a feeling" by the Black-eyed peas?
6. The American cancer society raises money for cancer research.
7. I was happy to improve my gpa from 3.1 to 3.4 last semester.
8. Where did you buy that Seattle mariners t-shirt?
9. The doctor charted the growth of the tumor using an s-curve.
10. The man read a copy of *gq* magazine in New York City's central park.
11. Jill was promoted to chief operating officer (ceo) this july.

Practice B   Read the paragraph below. Then write down the words that need to be capitalized.

> On our way to the Kansas city royals game, my friend Ted and I got   *1*
>
> in an argument over our favorite music. He likes coldplay, while I prefer
>
> radiohead. His favorite song is "Vida la viva." My favorite is "Fake plastic
>
> trees." But as we argued about the merits of each band, we completely
>
> missed our exit to the stadium. Ted suggested we perform a u-turn.   *5*
>
> Instead, I used my gps to find a new route. Luckily, we made it to the
>
> ballpark in time to grab a hot dog and coke before the opening pitch.

LO4 Other Capitalization Rules II

Words Used as Names

Capitalize words like *father, mother, uncle, senator,* and *professor* only when they are parts of titles that include a personal name or when they are substitutes for proper nouns (especially in direct address).

> Hello, **Senator** Feingold. (*Senator* is part of the name.)
>
> It's good to meet you, **Senator.** (*Senator* is a substitute for the name.)
>
> Our **senator** is an environmentalist.
>
> Who was your chemistry **professor** last quarter?
>
> I had **Professor Williams** for Chemistry 101.
>
> Good morning, **Professor.**

NOTE: To test whether a word is being substituted for a proper noun, simply read the sentence with a proper noun in place of the word. If the proper noun fits in the sentence, the word being tested should be capitalized. Usually the word is not capitalized if it follows a possessive—*my, his, our, your,* and so on.

> Did **Dad** (Brad) pack the stereo in the trailer? (*Brad* works in the sentence.)
>
> Did your **dad** (Brad) pack the stereo in the trailer?
> (*Brad* does not work in the sentence; the word *dad* follows *your.*)

Titles of Courses

Words such as *technology, history,* and *science* are proper nouns when they are included in the titles of specific courses; they are common nouns when they name a field of study.

> Who teaches **Art History 202**? (title of a specific course)
>
> Professor Bunker loves teaching **history.** (a field of study)

Internet and E-Mail

The words *Internet* and *World Wide Web* are capitalized because they are considered proper nouns. When your writing includes a Web address (URL), capitalize any letters that the site's owner does (on printed materials or on the site itself).

> When doing research on the **Internet**, be sure to record each site's **Web** address (URL) and each contact's **e-mail** address.

Correcting Capitalization

Practice A   In each sentence below, capitalize the appropriate words.

1. I met mayor Greg Ballard by chance today at the daily brew coffee shop.

2. When I was a freshman, I studied the history of roman art in art history 101.

3. Ever since I gained wireless access to the internet, I've spent hours each day on YouTube.

4. Let's hope dad can make it in time for our tee time.

5. In a speech to his constituents, congressman Paul Ryan called for fiscal responsibility.

6. My favorite class this semester is advanced forensics 332 with dr. Charles Wendell, a well-known professor.

7. My uncle Brad has no clue how to navigate the world wide web.

8. Elizabeth attended the Wayne State University senior Banquet.

9. In searching for exercise routines, Jack bookmarked a web address (url) for *men's health* magazine.

10. You will need to contact commissioner Sheffield for permission.

Practice B   Read the paragraph below. Then write down the words that need to be capitalized.

> Before Steve Jobs became ceo of apple Inc. and the brainchild behind   *1*
>
> Macintosh, he attended high school in the San Francisco bay Area, a
>
> region that is famously known as silicon valley. Jobs enrolled at Reed
>
> College in portland, Oregon, but dropped out after the first semester to
>
> return home to co-create apple. At the same time, other tech innovators   *5*
>
> flooded the area to create companies such as Hewlett-packard and Intel. It
>
> is also here where internet giants google and Yahoo! were founded. Today
>
> Silicon valley remains a region of technological innovation.

LO5 Real-World Application

Correct   In the following basic letter, capitalize the appropriate words. Then lowercase the words that shouldn't be capitalized. If a letter is capitalized and shouldn't be, put a lowercase editing mark through the letter.

Ball State university Volunteer Center
7711 S. Hampton drive
Muncie, IN 47302
July, 5 2010

Mr. Ryan Orlovich
Muncie parks Department
1800 Grant Street
Muncie, IN 47302

Dear superintendent Orlovich:

Last Saturday, the Ball State volunteer center committee met to discuss new volunteer opportunities for the upcoming semester. We are interested in putting together a service event at big oak park for the incoming Freshmen.

We would like to get in contact with someone from your department to set up a time and date for the event. We would prefer the event to take place between thursday, August 23, and Sunday, August 26. Also, we hope to design t-shirts for the volunteers and were wondering if your office knew of any sponsors who might be interested in funding this expenditure.

When you have time, please contact me by phone at 317-555-3980 or E-mail at ehenderson@bs23u.edu. (you may also e-mail the office at bsuvolunteerism@bs23u.edu.)

Yours Truly,

Liz Henderson

Liz Henderson

BSU Volunteer President

Special Challenge   Write a sentence that includes a colon followed by another sentence you want to emphasize. (See page 506).

27

Comma

> "The writer who neglects punctuation, or mispunctuates, is liable to be misunderstood for the want of merely a comma."
>
> —Edgar Allan Poe

Commas divide sentences into smaller sections so that they may be read more easily and more precisely. They also show which words belong together and which line up in parallel. Of all the punctuation marks, commas are used most frequently—and oftentimes incorrectly.

This chapter will guide you in the conventional use of commas. Understanding correct comma usage is an important step in becoming a college-level writer. Applying these rules will make your writing clearer and easier to follow.

Learning Outcomes

LO1 Use commas in compound sentences.

LO2 Use commas with introductory phrases and equal adjectives.

LO3 Use commas between items in a series.

LO4 Use commas with appositives and nonrestrictive modifiers.

LO5 Use commas in real-world writing.

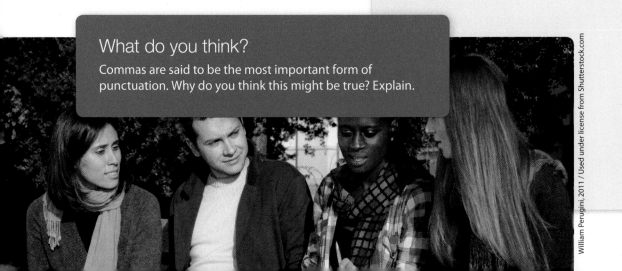

What do you think?

Commas are said to be the most important form of punctuation. Why do you think this might be true? Explain.

LO1 In Compound Sentences and After Introductory Clauses

The following principles will guide the use of commas in your writing.

In Compound Sentences

Use a comma before the coordinating conjunction *(and, but, or, nor, for, yet, so)* in a compound sentence.

Heath Ledger completed his brilliant portrayal as the Joker in *The Dark Knight*, **but** he died before the film was released.

NOTE: Do not confuse a compound verb with a compound sentence.

Ledger's Joker became instantly iconic and won him the Oscar for best supporting actor. *(compound verb)*

His death resulted from the abuse of prescription drugs, but it was ruled an accident. *(compound sentence)*

After Introductory Clauses

Use a comma after most introductory clauses.

Although Charlemagne was a great patron of learning, he never learned to write properly. (adverb dependent clause)

When the clause follows the independent clause and is not essential to the meaning of the sentence, use a comma. This comma use generally applies to clauses beginning with *even though, although, while,* or some other conjunction expressing a contrast.

Charlemagne never learned to write properly, **even though he continued to practice.**

NOTE: A comma is *not* used if the dependent clause following the independent clause is needed.

CONSIDER THE TRAITS

Make sure to use both a comma and a coordinating conjunction in a compound sentence, or you will create a comma splice or a run-on.

Correcting Comma Errors

Correct For each sentence below, add a comma before the coordinating conjunction (*and, but, or, nor, for, so, yet*) if the clause on each side could stand alone as a sentence. Write "correct" if the conjunction separates word groups that can't stand alone.

1. I was sick of sitting around on the couch, so I drove over to the driving range. _____

2. Her cell phone rang, but she decided against answering it. _____

3. Maria downloaded some new music and imported it on her iPod. *correct*

4. I wanted to finish my assignment, but I couldn't turn away from the *House* marathon. _____

5. Should I put a down payment on a new car, or should I save my money for a new apartment? _____

6. Kelly is studying frog populations in the rain forest, and she hopes to publish her work. _____

7. Ryan wanted to make a new style of chili, but he lost the recipe. _____

8. Trisha was looking forward to the baseball game, but it got rained out. _____

Correct For each sentence below, add a comma after any introductory clauses. If no comma is needed, write "correct" next to the sentence.

1. While Becca prefers grilled salmon, Mia's favorite food is sushi. _____

2. Although the water conditions were perfect, I couldn't catch a wave to save my life. _____

3. Perhaps I should rethink my major because I don't enjoy the classes. *correct*

4. Even though the Cubs haven't won a World Series since 1901, I still cheer for them. _____

5. While *American Idol* is popular in America, *Britain's Got Talent* is the craze in England. _____

LO2 With Introductory Words and Equal Adjectives

After Introductory Phrases

Use a comma after introductory phrases.

In spite of his friend's prodding, Jared decided to stay home and study.

A comma is usually omitted if the phrase follows an independent clause.

Jared decided to stay home and study **in spite of his friend's prodding.**

You may omit a comma after a short (four or fewer words) introductory phrase unless it is needed to ensure clarity.

At 10:32 p. m. he would quit and go to sleep.

To Separate Adjectives

Use commas to separate adjectives that equally modify the same noun. Notice in the examples below that no comma separates the last adjective from the noun.

You should exercise regularly and follow a **sensible, healthful** diet.

A good diet is one that includes lots of **high-protein, low-fat** foods.

To Determine Equal Modifiers

To determine whether adjectives modify a noun equally, use these two tests.

1. Reverse the order of the adjectives; if the sentence is clear, the adjectives modify equally. (In the example below, *hot* and *crowded* can be switched, but *short* and *coffee* cannot.)

   Matt was tired of working in the **hot, crowded** lab and decided to take a **short coffee** break.

2. Insert *and* between the adjectives; if the sentence reads well, use a comma when *and* is omitted. (The word *and* can be inserted between *hot* and *crowded,* but *and* does not make sense between *short* and *coffee.*)

Correcting Comma Errors

Correct If a comma is needed after the introductory phrase, write the words before and after the comma, with it between them. If no comma is needed, write "correct."

1. Before you can receive your diploma␣you will need to pay your unpaid parking tickets.   _____

2. At Central Perk Ross, Rachel, and the gang sipped coffee and exchanged barbs.   _correct_

3. In accordance with state law␣Hanna decided against sending a text message while driving on the interstate.   _____

4. On the other hand pursuing the wrong type of adrenaline high can be destructive.   _correct_

5. After handing in her paper␣Eva felt a great wave of relief.   _____

6. Eva felt a great wave of relief after handing in her paper.   _correct_

7. Based on his primary research␣Andy came up with a preliminary hypothesis.   _____

8. To save a few dollars␣Stephanie rode her bike to work.   _____

Correct For each sentence below, determine whether or not a comma is needed to separate the adjectives that modify the same noun. Add any needed commas. Write "no" next to the sentence if a comma is not needed.

1. The **long␣difficult** exam took a lot out of me.   _____

2. Last night I went to a **fun graduation** party.   _no_

3. A good concert includes many **memorable␣hair-raising** moments.   _____

4. A **thoughtful␣considerate** friend goes an extra mile to make you smile.   _____

5. I could really use a **relaxing back** massage.   _no_

6. When dressing for skiing, consider wearing a **thick␣well-insulated** jacket.   _____

LO3 Between Items in a Series and Other Uses

Between Items in Series

Use commas to separate individual words, phrases, or clauses in a series. (A series contains at least three items.)

Many college students must balance studying with **taking care of a family, working, getting exercise, and finding time to relax.**

Do not use commas when all the items are connected with *or, nor,* or *and.*

Hmm . . . should I study **or** do laundry **or** go out?

To Set Off Transitional Expressions

Use a comma to set off conjunctive adverbs and transitional phrases.

Handwriting is not**, as a matter of fact,** easy to improve upon later in life; **however,** it can be done if you are determined enough.

If a transitional expression blends smoothly with the rest of the sentence, it does not need to be set off.

If you are **in fact** coming**,** I'll see you there.

To Set Off Dialogue

Use commas to set off the words of the speaker from the rest of the sentence. Do not use a comma before an indirect quotation.

"Never be afraid to ask for help," advised Ms. Kane

"With the evidence that we now have," Professor Thom said**, "many scientists believe there could be life on Mars."**

To Enclose Explanatory Words

Use commas to enclose an explanatory word or phrase.

Time management**, according to many professionals,** is an important skill that should be taught in college.

Correcting Comma Errors

Correct   Indicate where commas are needed. Write the words before and after the comma, showing the comma between them.

1. I'm looking forward to graduation‸ summer vacation‸ and moving into a new apartment.

2. A new strain of virus‸ according to biologists‸ could cause future outbreaks of poultry disease.

3. "To confine our attention to terrestrial matters would be to limit the human spirit" said Stephen Hawking.

4. I need you to pick up two jars of peanut butter, a half-gallon of skim milk‸ and snacks for the party.

5. I enjoy live music; however‸ I don't like big crowds.

6. "With all the advancements in technology‸" Sara said, "you'd think we would have invented a quicker toaster by now."

7. Eighty percent of states‸ as a matter of fact‸ are in financial trouble.

8. We can meet up at either the library‸ the student union‸ or memorial hall.

9. The difference between perseverance and obstinacy‸ according to Henry Ward Beecher‸ is that one comes from strong will, and the other from a strong won't.

10. Chicago, Detroit‸ and Indianapolis are the most-populated cities in the Midwest.

Correct   Indicate where commas are needed. Write the line number and the words before and after the comma, showing the comma between them.

> The Erie Canal is a man-made waterway that connects the Atlantic   *1*
> Ocean to Lake Erie. It was the first transportation system to connect the
> eastern seaboard and the Great Lakes‸ was faster than carts pulled by
> animals‸ and significantly cut transportation time. "The opening of the
> Erie Canal to New York in 1825 stimulated other cities on the Atlantic   *5*
> seaboard to put themselves into closer commercial touch with the West‸"
> said John Moody. Since the 1990s the canal is mostly home to recreational
> traffic; however‸ some cargo is still transported down the waterway.

LO4 With Appositives and Other Word Groups

To Set Off Some Appositives

A specific kind of explanatory word or phrase called an **appositive** identifies or renames a preceding noun or pronoun.

Albert Einstein, **the famous mathematician and physicist,** developed the theory of relativity.

Do not use commas if the appositive is important to the basic meaning of the sentence.

The famous physicist **Albert Einstein** developed the theory of relativity.

With Some Clauses and Phrases

Use commas to enclose phrases or clauses that add information that is not necessary to the basic meaning of the sentence. For example, if the clause or phrase (in boldface) were left out of the two examples below, the meaning of the sentences would remain clear. Therefore, commas are used to set off the information.

The locker rooms in Swain Hall, **which were painted and updated last summer,** give professors a place to shower. (nonrestrictive clause)

Work-study programs, **offered on many campuses,** give students the opportunity to earn tuition money. (nonrestrictive phrase)

Do not use commas to set off necessary clauses and phrases, which add information that the reader needs to understand the sentence.

Only the professors **who run at noon** use the locker rooms. (necessary clause)

Using "That" or "Which"

Use *that* to introduce necessary clauses; use *which* to introduce unnecessary clauses.

Campus jobs **that are funded by the university** are awarded to students only. (necessary)

The cafeteria, **which is run by an independent contractor,** can hire nonstudents. (unnecessary)

Correcting Comma Errors

Correct Indicate where commas are needed in the following sentences. If no commas are needed, write "correct."

1. John D. Rockefeller, the famous American philanthropist and oil executive, is sometimes referred to as the richest person in history.
   _____

2. The new library, which is scheduled to open in July, will include three different computer labs.
   _____

3. The renowned trumpeter Louis Armstrong sang the song "What a Wonderful World."
   correct

4. Kansas City, along with Memphis, Tennessee, is known for its delicious barbecue.
   _____

5. Judge Sonya Sotomayer, the first Hispanic Supreme Court justice, was confirmed into office in 2009.
   _____

6. The book *The Notebook*, which was later adapted into a movie, was written by Nicolas Sparks.
   _____

Write The following sentences contain clauses using *that*. Rewrite the sentences with clauses using *which*, and insert commas correctly. You may need to reword some parts.

1. The road construction that delayed traffic yesterday should be completed by the end of the week.
   The road construction, which delayed traffic yesterday, should be completed by the end
   of the week.

2. The homework that Dr. Grant assigned yesterday will consume the next two weeks of my life.
   The homework, which Dr. Grant assigned yesterday, will consume the next two weeks of my life.
   _____

3. The earplugs that we bought before the race made the deafening noise more bearable.
   The earplugs, which we bought before the race, made the deafening noise more bearable.
   _____

Vocabulary

appositive
a noun or noun phrase that renames another noun right beside it

LO5 Real-World Application

Correct Indicate where commas are needed in the following e-mail message. Write the line number and the words before and after the comma, showing it between them.

Send	Attach	Fonts	Colors	Save As Draft

To: Tyler Hoffman <thoffman@ucsc.edu>

Subject: Carrie Andritz <candritz@ucsc.edu>

Attach: Letter of Recommendation for Tyler Hoffman

Dear Professor Andritz: 1

I enjoyed meeting with you today to discuss my letter of recommendation. You know the quality of my academic work my qualities as a person and my potential for working in the marketing industry.

As my professor for Marketing 303 and Economics 401 you have witnessed my   5
hardworking nature. As my adviser you know my career plans and should have a good sense of whether I have the qualities needed to succeed in the fast-paced competitive marketing industry.

Please send your letter to Craig Emmons human resources director at FastTech by April 14. If you have any questions please call me at (324) 472-3489.   10

Sincerely,

Tyler Hoffman

CONSIDER THE WORKPLACE ————————————————
Correct comma use is critical for clear business communication.

28

"A fine quotation is a diamond on the finger of a man of wit, and a pebble in the hand of a fool."
—Joseph Roux

Quotation Marks and Italics

Much of the time, language flows from us as naturally as breathing. We think; we speak; someone hears and responds—all without consciously thinking about the words.

Sometimes, however, we have need to note a word as a word, to call attention to a phrase in a special sense, to use an apt or time-honored quotation from someone else, or to mark the title of a work. In such cases, quotation marks and italics allow us to indicate this special use of language.

Learning Outcomes

LO1 Understand the use of quotation marks.

LO2 Understand the use of italics.

LO3 Apply quotation marks and italics in a real-world document.

What do you think?
Study the image and quotation. What makes the gemstones in the photo valuable? In what way does this relate to the Joseph Roux quotation?

LO1 Quotation Marks

To Punctuate Titles (Smaller Works)

Use quotation marks to enclose the titles of smaller works, including speeches, short stories, songs, poems, episodes of audio or video programs, chapters or sections of books, unpublished works, and articles from magazines, journals, newspapers, or encyclopedias. (For other titles, see page 526.)

Speech:	"The Cause Endures"
Song:	"Head Like a Hole"
Short Story:	"Dark They Were, and Golden Eyed"
Magazine Article:	"The Moral Life of Babies"
Chapter in a Book:	"Queen Mab"
Television Episode:	"The Girl Who Was Death"
Encyclopedia Article:	"Cetacean"

Placement of Periods and Commas

When quoted words end in a period or comma, always place that punctuation inside the quotation marks.

"If you want to catch the train," Grace said, "you must leave now."

Placement of Semicolons and Colons

When a quotation is followed by a semicolon or colon, always place that punctuation outside the quotation marks.

I finally read "Heart of Darkness"; it is amazingly well written!

Placement of Exclamation Points and Question Marks

If an exclamation point or a question mark is part of the quotation, place it inside the quotation marks. Otherwise, place it outside.

Marcello asked me, "Are you going to the Dodge Poetry Festival?" What could I reply except, "Yes, indeed"?

For Special Words

Quotation marks can be used (1) to show that a word is being referred to as the word itself; (2) to indicate that it is jargon, slang, or a coined term; or (3) to show that it is used in an ironic or sarcastic sense.

(1) Somehow, the term "cool" has survived decades.
(2) The band has a "wicked awesome" sound.
(3) I would describe the taste of this casserole as "swampy."

Using Quotation Marks

Correct   For the following sentences, insert quotation marks where needed.

1. Kamala loves to listen to the song "I Take Time" over and over and over.

2. Ray Bradbury's short story "A Sound of Thunder" has been republished many times.

3. Fast Company published an article today called "How Google Wave Got Its Groove Back."

4. Angelo told Arlena, "I have a guy who can fix that fender."

5. Arlena asked, "How much will it cost me?"

6. Was she thinking, "This car is driving me into bankruptcy?"

7. This is the message of the article "Tracking the Science of Commitment": Couples that enhance one another have an easier time remaining committed.

8. I love the article "Tall Tales About Being Short"; it challenged my preconceptions about the effect of height on a person's life.

9. How many examples of the word "aardvark" can you find on this page?

10. Is anyone else here tired of hearing about his "bling bling"?

Write   Write a sentence that indicates the actual meaning of each sentence below.

1. Hoyt's great Dane "skipped" across the floor and "settled" its bulk across his lap.

   (AWV) Hoyt's great Dane thundered across the floor and planted its bulk across his lap.

2. Our baked goods are always "fresh."

   Our baked goods are always stale.

3. And so began another "wonderful" day of marching through a "fairyland" of bugs.

   And so began another miserable day of marching through a swarm of bugs.

LO2 Italics

To Punctuate Titles (Larger Works)

Use italics to indicate the titles of larger works, including newspapers, magazines, journals, pamphlets, books, plays, films, radio and television programs, movies, ballets, operas, long musical compositions, CD's, DVD's, software programs, and legal cases, as well as the names of ships, trains, aircraft, and spacecraft. (For other titles, see page 524.)

Magazine: *Wired*	**Newspaper:** *Washington Post*
Play: *Night of the Iguana*	**Journal:** *Journal of Sound & Vibration*
Film: *Bladerunner*	**Software Program:** *Paint Shop Pro*
Book: *Moby Dick*	**Television Program:** *The Prisoner*

For a Word, Letter, or Number Referred to as Itself

Use italics (or quotation marks—see page 524) to show that a word, letter, or number is being referred to as itself. If a definition follows a word used in this way, place that definition in quotation marks.

The word *tornado* comes to English from the Spanish *tronar,* which means "to thunder."

I can't read your writing; is this supposed to be a *P* or an *R*?

For Foreign Words

Use italics to indicate a word that is being borrowed from a foreign language.

Je ne sais pas is a French phrase that many English speakers use as a fancy way of saying "I don't know what."

For Technical Terms

Use italics to introduce a technical term for the first time in a piece of writing. After that, the term may be used without italics.

The heart's *sternocostal* surface—facing toward the joining of sternum and ribs— holds the heart's primary natural pacemaker. If this sternocostal node fails, a lower, secondary node can function in its place.

NOTE: If a technical term is being used within an organization or a field of study where it is common, it may be used without italics even the first time in a piece of writing.

Using Italics

Correct For the following sentences, underline words that should be in italics.

1. I almost couldn't finish Stephenie Meyer's second book, _New Moon_, because of its deep emotion.

2. What is your favorite part of the movie _Avatar_?

3. The Spanish say _duende_ to describe a transcendent, creative passion.

4. Was the aircraft carrier _Enterprise_ named after the vessel from the _Star Trek_ series or the other way around?

5. You might use the term _bonhomie_ to describe our relationship.

6. One thing I love about the _MS Word_ program is its "Track Changes" feature.

7. In this course, we will use the term _noetics_ as an indication of deep-felt self-awareness, beyond mere consciousness.

8. How am I supposed to compete at _Scrabble_ when all I have is an _X_ and a _7_.

9. Wait, that's not a _7_; it's an _L_.

10. That, ladies and gentleman, is what we in show business call a _finale_!

Write Write three sentences, each demonstrating your understanding of one or more rules for using italics.

1. Answers will vary.

2.

3.

LO3 Real-World Application

Practice In the following business letter, underline any words that should be italicized and add quotation marks where needed.

<u>Brideshead Publishing</u>
1012 Broadway
New York, New York 10011

May 13, 2010   *1*

Neva Konen
4004 W. Obleness Parkway
Hollenshead, New Hampshire 03305

Dear Neva Konen: *5*

Thank you for your recent novel submission entitled <u>A Time of Dimly Perceived Wonders</u>, which I read with great interest. The setting is richly portrayed, and the main characters are at the same time both mysterious and familiar, conveying a certain <u>je ne sais quas</u> about themselves. For example, although his words land strangely on my ear, still I am overwhelmed with feelings of kinship for Anibal when he cries out "I could've et 'em up   *10* right there 'n' then." Similarly, when at the end Kandis softly croons the words of "Come One, Come All, to the Family Reunion," I feel I'm being called home myself, although I've never actually seen the Appalachians.

While I greatly enjoyed the novel, and it would certainly receive an "A" in my Creative Writing Seminar at Midtown College, I do have a few concerns. For one thing, the title   *15* seems long and somewhat vague; I'd recommend <u>Foggy Mountain Memories</u>, instead. Also, it seems unnecessary to print the full text of Abraham Lincoln's "Gettysburg Address" and Martin Luther King, Jr.'s "I Have a Dream" speech in the chapter entitled "A Few Words of Hope." Modern readers are certainly familiar with both speeches. It should be enough to merely include a few phrases, such as "Four score and seven years ago," and "Let   *20* freedom ring from Lookout Mountain of Tennessee."

If you are willing to accept changes such as these, I believe we can work together to make your novel a commercial success. Please review the enclosed contract and return it to me at your earliest convenience.

Sincerely,   *25*

Christene Kaley

Christene Kaley

29

> "If the English language made any sense,
> a catastrophe would be an apostrophe with fur."
> —Doug Larson

Other Punctuation

You may be surprised to discover that the words *catastrophe* and *apostrophe* have something in common. Both come from the Greek word for "turn." An apostrophe simply turns away, but a catastrophe overturns.

Sometimes the use of apostrophes becomes a catastrophe. Apostrophes shouldn't be used to form plurals of words. Their main use is to form possessives and contractions. The rules and activities in this chapter will help you understand their usage and avoid an apostrophe catastrophe.

This chapter also provides guidelines for the rules and correct usage of semicolons, colons, hyphens, and dashes.

Learning Outcomes

LO1 Use apostrophes for contractions and possessives.

LO2 Use semicolons and colons correctly.

LO3 Understand hyphen use.

LO4 Use dashes well.

LO5 Apply apostrophes in real-world documents.

LO6 Apply punctuation in real-world documents.

What do you think?

Why do you think *apostrophe* comes from the word "to turn away?"

Gary James Calder, 2011 / Used under license from Shutterstock.com

LO1 Contractions and Possessives

Apostrophes are used primarily to show that a letter or number has been left out, or that a noun is possessive.

Contractions

When one or more letters are left out of a word, use an apostrophe to form the **contraction**.

don't	he'd	would've
(*o* is left out)	(*woul* is left out)	(*ha* is left out)

Missing Characters

Use an apostrophe to signal when one or more characters are left out.

class of '16	rock 'n' roll	good mornin'
(*20* is left out)	(*a* and *d* are left out)	(*g* is left out)

Possessives

Form possessives of singular nouns by adding an apostrophe and an *s*.

Sharla's pen	the man's coat	*The Pilgrim's Progress*

Singular Noun Ending In *s* (One Syllable)

Form the possessive by adding an apostrophe and an *s*.

the boss's idea	the lass's purse	the bass's teeth

Singular Noun Ending In *s* (Two Or More Syllables)

Form the possessive by adding an apostrophe and an *s*—or by adding just an apostrophe.

Kansas's plains	*or*	Kansas' plains

Plural Noun Ending In *s*

Form the possessive by adding just an apostrophe.

the bosses' preference	the Smiths' home
the girl's ball	the girls' ball
(*girl* is the owner)	(*girls* are the owners)

Plural Noun Not Ending In *s*

Form the possessive by adding an apostrophe and an *s*.

the children's toys	the women's room

Forming Contractions and Possessives

Write For each contraction below, write the words that formed the contraction. For each set of words, write the contraction that would be formed.

1. they're _they are_
2. you've _you have_
3. Charlie is _Charlie's_
4. wouldn't _would not_
5. we have _we've_

6. have not _haven't_
7. I would _I'd_
8. I had _I'd_
9. won't _will not_
10. will not _won't_

Rewrite Rework the following sentences, replacing the "of" phrases with possessives using apostrophes.

1. The idea of my friend is a good one.

   My friend's idea is a good one.

2. I found the flyer of the orchestra.

   I found the orchestra's flyer.

3. The foundation of the government is democracy.

   The government's foundation is democracy.

4. He washed the jerseys of the team.

   He washed the team's jerseys.

5. I went to the house of the Kings.

   I went to the Kings' house.

6. The plan of the managers worked well.

   The managers' plan worked well.

7. I like the classic albums of Kiss.

   I like Kiss's classic albums.

8. I graded the assignment of Ross.

   I graded Ross's assignment.

9. The pastries of the chef were delicious.

   The chef's pastries were delicious.

10. The books of the children covered the floor.

    The children's books covered the floor.

Vocabulary

contraction
word formed by joining two words, leaving out one or more letters (indicated by an apostrophe)

LO2 Semicolons and Colons

Semicolons and colons have specific uses in writing.

Semicolon

A **semicolon** can be called a soft period. Use the semicolon to join two sentences that are closely related.

> The job market is improving; it's time to apply again.

Before a Conjunctive Adverb

Often, the second sentence will begin with a conjunctive adverb *(also, besides, however, instead, meanwhile, therefore)*, which signals the relationship between the sentences. Place a semicolon before the conjunctive adverb, and place a comma after it.

> I looked for work for two months; however, the market is better now.

With Series

Use a semicolon to separate items in a series if any of the items already include commas.

> I should check online ads, headhunting services, and position announcements; compile a list of job openings; create a résumé, an e-résumé, and a cover letter; and apply, requesting an interview.

Colon

The main use of a **colon** is to introduce an example or a list.

> I've forgotten one other possibility: social networking.
> I'll plan to use the following: LinkedIn, Twitter, and Facebook.

After Salutations

In business documents, use a colon after **salutations** and in memo headings.

> Dear Mr. Ortez: To: Lynne Jones

Times and Ratios

Use a colon to separate hours, minutes, and seconds. Also use a colon between the numbers in a ratio.

> 7:35 p.m.   6:15 a.m.   The student-teacher ratio is 30:1.

Using Semicolons and Colons

Correct   Add semicolons and commas as needed in the sentences below.

1. Searching for a job is nerve-wracking however it's also about possibilities.

2. Don't think about rejections think about where you could be working.

3. Each résumé you send is a fishing line then you wait for a nibble.

4. Put out dozens of lines also give yourself time.

5. Make sure that you have a strong résumé e-résumé and cover letter that you consult social networks local newspapers and friends and that you keep your spirits up.

6. It doesn't cost much to send out résumés therefore send out many.

7. Job searching can feel lonely and frustrating rely on friends and family to help you through.

8. Ask people if you can use them as references don't provide the list of references until requested.

9. When you interview, wear professional clothing show up at the right place at the right time and armed with any information you need and be confident.

10. Try to enjoy the process it is the gateway to your future.

Correct   Add colons where needed in the sentences below.

1. Use your social resources contacts, references, and organizations.

2. Call for an appointment between 9 00 a.m. and 4 00 p.m.

3. Remember a response rate of 1 10 is good for résumés submitted.

4. Politely start your cover letter with a salutation "Dear Mrs. Baker."

5. For an interview, remember these three keys Be punctual, be polite, and be professional.

6. Here's one last piece of advice Be yourself.

Vocabulary

semicolon
a punctuation mark (;) that connects sentences and separates items in some series

colon
a punctuation mark (:) that introduces an example or list and has other special uses

salutation
the formal greeting in a letter; the line starting with "Dear"

LO3 Hyphens

A **hyphen** joins words to each other or to letters to form compounds.

Compound Nouns

Use hyphens to create **compound nouns**.

city-state	fail-safe	fact-check	one-liner	mother-in-law

Compound Adjectives

Use hyphens to create **compound adjectives** that appear before the noun. If the adjective appears after, it usually is not hyphenated.

peer-reviewed article   an article that was peer reviewed
ready-made solution   a solution that is ready made

NOTE: Don't hyphenate a compound made from an -*ly* adverb and an adjective, or a compound that ends with a single letter.

newly acquired songs (*ly* adverb)   grade B plywood (ending with a letter)

Compound Numbers

Use hyphens for **compound numbers** from twenty-one to ninety-nine. Also use hyphens for numbers in a fraction and other number compounds.

twenty-two	fifty-fifty	three-quarters	seven thirty-seconds

With Letters

Use a hyphen to join a letter to a word that follows it.

L-bracket	U-shaped	T-shirt	O-ring	G-rated	x-ray

With Common Elements

Use hyphens to show that two or more words share a common element included in only the final term.

We offer low-, middle-, and high-coverage plans.

Using Hyphens

Correct Rewrite the following sentences. Add hyphens as needed.

1. The secretary-treasurer recorded the vote as four-five.

   _____

2. We had to x-ray twenty-one people today.

   _____

3. Cut each board at seven-and-three-sixteenths inches.

   _____

4. The statistics on low-, middle-, and high-income households are ready.

   _____

5. A double-insulated wire should be used for high-voltage applications.

   _____

6. The x-axis shows months and the y-axis shows dollar amounts.

   _____

7. The tax-rate table shows I should pay twenty-eight cents.

   _____

8. My mother-in-law thinks I am quite a fine son-in-law.

   _____

9. The L-bracket measured eleven-sixteenths by twenty-seven thirty-seconds.

   _____

Vocabulary

hyphen
a short, horizontal line (-) used to form compound words

compound noun
a noun made of two or more

words, often hyphenated or spelled closed

compound adjective
an adjective made of two or more words, hyphenated

before the noun but not afterward

compound numbers
two-word numbers from twenty-one to ninety-nine

LO4 Dashes

Unlike the hyphen, the **dash** does more to separate words than to join them together. A dash is indicated by two hyphens with no spacing before or after. Most word-processing programs convert two hyphens into a dash.

For Emphasis

Use a dash instead of a colon if you want to emphasize a word, phrase, clause, or series.

Ice cream—it's what life is about.

I love two things about ice cream—making it and eating it.

Ice cream is my favorite dessert—cold, sweet, and flavorful.

To Set Off a Series

Use a dash to set off a series of items.

Rocky road, moose tracks, and chocolate-chip cookie dough—these are my favorite flavors.

Neapolitan ice cream—chocolate, strawberry, and vanilla—is my sister's favorite.

With Nonessential Elements

Use a dash to set off explanations, examples, and definitions, especially when these elements already include commas.

Ice milk—which, as you might guess, is made of milk instead of cream—provides a light alternative.

To Show Interrupted Speech

Use a dash to show that a speaker has been interrupted or has started and stopped while speaking.

"Could you help me crank this—"

"I've got to get more salt before—"

"It'll freeze up if you don't—Just give me a hand, please."

Using Dashes

Correct In the sentences below, add a dash where needed.

1. Which dessert would you prefer—brownies, apple pie, or ice cream?

2. I love the triple brownie surprise—a brownie with vanilla and chocolate ice cream covered in hot fudge.

3. Ice cream—it's what's for dinner.

4. "Could I have a taste of—" "You want to try some of—" "I want to try—um—could I try the pistachio?"

5. Bananas, ice cream, peanuts, and fudge—these are the ingredients of a banana-split sundae.

6. Making ice cream at home takes a long time—and a lot of muscle!

7. An electric ice-cream maker—which replaced arm power with a cranking motor—makes the job easier but less fun.

8. Nothing tastes better than the first taste of freshly made ice cream—nothing except perhaps the next taste.

9. Don't eat too quickly—brain-freeze.

10. A danger of ice cream—I'll risk it every time.

Correct Write your own sentence, correctly using dashes for each of the situations indicated below:

1. For emphasis:

   Answers will vary.

2. To set off a series:

3. With nonessential elements:

Mike Flippo, 2011 / Used under license from Shutterstock.com

Vocabulary

dash
long horizontal line that separates words, creating emphasis.

LO5 Real-World Application

Correct The following letter sounds too informal because it contains too many contractions. For any contractions you find, write the line number and full form of the word. Also, if you find any errors with apostrophes, write the line number and show the correct punctuation.

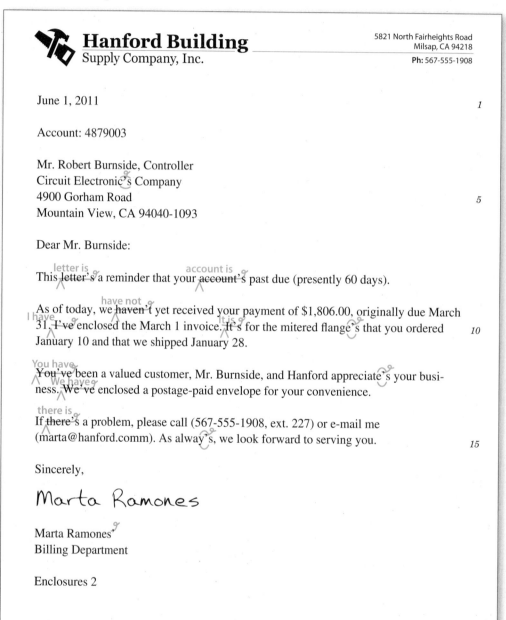

Hanford Building
Supply Company, Inc.

5821 North Fairheights Road
Milsap, CA 94218
Ph: 567-555-1908

June 1, 2011   *1*

Account: 4879003

Mr. Robert Burnside, Controller
Circuit Electronic's Company
4900 Gorham Road   *5*
Mountain View, CA 94040-1093

Dear Mr. Burnside:

This letter's a reminder that your account's past due (presently 60 days).

As of today, we haven't yet received your payment of $1,806.00, originally due March
31. I've enclosed the March 1 invoice. It's for the mitered flange's that you ordered   *10*
January 10 and that we shipped January 28.

You've been a valued customer, Mr. Burnside, and Hanford appreciate's your business. We've enclosed a postage-paid envelope for your convenience.

If there's a problem, please call (567-555-1908, ext. 227) or e-mail me
(marta@hanford.comm). As alway's, we look forward to serving you.   *15*

Sincerely,

Marta Ramones

Marta Ramones
Billing Department

Enclosures 2

LO6 Real-World Application

Correct Rewrite the following e-mail message, and insert semicolons, colons, hyphens, and dashes where necessary.

Send	Attach	Fonts	Colors	Save As Draft

To:	Felton Engineering Staff
Subject:	Ideas for Open House Displays

Hello, all: 1

September 1 that's the big open house when we will celebrate our new location. To help visitors understand what Felton Engineering does, I plan to set up displays heater designs, product applications, and aerospace technology.

Please help me by doing the following looking for blueprints, sketches, small   5
models, and prototypes that illustrate what we do identifying items that would interest visitors and setting them aside as you pack.

Then please respond to this e-mail with the following your name, the name of the product, the product number, and the type of display materials that you have.   10

Please respond no later than August 22. I will handle the other arrangements pick up your materials, set up the displays, and return the materials to you after the open house. Innovation it's what drives Felton Engineering!

Thanks,

Jilliane Seaforth

Glossary/Appendix

Understanding Assignments

You can use the STRAP strategy to analyze your writing and reading assignments. The strategy consists of answering questions about these five features: *subject, type, role, audience,* and *purpose.* Once you answer the questions, you'll be ready to get to work. This chart shows how the strategy works:

For Reading Assignments		For Writing Assignments
What specific topic does the reading address?	**Subject**	What specific topic should I write about?
What form (*essay, text chapter, article*) does the reading take?	**Type**	What form of writing (*essay, article*) will I use?
What position (*student, responder, concerned individual*) does the writer assume?	**Role**	What position (*student, citizen, employee*) should I assume?
Who is the intended reader?	**Audience**	Who is the intended reader?
What is the goal of the material?	**Purpose**	What is the goal (*to inform, to persuade*) of the writing?

For additional information, see pages 4–5.

Understanding the Reading Process

When reading academic texts, be sure to use the **reading process** to gain a full understanding of the material. This graphic shows the reading process in action. The arrows show how you may move back and forth between the steps.

The Reading Process

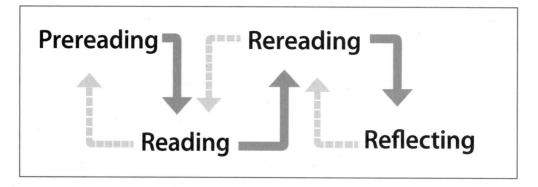

Prereading · Rereading · Reading · Reflecting

Key Terms to Remember

To use the reading process, you must understand each step in the process.

- **Prereading**—Becoming familiar with the text by reviewing the title, headings, etc.
- **Reading**—Read the text once for a basic understanding, using a reading strategy such as note taking
- **Rereading**—Complete additional readings as needed until you have a clear understanding of the material
- **Reflecting**—Evaluate your reading experience: *What have you learned? What questions to you still have?*

For additional information, see pages 13–15.

Understanding the Writing Process

When completing a writing assignment, be sure to use the writing process to help you do your best work. This graphic shows the writing process in action. The arrows show how you may move back and forth between the steps.

The Writing Process

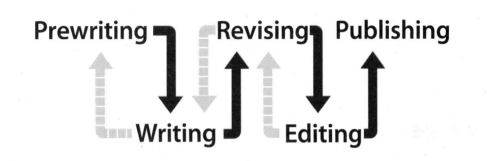

Key Terms to Remember

To use the writing process, you must understand each step in the process.

- **Prewriting**—Starting the process by analyzing the assignment, selecting a topic, gathering details, and finding a focus
- **Writing**—Writing a first draft using your prewriting as a guide
- **Revising**—Improving the content of a first draft
- **Editing**—Checking for style, grammar, mechanics, and spelling
- **Publishing**—Preparing your writing to share or submit

For additional information, see pages 70–75.

Using the Traits for Reading and Writing

The **traits** identify the key elements of written language. The traits help you to know what to look for when analyzing reading material. They also help you to know what to consider in your own writing.

The Traits of Written Language

Read to identify . . .	The Traits	Write to shape . . .
■ the topic. ■ the thesis (main point). ■ the key supporting details.	**Ideas**	■ a thesis or focus. ■ your thoughts on the topic. ■ effective supporting details.
■ the quality of the beginning, middle, and ending parts. ■ the organization of the supporting details.	**Organization**	■ an effective beginning, middle, and ending. ■ a logical, clear presentation of your supporting details.
■ the level of the writer's interest in and knowledge about the topic.	**Voice**	■ a voice that sounds interesting, honest, and knowledgeable.
■ the quality of the words. (Are they interesting and clear?)	**Word Choice**	■ words that are specific, clear, and fitting for the assignment.
■ the effectiveness of the sentences. (Do they flow smoothly, and are they clear?)	**Sentence Fluency**	■ smooth-reading, clear, and accurate sentences.
■ to what degree the writing follows conventions (and why or why not).	**Conventions**	■ paragraphs or essays that follow the conventions or rules.

Key Terms to Remember

To use the traits, you must understand what they mean.

- **Ideas**—The main point and supporting details
- **Organization**—The arrangement of the ideas
- **Voice**—The personality or tone of the writing
- **Word choice**—The words in writing
- **Sentences**—The sentences in writing
- **Conventions**—The rules governing correctness in writing

For additional information, see pages 70–75.

Understanding the Structure of Paragraphs and Essays

Paragraphs and essays follow a three-part structure. Knowing the purpose of each part will help you understand reading assignments and develop your own writing.

Three-Part Structure

Paragraph Structure

Topic Sentence
- Names the topic and focus

Body Sentences
- Provide supporting sentences
- Follows a pattern of organization

Closing Sentence
- Wraps up the paragraph

Essay Structure

Opening Part
- Introduces the topic
- Provides background information
- Identifies the main point or thesis

Middle Part
- Supports or develops the main point
- Follows one or more patterns of organization

Closing Part
- Summarizes the key ideas
- Restates the thesis
- Provides final thoughts or analysis

For additional information, see pages 54–55 and 76–81.

Understanding Strong Writing

The checklist below serves as a guide to strong writing. Your writing will be clear and effective when it can "pass" each point. This checklist is especially helpful during revising, when you are deciding how to improve your writing.

A Guide to Strong Writing

Ideas

☐ 1. Does an interesting and relevant topic serve as a starting point for the writing?

☐ 2. Is the writing focused, addressing a specific feeling about or a specific part of the topic? (Check the thesis statement.)

☐ 3. Are there enough specific ideas, details, and examples to support the thesis?

☐ 4. Overall, is the writing interesting and informative?

Organization

☐ 5. Does the writing form a meaningful whole—with opening, middle, and closing parts?

☐ 6. Does the writing follow a logical pattern of organization?

☐ 7. Do transitions connect ideas and help the writing flow?

Voice

☐ 8. Does the writer sound informed about and interested in the topic?

☐ 9. Does the writer sound sincere and genuine?

Word Choice

☐ 10. Does the word choice clearly fit the purpose and the audience?

☐ 11. Does the writing include specific nouns and verbs?

Sentence Fluency

☐ 12. Are the sentences clear, and do they flow smoothly?

☐ 13. Are the sentences varied in their beginnings and length?

Conventions

☐ 14. Does your writing follow the rules of the language?

For additional information, see pages 89–110.

Using a Peer Review Sheet

Sharing your writing at various stages is important, but it is especially important when you review and revise a first draft. The feedback that you receive will help you change and improve your essay.

Peer Review Sheet

Essay title: _____

Writer: _____

Reviewer: _____

1. Which part of the essay seems to work best—opening, middle, or closing? Why?

   _____

   _____

2. Which part of the essay needs work—opening, middle, or closing? Why?

   _____

   _____

3. Do the middle paragraphs clearly present each step of the process? Explain.

   _____

   _____

4. Do you understand the process after reading the essay?

   _____

   _____

5. Identify a phrase or two that shows the writer's level of interest.

   _____

   _____

Using Standard English

Standard English (SE) is English that is considered appropriate for school, business, and government. You have been learning SE throughout your years in school. The chart that follows shows the basic differences between non-Standard English (NS) and SE.

Differences in . . .	NS	SE
1. Expressing plurals after numbers	10 mile	10 miles
2. Expressing habitual action	He always be early.	He always is early.
3. Expressing ownership	My friend car . . .	My friend's car . . .
4. Expressing the third-person singular verb	The customer ask . . .	The customer asks . . .
5. Expressing negatives	She doesn't never . . .	She doesn't ever . . .
6. Using reflexive pronouns	He sees hisself . . .	He sees himself . . .
7. Using demonstrative adjectives	Them reports are . . .	Those reports are . . .
8. Using forms of *do*	He done it.	He did it.
9. Avoiding double subjects	My manager he . . .	My manager . . .
10. Using *a* or *an*	I need new laptop. She had angry caller.	I need a new laptop. She had an angry caller.
11. Using the past tense of verbs	Carl finish his . . .	Carl finished his . . .
12. Using *isn't* or *aren't* versus *ain't*	The company ain't . . .	The company isn't . . .

For additional information, see pages 389–565.

Understanding Word Parts

The next nine pages include common prefixes, suffixes, and roots. Many of our words are made up of combinations of these word parts.

Prefixes

Prefixes are those "word parts" that come *before* the root words (*pre* = before). Depending upon its meaning, a prefix changes the intent, or sense, of the base word. As a skilled reader, you will want to know the meanings of the most common prefixes and then watch for them when you read.

a, an [not, without] amoral (without a sense of moral responsibility), atypical, atom (not cuttable), apathy (without feeling), anesthesia (without sensation)

ab, abs, a [from, away] abnormal, abduct, absent, avert (turn away)

acro [high] acropolis (high city), acrobat, acronym, acrophobia (fear of height)

ambi, amb [both, around] ambidextrous (skilled with both hands), ambiguous, amble

amphi [both] amphibious (living on both land and water), amphitheater

ante [before] antedate, anteroom, antebellum, antecedent (happening before)

anti, ant [against] anticommunist, antidote, anticlimax, antacid

be [on, away] bedeck, belabor, bequest, bestow, beloved

bene, bon [well] benefit, benefactor, benevolent, benediction, bonanza, bonus

bi, bis, bin [both, double, twice] bicycle, biweekly, bilateral, biscuit, binoculars

by [side, close, near] bypass, bystander, by-product, bylaw, byline

cata [down, against] catalog, catapult, catastrophe, cataclysm

cerebro [brain] cerebral, cerebrum, cerebellum

circum, circ [around] circumference, circumnavigate, circumspect, circular

co, con, col, com [together, with] copilot, conspire, collect, compose

coni [dust] coniosis (disease that comes from inhaling dust)

contra, counter [against] controversy, contradict, counterpart

de [from, down] demote, depress, degrade, deject, deprive

deca [ten] decade, decathlon, decapod (10 feet)

di [two, twice] divide, dilemma, dilute, dioxide, dipole, ditto

dia [through, between] diameter, diagonal, diagram, dialogue (speech between people)

dis, dif [apart, away, reverse] dismiss, distort, distinguish, diffuse

dys [badly, ill] dyspepsia (digesting badly), dystrophy, dysentery

em, en [in, into] embrace, enslave

epi [upon] epidermis (upon the skin, outer layer of skin), epitaph, epithet

eu [well] eulogize (speak well of, praise), euphony, euphemism, euphoria

ex, e, ec, ef [out] expel (drive out), ex-mayor, exorcism, eject, eccentric (out of the center position), efflux, effluent

extra, extro [beyond, outside] extraordinary (beyond the ordinary), extrovert, extracurricular

for [away or off] forswear (to renounce an oath)

fore [before in time] forecast, foretell (to tell beforehand), foreshadow

hemi, demi, semi [half] hemisphere, demitasse, semicircle (half of a circle)

hex [six] hexameter, hexagon

homo [man] Homo sapiens, homicide (killing man)

hyper [over, above] hypersensitive (overly sensitive), hyperactive

hypo [under] hypodermic (under the skin), hypothesis

il, ir, in, im [not] illegal, irregular, incorrect, immoral

in, il, im [into] inject, inside, illuminate, illustrate, impose, implant, imprison

infra [beneath] infrared, infrasonic

inter [between] intercollegiate, interfere, intervene, interrupt (break between)

intra [within] intramural, intravenous (within the veins)

intro [into, inward] introduce, introvert (turn inward)

macro [large, excessive] macrodent (having large teeth), macrocosm

mal [badly, poorly] maladjusted, malady, malnutrition, malfunction

meta [beyond, after, with] metaphor, metamorphosis, metaphysical

mis [incorrect, bad] misuse, misprint

miso [hate] misanthrope, misogynist

mono [one] monoplane, monotone, monochrome, monocle

multi [many] multiply, multiform

neo [new] neopaganism, neoclassic, neophyte, neonatal

non [not] nontaxable (not taxed), nontoxic, nonexistent, nonsense

ob, of, op, oc [toward, against] obstruct, offend, oppose, occur

oct [eight] octagon, octameter, octave, octopus

paleo [ancient] paleoanthropology (pertaining to ancient humans), paleontology (study of ancient life-forms)

para [beside, almost] parasite (one who eats beside or at the table of another), paraphrase, paramedic, parallel, paradox

penta [five] pentagon (figure or building having five angles or sides), pentameter, pentathlon

per [throughout, completely] pervert (completely turn wrong, corrupt), perfect, perceive, permanent, persuade

peri [around] perimeter (measurement around an area), periphery, periscope, pericardium, period

poly [many] polygon (figure having many angles or sides), polygamy, polyglot, polychrome

post [after] postpone, postwar, postscript, posterity

pre [before] prewar, preview, precede, prevent, premonition

pro [forward, in favor of] project (throw forward), progress, promote, prohibition

pseudo [false] pseudonym (false or assumed name), pseudopodia

quad [four] quadruple (four times as much), quadriplegic, quadratic, quadrant

quint [five] quintuplet, quintuple, quintet, quintile

re [back, again] reclaim, revive, revoke, rejuvenate, retard, reject, return

retro [backward] retrospective (looking backward), retroactive, retrorocket

se [aside] seduce (lead aside), secede, secrete, segregate

self [by oneself] self-determination, self-employed, self-service, selfish

sesqui [one and a half] sesquicentennial (one and one-half centuries)

sex, sest [six] sexagenarian (sixty years old), sexennial, sextant, sextuplet, sestet

sub [under] submerge (put under), submarine, substitute, subsoil

suf, sug, sup, sus [from under] sufficient, suffer, suggest, support, suspend

super, supr [above, over, more] supervise, superman, supernatural, supreme

syn, sym, sys, syl [with, together] system, synthesis, synchronize (time together), synonym, sympathy, symphony, syllable

trans, tra [across, beyond] transoceanic, transmit (send across), transfusion, tradition

tri [three] tricycle, triangle, tripod, tristate

ultra [beyond, exceedingly] ultramodern, ultraviolet, ultraconservative

un [not, release] unfair, unnatural, unknown

under [beneath] underground, underlying

uni [one] unicycle, uniform, unify, universe, unique (one of a kind)

vice [in place of] vice president, viceroy, vice admiral

Numerical Prefixes

Prefix	Symbol	Multiples and Submultiples	Equivalent	Prefix	Symbol	Multiples and Submultiples	Equivalent
tera	T	10^{12}	trillionfold	centi	c	10^{-2}	hundredth part
giga	G	10^9	billionfold	milli	m	10^{-3}	thousandth part
mega	M	10^6	millionfold	micro	u	10^{-6}	millionth part
kilo	k	10^3	thousandfold	nano	n	10^{-9}	billionth part
hecto	h	10^2	hundredfold	pico	p	10^{-12}	trillionth part
deka	da	10	tenfold	femto	f	10^{-15}	quadrillionth part
deci	d	10^{-1}	tenth part	atto	a	10^{-18}	quintillionth part

Suffixes

Suffixes come at the end of a word. Very often a suffix will tell you what kind of word it is part of (noun, adverb, adjective, and so on). For example, words ending in *-ly* are usually adverbs.

able, ible [able, can do] capable, agreeable, edible, visible (can be seen)

ade [result of action] blockade (the result of a blocking action), lemonade

age [act of, state of, collection of] salvage (act of saving), storage, forage

al [relating to] sensual, gradual, manual, natural (relating to nature)

algia [pain] neuralgia (nerve pain)

an, ian [native of, relating to] African, Canadian, Floridian

ance, ancy [action, process, state] assistance, allowance, defiance, truancy

ant [performing, agent] assistant, servant

ary, ery, ory [relating to, quality, place where] dictionary, bravery, dormitory

ate [cause, make] liquidate, segregate (cause a group to be set aside)

cian [having a certain skill or art] musician, beautician, magician, physician

cule, ling [very small] molecule, ridicule, duckling (very small duck), sapling

cy [action, function] hesitancy, prophecy, normalcy (function in a normal way)

dom [quality, realm, office] freedom, kingdom, wisdom (quality of being wise)

ee [one who receives the action] employee, nominee (one who is nominated), refugee

en [made of, make] silken, frozen, oaken (made of oak), wooden, lighten

ence, ency [action, state of, quality] difference, conference, urgency

er, or [one who, that which] baker, miller, teacher, racer, amplifier, doctor

escent [in the process of] adolescent (in the process of becoming an adult), obsolescent, convalescent

ese [a native of, the language of] Japanese, Vietnamese, Portuguese

esis, osis [action, process, condition] genesis, hypnosis, neurosis, osmosis

ess [female] actress, goddess, lioness

et, ette [a small one, group] midget, octet, baronet, majorette

fic [making, causing] scientific, specific

ful [full of] frightful, careful, helpful

fy [make] fortify (make strong), simplify, amplify

hood [order, condition, quality] manhood, womanhood, brotherhood

ic [nature of, like] metallic (of the nature of metal), heroic, poetic, acidic

ice [condition, state, quality] justice, malice

id, ide [a thing connected with or belonging to] fluid, fluoride

ile [relating to, suited for, capable of] missile, juvenile, senile (related to being old)

ine [nature of] feminine, genuine, medicine

ion, sion, tion [act of, state of, result of] contagion, aversion, infection (state of being infected)

ish [origin, nature, resembling] foolish, Irish, clownish (resembling a clown)

ism [system, manner, condition, characteristic] heroism, alcoholism, Communism

ist [one who, that which] artist, dentist

ite [nature of, quality of, mineral product] Israelite, dynamite, graphite, sulfite

ity, ty [state of, quality] captivity, clarity

ive [causing, making] abusive (causing abuse), exhaustive

ize [make] emphasize, publicize, idolize

less [without] baseless, careless (without care), artless, fearless, helpless

ly [like, manner of] carelessly, quickly, forcefully, lovingly

ment [act of, state of, result] contentment, amendment (state of amending)

ness [state of] carelessness, kindness

oid [resembling] asteroid, spheroid, tabloid, anthropoid

ology [study, science, theory] biology, anthropology, geology, neurology

ous [full of, having] gracious, nervous, spacious, vivacious (full of life)

ship [office, state, quality, skill] friendship, authorship, dictatorship

some [like, apt, tending to] lonesome, threesome, gruesome

tude [state of, condition of] gratitude, multitude (condition of being many), aptitude

ure [state of, act, process, rank] culture, literature, rupture (state of being broken)

ward [in the direction of] eastward, forward, backward

y [inclined to, tend to] cheery, crafty, faulty

Roots

A *root* is a base upon which other words are built. Knowing the root of a difficult word can go a long way toward helping you figure out its meaning—even without a dictionary. For that reason, learning the following roots will be very valuable in all your classes.

acer, acid, acri [bitter, sour, sharp] acrid, acerbic, acidity (sourness), acrimony

acu [sharp] acute, acupuncture

ag, agi, ig, act [do, move, go] agent (doer), agenda (things to do), agitate, navigate (move by sea), ambiguous (going both ways), action

ali, allo, alter [other] alias (a person's other name), alibi, alien (from another place), alloy, alter (change to another form)

alt [high, deep] altimeter (a device for measuring heights), altitude

am, amor [love, liking] amiable, amorous, enamored

anni, annu, enni [year] anniversary, annually (yearly), centennial (occurring once in 100 years)

anthrop [man] anthropology (study of mankind), philanthropy (love of mankind), misanthrope (hater of mankind)

anti [old] antique, antiquated, antiquity

arch [chief, first, rule] archangel (chief angel), architect (chief worker), archaic (first, very early), monarchy (rule by one person), matriarchy (rule by the mother)

aster, astr [star] aster (star flower), asterisk, asteroid, astronomy (star law), astronaut (star traveler, space traveler)

aud, aus [hear, listen] audible (can be heard), auditorium, audio, audition, auditory, audience, ausculate

aug, auc [increase] augur, augment (add to; increase), auction

auto, aut [self] autograph (self-writing), automobile (self-moving vehicle), author, automatic (self-acting), autobiography

belli [war] rebellion, belligerent (warlike or hostile)

bibl [book] Bible, bibliography (list of books), bibliomania (craze for books), bibliophile (book lover)

bio [life] biology (study of life), biography, biopsy (cut living tissue for examination)

brev [short] abbreviate, brevity, brief

cad, cas [to fall] cadaver, cadence, caducous (falling off), cascade

calor [heat] calorie (a unit of heat), calorify (to make hot), caloric

cap, cip, cept [take] capable, capacity, capture, reciprocate, accept, except, concept

capit, capt [head] decapitate (to remove the head from), capital, captain, caption

carn [flesh] carnivorous (flesh eating), incarnate, reincarnation

caus, caut [burn, heat] caustic, cauterize (to make hot, to burn)

cause, cuse, cus [cause, motive] because, excuse (to attempt to remove the blame or cause), accusation

ced, ceed, cede, cess [move, yield, go, surrender] procedure, secede (move aside from), proceed (move forward), cede (yield), concede, intercede, precede, recede, success

centri [center] concentric, centrifugal, centripetal, eccentric (out of center)

chrom [color] chrome, chromosome (color body in genetics), chromosphere, monochrome (one color), polychrome

chron [time] chronological (in order of time), chronometer (time measured), chronicle (record of events in time), synchronize (make time with, set time together)

cide, cise [cut down, kill] suicide (killing of self), homicide (human killer), pesticide (pest killer), germicide (germ killer), insecticide, precise (cut exactly right), incision, scissors

cit [to call, start] incite, citation, cite

civ [citizen] civic (relating to a citizen), civil, civilian, civilization

clam, claim [cry out] exclamation, clamor, proclamation, reclamation, acclaim

clud, clus, claus [shut] include (to take in), conclude, claustrophobia (abnormal fear of being shut up, confined), recluse (one who shuts himself away from others)

cognosc, gnosi [know] recognize (to know again), incognito (not known), prognosis (forward knowing), diagnosis

cord, cor, cardi [heart] cordial (hearty, heartfelt), concord, discord, courage, encourage (put heart into), discourage (take heart out of), core, coronary, cardiac

corp [body] corporation (a legal body), corpse, corpulent

cosm [universe, world] cosmic, cosmos (the universe), cosmopolitan (world citizen), cosmonaut, microcosm, macrocosm

crat, cracy [rule, strength] democratic, autocracy

crea [create] creature (anything created), recreation, creation, creator

cred [believe] creed (statement of beliefs), credo (a creed), credence (belief), credit (belief, trust), credulous (believing too readily, easily deceived), incredible

cresc, cret, crease, cru [rise, grow] crescendo (growing in loudness or intensity), concrete (grown together, solidified), increase, decrease, accrue (to grow) crit [separate, choose] critical, criterion (that which is used in choosing), hypocrite

cur, curs [run] concurrent, current (running or flowing), concur (run together, agree), incur (run into), recur, occur, precursor (forerunner), cursive

cura [care] curator, curative, manicure (caring for the hands)

cycl, cyclo [wheel, circular] Cyclops (a mythical giant with one eye in the middle of his forehead), unicycle, bicycle, cyclone (a wind blowing circularly, a tornado)

deca [ten] decade, decalogue, decathlon

dem [people] democracy (people-rule), demography (vital statistics of the people: deaths, births, and so on), epidemic (on or among the people)

dent, dont [tooth] dental (relating to teeth), denture, dentifrice, orthodontist

derm [skin] hypodermic (injected under the skin), dermatology (skin study), epidermis (outer layer of skin), taxidermy (arranging skin; mounting animals)

dict [say, speak] diction (how one speaks, what one says), dictionary, dictate, dictator, dictaphone, dictatorial, edict, predict, verdict, contradict, benediction

doc [teach] indoctrinate, document, doctrine

domin [master] dominate, dominion, predominant, domain

don [give] donate, condone

dorm [sleep] dormant, dormitory

dox [opinion, praise] doxy (belief, creed, or opinion), orthodox (having the correct, commonly accepted opinion), heterodox (differing opinion), paradox (contradictory)

drome [run, step] syndrome (run-together symptoms), hippodrome (a place where horses run)

duc, duct [lead] produce, induce (lead into, persuade), seduce (lead aside), reduce, aqueduct (water leader or channel), viaduct, conduct

dura [hard, lasting] durable, duration, endurance

dynam [power] dynamo (power producer), dynamic, dynamite, hydrodynamics

endo [within] endoral (within the mouth), endocardial (within the heart), endoskeletal

equi [equal] equinox, equilibrium

erg [work] energy, erg (unit of work), allergy, ergophobia (morbid fear of work), ergometer, ergonomic

fac, fact, fic, fect [do, make] factory (place where workers make goods of various kinds), fact (a thing done), manufacture, amplification, confection

fall, fals [deceive] fallacy, falsify

fer [bear, carry] ferry (carry by water), coniferous (bearing cones, as a pine tree), fertile (bearing richly), defer, infer, refer

fid, fide, feder [faith, trust] confidante, Fido, fidelity, confident, infidelity, infidel, federal, confederacy

fila, fili [thread] filament (a single thread or threadlike object), filibuster, filigree

fin [end, ended, finished] final, finite, finish, confine, fine, refine, define, finale

fix [attach] fix, fixation (the state of being attached), fixture, affix, prefix, suffix

flex, flect [bend] flex (bend), reflex (bending back), flexible, flexor (muscle for bending), inflexibility, reflect, deflect

flu, fluc, fluv [flowing] influence (to flow in), fluid, flue, flush, fluently, fluctuate (to wave in an unsteady motion)

form [form, shape] form, uniform, conform, deform, reform, perform, formative, formation, formal, formula

fort, forc [strong] fort, fortress (a strong place), fortify (make strong), forte (one's strong point), fortitude, enforce

fract, frag [break] fracture (a break), infraction, fragile (easy to break), fraction (result of breaking a whole into equal parts), refract (to break or bend)

gam [marriage] bigamy (two marriages), monogamy, polygamy (many spouses or marriages)

gastr(o) [stomach] gastric, gastronomic, gastritis (inflammation of the stomach)

gen [birth, race, produce] genesis (birth, beginning), genetics (study of heredity), eugenics (well born), genealogy (lineage by race, stock), generate, genetic

geo [earth] geometry (earth measurement), geography (earth writing), geocentric (earth centered), geology

germ [vital part] germination (to grow), germ (seed; living substance, as the germ of an idea), germane

gest [carry, bear] congest (bear together, clog), congestive (causing clogging), gestation

gloss, glot [tongue] glossary, polyglot (many tongues), epiglottis

glu, glo [lump, bond, glue] glue, agglutinate (make to hold in a bond), conglomerate (bond together)

grad, gress [step, go] grade (step, degree), gradual (step-by-step), graduate (make all the steps, finish a course), graduated (in steps or degrees), progress

graph, gram [write, written] graph, graphic (written, vivid), autograph (self-writing, signature), graphite (carbon used for writing), photography (light writing), phonograph (sound writing), diagram, bibliography, telegram

grat [pleasing] gratuity (mark of favor, a tip), congratulate (express pleasure over success), grateful, ingrate (not thankful) grav [heavy, weighty] grave, gravity, aggravate, gravitate

greg [herd, group, crowd] gregarian (belonging to a herd), congregation (a group functioning together), segregate (tending to group aside or apart)

helio [sun] heliograph (an instrument for using the sun's rays to send signals), heliotrope (a plant that turns to the sun)

hema, hemo [blood] hemorrhage (an outpouring or flowing of blood), hemoglobin, hemophilia

here, hes [stick] adhere, cohere, cohesion

hetero [different] heterogeneous (different in birth), heterosexual (with interest in the opposite sex)

homo [same] homogeneous (of same birth or kind), homonym (word with same pronunciation as another), homogenize

hum, human [earth, ground, man] humus, exhume (to take out of the ground), humane (compassion for other humans)

hydr, hydra, hydro [water] dehydrate, hydrant, hydraulic, hydraulics, hydrogen, hydrophobia (fear of water)

hypn [sleep] hypnosis, Hypnos (god of sleep), hypnotherapy (treatment of disease by hypnosis)

ignis [fire] ignite, igneous, ignition

ject [throw] deject, inject, project (throw forward), eject, object

join, junct [join] adjoining, enjoin (to lay an order upon, to command), juncture, conjunction, injunction

juven [young] juvenile, rejuvenate (to make young again)

lau, lav, lot, lut [wash] launder, lavatory, lotion, ablution (a washing away), dilute (to make a liquid thinner and weaker)

leg [law] legal (lawful; according to law), legislate (to enact a law), legislature, legitimize (make legal)

levi [light] alleviate (lighten a load), levitate, levity (light conversation; humor)

liber, liver [free] liberty (freedom), liberal, liberalize (to make more free), deliverance

liter [letters] literary (concerned with books and writing), literature, literal, alliteration, obliterate

loc, loco [place] locality, locale, location, allocate (to assign, to place), relocate (to put back into place), locomotion (act of moving from place to place)

log, logo, ogue, ology [word, study, speech] catalog, prologue, dialogue, logogram (a symbol representing a word), zoology (animal study), psychology (mind study)

loqu, locut [talk, speak] eloquent (speaking well and forcefully), soliloquy, locution, loquacious (talkative), colloquial (talking together; conversational or informal)

luc, lum, lus, lun [light] translucent (letting light come through), lumen (a unit of light), luminary (a heavenly body; someone who shines in his or her profession), luster (sparkle, shine), Luna (the moon goddess)

magn [great] magnify (make great, enlarge), magnificent, magnanimous (great of mind or spirit), magnate, magnitude, magnum

man [hand] manual, manage, manufacture, manacle, manicure, manifest, maneuver, emancipate

mand [command] mandatory (commanded), remand (order back), mandate

mania [madness] mania (insanity, craze), monomania (mania on one idea), kleptomania, pyromania (insane tendency to set fires), maniac

mar, mari, mer [sea, pool] marine (a soldier serving on shipboard), marsh (wetland, swamp), maritime (relating to the sea and navigation), mermaid (fabled sea creature, half fish, half woman)

matri [mother] maternal (relating to the mother), matrimony, matriarchate (rulership of women), matron

medi [half, middle, between, halfway] mediate (come between, intervene), medieval (pertaining to the Middle Ages), Mediterranean (lying between lands), mediocre, medium

mega [great, million] megaphone (great sound), megalopolis (great city; an extensive urban area including a number of cities), megacycle (a million cycles), megaton

mem [remember] memo (a reminder), commemoration (the act of remembering by a memorial or ceremony), memento, memoir, memorable

meter [measure] meter (a metric measure), voltameter (instrument to measure volts), barometer, thermometer

micro [small] microscope, microfilm, microcard, microwave, micrometer (device for measuring small distances), omicron, micron (a millionth of a meter), microbe (small living thing)

migra [wander] migrate (to wander), emigrate (one who leaves a country), immigrate (to come into the land)

mit, miss [send] emit (send out, give off), remit (send back, as money due), submit, admit, commit, permit, transmit (send across), omit, intermittent (sending between, at intervals), mission, missile

mob, mot, mov [move] mobile (capable of moving), motionless (without motion), motor, emotional (moved strongly by feelings), motivate, promotion, demote, movement

mon [warn, remind] monument (a reminder or memorial of a person or an event), admonish (warn), monitor, premonition (forewarning)

mor, mort [mortal, death] mortal (causing death or destined for death), immortal (not subject to death), mortality (rate of death), mortician (one who prepares the dead for burial), mortuary (place for the dead, a morgue)

morph [form] amorphous (with no form, shapeless), metamorphosis (a change of form, as a caterpillar into a butterfly), morphology

multi [many, much] multifold (folded many times), multilinguist (one who speaks many languages), multiped (an organism with many feet), multiply

nat, nasc [to be born, to spring forth] innate (inborn), natal, native, nativity, renascence (a rebirth, a revival)

neur [nerve] neuritis (inflammation of a nerve), neurology (study of nervous systems), neurologist (one who practices neurology), neural, neurosis, neurotic

nom [law, order] autonomy (self-law, self-government), astronomy, gastronomy (art or science of good eating), economy

nomen, nomin [name] nomenclature, nominate (name someone for an office)

nov [new] novel (new, strange, not formerly known), renovate (to make like new again), novice, nova, innovate

nox, noc [night] nocturnal, equinox (equal nights), noctilucent (shining by night)

numer [number] numeral (a figure expressing a number), numeration (act of counting), enumerate (count out, one by one), innumerable

omni [all, every] omnipotent (all-powerful), omniscient (all-knowing), omnipresent (present everywhere), omnivorous

onym [name] anonymous (without name), synonym, pseudonym (false name), antonym (name of opposite meaning)

oper [work] operate (to labor, function), cooperate (work together)

ortho [straight, correct] orthodox (of the correct or accepted opinion), orthodontist (tooth straightener), orthopedic (originally pertaining to straightening a child), unorthodox

pac [peace] pacifist (one for peace only; opposed to war), pacify (make peace, quiet), Pacific Ocean (peaceful ocean)

pan [all] panacea (cure-all), pandemonium (place of all the demons, wild disorder), pantheon (place of all the gods in mythology)

pater, patr [father] paternity (fatherhood, responsibility), patriarch (head of the tribe, family), patriot, patron (a wealthy person who supports as would a father)

path, pathy [feeling, suffering] pathos (feeling of pity, sorrow), sympathy, antipathy (feeling against), apathy (without feeling), empathy (feeling or identifying with another), telepathy (far feeling; thought transference)

ped, pod [foot] pedal (lever for a foot), impede (get the feet in a trap, hinder), pedestal (foot or base of a statue), pedestrian (foot traveler), centipede, tripod (three-footed support), podiatry (care of the feet), antipodes (opposite feet)

pedo [child] orthopedic, pedagogue (child leader; teacher), pediatrics (medical care of children)

pel, puls [drive, urge] compel, dispel, expel, repel, propel, pulse, impulse, pulsate, compulsory, expulsion, repulsive

pend, pens, pond [hang, weigh] pendant pendulum, suspend, appendage, pensive (weighing thought), ponderous

phil [love] philosophy (love of wisdom), philanthropy, philharmonic, bibliophile, Philadelphia (city of brotherly love)

phobia [fear] claustrophobia (fear of closed spaces), acrophobia (fear of high places), hydrophobia (fear of water)

phon [sound] phonograph, phonetic (pertaining to sound), symphony (sounds with or together)

photo [light] photograph (light-writing), photoelectric, photogenic (artistically suitable for being photographed), photosynthesis (action of light on chlorophyll to make carbohydrates)

plac [please] placid (calm, peaceful), placebo, placate, complacent

plu, plur, plus [more] plural (more than one), pluralist (a person who holds more than one office), plus (indicating that something more is to be added)

pneuma, pneumon [breath] pneumatic (pertaining to air, wind, or other gases), pneumonia (disease of the lungs)

pod (see ped)

poli [city] metropolis (mother city), police, politics, Indianapolis, Acropolis (high city, upper part of Athens), megalopolis

pon, pos, pound [place, put] postpone (put afterward), component, opponent (one put against), proponent, expose, impose, deposit, posture (how one places oneself), position, expound, impound

pop [people] population, populous (full of people), popular

port [carry] porter (one who carries), portable, transport (carry across), report, export, import, support, transportation

portion [part, share] portion (a part; a share, as a portion of pie), proportion (the relation of one share to others)

prehend [seize] comprehend (seize with the mind), apprehend (seize a criminal), comprehensive (seizing much, extensive)

prim, prime [first] primacy (state of being first in rank), prima donna (the first lady of opera), primitive (from the earliest or first time), primary, primal, primeval proto [first] prototype (the first model made), protocol, protagonist, protozoan

psych [mind, soul] psyche (soul, mind), psychiatry (healing of the mind), psychology, psychosis (serious mental disorder), psychotherapy (mind treatment), psychic

punct [point, dot] punctual (being exactly on time), punctuation, puncture, acupuncture

reg, recti [straighten] regiment, regular, regulate, rectify (make straight), correct, direction

ri, ridi, risi [laughter] deride (mock, jeer at), ridicule (laughter at the expense of another, mockery), ridiculous, derision

rog, roga [ask] prerogative (privilege; asking before), interrogation (questioning; the act of questioning), derogatory

rupt [break] rupture (break), interrupt (break into), abrupt (broken off), disrupt (break apart), erupt (break out), incorruptible (unable to be broken down)

sacr, sanc, secr [sacred] sacred, sanction, sacrosanct, consecrate, desecrate

salv, salu [safe, healthy] salvation (act of being saved), salvage, salutation

sat, satis [enough] satient (giving pleasure, satisfying), saturate, satisfy (to give pleasure to; to give as much as is needed)

sci [know] science (knowledge), conscious (knowing, aware), omniscient (knowing everything)

scope [see, watch] telescope, microscope, kaleidoscope (instrument for seeing beautiful forms), periscope, stethoscope

scrib, script [write] scribe (a writer), scribble, manuscript (written by hand), inscribe, describe, prescribe

sed, sess, sid [sit] sediment (that which sits or settles out of a liquid), session (a sitting), obsession (an idea that sits stubbornly in the mind), possess, preside (sit before), president, reside, subside

sen [old] senior, senator, senile (old; showing the weakness of old age)

sent, sens [feel] sentiment (feeling), consent, resent, dissent, sentimental (having strong feeling or emotion), sense, sensation, sensitive, sensory, dissension

sequ, secu, sue [follow] sequence (following of one thing after another), sequel, consequence, subsequent, prosecute, consecutive (following in order), second (following "first"), ensue, pursue

serv [save, serve] servant, service, preserve, subservient, servitude, conserve, reservation, deserve, conservation

sign, signi [sign, mark, seal] signal (a gesture or sign to call attention), signature (the mark of a person written in his or her own handwriting), design, insignia (distinguishing marks)

simil, simul [like, resembling] similar (resembling in many respects), assimilate (to make similar to), simile, simulate (pretend; put on an act to make a certain impression)

sist, sta, stit [stand] persist (stand firmly; unyielding; continue), assist (to stand by with help), circumstance, stamina (power to withstand, to endure), status (standing), state, static, stable, stationary, substitute (to stand in for another)

solus [alone] soliloquy, solitaire, solitude, solo

solv, solu [loosen] solvent (a loosener, a dissolver), solve, absolve (loosen from, free from), resolve, soluble, solution, resolution, resolute, dissolute (loosened morally)

somnus [sleep] insomnia (not being able to sleep), somnambulist (a sleepwalker)

soph [wise] sophomore (wise fool), philosophy (love of wisdom), sophisticated

spec, spect, spic [look] specimen (an example to look at, study), specific, aspect, spectator (one who looks), spectacle, speculate, inspect, respect, prospect, retrospective (looking backward), introspective, expect, conspicuous

sphere [ball, sphere] stratosphere (the upper portion of the atmosphere), hemisphere (half of the earth), spheroid

spir [breath] spirit (breath), conspire (breathe together; plot), inspire (breathe into), aspire (breathe toward), expire (breathe out; die), perspire, respiration

string, strict [draw tight] stringent (drawn tight; rigid), strict, restrict, constrict (draw tightly together), boa constrictor (snake that constricts its prey)

stru, struct [build] construe (build in the mind, interpret), structure, construct, instruct, obstruct, destruction, destroy

sume, sump [take, use, waste] consume (to use up), assume (to take; to use), sump pump (a pump that takes up water), presumption (to take or use before knowing all the facts)

tact, tang, tag, tig, ting [touch] contact, tactile, intangible (not able to be touched), intact (untouched, uninjured), tangible, contingency, contagious (able to transmit disease by touching), contiguous

tele [far] telephone (far sound), telegraph (far writing), television (far seeing), telephoto (far photography), telecast

tempo [time] tempo (rate of speed), temporary, extemporaneously, contemporary (those who live at the same time), pro tem (for the time being)

ten, tin, tain [hold] tenacious (holding fast), tenant, tenure, untenable, detention, content, pertinent, continent, obstinate, abstain, pertain, detain

tend, tent, tens [stretch, strain] tendency (a stretching; leaning), extend, intend, contend, pretend, superintend, tender, extent, tension (a stretching, strain), pretense terra [earth] terrain, terrarium, territory, terrestrial

test [to bear witness] testament (a will; bearing witness to someone's wishes), detest, attest (bear witness to), testimony

the, theo [God, a god] monotheism (belief in one god), polytheism (belief in many gods), atheism, theology

therm [heat] thermometer, therm (heat unit), thermal, thermostat, thermos, hypothermia (subnormal temperature)

thesis, thet [place, put] antithesis (place against), hypothesis (place under), synthesis (put together), epithet

tom [cut] atom (not cuttable; smallest particle of matter), appendectomy (cutting out an appendix), tonsillectomy, dichotomy (cutting in two; a division), anatomy (cutting, dissecting to study structure)

tort, tors [twist] torture (twisting to inflict pain), retort (twist back, reply sharply), extort (twist out), distort (twist out of shape), contort, torsion (act of twisting, as a torsion bar)

tox [poison] toxic (poisonous), intoxicate, antitoxin

tract, tra [draw, pull] tractor, attract, subtract, tractable (can be handled), abstract (to draw away), subtrahend (the number to be drawn away from another)

trib [pay, bestow] tribute (to pay honor to), contribute (to give money to a cause), attribute, retribution, tributary

turbo [disturb] turbulent, disturb, turbid, turmoil

typ [print] type, prototype (first print; model), typical, typography, typewriter, typology (study of types, symbols), typify

ultima [last] ultimate, ultimatum (the final or last offer that can be made)

uni [one] unicorn (a legendary creature with one horn), unify (make into one), university, unanimous, universal

vac [empty] vacate (to make empty), vacuum (a space entirely devoid of matter), evacuate (to remove troops or people), vacation, vacant

vale, vali, valu [strength, worth] valiant, equivalent (of equal worth), validity (truth; legal strength), evaluate (find out the value), value, valor (value; worth)

ven, vent [come] convene (come together, assemble), intervene (come between), venue, convenient, avenue, circumvent (come or go around), invent, prevent

ver, veri [true] very, aver (say to be true, affirm), verdict, verity (truth), verify (show to be true), verisimilitude

vert, vers [turn] avert (turn away), divert (turn aside, amuse), invert (turn over), introvert (turn inward), convertible, reverse (turn back), controversy (a turning against; a dispute), versatile (turning easily from one skill to another)

vic, vicis [change, substitute] vicarious, vicar, vicissitude

vict, vinc [conquer] victor (conqueror, winner), evict (conquer out, expel), convict (prove guilty), convince (conquer mentally, persuade), invincible (not conquerable)

vid, vis [see] video, television, evident, provide, providence, visible, revise, supervise (oversee), vista, visit, vision

viv, vita, vivi [alive, life] revive (make live again), survive (live beyond, outlive), vivid, vivacious (full of life), vitality

voc [call] vocation (a calling), avocation (occupation not one's calling), convocation (a calling together), invocation, vocal

vol [will] malevolent, benevolent (one of goodwill), volunteer, volition

volcan, vulcan [fire] volcano (a mountain erupting fiery lava), volcanize (to undergo volcanic heat), Vulcan (Roman god of fire)

volvo [turn about, roll] revolve, voluminous (winding), voluble (easily turned about or around), convolution (a twisting)

vor [eat greedily] voracious, carnivorous (flesh eating), herbivorous (plant eating), omnivorous (eating everything), devour

zo [animal] zoo (short for zoological garden), zoology (study of animal life), zodiac (circle of animal constellations), zoomorphism (being in the form of an animal), protozoa (one-celled animals)

The Human Body

capit	head	**gastro**	stomach	**osteo**	bone
card	heart	**glos**	tongue	**ped**	foot
corp	body	**hema**	blood	**pneuma**	breathe
dent	tooth	**man**	hand	**psych**	mind
derm	skin	**neur**	nerve	**spir**	breath

For additional information, see page 25.

Glossary

A

abstract
something that can't be sensed (seen, heard, etc.); a feeling or idea

abstract nouns
nouns referring to ideas or conditions that cannot be sensed

academic sentences
usually longer sentences with multiple layers of meaning; reveal careful thought on the part of the writer

academic voice
the tone or style used in most textbooks and professional journals; formal and serious

action verb
word functioning as a verb that expresses action

active voice
the voice created when a subject is acting

adjective
a word that modifies a noun or pronoun

adjective phrase or clause
a dependent clause functioning as an adjective

adverb
word that modifies a verb, an adjective, an adverb, or a whole sentence

adverb clause
a dependent clause functioning as an adverb

agree in number
when subject and verb are both singular or both plural

ambiguous
unclear or confusing

annotate
to add comments or make notes in a text

antecedent
the noun or pronoun that a pronoun refers to or replaces

APA
American Psychological Association; provides documentation guidelines for the social sciences

appositive
a noun or non phrase that renames another noun right beside it; usually set off by commas

apostrophe
a punctuation mark (') used to show that a letter or number has been left out or that a word is possessive

argumentation
a discussion or course of reasoning aimed at demonstrating truth or falsehood; relies on logic and sound reasoning

article
common noun markers (*a, an,* or *the*)

audience
the intended reader of a text

auxiliary verbs
helping verbs used with the main verb to indicate tense and other things

B

base word (root)
the word part or base upon which other words are built (help is the base for the word helpful)

"be" verb
forms of the verb "be" (*is, are, was, were*); function as linking verbs

C

causal connection
the link between the causes and effects of a topic; usually identified in the thesis statement

causes
the reasons for an action or a condition

chronological
organized by time

citations
sources referred to in research; occur within the text and in a listing at the end of the report

claim
the position or thesis developed in an argument essay

classification
the act of arranging or organizing according to classes or categories

closing
the final part of writing; a closing sentence in a paragraph, a closing paragraph (or two) in an essay

cluster
a strategy to generate ideas graphically; used to select topics and to gather details about a topic

colon
a punctuation mark (:) that introduces an example or list

comma splice
a sentence error that occurs when two sentences are connected with only a comma

common noun
a general noun, not capitalized

comparison-contrast
showing how two or more subjects are similar and different

complete predicate
the predicate with modifiers and objects

complete subject
the subject with modifiers

complex sentences
a sentence with an independent and dependent clause

compound adjective
an adjective made of two more words, hyphenated before the noun, but not afterward (*ready-made meals*)

compound-complex sentences
a sentence with two or more independent clauses and one or more dependent clauses

compound noun
noun made up of two or more words (*editor in chief*)

compound predicate
two or more predicates joined by *and* or *or*

compound sentence
two or more simple sentences joined with a coordinating conjunction that share the same verb

compound subject
two or more subjects connected by *and* or *or*

concrete nouns
nouns referring to something that can be sensed

conjunction
word or word group that joins parts of a sentence

content
the ideas and meaning developed in a piece of writing

context
the part of a text that surrounds a particular word; helps determine the word's meaning

contraction
word formed by joining two words, leaving out one or more letters (indicated by an apostrophe)

conventions
the rules governing the standard use of the language

coordinating conjunctions
conjunction that joins grammatically equal parts

correlative conjunctions
pair of conjunctions that stress the equality of the parts that are joined

count nouns
nouns that name things that can be counted (*pens, votes, people*)

counterarguments
opposing positions or arguments

cycle chart
a graphic organizer that identifies the steps in a recurring process

D

dangling modifiers
a modifying word, phrase, or clause that appears to modify the wrong word

dash
long horizontal line (—) that separates words or ideas, creating emphasis

declarative sentence
a sentence that express a basic statement

deductive thinking
following a thesis (main idea) with supporting reasons, examples, and facts

definite article
the word *the*

definition
the formal statement or explanation of a meaning of a word

delayed subject
a subject that appears after the verb

demonstrative adjective
a demonstrative pronoun (*this, that, those*) used as an adjective

dependent clause
a group of words with a subject and verb that does not express a complete thought

description
the creation of an image of a person, place, thing, or idea

dialogue
conversation between two or more people

direct object
a word that follows a transitive verb

documentation guidelines
rules to follow for giving credit for the ideas of others used in a report; MLA and APA provide two common sets of documentation rules

double negative
the nonstandard use of two negatives to express a single negative idea (*I hardly can't sleep*)

double preposition
the nonstandard use of two prepositions together (*off of*)

double subject
error created by following a subject with a pronoun

E

editing
checking revised writing for style, grammar, punctuation, capitalization, and spelling errors

effects
circumstances brought about by a cause or an action

essay
a short piece of writing that uses facts and details to support a claim (thesis)

example
details that demonstrate or show something

exclamation mark
a punctuation mark (!) used at the end of an exclamatory sentence or a word that indicates strong emotion

exclamatory sentence
a sentence that expresses strong emotion

F

feminine
female

first draft
a first attempt to develop writing

focus
a particular part or feeling about topic that is emphasized in a piece of writing; usually expressed in a thesis statement

formal English
a serious, straightforward style used in most academic writing; objective (sticks to the facts)

fragment
a group of words that does not express a complete thought

freewriting
a prewriting strategy involving rapid, nonstop writing; helps in selecting a topic and gathering details about it

future tense
verb tense indicating that action will happen later

G

gathering grid
a graphic organizer used to identify or gather different types of defining details

gender
masculine, feminine, neuter, or indefinite

gerund
a verb form that ends in *ing* and is used as a noun

graphic organizers
clusters, lists, charts, and other visuals that help writers explore and arrange ideas

H

helping (auxiliary) verb
verbs that work with a main verb to form different tenses and so on

hyphen
a short, horizontal line (-) used to form compound words (*in-service*)

I

ideas
the first and main trait of writing; includes the main idea plus supporting details

idiom
a common expression whose meaning is different from its literal meaning (*hit the roof*)

illogical
without logic; senseless, false, or untrue

illustration
the act of clarifying or explaining in writing

implied subject
the word you assumed to begin command sentences

indefinite article
the words *a* or *an*

indefinite adjective
an indefinite pronoun (*man, much, some*) used as an adjective

indefinite pronoun
a pronoun such as *someone* or *everything* that does not refer to a specific person or thing

independent clause
a group of words with a subject and verb that expresses a complete thought

indirect object
a word that comes between a transitive verb and a direct object

K

KWL
a reading strategy, identifying what the reader knows, wants to learn, and eventually learns

inductive thinking
presenting specific details first and concluding with the thesis (main point)

inferences
a logical conclusion that can be made about something that is not actually said or stated in a text

infinitive
a verb form that begins with *to* and can used as a noun (or as an adjective or adverb)

informal English
a relaxed style used in most personal essays; subjective (contains the writer's thoughts and feelings)

interrogative sentence
a sentence that asks a question

italics
a special type style like *this* used to identify titles of books moves, etc.; functions the same as underlining

items in a series
three or more words, phrases, or clauses that are grammatically the same; set off by commas

interjection
a word or phrase that expresses strong emotion

intransitive verb
action verb that does not transfer action to a direct object

irregular verb
a verb in which the principal parts are different words (*give, gave, given*)

L

levels of detail
details that contain differing levels of clarifying support

line diagram
a graphic organizer used to identify the main idea and examples in writing

linking verb
verb that connects the subject with a noun or another word; "be" verbs (*is, are, was, were*) are linking verbs

listing
a strategy used to gather ideas for writing

M

main idea (main point)
the idea that is developed in a piece of writing

masculine
male

misplaced modifier
a modifying word, phrase, or clause that has been placed incorrectly in a sentence

MLA
Modern Language Association; provides documentation guidelines for use in the humanities (literature, history, philosophy, etc.)

N

narration
the sharing of a story; a personal narrative shares a true story

neuter
neither male nor female

nominative case
used as a subject or a subject complement

noncount noun
nouns that name things that cannot be counted (*ice, plastic, sunshine*)

noun
a word that names a person, place, thing, or idea

noun clause
a dependent clause that functions as a noun

noun phrase
a noun plus its modifiers

number
singular or plural

O

objective
sticking to the facts; uninfluenced by personal feelings

objective case
used as a direct object, an indirect object, or an object of a preposition

organization
the second important trait; deals with the arranged of ideas

organized list
an outline-like graphic used to keep track of the information in a report and other forms of writing; customized for personal use

outline
an orderly graphic representation of ideas, following specific rules for arrangement

P

paragraph
a distinct division of writing containing a topic sentence, body sentences, and a closing sentence; usually develops one specific topic

paraphrase
a form of summary writing with explanations and interpretations; may be as long or longer than the source text

participle
verbal ending in *ing* or *ed* and functioning as an adjective

passive voice
the voice created when a subject is being acted upon

past tense
verb tense indicating that action happened earlier

perfect tense
verb tense that expresses completed action

person
whether the pronoun is speaking, being spoken to, or being spoken about

personal voice
sounds informal and somewhat relaxed; subjective (including the writer's thoughts and feelings)

persuasion
a form of discourse attempting to convince a audience; may appeal to emotion as well as logic

phrase
a group of words that lacks a subject or predicate or both

plagiarism
using the words and thoughts of others without crediting them; intellectual stealing

plot
the different parts of a story that create suspense

plural
referring to more than one thing

points of comparison
the special elements or features used to make a comparison (size, strength, appearance, etc.)

possessive
used to show ownership

predicate
the part of the sentence that tells or asks something about the subject

predicate adjective
adjective that appears after a linking verb

prefix
word parts that come before the base word (*un* is a prefix in *unwind*)

prepositional phrase
a group of words with a preposition, an object, and any modifiers

prereading
becoming familiar with a text by reviewing the title, heading, etc.

present tense
verb tense indicating that action is happening now

prewriting
starting the writing process by analyzing the assignment, selecting a topic, gathering details, and finding a focus

primary sources
information collected directly, such as through firsthand experiences

process
a series of actions, steps, or changes bringing about a result

progressive tense
verb tense that expresses ongoing action

pronoun
word that takes the place of a noun or another pronoun

proper adjective
an adjective based on the name of a specific person, place, thing, or idea; capitalized

proper noun
the specific name of a person, place, thing, or idea; capitalized

publishing
preparing writing to share or submit

purpose
the reason for writing (to inform, to entertain, to persuade, etc.)

Q

question mark
a punctuation mark (?) used an the end of an interrogative sentence (question)

quotation
the specific thoughts or words of other people used in writing

quotation marks
punctuation marks (" ") that set off certain titles, special words, and the exact words spoken by someone

R

rambling sentence
a sentence error that occurs when a long series of separate ideas are connected by one connecting word after another

reading
the second step in the reading process; getting a basic understanding of the text

reading process
a process helping a reader gain a full understanding of a text

rereading
part of the reading process; consists of additional readings and analysis after the first reading

research report
a carefully planned form of informational writing, ranging in length from two or three pages on up

revising
improving the content of a first draft

relative clause
a dependent group of words beginning with a relative pronoun and a verb

relative pronoun
a word—that, which, who, whom—that introduces a relative clause

root (base word)
the word part (base) upon which other words are built (*help* is the base in *helpful*)

run-on sentence
a sentence error when two sentences are joined without punctuation or a connecting word

S

satiric voice
the use of humor, fake praise, or sarcasm (ridicule) to make fun of someone or something

secondary sources
information gained through reading what others have learned about a topic

semicolon
a punctuation mark (;) that connects sentences and separates items in some series

sensory details
specific sights, sounds, smells, textures, and tastes

sentences
the thoughts that carry the meaning in discourse; one of the key traits

sequencing
the following of one thing after another

shift in person
when first, second, and/or third person are improperly mixed in a sentence

shift in tense
more than one verb tense improperly used in a sentence

simple predicate
the verb and any helping verbs without modifiers or objects

simple sentence
a complete thought (containing a subject and a verb)

simple subject
the subject without any modifiers

singular
referring to one thing

spatial
organization related to location; often used in descriptions

SQ3R
a reading strategy consisting of survey, question, read, recite, and review

Standard English
English considered appropriate for school, business, and government

story line
the parts of a plot or story; includes exposition, rising action, climax, and resolution

STRAP strategy
a strategy to analyze writing and writing assignments

subject
the part of a sentence that tells who or what the sentence is about

subject complement
as word that follows a linking verb and renames or describes the subject

subjective
including a writer's personal thoughts and feelings

subordinate clause
word group that begins with a subordinating conjunction and has a subject and verb but can't stand alone as a sentence

subordinating conjunction
word or word groups that connects clauses of different importance

summarizing
the process of presenting the core of a text in a condensed form

suffix
a word part coming after a base word (*ful* is a suffix in *healthful*)

T

T-chart
A graphic organizer used to list causes and effects

tense
tell whether the action (verb) happens in the past, present, future, etc.

thesis statement
the statement of the main idea or focus of an essay; usually appears early in the text (often at the end of the first paragraph)

time line
a graphic organizer used to list ideas or events in chronological order

topic sentence
the statement of the main idea in a paragraph

transitions
words and phrases that link ideas in writing

transitive verb
action verb that transfers action to a direct object

traits
the main elements or features in writing; includes ideas, organization, voice, word choice, sentences, and conventions

U

usage error
using the wrong word (*they're* instead of *their*)

V

Venn diagram
a graphic organizer (two intersecting circles) used to identify similarities and differences for comparative writing

verb
A word that expresses action or a state of being

verb phrase
the main verb and any auxiliary verbs

verbal
a construction formed from a verb but functioning as a noun, adjective, or adverb (gerund, participle, or infinitive)

voice
the personality or tone in a piece of writing; one of the traits

W

word choice
the choice of words in a piece of writing; one of the traits

writing (the first draft)
the first attempt to develop a piece of writing; one of the steps in the writing process

writing process
a series of steps to follow to develop a piece of writing; includes prewriting, writing, revising, editing, and publishing

Photo Credits:

Page iv: Evangelos, 2011 / Used under license from Shutterstock.com
Page vii: Jaimie Duplass, 2011 / Used under license from Shutterstock.com
Page ix: JeniFoto, 2011 / Used under license from Shutterstock.com
Page xii: Andresr, 2011 / Used under license from Shutterstock.com
Page 1: Falconia, 2011 / Used under license from Shutterstock.com
Page 3: Supri Suharjoto, 2011 / Used under license from Shutterstock.com
Page 11: kRie, 2011 / Used under license from Shutterstock.com
Page 14: Robert Kneschke, 2011 / Used under license from Shutterstock.com
Page 17: Skyline, 2011 / Used under license from Shutterstock.com
Page 19: I.Quintanilla, 2011 / Used under license from Shutterstock.com
Page 29: Galina Barskaya, 2011 / Used under license from Shutterstock.com
Page 32: leungchopan, 2011 / Used under license from Shutterstock.com
Page 33: Piotr Tomicki, 2011 / Used under license from Shutterstock.com
Page 34: Supri Suharjoto, 2011 / Used under license from Shutterstock.com
Page 35: lev radin, 2011 / Used under license from Shutterstock.com
Page 39: Aksana Yakupava, 2011 / Used under license from Shutterstock.com
Page 56: Arkorn, 2011 / Used under license from Shutterstock.com
Page 60: Lepas, 2011 / Used under license from Shutterstock.com
Page 65: Yuri Arcurs, 2011 / Used under license from Shutterstock.com
Page 70: Supri Suharjoto, 2011 / Used under license from Shutterstock.com
Page 74: Patryk Kosmider, 2011 / Used under license from Shutterstock.com
Page 78: svry, 2011 / Used under license from Shutterstock.com
Page 81: kosam, 2011 / Used under license from Shutterstock.com
Page 87: Rido, 2011 / Used under license from Shutterstock.com
Page 101: OLJ Studio, 2011 / Used under license from Shutterstock.com
Page 102: Samot, 2011 / Used under license from Shutterstock.com
Page 107: travis manley, 2011 / Used under license from Shutterstock.com
Page 109: Hirurg, 2011 / Used under license from Shutterstock.com
Page 111: Jan van der Hoeven, 2011 / Used under license from Shutterstock.com
Page 112: Ljupco Smokovski, 2011 / Used under license from Shutterstock.com
Page 121: ARENA Creative, 2011 / Used under license from Shutterstock.com
Page 122: Daniel Ochoa IFOTOCHOA, 2011 / Used under license from Shutterstock.com
Page 130: Justin Mair, 2011 / Used under license from Shutterstock.com
Page 132: Athanasia Nomikou, 2011 / Used under license from Shutterstock.com
Page 133: Dean Mitchell, 2011 / Used under license from Shutterstock.com
Page 135: Glenda M. Powers, 2011 / Used under license from Shutterstock.com
Page 137: Evangelos, 2011 / Used under license from Shutterstock.com
Page 141: Blaj Gabriel, 2011 / Used under license from Shutterstock.com
Page 144: Kayros Studio "Be Happy!", 2011 / Used under license from Shutterstock.com
Page 145: Lane V. Erickson, 2011 / Used under license from Shutterstock.com
Page 148: Vitaly Korovin, 2011 / Used under license from Shutterstock.com
Page 152: absolute-india, 2011 / Used under license from Shutterstock.com
Page 154: Katrina Brown, 2011 / Used under license from Shutterstock.com
Page 156: suphakit73, 2011 / Used under license from Shutterstock.com
Page 157: Diego Cervo, 2011 / Used under license from Shutterstock.com
Page 159: lev radin, 2011 / Used under license from Shutterstock.com
Page 161: funflow, 2011 / Used under license from Shutterstock.com
Page 169: Mike Flippo, 2011 / Used under license from Shutterstock.com
Page 170: Jaimie Duplass, 2011 / Used under license from Shutterstock.com
Page 174: Nathalie Speliers Ufermann, 2011 / Used under license from Shutterstock.com
Page 181: Monkey Business Images, 2011 / Used under license from Shutterstock.com
Page 183: Arthur R., 2011 / Used under license from Shutterstock.com
Page 184: Matt Antonino, 2011 / Used under license from Shutterstock.com
Page 189: william casey, 2011 / Used under license from Shutterstock.com
Page 193: Konstantin Sutyagin, 2011 / Used under license from Shutterstock.com
Page 198: sdecoret, 2011 / Used under license from Shutterstock.com
Page 202: Lightspring, 2011 / Used under license from Shutterstock.com
Page 204: Semisatch, 2011 / Used under license from Shutterstock.com
Page 205: Jenkedco, 2011 / Used under license from Shutterstock.com
Page 207: ARTEKI, 2011 / Used under license from Shutterstock.com
Page 209: Piti Tan, 2011 / Used under license from Shutterstock.com
Page 211: szefei, 2011 / Used under license from Shutterstock.com
Page 217: Lisa F. Young, 2011 / Used under license from Shutterstock.com
Page 218: Rido, 2011 / Used under license from Shutterstock.com
Page 222: Amy Johansson, 2011 / Used under license from Shutterstock.com
Page 229: Robert Kneschke, Schaumburg, 2011 / Used under license from Shutterstock.com

Page 231: Mark Atkins, 2011 / Used under license from Shutterstock.com
Page 232: Mike Flippo, 2011 / Used under license from Shutterstock.com
Page 237: OLJ Studio, 2011 / Used under license from Shutterstock.com
Page 239: ifong, 2011 / Used under license from Shutterstock.com
Page 241: Harris Shiffman, 2011 / Used under license from Shutterstock.com
Page 248: JPerez, 2011 / Used under license from Shutterstock.com
Page 250: Falko Matte, 2011 / Used under license from Shutterstock.com
Page 253: Carlos E. Santa Maria, 2011 / Used under license from Shutterstock.com
Page 255: Vladislav Gajic, 2011 / Used under license from Shutterstock.com
Page 261: Dasha Rusanenko, 2011 / Used under license from Shutterstock.com
Page 265: Justin Black, 2011 / Used under license from Shutterstock.com
Page 277: michaeljung, 2011 / Used under license from Shutterstock.com
Page 279: Hervé Hughes/Hemis/Corbis
Page 280: R. Gino Santa Maria, 2011 / Used under license from Shutterstock.com
Page 285: Shamleen, 2011 / Used under license from Shutterstock.com
Page 289: Christos Georghiou, 2011 / Used under license from Shutterstock.com
Page 298: Casper Simon, 2011 / Used under license from Shutterstock.com
Page 300: Leah-Anne Thompson, 2011 / Used under license from Shutterstock.com
Page 301: ene, 2011 / Used under license from Shutterstock.com
Page 303: arindambanerjee, 2011 / Used under license from Shutterstock.com
Page 309: Marquis, 2011 / Used under license from Shutterstock.com
Page 313: dominique landau, 2011 / Used under license from Shutterstock.com
Page 322: ER_09, 2011 / Used under license from Shutterstock.com
Page 325: Monkey Business Images, 2011 / Used under license from Shutterstock.com
Page 327: Lichtmeister, 2011 / Used under license from Shutterstock.com
Page 329: ajt, 2011 / Used under license from Shutterstock.com
Page 330: maxstockphoto, 2011 / Used under license from Shutterstock.com
Page 333: Artur Synenko, 2011 / Used under license from Shutterstock.com
Page 337: Supri Suharjoto, 2011 / Used under license from Shutterstock.com
Page 338: Alperium, 2011 / Used under license from Shutterstock.com
Page 343: Omer N Raja, 2011 / Used under license from Shutterstock.com
Page 344: Marie Lumiere, 2011 / Used under license from Shutterstock.com
Page 347: arbit, 2011 / Used under license from Shutterstock.com
Page 349: hektor2, 2011 / Used under license from Shutterstock.com
Page 351: Michiel de Wit, 2011 / Used under license from Shutterstock.com
Page 360: Supri Suharjoto, 2011 / Used under license from Shutterstock.com
Page 363: pheral creative, 2011 / Used under license from Shutterstock.com
Page 365: Volodymyr Krasyuk, 2011 / Used under license from Shutterstock.com
Page 367: Diego Barbieri, 2011 / Used under license from Shutterstock.com
Page 370: ajt, 2011 / Used under license from Shutterstock.com
Page 373: Monkey Business Images, 2011 / Used under license from Shutterstock.com
Page 379: Perry Correll, 2011 / Used under license from Shutterstock.com
Page 389: WilleeCole, 2011 / Used under license from Shutterstock.com
Page 393: Yuri Arcurs, 2011 / Used under license from Shutterstock.com
Page 396: Rubberball/Corbis
Page 404: Ocean/Corbis
Page 409: Jose Ignacio Soto, 2011 / Used under license from Shutterstock.com
Page 417: Galyna Andrushko, 2011 / Used under license from Shutterstock.com
Page 418: webphotographer / istockphoto.com
Page 429: gary718, 2011 / Used under license from Shutterstock.com
Page 433: SeDmi, 2011 / Used under license from Shutterstock.com
Page 435: Steve Collender, 2011 / Used under license from Shutterstock.com
Page 437: Christopher Elwell, 2011 / Used under license from Shutterstock.com
Page 443: paul prescott, 2011 / Used under license from Shutterstock.com
Page 457: Evgeniya Moroz, 2011 / Used under license from Shutterstock.com
Page 477: william casey, 2011 / Used under license from Shutterstock.com
Page 480: InavanHateren, 2011 / Used under license from Shutterstock.com
Page 484: AYAKOVLEV, 2011 / Used under license from Shutterstock.com
Page 487: Jessmine,, 2011 / Used under license from Shutterstock.com
Page 488: Piotr Wawrzyniuk, 2011 / Used under license from Shutterstock.com
Page 491: Cheryl Casey, 2011 / Used under license from Shutterstock.com
Page 496: Margoe Edwards, 2011 / Used under license from Shutterstock.com
Page 497: VR Photos, 2011 / Used under license from Shutterstock.com
Page 503: Dariusz Sas, 2011 / Used under license from Shutterstock.com
Page 508: Robert J. Beyers II, 2011 / Used under license from Shutterstock.com
Page 513: William Perugini, 2011 / Used under license from Shutterstock.com
Page 517: Steve Mann, 2011 / Used under license from Shutterstock.com
Page 523: Tom Mc Nemar, 2011 / Used under license from Shutterstock.com
Page 527: AntonSokolov, 2011 / Used under license from Shutterstock.com
Page 529: Gary James Calder, 2011 / Used under license from Shutterstock.com
Page 537: Mike Flippo, 2011 / Used under license from Shutterstock.com

Models:

Page 34: "Be Advised! Advising Mistakes Students Make," from STALEY/STALEY. *FOCUS on College and Career Success,* 1E. © 2012 Wadsworth, a part of Cengage Learning, Inc.

Page 35 "Status and Style" from BRYM/LIE. *Sociology: Your Compass for a New World,* 2E. © 2006 Thompson, a part of Cengage Learning, Inc.

Page 38 "Dietary Diversity" from HALES. *An Invitation to Health,* 7E. © 2012 Brooks/Cole, a part of Cengage Learning, Inc.

Page 53 "TV and Your Health" from HALES. *An Invitation to Health,* 7E. © 2012 Brooks/Cole, a part of Cengage Learning, Inc.

Page 53 "About Race" from STALEY/STALEY. *FOCUS on College and Career Success,* 1E. © 2012 Wadsworth, a part of Cengage Learning, Inc.

Page 129 Joseph T. O'Connor, "A View From Mount Ritter." From Newsweek, May 25, 1998. Copyright © 1998 Newsweek/Daily Beast Company LLC. All rights reserved. Used by permission and protected by the Copyright Laws of the United States. The printing, copying, redistribution, or retransmission of the Material without the express written permission is prohibited.

Page 153 Brent Staples, "A Brother's Murder." From The New York Times, March 30, 1986. © Copyright 1986 The New York Times/Daily Beast Company LLC. All rights reserved. Used by permission and protected by the Copyright Laws of the United States. The printing, copying, redistribution, or retransmission of the Material without the express written permission is prohibited.

Page 162 "Groupthink" from BRYM/LIE. *Sociology: Your Compass for a New World,* 2E. © 2006 Thompson, a part of Cengage Learning, Inc.

Page 186 "The Three Most Difficult Words" from HALES. *An Invitation to Health,* 7E. © 2012 Brooks/Cole, a part of Cengage Learning, Inc. Reproduced by permission. www.cengage.com/permissions

Page 201 "What is psychology and what are its goals?" from COON/MITTERER. *Psychology: A Journey,* 4E. © 2011 Wadsworth, a part of Cengage Learning, Inc.

Page 210 "Crime-Scene Investigation of Blood" from BERTINO. *Forensic Science: Fundamentals and Investigations,* Copyright 2012 Wadsworth, a part Cengage Learning, Inc.

Page 225 "What to Do During the Test" from ELLIS. *Becoming a Master Student,* 13E. ©2011 Wadsworth, a part of Cengage Learning, Inc. Reproduced by permission. www.cengage.com/permissions

Page 234 "Effective Discipline" from COON/MITTERER. *Psychology: A Journey,* 4E. © 2011 Wadsworth, a part of Cengage Learning, Inc.

Page 258 "Burning Tropical Rainforests and Climate Change" from MILLER. *Living in the Environment,* 17E. © 2012 Brooks/Cole, a part of Cengage Learning, Inc.

Page 273 "Cramming: Does 'All or Nothing' Really Work?" from STALEY/STALEY. *FOCUS on College and Career Success,* 1E. © 2012 Wadsworth, a part of Cengage Learning, Inc. Reproduced by permission. www.cengage.com/permissions

Page 282 "Cross-Cultural Miscues" from FERRARO/ANDREATTA. *Cultural Anthropology: An Applied Perspective,* 9E. © 2012 Wadsworth, a part of Cengage Learning, Inc.

Page 321 "What Exactly Is a Frivolous Lawsuit?" from FLEMMING, *Reading for thinking,* 7E. © 2012 Cengage Learning. Reproduced by permission. www.cengage.com/permissions

Page 330 Marvin Harris, "How Our Skins Got Their Color," Our Kind: Who We Are, Where We Came From, and Where We Are Going, Harper Collins, 1989.

Page 333 "Get Physically Energized" from STALEY/STALEY. *FOCUS on College and Career Success,* 1E. © 2012 Wadsworth, a part of Cengage Learning, Inc.

Page 338 "Why Should We Protect Sharks?" from MILLER. *Living in the Environment,* 17E. © 2012 Brooks/Cole, a part of Cengage Learning, Inc.

Page 340 "Six Degrees of Kevin Bacon" from BRYM/LIE. *Sociology: Your Compass for a New World,* 2E. © 2006 Thompson, a part of Cengage Learning, Inc.

Page 346 "Life Stages" from SIMMERS. *Diversified Health Occupations,* 7E. © 2009 Delmar Learning, a part of Cengage Learning, Inc. Reproduced by permission. www.cengage.com/permissions

Page 357 "Forgiving" from HALES. *An Invitation to Health,* 7E. © 2012 Brooks/Cole, a part of Cengage Learning, Inc.